SAGE was founded in 1965 by Sara Miller McCune to support the dissemination of usable knowledge by publishing innovative and high-quality research and teaching content. Today, we publish over 900 journals, including those of more than 400 learned societies, more than 800 new books per year, and a growing range of library products including archives, data, case studies, reports, and video. SAGE remains majority-owned by our founder, and after Sara's lifetime will become owned by a charitable trust that secures our continued independence.

Los Angeles | London | New Delhi | Singapore | Washington DC | Melbourne

LAND AND LABOUR IN INDIAN AGRICULTURE

Thank you for choosing a SAGE product!
If you have any comment, observation or feedback,
I would like to personally hear from you.

Please write to me at **contactceo@sagepub.in**

Vivek Mehra, Managing Director and CEO, SAGE India.

Bulk Sales

SAGE India offers special discounts
for purchase of books in bulk.
We also make available special imprints
and excerpts from our books on demand.

For orders and enquiries, write to us at

Marketing Department
SAGE Publications India Pvt Ltd
B1/I-1, Mohan Cooperative Industrial Area
Mathura Road, Post Bag 7
New Delhi 110044, India

E-mail us at **marketing@sagepub.in**

Subscribe to our mailing list
Write to **marketing@sagepub.in**

This book is also available as an e-book.

LAND AND LABOUR IN INDIAN AGRICULTURE

Discourses on Growth and Equity

Social Change in Contemporary India

Series Editor: Manoranjan Mohanty

Volume II

Edited by

PRASHANT K. TRIVEDI

Los Angeles | London | New Delhi
Singapore | Washington DC | Melbourne

Copyright © Council for Social Development, 2021

All rights reserved. No part of this book may be reproduced or utilized in any form or by any means, electronic or mechanical, including photocopying, recording or by any information storage or retrieval system, without permission in writing from the publisher.

First published in 2021 by

SAGE Publications India Pvt Ltd
B1/I-1 Mohan Cooperative Industrial Area
Mathura Road, New Delhi 110 044, India
www.sagepub.in

SAGE Publications Inc
2455 Teller Road
Thousand Oaks, California 91320, USA

SAGE Publications Ltd
1 Oliver's Yard, 55 City Road
London EC1Y 1SP, United Kingdom

SAGE Publications Asia-Pacific Pte Ltd
18 Cross Street #10-10/11/12
China Square Central
Singapore 048423

Published by Vivek Mehra for SAGE Publications India Pvt. Ltd. Typeset in 10.5/13pt Bembo by Fidus Design Pvt. Ltd, Chandigarh.

Library of Congress Control Number: 2020951604

ISBN: 978-93-5388-734-6 (HB)

SAGE Team: Rajesh Dey, Syed Husain Naqvi, Sonam Rana, Aishna Bhatt and Rajinder Kaur

Contents

List of Abbreviations vii
About the Series ix
Foreword by Manoranjan Mohanty xiii
Introduction xvii

Section I: The Land Question
Sectional Introduction

Chapter 1	Kin, Clan and Land Reforms in Bihar Villages R. A. P. Singh	7
Chapter 2	Land Alienation of Tribals in the Jharkhand Region of Bihar: Process and Pattern Ramesh Sharan, Amar Kumar Singh and S. L. Batra	19
Chapter 3	Triple Exclusion of Dalits in Landownership in Kerala C. R. Yadu and C. K. Vijayasuryan	53
Chapter 4	Contextualizing Women's Rights and Entitlements to Land: Insights from Gujarat Meera Velayudhan	73

Section II: The Agrarian Structure
Sectional Introduction

Chapter 5	Agrarian Structure and the Rural Poor: Review of Perspectives P. C. Joshi	107
Chapter 6	Role of Peasant Economy in Capitalist Development: Case Study of a Maharashtra Village Sulabha Brahme	121

Chapter 7	Micro-regional Planning for the Management of Agriculture *Prodipto Roy*	139
Chapter 8	Agricultural Modernization in Rural Maharashtra: Myth and Reality *B. B. Mohanty*	168
Chapter 9	Green Revolution Revisited: The Contemporary Agrarian Situation in Punjab *Swarup Dutta*	188

Section III: The Globalization Era
Sectional Introduction

Chapter 10	Changing Structure and Organization of Agriculture and Small Farmers in India *Sukhpal Singh*	219
Chapter 11	Shifting Pattern of Agricultural Space: Evolution of Contract Farming in Punjab *Mahesh Pratap Singh*	252
Chapter 12	Employment Patterns among Agricultural Labourers in Rural Punjab *Gurmanpreet Singh and Kamaljit Singh*	279
Chapter 13	Agriculture Security: How to Attain It *Pushpa M. Bhargava*	303

About the Editors and Contributors	335
Index	340

List of Abbreviations

BMP	Bihar Military Police
CD	Community development
CNT	Chotanagpur Tenancy
CPRs	Common property resources
CSD	Council for Social Development
DC	Deputy commissioner
ERTS	Earth Resources Technical Satellite
FCI	Food Corporation of India
FDI	Foreign direct investment
GDP	Gross domestic product
GM	Genetically manipulated
HEC	Heavy Engineering Corporation
HYV	High-yielding varieties
ICAR	Indian Council of Agricultural Research
IPM	Integrated pest management
KVKs	Krishi Vigyan Kendras
MGNREGS	Mahatma Gandhi National Rural Employment Guarantee Scheme
MSP	Minimum support prices
NCPHs	Non-cultivating peasant households
NGOs	Non-governmental organizations
NREGS	National Rural Employment Guarantee Scheme
OBC	Other Backward Castes
PAFC	Punjab Agro Foodgrains Corporation
PDS	Public distribution system
PP	Purchase price
SAR	Scheduled Area Regulation
SCs	Scheduled Castes
SEZs	Special economic zones
SPT	Santhal Parganas Tenancy
STs	Scheduled Tribes
WTO	World Trade Organization

About the Series

Social Change in Contemporary India is a series of thematic volumes carrying selected articles from the journal *Social Change*, which is celebrating its Golden Jubilee. They are offered as important contributions capturing the momentous experience of the people of India and their institutions since Independence.

Social change in Independent India has gone through three distinct phases. The first two decades saw the impact of the freedom struggle in most arenas, where policymakers and the common people shared some perspectives to initiate concrete steps to reduce poverty, hunger and scarcities, with the objective of making progress towards the goals enshrined in the Constitution of India. Planned development with a focus on industrialization, the Green Revolution in agriculture, the construction of educational institutions of high quality and, above all, the promotion of democratic institutions and procedures to meet the aspirations of all sections of society, characterized most of this era. The pluralistic character of Indian society, culture and polity was acknowledged, and some important policy initiatives emerged.

But by the late 1960s, the crisis of this model had already surfaced. Food riots in 1966, the Naxalbari uprising in 1967 and the beginning of non-Congress governments in many states were symptoms of the emerging environment. That heralded the second phase, from 1970 to 1990, which witnessed the unfolding of the most major contradictions in the Indian Republic. The assertion of the rights by ethnic groups in different parts of the country was responded to by a certain centralization of power by the Union government, which in turn was challenged by the emergence of strong regional parties and movements. Poverty eradication was prominent on the agenda, but progress was tardy. Education and health facilities expanded, but not to the extent needed. An Indian middle class did emerge but was increasingly alienated from the masses. Challenges accumulated leading to mass movements and the Republic saw the declaration of Emergency followed by the rule of alternative forces and the return of the Congress to power. In the process, civil society organizations pursuing citizens' rights emerged and the struggle for democratic rights continued to expand. Internal disturbances, communal riots and atrocities on Dalits, minorities and women occurred from time to time. But the democratic structure continued to get consolidated and people's consciousness to defend constitutional values continued to grow.

In 1991, neoliberal economic reforms were launched in the wake of a serious economic crisis. At that time, India was also experiencing a social upsurge over the rights of Dalits, backward classes, religious minorities and women. By this time, environmental issues had also acquired much attention. Thus, the third phase began. The Indian elite, cutting across the dominant political parties, accepted the agenda of globalization, liberalization and privatization. Mobilization on caste and religious issues took a new turn, with Hindu nationalist forces becoming stronger. Initially, through its alliance of parties, the Congress was able to stem this trend. For a decade, they handled contradictions by a strategy that promoted rapid economic growth, tried to provide rural employment and food security to the poor and addressed the grievances of minorities. But corruption and inefficiency made them unpopular and a BJP-led government came to power. This third phase of neoliberal growth, steered by Hindu nationalism, is in full swing, though alternative forces have continued to occupy a significant space.

This story of Independent India is captured by scholars and commentators as it unfolded during the past 50 years as contributions to the Council for Social Development's social science quarterly, *Social Change*. They narrate the multidimensional dynamics of social change experienced by various sections of people at the local, regional and national levels, as well as in the global context. We have decided to share these contributions on specific themes in several volumes with a wider readership for good reasons.

First, *Social Change* is a unique, interdisciplinary journal that covers not only research papers in social sciences but also policy analysis and reports from the field in areas of social development. Right from the start, Durgabai Deshmukh, the founder of the Council of Social Development, wanted theory, policy and ground-level experience to be integrated, each benefitting from the other. So each volume in this series has papers by authors defining concepts, explaining theoretical frameworks, analysing policies and presenting survey results and other evidences from rural, urban and tribal areas.

Second, the journal carried contributions from not only senior scholars such as Nirmal Kumar Bose, B. N. Ganguly, T. N. Madan and B. K. Roy Burman, policymakers like C. D. Deshmukh and social activists such as Devaki Jain but also from a large number of young academics from all over the country who used the forum to present their findings from their most important research projects. Some of them later became eminent academics and important policymakers. The contributions by these writers over a 50-year period can help us identify key points in the history of policymaking as well as discourses during the three major phases of contemporary India. Some contributions clearly impacted public discourses and the policy process. Thus, we are able to capture shifts in policy in the early 1970s, when the state took many active initiatives, and also the big change in 1991, when a new role of the state was visible in the economy, giving a substantial role to the private sector. That trend continued in the first two decades of the 21st century. We may note the changing perspectives and linkage with global processes not only on theoretical issues of social development but also on policy debates concerning questions such as the privatization of health, education, rural development, forestry and environment. Their implications for people's welfare and human rights were also dealt with by many authors in recent years.

Third, an equally important consideration underlying these volumes is the fact that the Council for Social Development has a mission to serve the interests of marginalized groups: its research, publications, advocacy and, indeed, this journal reflects that commitment. Therefore, the volumes carry articles on selected themes such as health, education, poverty, agriculture with special focus on the marginalized groups, including Adivasis, Dalits, minorities, women, and urban and rural poor. Each of these volumes reflects what has been done in respect of the specific marginalized groups and analyses the nature of the development experience from the vantage point of the marginalized.

Each volume is edited by an expert who has done considerable work on the subject. A major and substantive introduction by the editor of the volume not only puts the papers in perspective but also identifies the strengths as well as the gaps in the treatment of the subject.

The editor's 'Introduction' also addresses current concerns in theory and policy, discourse and practice, and presents suggestions for further thinking and action. These volumes are designed as studies on a theme for ready reference and use by students, researchers and general readers.

Manoranjan Mohanty
Series Editor

Foreword

The lockdown enforced as a response to COVID-19 beginning late March 2020 has put on the forefront the plight of the millions of migrant labourers who were forced to leave for their villages. For weeks they were on the road, some on bicycles, many walking, some dying on the way. After the governments organized trains to take these weary travellers to their destination, at the end of the next two months only about 40 per cent had reached their villages. Of them, only a small proportion got engaged in the Mahatma Gandhi National Rural Employment Guarantee Scheme (MGNREGS) and majority were still waiting for employment. This experience squarely brought to the fore the persisting crisis in rural India where lack of employment compelled the rural poor to migrate to far-off places in search of work. Despite many achievements such as raising the production of food grains, reduction of poverty and expanding irrigation facilities and rural infrastructure, large masses of rural population suffer from hunger, malnutrition and absence of basic livelihood amenities such as housing and drinking water even after seven decades of Independence. Even when the central government announced its economic measures in the midst of the COVID outbreak, the agenda announced for the farmers reflected little understanding of the reasons as to why rural India continued to suffer until today.

This volume of selected contributions from *Social Change* spanning five decades presents a set of materials which focus on the land question as the key to agrarian transformation. The abandonment of land reforms has made every policy intervention either unproductive or iniquitous. The Green Revolution vastly increased the extent of food grain production, but it made rural society even more unequal and irreversibly devastated the natural resources of the region. Introduction of reform measures in the wake of globalization that gradually removed market restrictions and sought to link the Indian agricultural production to the world market further consolidated the unequal structure in the Indian countryside. Agricultural growth remains low and rural economy depressed. As a result, inequality and deprivation persist at multiple levels—between states; between regions; within states; between classes of rich peasantry and the poor and the landless; between upper, middle castes who own land, on the one hand, and the tenant farmers and agricultural labourers, most of whom are Dalits, Adivasis and lower backward castes, on the other. Due to the persistence of poverty and the low-level of livelihood conditions, the purchasing power of the vast rural masses remained low and their physical abilities did not grow adequately, thus adversely affecting the overall productive strength of the economy and society. Women and children became the direct victims of this unequal development and failed rural transformation. The artisans became agricultural labourers as the demand for their skills nearly disappeared. The poverty alleviation programmes including MGNREGA and food security measures, though well-intentioned, only marginally addressed the problem of destitution. Rural crisis persisted because majority of the population did not have adequate access to and control over productive assets, especially land.

The unfolding of this story of India's countryside is chronicled in this volume covering three phases of agrarian policies in India. The institutional reforms of the early decades after Independence when zamindari abolition took place and some important land reform measures were initiated showed some promise of moving on the path of 'growth with equity'. We have accounts from different parts of India including Bihar, Kerala and Gujarat to show the pattern and extent of land reforms. How the rights of women, Dalits and Adivasis were structurally undermined in the Indian land reform scenario comes out very clearly in these essays. The targeted distribution of titles to small patches of land in some states to the Scheduled Castes (SCs) and Scheduled Tribes (STs) was a poor substitute for what was needed. In the next phase, the Green Revolution years, India's policymakers were preoccupied with raising farm productivity through technological inputs. That perspective of 'modernization' of agriculture continued to dominate the thinking of India's elite until today. The essays in this volume sharply assess the effects of the Green Revolution on the agrarian structure and examine the extent of capitalist development in agriculture. In reality, rich farmers who symbolize capitalist trends also use Dalit and Adivasi labour, even bonded labour in many cases. The Punjab study shows many striking features of this complex process which is examined in another essay on the debate on the mode of production. The post-1991 era of globalization not only reaffirmed the techno-capitalist strand of the Green Revolution but also added many new initiatives such as 'contract farming', cyber management and insurance-based support system rather than public investment in social and physical infrastructure in the countryside. During this period, the ideas of institutional reforms like 'land to the tiller' were buried forever.

This volume captures the principal concerns of the discourse on the agrarian question in India presenting studies which are empirically grounded and theoretically interpreted from the vantage point of the rural poor. Celebrated essays by eminent experts such as P. C. Joshi and Sulabha Brahme who had major influence on the debates on the rural transformation make it a valuable volume. A detailed blueprint to achieve agricultural security in India by the eminent scientist P. M. Bhargava makes the volume extremely useful. The Introduction by Prashant Trivedi is a comprehensive, analytical essay on the agrarian question in India from the perspective of land, labour and social transformation. He puts the contributions in the larger perspective of the discourse on agrarian question by highlighting the points of debate and the critical issues therein. Having done considerable work on the land question and the experience of Dalits, women and minorities in various regions of rural India, especially in Uttar Pradesh, Trivedi brings to the volume his rich insights in his Introduction. A former colleague of ours in the Council for Social Development, he continues major research projects on the agrarian studies currently at the Giri Institute of Development Studies, Lucknow. I am thankful to him for his undertaking to edit this volume.

This valuable work embodying 50 years of discourses on the agrarian question in India, with focus on land and labour, not only tells us why the rural crisis persists in India but also where interventions are urgently needed.

Manoranjan Mohanty
Council for Social Development
New Delhi

Introduction
Revisiting Agrarian Question
Land, Labour and Development

Besides education, health, tribal, Dalit and gender studies, rural India has been a major preoccupation of *Social Change*. A clear trajectory of deliberations on policy, performance and trends on land, agriculture and rural development emerges when one connects the dots seen in the articles published in the journal over the last 50 years. This volume is an attempt precisely in this direction looking at the issue of agricultural development as a means of improving the quality of life in rural areas. The articles published in *Social Change* represent the principal concerns of social science research of their time, tracing the evolution of the discourse, capturing shifts not only in policymaking but also the emerging ground realities.

Following its mandate of encouraging social science research on food security, inequality and poverty from the standpoint of marginalized groups, *Social Change* has for over five decades conceived the land and agrarian question central to its area of concerns. Significantly, 50 years of *Social Change* has also coincided with the period of the most engaging debates in the field of agrarian studies. Thus, empirically robust and theoretically rigorous pieces often have found space in the pages of this journal. Selection of these articles from a large pool of papers has offered an interesting view of the different strands of this debate.

Social science research on the agrarian sector in Independent India can be considered in three separate yet continuous phases identified taking state's outlook vis-à-vis agriculture as a marker: the years of institutional reforms, the Green Revolution period and the globalization era. In the first period, the state initiated major institutional changes in the land tenure system. Social science research responded with a critique of the land reform architecture which was marked by particularly ill-conceived key concepts that actually defeated the very objectives against a powerful backlash unleashed by the landlord class. Social oppression rooted in land relations, persisting landlessness and related agrarian problems were other major academic preoccupations.

Faced with the reality of mass hunger and in an attempt to achieve self-sufficiency in food, the state threw its weight behind agriculture during the second phase. Mainstream social sciences, particularly economics, applauded these initiatives, at the same time highlighting some implementation issues. Critical perspectives identified some emerging tensions, especially the rising inequality seen both vertically and horizontally. This period was most fruitful for agrarian studies since two major debates of enduring relevance emerged: the inverse farm size productivity relationship debate and the mode of production debate.

But the period after this was clearly crisis ridden, both for agriculture and social science research. Agriculture and more than that workers engaged in the sector slipped into despair as the state for over three decades looked away, leaving this sector vulnerable to the vagaries of the market. In the absence of any conceptual breakthrough, social science scholars found themselves repeating earlier theories, often resorting to concepts developed in different contexts. An increasingly funding-agency-driven research agenda further aided this decline in scholarship.

In the era of institutional reforms, the twin planks of equity and growth that were a driving force in Independent India's early decades were reflected in the overhauling of land relations. Since then, the land question continued to evolve with new dimensions added to it. It was no surprise then that *Social Change* was a witness to every twist and turn in this deliberation. The four articles chosen from a large repository of the journal representing this period showed concerns of different time periods and of diverse segments of society which constituted the section of the land question. The debate on land relations was to come under a scathing attack for its gender-blind approach and neglect of women farmers who were major contributors to farming in India. *Social Change* responded to this theoretical crisis with articles in this section capturing crucial aspects of land rights of women.

Later, when the delicate balance between equity and growth tilted in favour of the latter in the second phase of policy initiatives on land

and agriculture, they were identified and closely analysed by scholars in the journal. The modernization perspective might have held sway in the Green Revolution debate for a very long time, but academic critiques offered an alternative view. The article chosen on the Green Revolution familiarized readers with both sides of the debate, while the modernization perspective was subjected to thorough scrutiny in another article. Yet another article discusses in detail the key role of planning in agriculture giving a taste of the 1970s policy environment. The Green Revolution discussion triggered another debate on the basic transformation of the agrarian structure. The two articles included in this section of the volume introduce the debate's various dimensions. The first is an empirical study that has captured ground-level processes from the perspective of the peasantry and the other is a theoretical study that engages with major arguments made in this debate. With these diverse themes, perspectives and spatial locations, the section on agrarian structure has emerged as the richest part of the volume.

A major rupture in this debate took place with the onset of new economic policies oriented towards privatization, liberalization and globalization. With the state turning its attention towards other sectors of the economy, social science literature found itself discussing the possibility and desirability of the survival of small farming in the wake of increasing capital-intensive nature of agriculture. 'Contract farming' figured in these debates both as a challenge and solution to the ensuing crisis. The discourse on the 'agriculture–food' dyad is touched upon from a 'security' perspective. The four chapters constituting the section on the globalization era deliberate upon challenges facing the entire agrarian sector and people dependent on it in contemporary times.

THE LAND QUESTION

The land question was a major concern of social science study in post-Independence India. Articles published in *Social Change* often approached the land question from the perspective of the marginalized, mainly the landless, marginal and small farmers, Dalits, Adivasis and women. Articles often examined and questioned state intervention in land relations in the form of redistributive land reforms, presumably premised on the notion of equity in landownership and growth in agricultural production. As part of this overall strategy, the state also tried to check the alienation of land from marginalized communities. Selected articles in the first section of the volume would give the reader a glimpse of the debates on the redistributive aspect of the land question from the perspective of the marginalized.

The equity question was of crucial concern for a newly independent country, a country that had been dreaming of a better future for its people during its long struggle against colonial rule. Liberation from social oppression and economic exploitation, both closely intertwined in the rural power structure, had for decades caught the imagination of the peasantry which had erupted into uprisings on several occasions against landlords and their colonial masters during one century before Independence.

> After freedom from colonial rule hopes were high that the new national government would keep the promise given to their peasant supporters by liberating them from the domination of big landlords, most of whom had collaborated with the British. This was one of the reasons why the Indian National Movement had taken an antagonistic position against [the] semi-feudal landlord class created and strengthened by [the] colonial administration by modifying [the] Indian tenure system. (Myrdal, 1968, pp. 1302–1306)

With most of India's population living in rural areas and largely dependent on agriculture, access to land came to be seen as a means of poverty alleviation.

REDISTRIBUTIVE LAND REFORMS

Seeking to decolonize the land revenue system and ensure equity as well as productivity, the Indian state adopted massive land reforms soon after Independence beginning with the abolition of all intermediaries between the state and the actual tiller. The reforms aimed at the elimination of intermediaries, bringing cultivators in direct contact with the state, converting them into owners of cultivated agricultural land and reducing the gap between the rich and the poor in rural areas were seen as initiatives to encourage entrepreneurship in agriculture and harmony in the countryside (Newell, 1972).

Additionally, this was thought to be a way of providing conducive conditions for the penetration of capitalist relations in agriculture while maintaining pre-capitalist forms of domination. In a nutshell, it allowed old-type landlords to convert themselves into capitalist landlords by changing forms of domination from 'indirect cultivation through tenants to direct cultivation through hired labour' (Patnaik, 1983, p. 9). Given these peculiarities, the reforms did not have the desired impact on agrarian sector in terms of tilting the balance of class relations in favour of peasantry and creating demand for the entire economy and boosted investment (Ramachandran, 2011).

Under the new conditions, the land was supposed to become a commodity, freely traded in the market discarding prestige attached to it. In pre-capitalist societies, social and political functions attached to land never allowed it to attain purely economic form. Land reforms in India fell short of breaking this impasse by allowing land as a factor of production to assume autonomy from landed property and landowner (Namboodiripad, 1984).

Equally important was the view that saw land reforms as a tool for 'disempowerment' of the rural elite rather than just empowerment of the poor. Democratizing rural society was considered essential for the success of developmental initiatives and participatory governance including cooperatives and Panchayati Raj (Bandyopadhyay, 2002). It was keeping this in mind that the distribution of ceiling surplus land was considered a cardinal element of a comprehensive land reforms programme. Authors might call it a 'private property bias' in land reforms (Borras, 2006) but ignoring the political dimension of the land reform would be to disregard the fact that land relations in India had been traditionally intermeshed with social and political relations.

Some policymakers could have been apprehensive that radical land reforms would slow down the pace of industrialization due to a decrease in the 'distress sale' of food grains needed for country's swelling urban population (Myrdal, 1968). But on account of productivity in agriculture, the economic argument tilted in favour of land reforms. The underlying assumption here was that smaller holdings tended to be more productive than larger ones and cultivators with secured ownership rights would invest in productivity-enhancing paraphernalia and technology. However, empirical observations cited by Basu testified that the impact of land reforms on poverty alleviation was mixed on productivity enhancement in general and positive in states where these measures were implemented strictly. In an imperfect property rights regime and in a sluggish land market, state intervention in favour of the rural poor was considered desirable from the equity point of view too (Basu, 2012; Ghatak & Roy, 2007).

Relationship between farm size and productivity received widespread attention in academia since Sen (1964) argued about the inverse relationship between the two. The conceptual framework of this debate received a major challenge from the research work that did not find land size a true measure of the scale of the economy (Patnaik, 1987). However, recent studies (Chand et. al, 2011) found smallholdings, in terms of acreage, to be more productive than large farms with a caution that per capita productivity of the former was lower given larger number of people dependent on them.

Proceeding from the vantage point of making a limited overhaul of landownership structure, the Indian state opted for a particular model of 'redistributive land reforms' that completely removed landlords from their statutory role of revenue collection but made little dent in their ownership of large tracts of best quality agricultural land in a village. They were allowed to retain *khudkasht* (self-cultivated) land. However, under the Indian Constitution, land reforms fall in the state subject list and the provisions of law and its implementations differ across states. But the successful abolition of intermediaries of various nomenclatures alongside the complete failure of ceiling provisions (with a few exceptions) was the common experience found in all the states.

Another aspect of land reforms that had a crucial bearing for the large mass of peasantry was tenancy reforms. In the colonial period, tenants were differentiated on the basis of their status in revenue records. Recorded tenants often had hereditary occupations on a cultivated piece of land, while oral tenants on *khudkasht* lands of intermediaries did not have any formal claim. This crucial difference between these broad set of tenants turned out to be a defining point in post-Independence India. The superior tenants were major beneficiaries of these reforms as they received freehold ownership of their cultivated land, while the failure of tenancy laws to distinguish and protect both kinds of tenants proved to be disastrous for unrecorded tenants (Myrdal, 1968; Thorner,

1956). They were forced to become landless agricultural labour after being evicted by landlords for fear of losing 'self-cultivated' land (Patnaik, 1983), while superior tenants turned out to be agricultural entrepreneurs in many parts of the country. It was important to note here that a larger section of superior tenants was from peasant *jatis* (caste) that later constituted the upper crust of the Other Backward Castes (OBC) and a huge chunk of oral tenants came from Dalit *jatis*.

The owner–cultivator model was the professed goal of the land reforms programme in India but given the wide inequalities in the ownership of agricultural land, tenancy persisted even after the first phase of land reforms. Land ceilings were introduced across states beyond which a person could not hold land in rural areas. The imposition of the ceiling was supposed to curb inequality in landownership and limit the scope for tenancy. After the failure of ceiling to fetch any meaningful results in the 1960s, these limits were lowered down in the 1970s but again to no avail.

Social science research has offered three broad explanations for this peculiar experience of land reforms in India, namely the abolition of intermediaries alongside the maintenance of land inequality. First, there were sharp differences in the national and regional leadership of the Congress party that formed governments at the centre and states soon after Independence. The landed gentry dominated in the elected governments, bureaucracy and judiciary in states (Newell, 1972). Second, the entire design of land reforms was to facilitate the reincarnation of erstwhile landlords to capitalist landlords (Patnaik, 1976). Third, the emerging capitalist class in India and feudal class that had an antagonistic relationship during the colonial period, the former opposing imperial rule while later providing the social base to it, came to form a coalition that was reflected in this distorted version of land reforms (Namboodiripad, 1984).

SOCIOLOGY OF LAND REFORMS

Land reform as a field of study has been mostly dominated by economists, political-economists and policymakers. Contributions by political scientists, historians and sociologists have been few and far between but they have illuminated the hitherto dark corners of this debate.

Their contributions have investigated the dynamics and negotiations of changing land relations under the impact of these reforms with social institutions and power structure. They focused their attention beyond the immediate problems of productivity, investment and income.

These studies looked at land reforms as the quest of the ruling elite to expand its base beyond the old middle class, decadent feudal class and rich peasantry to stabilize the political system. They wanted to include the newly emerging middle class from the SC and ST background who often came from landless and poor peasantry. Because of their unique approach, sociologists saw land reforms not just as a measure of economic and administrative planning but also in terms of political and social planning. They also probed the way caste was used as a tool by intermediaries and rich peasants who were entrenched in rural power structure against sharecroppers and tenants (Roy Burman et al., 1974).

A sociological perspective on land reforms also considered it as a response to the growing contradictions in our agrarian system and potential unrest in society. Sociological research also underlined the emergence of a new middle peasantry after the abolition of intermediaries and imposition of ceilings that developed a vested interest in the rural power structure to keep landless agricultural labourers dependent on it (Roy Burman et al., 1974).

Besides economic logic, the important role played by social ideology was also underlined by this viewpoint. Sociologists argued that the land reform programme was initiated to 'give concrete shape to the liberal ethos of the elite'. They also pointed out that the ideology of land reforms believed that land belonged to the actual tiller (Roy Burman et al., 1974).

Further, the sociological perspective on land reforms looked at it from the prism of social movements. It was argued that only people's movements could ensure that fruits of this policy reached intended beneficiaries. More importantly, sociopolitical mobilization ensured that they could hold on to the land against the wishes of the powerful rural elite. Under this view, the movement did not need to be outside the establishment, even the state could initiate a movement in favour of the implementation of these reforms (Roy Burman et al., 1974).

Major sociological studies alerted us about the breakdown of the traditional web of relationships under the impact of a massive restructuring of land relations that formed the bedrock of social institutions, including the *jajmani* system. This viewpoint underlined the institutional vacuum that had emerged in the wake of the replacement of traditional reciprocal relationships by contractual relations and the increasing sense of insecurity (Roy Burman et al., 1974).

Sociologists argued that the ruling establishment of India prioritized the problem of production, delinking it from the question of mass poverty during the first phase of land reforms and tilted towards landlords and rich peasantry, while during second phase considered it from the perspective of rural poor ignoring the problem of growth of the rural economy (Roy Burman et al., 1974). Moreover, they felt that it was not merely about the choice of economic strategy or simply prioritizing one class over another, but it involved questions about society, as a whole.

> To ask what kind of land reforms, we should have is to ask what kind of production system or economic system are we going to have; what kind of social system are we going to have; what kind of political structure are we going to have in India. Land reforms affect not only the top and the bottom layers but the mode of life of the entire rural society: the masses that live in the villages. Are we going to have a society which calls itself modern but continues as a quasi-modern or disguised feudal society. (Roy Burman et al., 1974, p. 61)

MARKET-BASED LAND REFORMS

Another twist to this story came in the changing political and economic environment from the 1990s onwards. A powerful opinion sought to shift the discourse of land reforms from the site of the state to the site of the market, arguing that governments must refrain from intervening in land-related matters and problems would better be handled by the market. 'Deregulation' was the mantra of this deliberation. They advocated the lifting of restrictions on the agricultural land market in the form of sale land-use conversion, ceiling limits, sale of land belonging to SC/ST owners to non-SC/ST buyers. They also demanded that agricultural land tenancy should be legalized where it was prohibited and terms of tenancy must be left to the market where tenancy *per se* was not banned but terms of contract were regulated by the law.

Mainly led by a multilateral organization like the World Bank, this debate argued that the regulation of land markets did more harm than good to farmers. For instance, they claimed that restriction on the sale of land belonging to SCs and STs to those outside this category depressed the value of their asset. Similarly, ceilings on agricultural land discouraged corporations to enter the land market, keeping it relatively inactive. Further, restrictions on land leases were blamed for the practice of oral tenancy and unprotected tenants.

Social science literature pointed out some fallacies in the basic premise of this argument. It underlined that land reforms by definition in the form of state intervention in land relations favoured the land poor. They were undertaken precisely because markets did not deliver redistribution that formed the basis for progressive social change. Looking at the debate from this perspective, land reforms through the market were actually a contradiction in terms (Ramachandran, 2011). It was repeatedly pointed out that imposition of ceilings on agricultural land and its distribution was the cardinal principal of the land reforms agenda that had evolved during the freedom movement.

Critics of market-based reforms further pointed out that the persistence of small tenancy reflected a skewed landownership structure where those who owned the land did not cultivate it and those who cultivated it did not own it. The entire architecture of land reforms was designed to correct this anomaly. Redistributive land reforms might not have achieved their stated goal but watering down their provisions would amount to the total surrender of the Indian state before powerful landowning classes. Underlining the historical context in which protections for marginalized groups were enacted, they argued the continued relevance of these provisions given the peasantry's mounting debt burden, the persistence of powerful groups in rural areas who kept an eye on the land owned by the poor and the growing interest of urban capital on agricultural land both for speculative purposes and construction. It was also pointed out that market forces had already exploited loopholes in the law to alienate land owned by marginalized groups (Saxena, 2016). By doing away with these statutory protections outrightly would create havoc for poor peasants.

One important strand in this debate referred to the persisting caste–tenancy relationship to critique the strategy of using leasing as the main channel of providing 'access' to land rather than ensuring 'ownership' through redistributive provisions. It was pointed out that this strategy reinforced the historical caste–tenancy relationship that left Dalits and other poorer castes dependent on landowning castes while secured ownership weakened the caste–land congruence (Mohanty, 2001). Redistributive measures raised productivity, alleviated poverty and provided an asset base for diversification, none of which could be achieved in 'accessing land through a tenancy approach'.

Market-based reforms were also critiqued for their minimalist approach that sought to replace agricultural land with homestead plots. The new discourse almost sidetracked the question of agricultural land by offering a relatively bigger homestead plot that could be used for both residence and cultivation of vegetables and other crops and animal farming. Land reforms included both agricultural land and house sites that received a concrete shape in the form of state laws.

The recent push towards updating and computerization of land records, consolidation of revenue laws and similar administrative initiatives could give a respite to farmers from cumbersome bureaucratic procedures, but they were more in the nature of land management aimed at activating land market. From the market-based approach, they were seen and presented as land reforms.

In essence, the market-based approach appeared more interested in providing a free run to capital rather than reforms. These almost ready-made prescriptions were often offered to many post-colonial countries ignoring their histories and more importantly their sociology.

REVERSAL OF LAND REFORMS

Since the 1990s, when the Indian state espoused the goal of a free market economy and proceeded to decontrol the country, sector by sector, giving free rein to market forces to determine outcomes, land reforms did not remain untouched. Sweeping changes such as privatization, liberalization and globalization became the mantra for the economic policy of these three decades. Under the influence of this entirely changed outlook, the architecture of redistributive land reforms began to be seen merely as inconvenient baggage from the past. It was often argued that these reform measures, if at all meaningful at a particular historical juncture, had outlived their utility, and they were nothing more than a drag on the further development of agricultural productivity.

This discourse started entering legal architecture in many states. The NITI Aayog recently proposed a framework tenancy bill for the consideration of state legislatures. The bill provided for the leaving terms of tenancy to market force provided the lessee entered into a written agreement with the lessor. Similarly, the new Revenue Code of Uttar Pradesh watered down the restrictions on the sale of SC/ST land to non-SC/STs. Several other instances could be cited where ceiling limits, land-use change procedures were amended initiating the reversal of whatever land reforms had taken place in India (Saxena, 2016).

CHANGING LAND RELATIONS

Modifications by the colonial administration had created an atypical model of intermediaries, especially in northern and eastern India, which was different from models found in the West and distinct from its previous incarnation of the pre-British era. It combined rent-seeking traits of semi-feudalism with rights to transfer the land by the sale of a capitalist landlord (Myrdal, 1968). Social science literature often described the abolition of intermediaries by distinguishing between a statutory role and property relations, while the former was neutralized, the latter was short of any radical change. As is famously described by Thorner (1956, p. 27) in the case of Uttar Pradesh, the land tenure pattern resembled in the pre- and post-era of abolition:

> In sum, the Uttar Pradesh Zamindari Abolition Act has provided for a new hierarchy of tenure-holders in place of old one; but the two are recognisably similar. At the top are [the] *bhumidars*, below them [the] *sirdars*, and still further down the *asamis*. At the bottom of the heap remain the mass of cropsharers and landless labourers. The *zamindars* have disappeared but these same persons have been confirmed as landholders, often of very substantial tracts of best quality of land.

The new lease of life to landlords was also given by the compensation offered to them for the loss of their rent collection rights. Interestingly, funds for this scheme were collected from tenants willing to obtain a secured status. Thorner (1956, p. 27) rightly said, '…the same peasants who were bearing the burden of maintaining zamindaris had to pay [the] full cost for the removal of this burden'. However, this 'compensation' was also seen as 'capitalised form of feudal rent that became part of the market price of the land' (Namboodiripad, 1984, p. 6).

Another idea that was travelling along with the proposal to abolish intermediaries was the imposition of a maximum ceiling on the ownership of agricultural land but it took concrete shape only after the first one failed to make a serious dent in the existing landownership structure. No other land reform measure ignited such a fierce debate, both in academia and policy circles, as ceiling provisions. One group of researchers argued that land as a factor of production was perfectly divisible and a larger availability of labour per unit land would ensure a higher output on small farms (Rao, 1972). However, policymakers were not as confident about a productivity rise and pushed ceiling proposals on the equity plank (Ladejinsky, 1972).

Ladejinsky (1972, p. 402) aptly captures the mood of policy debates of that time:

> There are many striking features of the Plans *vis-a-vis* the ceilings. The first one is that whereas the agricultural part of the Plans justifiably stressed the rise in agricultural production, the ceilings have never been looked upon as a means to the same end; the impression is one of treating the issue in a vacuum. Second, and as a corollary of the first, the justification given for advocating the ceilings rests only on ideological rather than practical grounds as well.

Stiff political opposition from the landowning classes and their interest groups could be one reason that the failure of ceiling measures was worse than any other land reforms initiative. Hardly 1.7 per cent of the country's land area was declared as ceiling surplus under state-wise limits and approximately 1 per cent was distributed (Misra & Puri, 2000, cited in Ghatak & Roy, 2007). However, this average figure did not reveal state-wise variations. West Bengal under the Left distributed around 20 per cent of the land dispersed under this programme in the entire country (Ghatak & Roy, 2007), while large states like Uttar Pradesh merely distributed 0.58 per cent of its area under this programme. Other large states too performed much below expected potential.

That the ceiling was a political question rather than an issue merely based on economic rationality was also reflected in the kind of opposition it witnessed. Other studies also underlined that the ceiling programme in India was not politically acceptable (Dandekar & Rath, 1971, cited in Ladejinsky, 1972). The dilemma about productivity would have further weakened the establishment's resolve to take it forward. One could count the many loopholes in the law that helped landowners evade ceilings, including exemptions: very high ceilings in the first phase, absolute confusion about considering family or individual as a unit, so on and so forth. Simply blaming faulty implementation would be akin to deliberately keeping ourselves in the dark. The reality was that '...enforcement was not a problem; there was little to enforce' (Ladejinsky, 1972).

Another parallel stream of land reforms that continued since the colonial period was often referred to as tenancy reforms. Abolition of intermediaries and ceiling, on the one side, and tenancy reforms, on the other, emanated from different approaches. The first sought to abolish all interests in land between the actual tiller and the state, regularize possession of cultivated land in the name of tenants and in effect confer ownership on the cultivators of land. The basis of this policy was that only those who cultivated it should own the land and those who did not till it should not own it. This approach had the potential of transferring large tracts of agricultural land to cultivating households from big landlords and the so-called upper-caste people who traditionally maintained a distance from any kind of manual labour (Appu, 1975).

The second sought to protect tenants while they were cultivating land owned by others. The first approach was considered to be more radical because it changed property relations. And admittedly the second one assumed that it was '...practical and worthwhile to look at the entire problem of tenancy reform from the limited, short term point of view of stepping agricultural production' (Appu, 1975, p. 1357). For historical reasons, both approaches continued in post-colonial India. One could see variations across states in their legal enactments on tenancy, broadly classified into two groups for easier comprehension as 'regulated tenancy' and 'no tenancy'.

The antecedent to contemporary tenancy reforms could be traced back to the crisis management policy adopted by the colonial administration when the disastrous consequences of the Permanent Settlement enacted in 1793 on India's peasantry became difficult to ignore. In a comprehensive review of policy initiatives on the tenancy question, Appu (1975) argued that the main points of intervention, namely rent, security of tenure and conferment of right to ownership on tenants were formed on three broad policy templates at the national level: fixing of the higher ceiling of rent to one-fifth or one-fourth of the gross produce, permanent rights to the tenant on cultivated land with a rider of a limited right of resumption to the landowner and finally the tenants right of ownership on non-resumable land.

Like any another land reform law, the definition of key variables decided the fate of tenancy laws in the states even before they were implemented. Appu (1975) identified such terms 'tenant', 'personal cultivation', 'right to resumption' and 'voluntary surrender' that would have consequences for millions of tenants across states. While most states considered a person who cultivated land owned by another person on payment of rent, cash or kind or a combination of both a tenant, some states such as Uttar Pradesh and West Bengal initially did not treat those cultivators as 'tenants' who paid their rents as a share of produce. This effectively excluded a large number of sharecroppers from the purview of tenancy regulations (Appu, 1975).

The definition of personal cultivation proved to be even more contentious. It was recommended to include at least three qualifying criteria to declare a particular holding under self-cultivation. It included that the entire risk of cultivation was to be borne by the 'landowner', the 'personal supervision by the owner or her family member' and 'performance of manual labour'. Out of these, the third one faced the stiffest opposition and was finally dropped in suggestions regarding the definition of personal cultivation except when the right to the resumption of land was exercised by the owner. However, most states did not include even this modified definition in their laws on tenancy (Appu, 1975).

Policymakers in India after a prolonged debate settled on balancing between the rights of small landowners and tenants and offered a graded schema with regard to the resumption of land under a tenancy for 'self-cultivation' on 'general grounds'. Like the notion of self-cultivation, 'general grounds were never properly defined' (Appu, 1975). However, all these meticulous exercises in hair-splitting and verbal jugglery inspired by solicitude for the so-called 'small owners' and anxiety to balance nicely the conflicting interests of landowners and tenants, seemed to have been undertaken, ignoring the realities of the power equation in the Indian countryside and the character and capability of the administrative machinery. (Appu, 1975 p. 1345)

Similarly, power equations in rural areas ensured that all forcible ejectments were recorded as 'voluntary surrender' by the tenant on 'persuasion' of the landowner. The fate of provisions regarding fair rent could not have been different. They remained on paper (Appu, 1975).

Tenancy reforms in India proved to be successful only in those states where both a powerful mobilization of the peasantry and state machinery invested their energy. It depended on the political atmosphere rather than administrative procedures. It was and is a political question. Ghatak and Roy (2007) argued that the Left-ruled West Bengal and Kerala were the two most successful states in India in terms of land reforms. 'These two states accounted for 11.75 and 22.88 per cent, respectively, of the total number of tenants conferred ownership rights (or protected rights) up to 2000, despite being home to only 7.05 and 2.31 per cent of India's population, respectively' (Ghatak & Roy, 2007, p. 253).

However, the situation was quite different in most other states where the oral tenancy was still widely practised. In these states, landowners did not even allow the registration of tenants, leave aside following rules on rent and security of tenancy. Various commentators tried to analyse reasons for the failure of tenancy laws in these states, but the following lines capture the essence of failure of tenancy reforms in India.

> When the labour force is large and rapidly growing, the demand for land is so acute that land owners can easily claim 50 percent or more of the gross output of their sharecropper; in such a situation it is strikingly naive to think that the economic position of sharecropper might be improved by statutory limiting landlord's share to one sixth. (Myrdal, 1968, p. 1327)

In a nutshell, landowners were so powerful in the lease market that they did not allow any regulation come in their way of dictating terms.

However, this was not true in cases of 'reverse tenancy' where rich peasants leased in land from marginal holdings. In these cases, the lessor decided the terms of the tenancy. Studies also confirmed that terms were mostly dictated by the more powerful party in a lease contract, and it reproduced an unequal power relationship between individual households and castes (Trivedi, 2011).

This was not to claim that land reforms had not made any contribution in favour of the landless and poor peasants. After the failure of the distribution of ceiling surplus land, following guidelines by the centre, many states initiated the distribution of government land to land-poor households. This programme was rather successful in many states. For instance, more than a million hectares of land was distributed to approximately 3.6 million households in Uttar Pradesh up to 2008, a majority of them belonging to SC/ST category. This initiative proved to be very helpful in curbing landlessness but in many instances unfortunately land distributed under this programme was not fit for cultivation. Besides, the distribution of common land reduced the area that was available to the village community for several other purposes other than cultivation. The dependence of the poor on the village commons was much higher than households with an asset base (Jodha, 1986; Ostrom, 1990).

The performance of the other two initiatives, namely land consolidation and land records updation and digitization, has varied across states. Some larger states like Bihar were lagging behind others on both counts, whereas Uttar Pradesh performed very well, especially in land consolidation. The positive impact of land consolidation on agricultural productivity was beyond doubt. It was not just a coincidence that states that had been ahead in land consolidation were also forerunners in adopting the Green Revolution agricultural practices.

After more than seven decades of land reforms, contemporary landownership was marked by a preponderance of 'functionally landless' holdings. Reported landlessness might be less than one-tenth of all the holdings but around two-thirds holdings were 'effectively landlessness' in terms of a land size capable of generating some income (Yadu & Satheesha, 2016). This situation reflected the utter failure of state intervention in the landownership structure. Often it was claimed that the average size of holding was coming down and the Indian agrarian scene was increasingly dominated by smaller size of holdings. However, it needs to be mentioned that decreasing the size of holdings had less to do with state interventions and even less with market transactions. It was mainly due to generational subdivision of holdings. Because of this, the caste and landownership congruence was not broken. In any village, the original group of landowners still held most of the land it owned during the time of Independence, despite the smaller size of individual holdings.

Another characteristic of this kind of changes in the landownership pattern was the persistence of inequality between individuals and groups. It never allowed the wide gap between groups to close down, leave aside bridging it. At the all-India level, this phenomenon could be seen in the top around 2 per cent holdings owing approximately 25 per cent of the area, while the bottom 75 per cent owned close to 30 per cent of the area in 2012–2013 (Yadu & Satheesha, 2016). Since the original group retained its interest in land, it also preserved the power associated with it.

The concealed tenancy was an obvious outcome of this kind of a landownership structure. Land might be open to market transactions, but it had not shed its sociopolitical dimensions completely. Additionally, it was also seen as an asset. This situation forbade absentee landowners to sell their land. Resident owners who diversified into other occupations or their major source of income shifted outside the agriculture sector also preferred to retain their land. After the unsuccessful attempt by the state to redistribute this kind of land to the actual tiller, the gap created by huge anomalies in landownership was filled by tenancy. On whatever exploitative terms, the poor then have no other means to access land other than through tenancy.

THE AGRARIAN STRUCTURE

Land relations do not exist in isolation, but they form the basis of a broader set of relationships often referred to as agrarian structure. Studies on agrarian structure have been a compelling preoccupation of political economy, sociology, economics, political science, development studies and other social sciences in India like many other post-colonial countries. One of the most engaging debates of this genre that drew the attention of a variety of scholars and approaches through the 1970s probed the question of penetration of capitalist relations in Indian agriculture. Often referred to as 'mode of production' debate, drawn from the main dispute to characterize production relations in Indian agriculture as 'semi-feudal', 'pre-capitalist', 'colonial', dual' or 'capitalist' (Thorner, 1982), participants investigated various aspects of agrarian relations in a Marxist political economy framework.

While debating 'capitalist development in agriculture' that could be understood concerning 'change in internal relations of production' and 'class structure in agrarian sector', scholars frequently resorted to the concept of 'peasant differentiation'—a dynamic process that leads to the polarization of the otherwise homogenous peasantry into a rich peasant and landless labourer (Patnaik, 2007, pp. 16–17). It had been pointed out earlier that the three readings of the classical agrarian question transition of peasant economy to capitalism, mobilization of resources for industrial development by the appropriation of surplus generated in agriculture and political question of alliances set the terms of this lively debate (Shah & Harriss-White, 2011, p. 13).

Primarily, the debate centred around the question of whether a progressive change of replacement of pre-capitalist relations by capitalist relations which would take the agrarian economy to a new level of development was taking place in India. Further, the dynamics and nature of this change were discussed to understand constraints in this process (Nadkarni, 1991). However, the entire debate was focused on one sector that was agriculture and several studies were region specific but, later on, it was clarified that the narrow usage of the concept 'mode of production' in terms of a sector/region in a given 'social formation in transition' was not appropriate and it was about the extent and the nature of the development of capitalist tendency in agriculture (Patnaik, 1986, p. 37–38 cited in Nadkarni, 1991, p. 103). It was abundantly clear that 'development of capitalism could not be confined to one sector, it was a force that transformed all economic activities and social life' (Namboodiripad, 1984, p. 5).

Thorner (1982) summarized various positions in this debate. Patnaik (1971a, 1971b, 1971c) took the position that capitalist relations in Indian agriculture had been penetrating deeply since Independence but the failure of land reforms to abolish landlordism and redistribute land had not allowed broadening its base. Patnaik further argued that in the absence of the desired transformation of land relations, small peasants had to pay high rents for want of any other means of subsistence without a commensurate rise in productivity. In this way, pre-capitalist rent acted as a major constraint for further development of capitalist relations. The rent barrier, Patnaik underlined, diverted investment away from irrigation, fertilizers and high-yield variety seeds that could boost output and surplus per unit area of land. To Patnaik, investment in mechanization and labour displacement technologies was selective and targeted at enhancing surplus (cited in Thorner, 1982).

Omvedt (1981) also took an equally clear position on the penetration of capitalist relations. She identified several tendencies in the Indian rural settings including 'dependence of very high proportion of the rural population on wages', 'cultivators selling in the market albeit under duress', 'growth in the application of capital inputs', 'industrial production of means of production and acquisition via market', 'rural rich being primarily exploiter of labour-power of rural poor in their relationship with the latter' and 'free and mobile rural semi-proletariat' to conclude about the dominance of capitalist tendency (cited in Thorner, 1982, p. 2063). On the same lines, Gupta (1980) too argued that capitalism had prevailed over feudal institutions, but it neither appeared in all its virility nor had it developed uniformly all over India (cited in Thorner, 1982).

Those who supported the 'feudalism thesis' underlined the role of imperialism and characterized India's agrarian sector as 'semi-colonial and semi-feudal'. It was argued that the 'feudal mode of production and feudal social formation' persisted in an 'assimilative form, running over a variety of proportionately between feudal mode and capitalist mode'. Further, 'Though capitalism has come, the pre-capitalist mode is still prevalent, and capitalist development is arrested primarily by the influence of imperialism' (Sen Gupta, 1977 cited in Thorner, 1982, p. 2061).

Chattopadhyay's (1980) thesis of 'dual role of capitalism *vis-à-vis* pre-capitalist' in terms of 'both preservation and destruction of older forms', and this being a universal phenomenon not just confined to colonies and semi-colonies, was a substantive contribution to the mode of production debate (cited in Thorner, 1982 p. 2062). But Lin's (1980) formulation of 'dual mode of production' in which capitalist and pre-capitalist modes infused into each other to 'constitute a single mode with dual characteristics' with 'accommodating and conflicting internal dynamics' did not yield expected responses in the debate (cited in Thorner, 1982). Rudra (1981) added a new dimension to the debate by bringing in the role of ideology and criticized other participants for ignoring social, cultural and religious institutions (Thorner, 1982).

What has muddied the water for researches on agrarian relations is the recovery of a mixed bag of evidence that lends support to various hypotheses. It was not strange for a periphery social formation. The empirical data collected by participants in the debate pointed to the existence of large-scale small tenancy, the concentration of land in the hands of landlords and prevalence of small landholdings to make a case of feudal relations. Survival of older practices such as the interlocking of markets, usury and extra-economic constraints further strengthened their case. Simultaneously, the tendency of intensive farming using hired labour was unmistakably becoming a principal mode of exploitation of rural labour replacing tenancy. This, along with evidence of relatively free labour liberated from debt bondage, servile and traditionally tied status, and investment in technology for increased and market-oriented production, gave credence to the capitalist thesis (Thorner, 1982). But keeping in mind Rao (1990) that 'what is becoming is more important than what is' (cited in Nadkarni, 1991, p. 100), the direction of change was unquestionably capitalist.

More important was the theorization upon which this empirical evidence was assessed and critiqued. For instance, the question of tenancy was looked at from various standpoints to arrive at contradictory conclusions. One position in this debate, including some of the ardent supporters of the capitalist thesis, considered small tenancy as an indicator of semi-feudal social formation. But this conceptual congruence between feudalism and tenancy faced stiff criticism by Chakraborty (1981, pp. 5–14) who argued that tenancy was becoming compatible with emerging capitalist relations, and it 'takes different forms and embodies different mixtures of capitalist and pre-capitalist relations under different historical conditions'. She further clarified her position that the relations of production involved in the diversion of agricultural surplus in the form of land rent were feudal but that did not make tenancy itself feudal or semi-feudal (cited in Thorner, 1982,

p. 2062). Citing Marx's theory of ground rent, Namboodiripad (1984) also argued that with the development of capitalism, small tenant farmers either earned freehold ownership of land or reincarnated themselves into capitalist tenant farmer transforming their obligatory relationship with the landlord into a contractual relationship in money form.

Similar was the case with wage labour which was often taken as an indicator of capitalist tendency. But Patnaik (1983) refused to accept this formulation citing the history of the evolution of a class of agricultural labour in India. She pointed out that unlike in the West where propertyless wage labour emerged alongside an 'enclosure movement', due to the caste system in India, they existed long before the onset of capitalist relations. Mostly belonging to the 'untouchable castes' and forbidden to hold land, they were forced into menial jobs. However, these people constituted only a part of the modern working class in India, the larger part came from the pauperized peasantry. Patnaik concluded that the presence of a large chunk of wage labour could be a necessary condition to characterize a social formation as the capitalist, reinvestment of appropriated surplus for further expansion being a sufficient condition.

One of the major contributions of the mode of production debate was the development of a methodology for the study of agrarian relations. The first question that needed to be addressed related to the assessment of class composition in rural society. The rampant usage of land–class–size categorization has continued to date but political economists long ago had identified limitations of this categorization. They pointed out that land size did not represent a scale of operation. Moreover, it was argued that 'class' signified a relationship between the producer and appropriator of surplus. Patnaik (1976 cited in Rahman, 1986) proposed a method of appreciating class composition based on the flow of surplus. The e-criterion identified five agrarian classes, that is, landlord, a rich peasant, middle peasant, a poor peasant and full-time labour. Collection of data was a major challenge in the operationalization of this method. Additionally, it was nearly impossible to find out households that were solely dependent on agriculture (Rahman, 1986).

Later Roemer (1982 cited in Rahman, 1986) proposed to identify agrarian classes taking into consideration self-employment, hiring out and hiring in by households. Bardhan (1984 cited in Rahman, 1986) applied this method in his study of rural West Bengal and identified five agrarian classes, that is, capitalist landlord, a rich farmer, family farmer, a poor peasant and landless labourer. Khan (1983 cited in Rahman, 1986) developed this method further by taking cognizance of both land and labour. But Rahman (1986) argued that an investigation into the agrarian relations as they existed in the Third World should not only consider land and labour but also farm implements, investible capital and so on. He opined that composite indices would be more useful in capturing contemporary agrarian realities. Ramachandran and Swaminathan (2014), and Swaminathan and Rawal (2015) also attempted a classification on the basis of multiple factors including the use of family and wage labour, ownership of means of production and level and diversification of incomes. Srivastava's (2016) index of class included diversification and non-agricultural sources. Development of such a composite index was a challenge considering the closer integration of the agrarian and non-agrarian sectors of the economy.

EMERGING AGRARIAN STRUCTURE

After a long hiatus, some recent works of this genre have rekindled the debate. Several responses have appeared in the recent past refuting Bernstein's (2004) proclamation that in the age of globalization, the agrarian question was dead. Tracing the history of the classical myth that the agrarian question was essentially of social and economic resources for the growth of industrialization, Moyo et. al. (2015) argued that under the burden of the backwardness–industrialization binary, the Eurocentric Marxist discourse ignored political questions such as land concentration and mass peasant population and reduced the agrarian question to the agrarian question of capital. They further argued that in Bernstein's schema, the agrarian question of labour was subsumed in the logic of capitalist development. In their powerful rebuttal, Moyo et al. (2015, p. 37) argued that the 'analytical rupture between the agrarian question of capital and the agrarian question of labour for the countries of South seemed to be misleading and certainly a misreading of the classical perspective in which question of capital and labour was viewed in an integrated fashion'. They further argued that the flow of capital did not necessarily lead to a transition in agriculture and elsewhere.

Another interesting debate was triggered recently on the question of non-cultivating peasant households (NCPHs). One position in this debate argued that NCPHs were 'too busy to farm' indicating that those households diversified into relatively more remunerative occupations and were loath to invest in agriculture for enhanced productivity. The increasing importance of these households rekindled debates on constraints to agrarian transformation. An alternative view in the debate pointed out that NCPHs were 'too poor to farm' in the context of increasing capital-intensive agriculture (Reddy & Shaw, 2013; Vijay, 2012). However, recent field studies (Trivedi, 2017) found NCPHs to be a heterogeneous group that included both classes of peasants. These studies indicated that both tendencies, rich and poor exiting agriculture, could be different facets of the same process.

Further, the persisting monopoly of original landowners over agricultural land was the characteristics of contemporary agrarian structure in India. This thriving landlordism controlled the land and political power, both closely interconnected with each other. However, this observation came with a rider indicating inter-caste and intra-caste inequalities. Across villages, landlessness and land poverty were not uncommon among the majority of the households who shared caste bonds with the biggest landowners of their village. Slight fissures were visible in this structure by way of sales of smaller and distant plots to mostly OBCs which had some implications for the rural power structure (Himanshu & Stern, 2016; Ramachandran, 2011; Saha, 2014; Srivastava, 2016; Trivedi, 2017).

This asymmetry in the landownership structure was reflected in often expanding the area under tenancy while a large number of agrarian households participated in the lease market. An increasing demand for land in the lease market weakened the bargaining power of tenants who had to concede to the terms dictated by the landowner. Sharecropping continued to be a major form of tenancy, but cash rents contracts were rising. Labour supply type of contracts were also found. 'Prevailing tenancy terms' has remained a myth, varying along the caste and landownership of both the parties, being the most exploitative when an 'upper-caste' landlord has leased out land to a Dalit landless household. Cash-rich OBC and SC households preferred to lease in land on the basis of cash rent, but landowners who had a final say in deciding terms chose sharecropping (Himanshu & Stern, 2016; Ramachandran, 2011; Saha, 2014; Srivastava, 2016; Trivedi, 2017).

The most interesting was the tendency of investing non-agricultural income in agriculture. Another remarkable aspect of the emerging agrarian scene was decreasing the proportion of households solely dependent on agriculture; however, most of them remained occupied in this sector. At the same time, the per unit of land income from cultivation remained stagnant for long periods while the revenue per unit of land was increasing due to cropping intensity, mechanization and cash crops. Poor and middle peasants incurred negative incomes from cultivation (Himanshu & Stern, 2016; Ramachandran, 2011; Saha, 2014; Srivastava, 2016; Trivedi, 2017). Despite the development of agriculture, the interlocking of credit and labour was not rare to find both in agriculture and allied activities (Rani, 2007).

AGRICULTURE IN THE PRE- AND DURING REFORMS PERIOD

Like other sectors of the economy, agriculture too underwent a colossal change under the impact of neoliberal globalization that was ushered in 1991, marking a milestone in history. It all started in the mid-1980s when the prime position of the sector, due in large measure to the Green Revolution, began to slide down. However, the package of high-yield variety seeds, chemical fertilizers and assured irrigation that was counterposed to 'red revolution' has more than one narratives but official story traced its needs to India's acute food grain crisis and dependence on imports majorly due to stagnant productivity during last one century under colonial rule. It represented the mood of the day when attaining self-sufficiency in agriculture and industry and overcoming dependence on foreign capital was considered the topmost priority of the newly independent nation.

This strategy paid off for India in terms of raising productivity and production. The country's food grain production increased rapidly in the first decade itself. Initially, the targeted areas having assured and sufficient irrigation and a class of 'progressive farmers' willing to invest in agriculture reaped the benefits of subsidized inputs, the government purchase at minimum support prices and deployment of new technology. Soon after, these farming practices disseminated to other areas and in the next two decades had overwhelmed entire rural India.

On the flip side, the Green Revolution turned out to be an ecological catastrophe. Growing wheat and later rice displacing locally suited varieties such as millets, pulses and oilseeds was an ill-conceived agricultural strategy both from the cultivation point of view and diets. Placing wheat and later rice over all other millets, pulses, oilseeds, etc., displaced locally suited varieties both from cultivation and diets turning country into nutrition deficit in the race of achieving food security. The forceful execution of mono-cropping, based on increasing control over nature, triggered a vicious cycle of loss of soil fertility, compensated by rising amount of fertilizers and water leading to escalating cost of cultivation (Kumar, 2019).

By the mid-1980s, the rise in productivity under the new practices had saturated and rise in costs had left farming unviable for a large section of farmers. The old support system of cultivation, seeds, manure, irrigation and so on had already been destroyed and even a partial withdrawal of the state from its supporting role proved to be devastating for the peasantry in a completely monetized, market-driven farm economy.

In this precarious situation, if there was one word that defined agriculture in India from the 1990s onwards, it was 'crisis'. If one was looking for a more charitable word, then perhaps 'distress' could fit the bill. But conceptually, both words would have different connotations. This was a period that saw an unprecedented number of farmer suicides, the very notion of which was heard of for the first time in a country that had a two-millennia-old history of settled agriculture. Social science research responded equally powerfully to this 'crisis', investigating causes behind this ensuing distress and critiquing the policy framework responsible for causing a catastrophe of this magnitude.

The first sign of this crisis was the rising gulf between agriculture and other sectors of the economy. The sector that used to contribute 29.6 per cent of the country's gross domestic product (GDP) in 1981–1982 had fallen to a mere 11.8 per cent in 2013–2014. However, during the same period, the fall in the share of population dependent on the sector was only marginal reflecting a sharp reduction in workers' productivity and dwindling income. The increasing divergence between the growth rate of agri-GDP and total GDP was another warning sign of deterioration. While agriculture grew at a rate of 2.9 per cent against 4.7 per cent of the economy during the 1980s, the respective figures were 2.8 per cent and 5.3 per cent during the 1990s. In the decade of 2000s, agriculture's growth rate plummeted down to 2.4 per cent, while the economy went up to 6.8 per cent (Roy, 2017). This way people engaged in the sector suffered at two interrelated levels—stagnation and overcrowding in agriculture and relative disadvantages due to the widening of the gap with other sectors.

The crisis was not an incident that occurred suddenly due to faulty policies of the state. It was in the making for a long time. When the state began to deprioritize agriculture, the agrarian structure was already plagued with huge anomalies, especially for the weakest sections of the peasantry. In other words, faulty policies superimposed on the huge concentration of land and failure of land reforms to transfer land to the tiller triggered a series of consequences that were devastating for the already pauperized peasantry. The conceptual distinction between 'agricultural crisis' and 'agrarian crises' makes it clear that the nature of the latter is institutional that demands radical changes like land reforms (Patnaik, 2002; Rao, 2009).

Interestingly, the symptoms and causes of this crisis intermeshed with each other making it difficult to isolate one from another. For instance, growing inequality between workers involved in the agrarian sector and the non-agrarian sector could be both the cause and effect of this crisis. Similarly, the growth of capital formation in agriculture has taken a beating after the 1980s (Chand, 2009). However, there were certain policy implications in the root of the crisis, direct or indirect, which were difficult to ignore. There was no denying the fact that at its root, declining public investment and the sharply decreasing share of agriculture in the formal credit severely hit the sector and people dependent on it. Similarly, the government's procurement policy was just a bit short of actually declaring that it was not interested in intervening in the marketing of agricultural produce. Similarly, pushing helpless Indian farmers to compete with large-scale, corporate-style farms with large-scale state support in the name of trade liberalization was equally dangerous. Price volatility in the international market too was identified as one of the major reasons for the suicides of farmers who were growing cash crops. Overall, the entire package of economic 'reforms' proved to be devastating for Indian peasantry at an unprecedented level (Reddy & Mishra, 2009).

The shrinking gap between input costs and output prices squeezed out whatever crop production profitability farmers had. They were pushed on both ends of their economics. Escalating prices of input items due to 'subsidy rationalization' coincided with most of them remaining out of the government network of procurement that left them to the mercy of private players. Some authors argued that input subsidies were bad since they diverted resources from capital investment. However, the fallacy of this argument lay in the assumption of fixity of resources available to agriculture (Agarwal, 2009). Needless to say, outside the government procurement network, the 'free market' was terrible for farmers. Crashing prices dominated during the harvest season, increasing barely a few months later when peasants needed to buy their household essentials. However, a significant section of peasantry did not have to even worry about that. They received a prefixed price for their produce from a creditor or input dealer debunking all talk of the end of interlocking.

However, one can claim that after the devastating late 1990s and the early 2000s, there was a recovery period when agriculture growth again picked up, increasing farmers' income. International market and terms of trade were also not unfavourable during that period. More than that, major state initiatives such as MGNREGA, farmers' debt relief scheme and the Forest Rights Act aided this recovery. Over and above, the government took initiatives to resolve at least the credit problem, doubling it in a short span. But this growth in credit flow to agriculture came with a rider. It was also due to an increase in 'indirect finance' rather than direct finance to cultivators. Further, the definition of indirect finance was amended to add several new items under its head. Moreover, there was a sharp increase in big tickets loans to agro-businesses, all accounted for under the umbrella title 'credit flow to agriculture' (Chavan & Ramakumar, 2007).

The 'crisis', the 'recovery' and again the plunge into another 'distress' has had varying effects and responses from different classes of farmers. A section of rich farmers might have been able to capitalize upon the opportunities thrown by the liberalization of trade, but it was generally the small and medium farmers who tried to diversify into capital-intensive, high-value crops who committed suicides in large numbers (Reddy & Mishra, 2009). It was these small farmers who witnessed the depletion in their assets, both land and livestock, under the burden of indebtedness (Patnaik, 2002).

However, the situation could have been redeemed if the state's obsession with productivity was replaced by the question of livelihood for farmers (Gulati et al., 2020). Further, the small farms could have been made viable provided they received support in terms of institutional cheap credit, marketing of produce at reasonable prices and technological innovations suitable for small farms (Reddy, 2011).

EMERGING AGENDA OF LAND AND AGRARIAN STUDIES

The most potent challenge to land and agrarian studies comes from the feminist perspective that questions the 'cognitive blackout' of women who have been a major contributor to agriculture from the beginning. An increasingly powerful stream of work has raised issues concerning women's land rights, their ownership of and control over other productive assets and participation in decision-making concerning agriculture. They have challenged social hierarchies that 'naturalize' women's subordinate status and cultural traditions that extend legitimacy to patriarchal institutions. Works of this genre interrogate closer linkages between patriarchies and resource ownership, often bringing in questions of sexuality (Agarwal, 1994; Kodoth, 2001; Razavi, 2007).

These arguments seek to demolish control of 'selected men' over not only private property but also resources controlled by state and community. They link property rights with 'women's struggle for equality' (Agarwal, 1994, p. 13). They critique land reforms for their gender-blind approach under the assumption that resources allocated to a household were equally shared between all members of a family (Razavi, 2007). Works of this genre have also questioned state policies for incorporating patriarchal families as homogenous entities irrespective of their caste, class and ethnicity (Kodoth, 2001). The narratives of women's struggle for land enrich this body of works (Kelkar, 1991). Gender-biased laws have received special attention in this discourse inviting critique and corrective measures (Saxena, n.d.).

In continuity with the feminist perspective, another area of social science research has questioned equality in landownership along caste lines. However, land and agrarian studies all along have been premised on the notion of equality but recent works prominently highlight deprivation among specific caste and ethnic groups, mostly Dalits and Adivasis. These studies have shown that given the close correspondence between social, political and economic, inequality in landownership has reinforced caste-based power equations (Mohanty, 2001; Sharma, 2007; Trivedi, 2011).

Combining a social justice perspective with concerns for the environment, recent works on common property resources (CPRs) and access of marginalized groups to them represent another emerging area of research. Various shades of these works reveal inclination either towards environmental studies or towards the rights of marginalized groups often located in their dilemma about the primacy of one of these planks. Further, works that interrogate access to CPRs from the perspective of the marginalized also face difficult choices when it comes to weighing individual rights versus collective rights.

The agenda of agrarian studies is an ever-evolving and dynamic process. All these emerging questions do not discount existing issues of agrarian reforms but further strengthen them. The present volume is an attempt to revisit the old formulations and emerging questions together to underline common concerns and diverse perspective that make this discourse lively.

REFERENCES

Agarwal, A. (2009). Harvest of despair. *Economic & Political Weekly*, 44(29), 38–39.
Agarwal, B. (1994). *A field of one's own—gender and land rights in South Asia*. Cambridge University Press.
Appu, P. S. (1975). Tenancy reform in India. *Economic & Political Weekly*, 10(33–35), 1339–13375.
Bandyopadhyay, D. (2002). The forgotten agenda. *Economic & Political Weekly*, 37(52), 5179–5181.
Bardhan, P. (1984). Agrarian class formation. In P. Bardhan (Ed.), *Land, labour and rural poverty: Essays in development economics*. Oxford University Press.
Basu, K. (2012). Land reform. In K. Basu & A. Maertens (Eds.), *The new Oxford companion to economics in India* (3rd ed.). Oxford University Press.

Bernstein, H. (2004). Changing before our very eyes: Agrarian questions and the politics of land in capitalism today. *Journal of Agrarian Change*, 4(1–2), 190–225.

Borras, S. M. Jr. (2006). Redistributive land reform in 'public' (forest) lands? Lessons from the Philippines and their implications for land reform theory and practice. *Progress in Development Studies*, 6(2), 123–145.

Chakraborty, A. (1981). Tenancy and Mode of Production. *Economic and Political Weekly*, XVI(13), *Review of Agriculture*, 5–14.

Chand, R. (2009). Capital formation in Indian agriculture: National and state level analysis. In D. N. Reddy & S. Mishra (Eds.), *Agrarian Crisis in India*. Oxford University Press.

Chand, R., Prasanna, P. A. L., & Singh, A. (2011). Farm size and productivity: Understanding the strengths of smallholders and improving their livelihoods. *Economic & Political Weekly*, XLVI(26–27), 5–11.

Chattopadhyay, P. (1980). Mode of production in Indian agriculture: An afterword. *Economic & Political Weekly*, XV(26), 85–88.

Chavan, P., & Ramakumar, R. (2007). Revival of agricultural credit in the 2000s: An explanation. *Economic & Political Weekly*, 42(52), 57–64.

Dandekar, V. M., & Rath, N. (1971). Poverty in India. *Economic & Political Weekly*, 6(2), 25–27, 29–43.

Ghatak, M., & Roy, S. (2007). Land reform and agricultural productivity in India: A review of the evidence. *Oxford Review of Economic Policy*, 23(2), 251–269.

Gulati, A., Kapur, D., & Burton, M. M. (2020). Reforming Indian agriculture. *Economic & Political Weekly*, 55(11), 35–42.

Gupta, D. (1980). Formal and real subsumption of labour under capital: The instance of 'share cropping'. *Economic & Political Weekly*, XV(39), 98, 106.

Himanshu, & Stern, N. (2016). How lives change: Six decades in a North Indian village. In Himanshu, P. Jha, & G. Rodgers (Eds.), *The changing villages in India: Insights from longitudinal research*. Oxford University Press.

Jodha, N. S. (1986). Common property resources and rural poor in dry regions of India. *Economic & Political Weekly*, 21(27), 1169–1181.

Kelkar, G. (1991). Agricultural labour, women and land rights in Bihar (India). *Peace Research*, 23(4), 37–47.

Khan, M. H. (1983). Class and agrarian transition in Pakistan. *The Pakistan Development Review*, XXII(3, Autumn), 129–162.

Kodoth, P. (2001). Gender, family and property rights—Questions from Kerala's land reforms. *Indian Journal of Gender Studies*, 8(2), 291–306.

Kumar, R. 2019. India's Green Revolution and Beyond-Visioning Agrarian Futures on Selective Reading of Agrarian Past. *Economic and Political Weekly*, LIV(34), 41–48.

Ladejinsky, W. (1972). Land ceilings and land reform. *Economic & Political Weekly*, 7(5–7), 401–408.

Lin, S. G. (1980). Theory of Dual Mode of Production in Post-Colonial India, in two parts. *Economic and Political Weekly*, XV(10), 516–529 and (11), 565–573.

Misra, S. K., & Puri, V. K. (2000). *Indian economy*. Himalaya Publishing.

Mohanty, B. B. (2001). Land distribution among scheduled castes and tribes. *Economic & Political Weekly, 36*(40), 3857–3868.

Moyo, S., Jha, P. & Yeros, P. (2015). The agrarian question in the 21st century. *Economic & Political Weekly, 50*(37).

Myrdal, G. (1968). Asian drama—An enquiry into the poverty of nations. Kalyani Publishers.

Nadkarni, M. V. (1991). The mode of production debate—A review article. *Indian Economic Review, XXVI*(1), 99–104.

Namboodiripad, E. M. S. (1984). The Marxist theory of ground rent: Relevance of the study of agrarian question in India. *Social Scientist, 12*(2), 3–15.

Newell, R. S. (1972). Ideology and realities: Land redistribution in Uttar Pradesh. *Pacific Affairs, 45*(2, Summer), 220–239.

Omvedt, Gail. (1981). Capitalist agriculture and rural classes in India. *Economic & Political Weekly, XVI*(52), 140–159.

Ostrom, E. (1990). *Governing the commons: The evolution of institutions for collective action*. Cambridge University Press.

Patnaik, U. (1971a). Capitalist development in agriculture—A note. *Economic & Political Weekly, VI*(39), 123–130.

Patnaik, U. (1971b). Capitalist development in agriculture: Further comment. *Economic & Political* Weekly, *VI*(52), 190–194.

Patnaik, U. (1971c). Capitalist Development in Agriculture: Further Comment. *Economic and Political Weekly, VI*(52), *Review of Agriculture*, 123–130.

Patnaik, U. (1976). Class differentiation within the peasantry—An approach to analysis of Indian agriculture. *Economic & Political Weekly, XI*(39), A82–A101.

Patnaik, U. (1983). On the evolution of class of agricultural labourers in India. *Social Scientist, 11*(7), 3–24.

Patnaik, U. (1986). *The agrarian question and the development of capitalism in India*. Oxford University Press.

Patnaik, U. (1987). *Peasant class differentiation—A study in method with reference to Haryana*. Oxford University Press.

Patnaik, U. (2002). Agrarian crisis and global deflationism. *Social Scientist, 30*(1–2), 3–30.

Patnaik, U. (2007). New data on arrested development of capitalism in Indian agriculture. *Social Scientist, 35*(7–8), 4–23.

Rahman, A. (1986). *Peasants and classes—A study in differentiation in Bangladesh*. Oxford University Press.

Ramachandran, V. K. (2011). Classes and class differentiation in India's countryside. *World Review of Political Economy, 2*(4), 646–670.

Ramachandran, V. K., & Swaminathan, M. (Eds.). (2014). *Dalit households in a village economy*. Tulika Books.

Rani, V. (2007). Casual labour contracts of agricultural labourers in East and West Uttar Pradesh. *Economic & Political Weekly, 42*(2), 154–160.

Rao, C. H. H. (1972). Ceiling on agricultural land-holding: It's economic rationale. *Economic & Political Weekly, 7*(26), A59, A61–A62.

Rao, R. S. (1990). *Agrarian Relations and Accumulation: The Mode of Production Debate in India*. In Patnaik U. (Ed.), Oxford University Press and Samiksha Trust, Bombay.

Rao, V. M. (2009). Farmers' distress in a modernising agriculture—The tragedy of upwardly mobile: An overview. In D. N. Reddy, & S. Mishra (Eds.), *Agrarian crisis in India*. Oxford University Press.

Razavi, S. (2007). Liberalisation and the debates on women's access to land. *Third World Quarterly, 28*(8), 1479–1500.

Reddy, B., & Shaw, A. (2013). New landlords—Too poor to farm or too busy to farm. *Economic & Political Weekly, 48*(38), 65–69.

Reddy, D. N. (2011). Small farms. In M. Mohanty (Ed.), *India social development report 2010—The land and the marginalized*. Oxford University Press.

Reddy, D. N., & Mishra, S. (Eds.). (2009). *Agrarian crisis in India*. Oxford University Press.

Roemer, J. (1982). *A general theory of exploitation and class*. Harvard University Press.

Roy Burman, B. K., Singh, Y., Oommen, T. K., Joshi, P. C., & Dube, S. C. (1974). Land reforms in a sociological perspective. *India International Centre Quarterly, 1*(1), 51–68.

Roy, S. D. (2017). Economic Reforms and Agricultural Growth in India. *Economic and Political Weekly, LII*(9), 67–72.

Rudra, A. (1981). Against feudalism. *Economic & Political Weekly, XVI*(52), 2133–2146.

Saha, P. (2014). Asset ownership and terms of tenancy contracts: Caste and class in a village in western UP. In A. Kumar Singh & S. Mehrotra (Eds.), *Land policies for equity and growth: Transforming the agrarian structure in Uttar Pradesh* (pp. 124–154). SAGE Publications.

Saxena, K. B. (2016). Preface. In P. K. Trivedi (Ed.), *Land to the tiller—Revisiting the unfinished land reform's agenda*. Books for Change.

Saxena, N. C. (n.d.). *Enhancement of property rights including land rights of women*. Theme paper. Planning Commission, Government of India.

Sen Gupta, N. (1977). Further on the mode of production in agriculture. *Economic & Political Weekly, XII*(26), 55–63.

Sen, A. K. (1964). Size of holdings and productivity. *Economic & Political Weekly, 16*(5–7), 323–326.

Shah, A., & Hariss-White, B. (2011). Resurrecting scholarship on agrarian transformation. *Economic & Political Weekly, 46*(39), 13–18.

Sharma, H. R. (2007). Land distribution and tenancy among different social groups. *Economic & Political Weekly, 42*(41), 4183–4185.

Srivastava, R. (2016). Assessing change: Land, labour and employment in an Eastern UP village, 1994–2012. In Himanshu, P. Jha, & G. Rodgers (Eds.), *The changing villages in India: Insights from longitudinal research*. Oxford University Press.

Swaminathan, M., & Rawal, V. (Eds.). (2015). *Socio-economic surveys of two villages in Rajasthan—A study of agrarian relations*. Foundation for Agrarian Relations.

Thorner, A. (1982). Semi-feudalism or capitalism—Contemporary debate on classes and modes of production of India. *Economic & Political Weekly, 17*(49–51).

Thorner, D. (1956). *The agrarian prospect in India*. University Press for the Delhi School of Economics.

Trivedi, P. K. (2011). Changing agrarian scene: Sociology of land, wages and indebtedness. In M. Mohanty (Ed.), *India social development report 2010—the land and the marginalized* (pp. 243–256). Oxford University Press.

Trivedi, P. K. (2017). Revisiting Senapur—Reflections on agrarian changes in North India. *Social Change, 47*(4), 509–525.

Vijay, R. (2012). Structural retrogression and rise of 'new landlords' in Indian agriculture: An empirical exercise. *Economic & Political Weekly, 47*(5), 37–45.

Yadu, C. R., & Satheesha, B. (2016). Agrarian question in India, indications from NSSO's 70th round. *Economic & Political Weekly, 51*(16), 20–23.

Section I
The Land Question

Sectional Introduction

The four chapters included in this section represent major concerns of the land discourse as it emerged in academic writing and social movements. First of all, they focus on the land rights of three major groups that were deprived of ownership of the most crucial productive asset, namely women, Dalits and Adivasis. Equally remarkable was the way these chapters linked the land question with the gender question, caste question and the ethnicity question. Significantly, these writings refused to discuss the issue of land ownership simply as a matter of economic concern but explored its social and political dimensions.

The first chapter by R. A. P. Singh explored changing social relations in the context of transforming landownership structure. Singh has argued that under the impact of land reforms, cooperation was replaced by conflict and competition within kin, clan and caste. To examine the consequence of land reforms on kinship ties, the author collected qualitative data from purposively selected 122 households of landlords, tenants and agricultural labourers from Begusarai district of North Bihar. Singh gave a narrative of cooperation among caste members during the zamindari period when intermediaries kept a large number of hangers-on and stick-wielders, mostly from their own trusted clan. During those days, people also helped each other with ploughs, oxen, seeds, and attached, hired or family labour. Singh has argued that it was a time of overlap between social relations and production processes.

In the contemporary period, economics appears to be separating from sociology with market-based contracts replacing traditional obligations.

Singh has further argued that legislations on landownership and wages, and farm technology unleashed economic forces that were causing the disintegration of the old system of cooperation and interdependence. Further, with the increasing importance of wealth, land-based conflicts were on the rise. Class interests were superseding caste interests, concluded Singh.

It was an interesting study that underlined the close correspondence between social and economic relations, a change in one reflecting a change in the other. However, the political economy literature conceived correlation between two aspects of a phenomenon as dialectical with causal relationship working both ways. Singh explored only one dimension; it would be very interesting to see how the equation worked another way around. This would precisely mean to explore caste's response to legislative changes brought by land reforms. A similar exploration could yield interesting insights into the negotiation between market and social relations.

The second chapter has focused on another important issue that has continued to be relevant in contemporary times. Alienation of land from marginalized groups as a result of actions by the state, market or powerful groups has been a major concern of social movements. Consequently, some protective provisions were incorporated in the revenue laws of all states. However, these provisions could have slowed down the pace of alienation, but it never came to a complete halt. Market forces always looked for and exploited loopholes in the protective legal shield.

The chapter by Ramesh Sharan, Amar Kumar Singh and S. L. Batra has interrogated pattern and causes of land alienation of Adivasis in Ranchi and Dumka districts of present-day Jharkhand. They considered alienation both at the community and individual level and for public projects and private interests. Sharan, Kumar and Batra found interesting changes in pattern and pace over some time, slowing down a bit since the 1980s. The authors have mentioned that the Chota Nagpur Tenancy (CNT) Act, 1908, and Santhal Pargana Tenancy Act, 1949, prohibited the transfer of land owned by a tribal family to a non-tribal person. As per the law, mortgaged land reverted back to the owner after seven years. Still, an alienation of tribal land continued with the changing dynamics, the investigation of which required a multi-stage random sampling of selected households for data collection in both districts.

Sharan, Kumar and Batra found four major means of land alienation, that is, mortgage, leasing out, sale and illegal encroachment, all forms overlapped with each other. For instance, mortgaging was supposed to be temporary but in most of the cases it resulted in permanent alienation. They also found that the non-tribals alienated over two-thirds of the total alienated land in the study areas, while the remaining one-third was transferred within Adivasi communities. After Scheduled Area Regulation (SAR) courts were set up in 1969, the momentum of alienation was somewhat checked. These mechanisms checked one prevalent method of collusive titling in which a tribal landowner used to declare that they were surrendering their mortgaged land to a non-tribal for the full and final settlement of loan that they could not pay anymore. Similarly, the *chaparbandi* method of declaring agricultural land protected under the CNT Act, a homestead plot and then selling it off was also checked by the SAR courts. Besides, awareness among Adivasis about the value of their land and their rights also protected their land to an extent.

Sharan, Kumar and Batra have justifiably focused on land transfers between tribals and non-tribals; however, they have also mentioned many transactions taking place within Scheduled Tribe groups. A further probe of these transfers would have revealed nature and extent of intra-tribes and inter-tribe transactions, further revealing emerging inequalities within the perceived egalitarian category.

The most professed goals of the land reforms programme all over the country have been to eradicate landlessness, put ownership in the hands of cultivators and break the caste–land link. All three objectives could have been achieved by putting ownership of cultivated land in the hands of Dalits who composed large sections of landless, informal tenants and agricultural labour and, most importantly, sanctioned based on their caste against holding any property including land. This is what made landownership among Dalits a test case of success of any land reform programme.

This perspective informed the work of C. R. Yadu and C. K. Vijayasuryan who looked at the impact of land reforms on Dalits. The authors underlined that the land-based caste system and caste-based landownership structure have denied Dalits holding this productive asset, crucial for mobility outside agriculture. They have argued that Dalits are historically forbidden to own land, bypassed by land reforms and excluded from the market. Their work showed that the caste–land link still persisted in Kerala, a state that successfully conferred the ownership right on the cultivating tenants of land leased by them and provided for homestead land. Yadu and Vijayasuryan have argued that the incidence of landlessness was high among Dalits due to the failure of the imposition of ceiling and distribution of surplus land among landless. While land concentration and monopoly of Brahmin landlords over land and rural power structure were considerably reduced, land reforms of the 1970s redistributed land from the upper stratum of the hierarchy to its middle rungs but the actual tiller of the land at the bottom remained landless.

Yadu and Vijayasuryan's story of land reforms in Kerala resembled the narrative of many other states where successful abolition of intermediaries, conferment of ownership rights on tenants coincided with the miserable failure of distribution of ceiling surplus land. The question needs to be asked why despite the huge variation in land tenures and social composition; it was mainly the middle-rung peasant castes that gained at the expense of poor peasantry during the redistributive land reforms across states. Equally important is a probe into caste–land congruence that has proved to be most resistant to reform in the face of a massive political-economic transformation.

Although the three chapters in this section highlight the whole problems of execution, the last one is the most important, since it highlights the basic fault in the very design of redistributive land reforms. While other works critiqued the gender bias in revenue laws, in general, and land reform policies, in particular, what distinguished Meera Velayudhan's work was a nuanced understanding of negotiation between social processes and legal architecture. In particular, she has captured the dynamics of exclusion of women from their land rights. Velayudhan's work has interrogated all three channels of landownership, that is, inheritance, state-mediated transfers and market transactions to conclude that none of these was free from biases against women.

First of all, she has argued that inheritance practices were patrilineal and land flowed down along the male line. Women only received rights of usage through their male relatives, often a father or a husband. Where women were entitled to the familial landed property, either based on local traditions or law, women appeared reluctant to claim it for fear of losing social benefits like their natal family's support. Velayudhan's work has also critiqued the biased manner which the bureaucracy adopts in cases of dispute arising out of women's claim over ancestral property.

The market might appear a 'level playing field' since in most countries women do have a legal right to buy land. But these equality claims do not go beyond appearances. A weak asset base and high dependence of women on men, both in terms of decision-making and access to finance, have left them handicapped actors in the market. The most fascinating part of Velayudhan's work is related to excuses trotted out by the family members of a woman for denying her claim over landed property. Interestingly, all the familiar pretexts such as fragmentation of land leading to lower efficiency, difficulty in managing land for a daughter who marries outside the fold and family disputes were all couched in the language of 'modernity'. Similarly, people adopted various forms of subterfuge to deny a woman her lawful share of the family property.

All four chapters taken together have offered a comprehensive critique of land reform policies in India. They also covered states located in the eastern, western and southern parts of the country. While providing a 'perspective from the below', they appeared to make the point that a critique from the standpoint of the marginalized could illuminate several dark spots in the discourse on land reforms. They also underlined the centrality of the land question in every epoch, beginning with the abolition of intermediaries and its social consequences, concern for the alienation of land owned by marginalized groups to the assertion of excluded groups over land as a matter of right. It is this centrality of the land question to the lives of people that keeps it relevant even today.

Chapter 1
Kin, Clan and Land Reform in Bihar Villages*

R. A. P. Singh

RESEARCH ANTECEDENTS

A brief reference to research antecedents in the field of kinship would be in order. We found that while very little attention has been paid to the study of kinship ties vis-à-vis land reform measures, several scholars have studied kinship with materialistic notion. Leach (1968, pp. 305–306) stands out as one of those when he says 'I want to insist that kinship systems have no 'reality' at all except in relation to land and property.' Other scholars have also noted that kinship handles strategic means of production—land (Djurfeldt & Lindberg, 1976, p. 125). Not only this but also the very phenomenon of 'rule' has been examined as an extension of kinship ties such as kin, clan, raja and rule (Fox, 1971). However, the rapid growth of population with resultant pressure on land (Srinivas, 1980, pp. 63–71) was felt, especially at the lower levels of the rural economic order. Land kept the members of the family together. Transition from agriculture to industry is loosening the ties; it is argued. New economic forces are favouring them to live separately (Beteille, 1964). Traditional kinship ties are inimical to wealth accumulation and under the pressure of new economic forces, those ties will gradually become weaker and finally would give way to more individualized economic activities which have drawn the interests of anthropologists also. It has been observed that the organization

---

* *Social Change*, 13(3), 1983.

of work, production and profit distribution and the concepts of savings and investment differs significantly from clan practices (Ciparisse, 1978). However, the hypothesis that kinship is inimical to wealth accumulation is disapproved in a study of Maya community in Chipas, Mexico (Thomas, 1978). Moreover, it has been noticed that kinship ties may further economic growth (Beteille, 1964). It has been observed that there is a close relationship between kinship and mode of production (Siskind, 1978). Kinship even plays instrumental role in economic activities (Bennett & Despres, 1960). The basic elements of kinship (Bennett, 1969) may be understood as a set of determinants of human social relations in a particular mode of production that is neither irreducible nor external. Godelier (1975) has recognized the place of kinship in economic as well as in social life and has stated that 'rationality' is relative. He would disagree with those who held the view that kinship syndrome cherishes elements of irrationality. He clarifies that in simpler societies kinship is both intra-structure and superstructure, but in a complex society like ours, kinship does not play the role of superstructure. He has further posited that kinship should not be considered as a cause of backwardness in a more complex society. Thus, kin-based or kin-oriented economic behaviour does not cause an academic anxiety in the thinking of Godelier. As a sharp contrast, Gough (1965) is another materialist who has identified indulgence in wider kinship network as a lifestyle of top-class and higher caste. Landed-class people are more kin oriented, whereas lower class people could afford very little of it. She has made a penetrating study of Brahmin kinship in a Tamil village.

It was Marriott (1952) who examined the consequences of various legislative measures in a village in Uttar Pradesh including the Tenancy and the Abolition of Zamindari Act and had reported that changes took place in various aspects of caste, clan and kinship. Kinship loyalty and sharing of resources were reported to be withering away. Aiyappan (1965, pp. 169–177) in his *Social Revolution in a Kerala Village*, has also reported a decline in the traditional relations among affine and friends and concluded that class interest was superseding caste interest.

After this brief perusal of a few studies, which provides us with a research direction, we would like to make statements regarding propositions of our undertaking. First of all, it should be noted that we have precluded here the examination of the impact of land reform measures at the family level (it has been done at length in the main study; rather, our aim is to examine the impact of land reform measures beyond the confines of the family). Thus, we intend to examine the aforementioned themes at the inter-household levels bound by threads of kinship, clan and caste. In the preceding pages, we have dealt with generated hypotheses emanating from the findings of a few studies. In the following text, we would examine a few collateral hypotheses facing our own field data, precisely related to kinship ties.

Hypotheses

1. Implementation of land reform measures has aroused mutual distrust among the kinsmen.
2. Land reform measures have let loose the force of conflict among the kin, clan and caste fellows.
3. As a consequence of the land reform, mutual cooperation in the process of production has been replaced by economic competition among the kinsmen.
4. The kin, clan and caste interest are being overtaken by the class interest.

Our data are qualitative in nature, thus, the entire text is based on case materials, as such we are not testing the hypotheses bit by bit. Rather, we are analysing the data in some sort of consolidated forms and presenting them in the following order: land concentration—kinship basis, kinship ties and the process of production; land-based conflict—general feature of the agrarian society, kinship, land reform and conflict. We would make statements with regard to our hypotheses after exposition of the case materials. Let us face the field data.

Land Concentration: Kinship Basis

In the past, especially during zamindari days, it was not customary for the zamindars to pay land rent and to become '*raiyats*' themselves. It would affect their status, and it was also possible that they would lose their zamindari. The alien government would take a different view about their competence to hold the office of zamindari. However, many tax farmers became land conscious and found a way out to own land—it was 'Benami' or *'farzi'* transaction of land in the names of some friends or relatives of the former zamindars. Sometimes, the owner of the land was family god and goddesses, a pet animal or a temple priest. Such practices became popular and enabled many zamindars to become big landlords. In many cases, the zamindars were only the owners of the land; cultivation was done by their tenants, while in some cases, the zamindars cultivated the land themselves.

It has been reported that the land was even a medium of exchange of goods and services. If in bad days some wealthy persons, say rich zamindars, fed some poor persons for a week or so, they would ask the debtors to get rid of the debts by selling their lands to the former. The land of the defaulters at paying land rent, even for petty amount, say 4 annas (1/4 of a rupee), was auctioned in favour of the men of zamindars themselves—friends or kinsmen.

In the past, the benami system of land ownership continued because of the fear of losing zamindari right. While during the later days—after Independence—due to the fear of the Land Ceiling Act, people began to purchase land within and outside family members in whose name negligible magnitude of the land stood. There was still another reason for benami purchase of land; it was to deprive other members of the family of the share in the newly purchased land. This could be explained like this: Mr X has four brothers; if he purchases land in his name or the name of any descendant of his family of origin, other members of the undivided family automatically become the shareholder in such property. Therefore, in order to hold exclusive right on the land, he would make a Benami purchasing; he would purchase the land in the name of his own brother-in-law or any other near relatives.

This can also be mentioned that during the past few decades, especially in agri-based society, the main source of power, prestige and income had been the land. Therefore, this urge for owning more and more land has let loose permanent land hunger among the peasantry. This could be explained like this that in urban areas, we find house hunger, and in rural areas, we find land hunger. The land has been dearer than brothers. This would be explained by mentioning a custom prevalent among the 'Chakwars'.* They had and still have a tradition of 'Jethansh' (primogeniture). Under the tradition, when division in the family would take place in a 'Chakwar family', first of all, the total land would be divided into 10 equal shares. First of all, the eldest brother would be given one share of the total. Then, the rest of the land would be equally divided amongst all the brothers. The practice is said to be legally recognized.

Kinship Ties and the Process of Production

There had been and still is great importance of social ties in the process of production in the rural economy. But due to the increasing intervention of new land reform measures, the process of production is getting separated from the mutual social bonds.

In the past, the big landowners and zamindars used to extend hospitality to their less fortunate kinsmen, not only in their bad days but also in good days also. A number of male relatives, also females in rare cases, would stay in the house of their wealthy zamindar relative; they would be provided with every kind of facility; their hobbies, such as wrestling and hunting, would be cared for; they would exhibit their importance whenever the patrons needed musclemen, toughs, *lathaits* (stick welders). It was customary for the zamindars to maintain a large number of hangers-on. Most of them were their trusted kinsmen. Now, as the economic conditions of zamindar's families have been shaken, the number of such dependents is also gradually being reduced.

In the plough-based cultivation, it was rather part of the system to mutually assist one another with plough, oxen, seeds, attached/hired labourers or personal labour; the system of mutual cooperation is becoming weaker, although the practice has not disappeared altogether; however, day by day its root is being dug up by new economic forces. Legislations regarding land ownership, wages and intervention of new farm technology—the green revolution—their combined effort is bound to disintegrate the old system of economic interdependence.

---

* Chakwars are considered superior segment of caste Bhumihar in this region.

In our sample villages, there are pump sets, threshers and tractors, their services are availed of on market payment basis. Traditional kind of cooperation has become actually a thing of the past. Due to increasing importance of wealth, there is competition among the members of the same kin group, intra-caste groups and inter-caste groups.

Many a time, the economic competition now takes the shape of conflict and leads to bloodshed.

Land-based Conflict: General Feature of the Agrarian Society

Inter-family disputes, inter-caste disputes for land or related to it have become almost daily routine affairs of the village life.

A few incidents stated further would throw some light on the nature of the conflict arising out of the new economic forces let loose at the doorstep of the rural communities.

In Kuberpur, Kurmi and Yadav are rivals. Other caste people take only sides. Basic fights originate from issues related to land and crops. Around the year 1975, a clash between the Kurmi and Yadav took place over encroachment on the standing crops. A pitched fight took place between them, there was, as alleged, one murder from each side. However, since then, there is no violent incident, but latent struggle is persisting.

In Champapur, Kurmi and Bhumihar do not see eye to eye as both want to capture economic and political power. However, there are few poor families of Bhumihar; in the past, they were landed peasantry who had sold their lands to their caste fellows.

In Sukhyapur, mostly Chakwar belong to the same clan, but now in terms of economic interest related to land, they are divided into two sub-classes, rich and the poor. First, they are working for cross purposes. Second, within the rich gentry, there are tension and squabbles related to land and share in the ancestral properties. Externally, it appears that everything is alright, but internally, there is a strong discontentment and dissatisfaction among them. Two prominent ex-zamindars belonging to the same clan have fought with guns. One of them is a family of money lender—usurer, the other is a family of the freedom fighter. Both are big landowners and progressive farmers. They want to let down others, and they want to excel each other overnight.

Saritapur is inhabited by medium-size farmers, except a few big landowners, where the new land reform measures have affected social relations at a larger scale. The new land reform measures have exposed the malpractices of ex-zamindars and have also aroused aspirations among the less fortunate. It does not matter, or it matters a little if the members are having kinship and caste affiliation. Economic motives appear on the surface at the slightest provocations from any other side.

Kinship, Land Reform and Conflict

As stated earlier, Aiyappan has reported in clear terms in his *Social Revolution in a Kerala Village* that class interest is superseding caste interest (Aiyappan, 1965, pp. 169–177) to a greater extent; similar conclusions can be drawn from the analysis of the following case materials:

1. In Saritapur, mostly persons belonging to the class of marginal farmers, sharecroppers and those who depend on animal husbandry set free their herd of cattle in the field of big landlords. The cattle destroy the standing crops. The fight between the intruders and the landowners has become a regular feature of the village. However, the persons involved are related by kinship and clan ties. They are Bhumihar by caste. The sharp economic disparity among members of the same kin group over a period of time has resulted in hostility. They are no more bound together by old zamindari right and privilege.
2. On account of the abolition of zamindari and implementation of the Land Ceiling Act, the rural people have become more individualistic (Dube, 1967, pp. 131–160, 222)[§] with regard to the land. W. R. Singh, the prominent ex-zamindar and landlord of Saritapur, is fighting with members of his own kin group on the issue of share in the land held jointly before the abolition of the zamindari. Late O. P. Singh, the father of W. R. Singh, submitted the *zamabandi* (land return) without specifying the claims of other members. The *zamabandi* (land return) submitted by late O. P. Singh included 'Benami' (*farzi*) land also. Although the family, in question, has

---

[§] See for the general trend of change in family and kinship system.

been identified as holding surplus land, other shareholders in the joint land are also likely to lose land, they are the victims of the clandestine role played by late O. P. Singh, the leader of the kin group. On the eve of the abolition of zamindari, he also got several pieces of '*gairmajarua*' (unoccupied land) settled in the names of his own family members and deprived the other distant kin. There is evidence of clear-cut polarization of two hostile groups having a common ancestral right in the landed property.
3. An ex-zamindar family head in Saritapur had settled some 6 bighas of land in the name of one of his own kin group members just before the abolition of the zamindari with the hope that land protected from government takeover by this means would be divided later on among all the members of the kin group. But the person in whose name the land in question had been settled earlier has declined to oblige the group of subsequent claimants.
4. Late L. Singh of Saritapur had purchased several bighas of land as 'Benami' (*farzi*). The daughters of one of his late sons, who have inherited the property, want to sell the lands, but all the shadow landowners have declined to sell the lands and to give the money to 'Benami' landowners. Many of the shadow landowners also happen to be the affinal kin of late L. Singh, but under the changed circumstances, they have changed their colours and are out to pocket the whole money themselves.
5. In Kuberpur, one Kurmi fellow—Garib Mahton—had purchased some 18 bighas of land from an *amla* (agent) of an absentee ex-zamindar long back. But later on, his own clan members in collaboration with other persons got the land registered from the ex-zamindar and showed him (Garib Mahton) the way. Not only this but also under duress, Garib Mahton has sold half of the land to a trio of powerful ex-zamindars and landlords (one purchaser of the land happens to be his clan member) obviously to pacify them so that he could peacefully cultivate on the rest of the land. However, the dispute is not over.
6. In Saritapur, one Bhumihar ex-Zamindar purchased a piece of land jointly with a Bania friend. Later on, the terms between them became strained. The Bania partner sold the better portion of the land to another Bhumihar friend. The new buyer entered into

the deal deliberately. Both the Bhumihar families involved in this land dispute belong to the same kin group. Resultantly, the land is lying barren. The former partner of the Bania does not approve the sale from the better portion of the land. During the best relation of Bhumihar–Bania friendship, the land was cultivated by a sharecropper, but after the new development, the land has been withdrawn from the tenant and, as stated earlier, is lying barren under the weight of dispute.

7. A big ex-zamindar of Sukhyapur had forfeited entire 20–25 bighas of land of one of his clan members on account of delay in the clearance of land rent on the eve of the zamindari abolition and had effected the settlement in favour of his close relatives. Even among the biggest ex-zamindar, kin-group people stoop so low and always try to protect their neck from the gallows of the Land Ceiling Act and divert the same to the other members, howsoever nearer, they may be. One such victim belonging to an ex-zamindar family, out of desperation, has got a red flag in his hands against his own kinsmen and has joined a militant political party.

In Champapur, one time, the biggest landlord family has now become a family of marginal farmers. The whole joint family has been broken into several units. They recall their landed property had been purchased by dubious means by their own caste fellows and clan members with whom their ancestors shared the glorious past.

Son Becomes Tenant of His Father: Saritapur

Dukhya Singh, a married man, had owned 2–3 bighas of land. He had no issue. His father who had four sons divided them with his own initiatives even when three of his sons were still minors. He unhesitatingly established his own household separately and got an equal share in landed property. His sons had taken to sharecropping as their own patches of land are quite inadequate to feed them. What happened to Dukhya Singh is that he made a contract with his father to cultivate a piece of land on a sharecropping basis. He cultivated the land on a sharecropping basis for three seasons. But when the sowing of the last rabi crop began, his father imposed on him a lease on land at the rate of 10 mounds per bigha. Dukhya Singh was under an obligation to pay 5 mounds of wheat to his father irrespective of the actual yield. Dukhya Singh was not willing to cultivate the land on a lease basis, he requested his father not to impose such a condition on him, but his father stuck to his decision. He also threatened him of taking back the land; in case, the terms and conditions were not acceptable to Dukhya Singh. Helpless Dukhya Singh accepted the terms and conditions as put forward by his father. However, it was so done with a view to maintain his relations with his parents. Dukhya Singh had no oxen of his own, he used to purchase plough during the sowing season at the rate of 20–25 per bigha. His brothers whose economic conditions have slightly improved and have become resourceful—they own oxen, cows, buffaloes and other agricultural implements, extend lip service to Dukhya Singh.

ANALYSIS AND FINDINGS

1. Our hypothesis is that the implementation of land reform measures has aroused mutual distrust among kinsmen stands valid. 'Benami' or '*farzi*' transaction of land has been questioned by shadow owners.
2. Our hypothesis is that land reform measures which have let loose forces of conflict among kin, clan and caste fellows are also retained on the basis of evidence pertaining to a land-based conflict and diverse interests emerging after abolition Zamindari.
3. Our third hypothesis is that as a consequence of land reform, mutual cooperation in the process of production has been replaced by economic competition among kinsmen stands verified. The ex-zamindars are cutting the number of their hangers-on. Moreover, exchange of plough, oxen, seeds and labour has become actually a thing of the past. In our sample villages, there are pump sets, threshers and tractors; their services are availed on a market rate.
4. Our fourth hypothesis is that kin, clan and caste interest which are being overtaken by the class interest are retained on the basis of evidence suggesting interest aggregation along class lines. People belonging to the same kin, clan and caste group are getting divided into sub-classes. They are working for cross purposes.

To conclude, our findings suggest that on account of the implementation of land reform measures, kinship is becoming weaker. Caste interest is getting overtaken by class interest. Tensions and weakening of the kinship ties are the manifestations of the future pattern of social structure in which economic interest will have the upper hand. And social tensions will be resolved, fought at the platform of class interest.

ACKNOWLEDGEMENTS

The author expresses gratitude to his Supervisor, Dr Yogendra Singh, Chairman, Centre for the Study of Social Systems, Jawaharlal Nehru University (JNU), New Delhi, and to the Indian Council of Social Science Research (ICSSR), New Delhi, for financial sponsorship of the project, 'A Study of the Social Consequences of Land Reform Measures in Bihar' which has been submitted recently. The author worked as a young social scientist fellow of the ICSSR, New Delhi, and was placed at the Centre for the Study of Social Systems, JNU, New Delhi, for the period 1980–1982.

REFERENCES

Aiyappan, A. (1965). *Social revolution in a Kerala village*. Asia Publishing House.

Bennett, J. W., & Despres, L. A. (1960). Kinship and instrumental activities: A theoretical inquiry. *American Anthropologist, 62*(2), 254–267.

Beteille, A. (1964). Family and social change in India and South Asia. *Economic Weekly, 2*(5–7), 237–244.

Ciparisse, G. (1978). An anthropological approach to socio-economic factors of development: The case of Zaire. *Current Anthropology, 19*(1), 37–41.

Djurfeldt, G., & Lindberg, S. (1976). *Behind poverty: The social formation in Tamil village*. Curzon Press.

Dube, S. C. (1967). *Indian village*. Harper and Row Publishers.

Fox, R. G. (1971). *Kin clan, raja and rule, state hinterland relations in preindustrial India*. University of California Press.

Godelier, M. (1975). *Rationality and irrationality in economics*. Verso, (x) 94–95, 103, 303–306, 317.

Gough, K. E. (1965). Brahman kinship in a Tamil village. *American Anthropologist, 58*(5), 826–853.

Leach, E. R. (1968). *Pul Eliya, a village in Ceylon: A study of land tenure and kinship*. Cambridge University Press.

Marriott, M. (1952). Social change in an Indian village. *Economic Development and Cultural Change, 1,* 145–155.
Siskind, J. (1978). Kinship and mode of production. *American Anthropologist, 80*(4), 860–872.
Srinivas, M. N. (1980). *India: Social structure.* Hindustan Publishing Corporation.
Thomas, J. S. (1978). Kinship and wealth in a Maya community. *Human Organization, 37*(1), 24–28.

Chapter 2

Land Alienation of Tribals in the Jharkhand Region of Bihar*
Process and Pattern

Ramesh Sharan, Amar Kumar Singh and S. L. Batra

Tribal land alienation happens to be one of the most important issues in Jharkhand, which has also attracted considerable attention in the past. The tribals in general and in Jharkhand particular have witnessed the continued alienation and encroachment on their resources both individual and community. The present chapter discusses, in brief, the process, pattern and causes of land alienation in the post-Independence period. This is based on a sample study conducted in Ranchi and Dumka districts of Jharkhand. The chapter outlines the mode and typology of land alienation in the two districts. The chapter points out the alienation of land, both for public projects and individuals, has continued in spite of various legislations. However, the process of alienation has slowed down since the 1980s, and the pattern of alienation has also changed.

In various phases of history, beginning from the mediaeval period to the modern day, the tribal communities in India have faced alienation of land and their common property. They have witnessed a continued encroachment on their traditional rights. In some cases, the outside communities were invited and, in some cases, they were subjugated by bigger powers. The advent of the colonial rule imposed new demands on the resources of tribals. The tribals revolted both violently and non-violently against such undue demands, leading to the recognition of their rights through Acts and Regulations made by the British

---

* *Social Change*, 29(3 & 4), 1999.

Government. However, in spite of the various legislation, the process of alienation of land continued both legally and illegally, overtly and covertly. There has been no respite to the tribals even in the post-Independence India. The tribal areas being rich in natural resources have attracted and are attracting considerable investment in mines, industries, hydel power and irrigation projects, which have led to both direct and indirect eviction of these communities. The improper and callous rehabilitation has further accentuated the problem. The urbanization and industrialization have also resulted in a considerable influx of migrant population putting pressure on the resources of the tribals living in the periphery of such urban centres.

The issue of tribal land alienation has attracted considerable attention in the past. There has been a large number of articles in journals, books and newspapers, which have pointed out the process and impact of various forms of tribal land alienation in the tribal regions of Bihar. One such study in the 1960s pointed out the various forms and means of land alienation in and around the city of Ranchi (Sinha, 1968). The study pointed out the illegal transfer of land continuing in Ranchi district primarily through collusive titles. The other means adopted were through getting *chaparbandi**, mortgage and even the outright sale. The study suggested many amendments in the Chotanagpur Tenancy (CNT) Act. It also recommended the appointment of a land commission to enquire into the land records. The study also pointed out the problems faced by the oustees from heavy engineering corporation (HEC), a public sector enterprise which was coming up then.

Another article during the late 1970s had observed that the problem of land alienation is complex and for which no easy solution can be found through legal and administrative action. The article had pointed out various illegal methods of tribal land alienation which include collusive title suits, de facto possession, transfer in false name by marrying tribal girls and so on (Thakur, 1977). Another article points out that most of the illegal transfers of land take place because of widespread indebtedness among the tribals. It also pointed out the alienation of tribal land due to development of industrial and mining projects on the tribal land by the migrant population (Gupta, 1977).

---

* Cleverly showing agricultural land as homestead plot in land records in order to evade restriction on the sale of agricultural land.

Yet another article drawing from micro and macro studies has traced the process of land alienation in the tribal region of Bihar right from the period of the British rule. The article points out that during the post-Independence period, the acquisition of land for the public purpose has been the major factor responsible for tribal land alienation. The continued deforestation has accentuated the agony of the tribals, the article points out (Iyer, 1993).

Another article, while pointing out the significance of land in tribal ethos and effect of land alienation on the tribals, brings out the loopholes in the protective legislation and administrative slackness in its implementation. The article has suggested many remedial measures, including involvement of non-government organizations in the implementation of the CNT and Santhal Parganas Tenancy (SPT) Act (Sinha, 1993).

One of the detailed studies was sponsored by the Ministry of Rural Development (Land Reforms), Government of India, and was conducted during the late 1980s on the problem, extent and remedies of land alienation of tribals in Chotanagpur and Santhal Pargana (Sinha, 1990). The study covered different typologies of villages and estimated that 18 per cent of the tribal families had alienated land in one form or the other. Sale (49.56%), mortgages (35.11%) and encroachment (4.89%) were observed to be the major causes of alienation. The study has also pointed out the dismal performance in restoration of land to the tribals after favourable verdict in the scheduled area regulation (SAR) cases.

In the aforementioned background, the chapter discusses, briefly, the process of land alienation of tribals, especially in the post-Independence period. The chapter is primarily concerned with land alienation to the individuals in contravention to the CNT Act, 1908, and the SPT Act, 1949. The chapter is based on a study conducted by the authors entitled 'A Study of Land Alienation of Tribals in Dumka and Ranchi districts of Bihar' sponsored by the Ministry of Rural Development, Government of India.

LEGAL FRAMEWORK

The study area is governed by the CNT Act, 1908, and the SPT Act, 1949. The Acts have been amended from time to time. The provisions of the Act prohibit the transfer of tribal land to non-tribals in the area. There is also a provision for restoration of illegally alienated land to the tribals. The Act also makes a provision for mortgage only for a limited period of seven years after which it is automatically restored to the tribal tenants. The Act also provides for the customary rights of the tribals. The SPT Act is even more restrictive than the CNT Act prohibiting the transfer of even non-tribal *raiyati* land. It is mandatory to obtain permission of the deputy commissioner (DC) in the case of transfer of the tribal land even to the non-tribals. Besides, the cases for the restoration of illegally alienated land could be instituted by DC sou motu or by the affected party itself. If a tribal files a case for the restoration, DC/state automatically becomes a party. There is also a provision for trying the cases filed for restoration under special courts meant for the purpose known as SAR courts for which SAR officers are deputed.

STUDY AREA AND SAMPLE

The study was conducted in two districts of Jharkhand region of Bihar, namely Ranchi and Dumka. A purposive multi-stage sampling method was used for the study. The sampling was done at three levels, namely circle, village and household level from the two districts. The revenue circles were so selected that they had a concentration of land acquisition (for public purpose) as well as the number of SAR cases in the circles. Altogether, 300 households from 13 villages from Dumka and 304 households from 13 villages from Ranchi were selected for the study.

The study covered six major scheduled tribes (ST) groups, namely Santal, Pahariya, Munda, Oraon, Loharas and Chik Baraik.

TYPOLOGY OF LAND ALIENATION IN THE STUDY AREA

During the study, the following typologies of land alienation have been identified:

1. Alienation due to land acquisition for public purpose

   a. *Acquisition with inbuilt rehabilitation package:* Under this category, the land oustees are not only paid compensation for land but also are given some rehabilitation package such as job, land, household plots and rehabilitation sites. HEC and irrigation project in the study area comes under this category.

    b. *Acquisition without any rehabilitation package:* There is considerable land acquisition under this category where only compensation for land is given. Such acquisitions include acquisitions for the Bihar Military Police (BMP), marketing yards, army and so on.

    c. Ongoing acquisition.

2. *Land alienation to individuals:* Alienation to the individuals can be to the tribals as well as to the non-tribals. The transfers can be grouped as follows:

    a. Transfer in contravention to the Acts.

        i. With cases filed for restoration/restoration pending after favourable verdict.

        ii. No cases filled for restoration.

    b. Transfer in consistence with the Act.

Land Alienation for Public Purpose: Results from the Sample Study

The study area included alienation for the public purpose for the irrigation project, industrial project, airport, railway, road and army/BMP/bazaar/dairy farm and so on and the voluntary organization. Altogether, 168 sample households in Dumka and 196 households in Ranchi districts reported land alienation for the public purpose and to the voluntary organization (Table 2.1). The sample households together have alienated 1,031.29 acres of land out of which 683.92 acres were for the irrigation purpose, 140.90 for industrial projects, 144.14 acres for airport, railway, road and so on, 62.13 acres for army, BMP, bazaar and so on and only 0.20 acres was alienated to the voluntary organization.

Dumka District

In Dumka, altogether 168 sample households selected from land alienation for a public purpose, 158 had alienated for irrigation project

Table 2.1 Land Alienation for Public Purpose

Public Purpose	Dumka Area (Acres)	Dumka No. of households	Ranchi Area (Acres)	Ranchi No. of Households
Irrigation project	501.39	158	182.53	63
Industrial project	–	–	140.90	43
Airport, railway and road	–	–	144.14	71
Army/BMP/bazaar/dairy	2.51	8	59.62	19
Voluntary organization	0.20	2	–	–
Total	504.10	168	527.19	196
Average per households	3.00		2.68	

Source: Author's own.

alienating around 501.39 acres of land which accounted for 99.54 per cent of the total land alienation. Only eight households reported alienation for dairy farm and bazaar measuring 2.51 acres of land, and only 0.20 acres were alienated to voluntary organizations. The average alienation per sample household works out to be 3.00 hectares in the district.

In Dumka, most of the land 501.29 acres for irrigation was alienated before 1960 only. Also, 0.10 acres were alienated between 1981 and 1985. For the category bazaar and dairy farm up to 1.06 acres in 1960 and 0.08 acres between 1961 and 1970 were alienated. Only about 1.27 acres have been alienated from 1985 to 1986. Between 1981 and 1990, 0.20 acres were alienated to one voluntary organization. Thus, the sample households in Dumka have alienated land before 1960, after which, these sample households have not alienated land for a public purpose. Most of the sample households were purposively selected; hence, such a result is not surprising.

Ranchi District

In Ranchi district, around 527.19 acres of land have been reported to be alienated by 196 sample households, out of which 182.53 acres of land were alienated for irrigation projects, 140.90 acres for industrial projects, 144.14 acres for public utilities such as airport, railway and road and 59.62 acres by the army, BMP and so on. The households have not alienated any land to the voluntary organizations. In comparison to Dumka, Ranchi has attracted more investment; as a result, the alienation of land has been not only relatively large in quantity but also has been for multiple purposes.

Land Alienation to Individuals

One of the important issues has been land alienation to individuals both tribals and non-tribals in contravention to the CNT and SPT Acts as well under the provisions of the Act. There has been continued land alienation of tribals to tribals as well as to non-tribals, though the process and pattern have changed over the years. From enquiries, it was revealed that four forms dominate in the transfer of tribal land, namely mortgage, leasing out, sale and illegal encroachments/eviction by influential people. Mortgage and leasing out are supposed to be temporary alienation while sale and encroachments are permanent in nature. However, all the forms are overlapping. Mortgaging and leasing out are supposedly temporary, but in fact, they turn out to be almost permanent alienation in most of the cases. Although the focus of the study was land alienation after the SAR, 1969, had been enacted in the area. Yet during the study, figures, earlier than 1970, were also obtained. This has been primarily based on the recall of the sample households.

QUANTUM OF LAND ALIENATION

The land alienation figures are given in Table 2.2. In Dumka, the land alienation, through four modes, namely mortgage, leasing out, encroachment and sale, works out to be 2.3 acres per household out of which 48.3 per cent households reported to have alienated land up to 1 acre, 15.3 per cent households between 1 and 2 acres, 13.3 per cent households between 2 and 4 acres and 23 per cent above 4 acres of land. The majority of the households fall in the category of 0–1 acre and above 4 acres category. In comparison, out of 304 sample households in Ranchi, 124 (40.8%) reported to have alienated the land above 4 acres, and 21.7 per cent between 2 and 4 acres. Around 16.8 per cent reported to have alienated the land between 1–2 acres and 19.7 per cent up to 1 acre. Three households in Ranchi did not report any alienation in the last 25 years as they were displaced from HEC and were landless. The extent of alienation to HEC was not known to them as the respondents' grandparents had been displaced who were not alive at the time of the survey.

Altogether, 956.78 acres of land reported to have been alienated by the sample households to individuals in the form of mortgage, encroachment and sale in Ranchi and Dumka districts, taken together, out of which 33 per cent had been to tribals, and 67 per cent had been to non-tribals (Table 2.3). Thus, non-tribals have alienated almost two-third of the tribal land in the study area. In Ranchi, the sample households reported to have alienated 840.97 acres of land out of which 31.69 per cent were to tribals, while 68.31 per cent were

Table 2.2 Land Alienation of Sample Households

Land Area (Acres)	No. of households	
	Dumka	Ranchi
Nil	–	3
0–1	145 (48.3)	60 (19.7)
1–2	46 (15.3)	51 (16.8)
2–4	40 (13.3)	66 (21.7)
4 & above	69 (23.0)	124 (40.6)

Note: Figures in bracket are in per cent.

Table 2.3 Land Alienation to Individuals by Sample Households

Mode	Dumka		Ranchi		Acres	
	1971–1996	Total	1971–1996	Total	1971–1996	Total
To tribal	41.01	49.17	81.15	266.50	122.16	315.67
To non-tribal	34.50	66.64	151.68	574.47	186.18	641.11
Total	75.51	115.81	232.83	840.97	308.34	956.78

by the non-tribals. Similarly, in Dumka, out of 115.81 acres of land alienated, 42.45 per cent had been to tribals and 57.55 per cent to non-tribals. Out of 950.78 acres alienated, 87.9 per cent had been in Ranchi and only 12.1 per cent in Dumka. In Ranchi district, land alienation per household has been higher than Dumka. This may be primarily because Ranchi has received more investment in both the public and private sector than Dumka due to which the urbanization and migration have been comparatively more.

Another important finding of the study is that out of 956.78 acres alienated by the sample households, 308.34 acres (32.2%) had been between 1971 and 1996 while the rest 67.8 per cent had been before 1970. It is interesting to note that there has been a decline in the land alienating after 1970 (which is after the SAR Act, 1969). Two possible explanations can be given for this. First, the initial phase of the public sector investment in and around Ranchi attracted considerable migrant population, and places like Ranchi were favoured by many to settle permanently. In the post-Independence period, cities like Dumka which were district headquarters also grew in size. In the initial phases, it seems that tribals were not able to understand the value of their land, especially near urban centres, and were duped by middlemen and agents in parting with their land through various methods such as collusive title suits and *chaparbandi*. It may be mentioned that in title suits, a tribal used to accept in the civil court that they had taken loan from a non-tribal, and they were unable to pay; hence, they were surrendering the land to the non-tribals for full and final settlement. The collusive titles were popular methods of alienating tribal land till the SAR Act, 1969, came into force. The second method has been *chaparbandi* which means declaring a plot as a homestead plot on which the restriction of the transfer did not apply as the restrictions are only for agricultural land in the CNT Act. Later on, due to the pressure by tribal leadership, the SAR Act, 1969, was enacted. The tribal consciousness has also increased. The large number of SAR cases filed by tribals and even by the government has slowly acted as a deterrent to the transfer of the tribal land.

The other interesting finding is that out of 308.34 acres of land alienated between 1971 and 1996 by the sample households, 75.5 per cent had been in Ranchi and 24.5 per cent in Dumka. Besides, 39.6 per cent had been to tribals and 60.4 per cent had been to non-tribals. If one compared the trend up to 1970 and beyond 1970, almost 69.5 per cent of the land was alienated to non-tribals and around 30.8 per cent to the tribals. The proportion of tribals to tribals alienation has increased while the proportion of alienation to non-tribals has declined.

Out of 840.97 acres of land alienated in Ranchi only, 27.78 per cent had been between 1971 and 1996 while 72.3 per cent had been before 1970. The proportion of land alienated in the post-1970 period has considerably declined. Similarly, out of 232.83 acres of land alienated in Ranchi between 1971 and 1996 around 34.8 per cent had been to tribals and 65.2 per cent to non-tribals, and it shows that non-tribals continue to be a major group alienating tribal land though their proportion is declining.

However, in Dumka district, out of 115.81 acres of land alienated, 65.2 per cent had been between 1971 and 1996, and only 34.8 per cent had been before 1970. Out of 75.51 acres of land alienated, 54.3 per cent had been to tribals and 46.7 per cent had been to the non-tribals. The trends in Dumka are, thus, quite different in comparison to Ranchi.

MODE OF LAND ALIENATION

Land alienation has been taken in two parts, one is nearly permanent alienation in terms of mortgage, encroachment and sale. Mortgage has been taken as continuing mortgage, that is, the mortgage which was continuing till the day of survey. Table 2.4 gives mode of land alienation of sample households up to 1996, while Table 2.5 gives alienation up to 1970, and Table 2.6 gives land alienation of the sample households.

ALIENATION IN PRE-1970 PHASE

Out of 648.44 acres of land reported to have been alienated by households 65.5 per cent had been by the way of sales, 28.9 per cent in the form of encroachment and 5.6 per cent in form of mortgage. The worst part is that the mortgages have continued for such a long period in spite of the regulations in the CNT Act and SPT Act. It seems up to 1970, the sale happened to be the most popular form of alienation. Out of 454.93 acres alienated to non-tribals, 74.2 per cent had been in form of sale primarily through collusive title suits, while 21.3 per cent were encroachment and 4.5 per cent in the form of mortgage, and out of 193.51 acres of land alienated to tribals, 45.1 per cent were in the form of sale. Also, 46.7 per cent by the way of encroachment and 8.2 per cent were in the form of mortgage. The encroachment had been primarily in the form that the purchase/alienated or have taken more land than what was actually negotiated for, and in some cases, the encroachment had been by the use of force.

In Ranchi, 608.14 acres had been reported to be alienated by the households out of which 67.8 per cent had been in the form of sale,

Table 2.4 Mode of Land Alienation of Sample Households

Mode of Alienation	Dumka			Ranchi			Overall		
	T	NT	Total	T	NT	Total	T	NT	Total
Mortgage	7.05	10.22	17.27	71.10	126.55	197.65	78.15	136.77	214.92
	(2.4)	(58.65)	(15.34)	(14.91)	(26.68)	(22.03)	(23.50)	(24.76)	(21.33)
	(22.47)	(24.35)							
Encroachment	28.84	28.57	57.41	92.13	83.46	175.59	120.97	112.03	233.00
			(42.87)	(49.57)	(34.57)	(14.53)	(20.88)	(38.32)	(17.48)
Sale	13.28	27.85	41.13	103.27	364.46	467.73	116.35	392.31	508.86
			(27.01)	(41.79)	(35.52)	(38.75)	(64.44)	(55.62)	(36.92)
			(61.19)	(53.18)					
Total	49.17	66.64	115.81	266.50	574.47	840.97	315.67	641.11	956.78
			(100.00)	(100.00)	(100.00)	(100.00)	(100.00)	(100.00)	(100.00)
			(100.00)	(100.00)					

Note: T = Tribal and NT = Non-tribal.

Table 2.5 Land Alienation of Sample Households up to 1970

Mode of Land Alienation	Dumka			Ranchi			Overall		
	T	NT	Total	T	NT	Total	T	NT	Total
Mortgage	–	2.00	2.00	15.87	18.45	34.27	15.87	20.47	36.27
		(6.30)	(4.00)	(8.6)	(4.4)	(5.7)	(8.2)	(4.5)	(5.6)
Encroachment	6.38	19.60	25.98	83.99	77.46	161.45	90.37	97.06	187.43
	(18.20)	(61.40)	(64.50)	(45.30)	(18.30)	(26.50)	(46.70)	(21.30)	(28.90)
Sale	1.78	10.34	12.32	85.49	326.93	412.42	87.27	337.47	424.74
	(21.80)	(32.80)	(30.60)	(46.10)	(77.30)	(67.80)	(45.10)	(74.20)	(65.50)
Total	8.16	31.94	40.30	185.35	422.79	608.14	193.51	454.93	648.44
	(100.00)	(100.00)	(100.00)	(100.00)	(100.00)	(100.00)	(100.00)	(100.00)	(100.00)

Notes: 1. Figures in bracket are in per cent.
2. T = Tribal and NT = Non-tribal.

Table 2.6 Land Alienation of Sample Households (1971–1996)

Mode of Land Alienation	Dumka			Ranchi			Overall		
	T	NT	Total	T	NT	Total	T	NT	Total
Mortgage	7.5	8.22	15.27	55.23	108.15	163.38	62.28	116.37	178.65
	(17.19)	(23.83)	(20.22)	(68.06)	(71.30)	(70.17)	(50.98)	(62.50)	(57.94)
Encroachment	22.46	8.97	31.43	8.14	6.00	14.14	30.60	14.97	45.57
	(54.77)	(26.00)	(41.62)	(10.03)	(3.96)	(6.07)	(25.05)	(8.04)	(14.78)
Sale	11.50	17.31	28.81	17.78	37.53	55.31	29.28	54.84	84.12
	(28.04)	(50.17)	(38.16)	(21.91)	(24.74)	(23.76)	(23.97)	(29.46)	(27.28)
Total	41.01	34.50	75.51	81.15	151.68	232.83	122.16	186.18	308.34
	(100.00)	(100.00)	(100.00)	(100.00)	(100.00)	(100.00)	(100.00)	(100.00)	(100.00)

Notes: 1. Figures in bracket are in per cent.
2. T = Tribal and NT = Non-tribal

26.5 per cent had been in the form of encroachment, and 5.7 per cent has been as mortgage. Out of 422.79 acres alienated to non-tribals, 77.3 per cent had been by way of sale, 18.3 per cent by the way of encroachment and 4.4 per cent by way of mortgage, and out of 185.35 acres alienated to tribals during the period, 46.1 per cent had been by the way of sale, 45.3 per cent by way of encroachment and only 8.6 per cent through mortgage. One of the surprising findings had been a considerable amount of land being alienated to the tribals in form of encroachment which means even tribals have encroached the upon tribal land in the study area.

In Dumka, only about 40.30 acres had been alienated by the household till 1970 out of which 30.6 per cent were in form of sale, 64.5 per cent by way of encroachment and 4.9 per cent by way of mortgage, and out of 31.94 acres alienated to non-tribals, 32.8 per cent had been by the way of sale, 61.4 per cent by way of encroachment and only 6.3 per cent in form of mortgage, and out of 8.16 acres alienated to tribals, 21.8 per cent had been by the way of sale and 78.2 per cent by the way of encroachment. It seems that before 1970 much tribal land was encroached both by tribals and non-tribals in Dumka.

ALIENATION IN POST-1970 PHASE

In the post-1970 phase, there were distinct trends worth noticing. In comparison to the pre-1970 phase, during this period, mortgage happens to be the most important mode accounting for 57.94 per cent followed by sale (27.28%) and encroachment (14.78). The importance of sale has thus declined substantially. This trend is visible for land alienated to both tribals and non-tribals. Out of 186.18 acres of land alienated to non-tribals during the period, 62.5 per cent had been by the way of mortgage, 8.04 per cent by the way of encroachment and 29.46 per cent by the way of sales. Similarly, out of 122.16 acres of land alienated to tribals, 50.98 per cent had been by way of mortgage, 25.05 per cent by encroachment and 23.97 per cent by the way of sales. However, there are differences in the modes of alienation in Ranchi and Dumka. In Ranchi, 70.1 per cent were by sale, while in Dumka, figures were 20.22 per cent through mortgage, 41.2 per cent by encroachment and 38.16 per cent by the way of sale.

In Ranchi, the mode is almost identical for both tribals and non-tribals. Out of 151.68 acres of land alienated to the tribals, 71.3 per cent had been through mortgage, 24.73 per cent by the way of sale and 3.96 per cent by encroachment. Similarly, out of 81.15 acres alienated to tribals, 68.06 per cent by the way of mortgage, 10.03 per cent by the way of encroachment and 21.91 per cent by the way of sale. It may be mentioned that in the post-1970 phase, owing to a number of SAR cases initiated for restoration increased in general awareness both amongst the tribals and the non-tribals regarding the SAR cases acting as a deterrent for non-tribals in buying the tribal land in urban areas. As a result, mortgage seems to be a convenient form of alienating land in the post-1970 period primarily because mortgage happens to be a convenient way for the tribals to procure money, sometimes, in dire needs, especially in the rural areas. In recent times, there has been growing housing finance from institutions which require that the land papers should be in proper order. It is quite natural that any land transferred in contravention to the CNT Act does not find favour with these institutions. Besides, there has also been pressure from tribal leaders, press, non-governmental organizations (NGOs) and other concerned people who have decelerated the process of alienation.

As stated earlier, in recent times, mortgage has become the easiest way of transfer of the tribal land when sale and other forms have become increasingly difficult. Although Section 46 of the CNT Act allows temporary alienation even to a non-tribal in two cases (a) mortgage for the period of five years (b) *bhugut bandha** mortgage for any period not exceeding seven years after which the land is supposed to be back to the tribals. But this has turned out to be permanent land alienation in reality because in the majority of cases, the tribal is unable to pay back the loan, and the land remains with the transferee for a considerable long period of time. There have been some cases where the tribal does not take back their land even if they have money but take others land as mortgage. However, the tribals in some of the cases consider that the land has been temporarily alienated, and they will get it back ultimately. In the result of the present survey, out of 39 households in Dumka, 38

---

* As per Chota Nagpur Tenancy Act, under 'Bhugut Bandha mortgage' land was temporarily transferred for cultivation to loan giver so that repayment of advanced amount and interest was extinguished by income arising out of land.

Table 2.7 Post-mortgage Status of Mortgagee

Status	No. of Households	
	Dumka	Ranchi
Temporarily alienated	38	98
	(97.4)	(94.2)
Owner-*bataidar* (land remained alienated)	–	1
		(1.0)
Ownership of alienated	1	5
Permanently transferred	(2.6)	(4.8)
Total cases	39	104

Note: Figures in brackets are in per cent.

(97.4%) felt that the land has been temporarily alienated while only 1 household reported to have alienated the land permanently. Similarly, in Ranchi, 98 (94.2%) out of 104 households reporting mortgages felt that the land has been temporarily alienated while one (1.0%) household reported to be owner *bataidar* on their own land and 5 (4.8%) reported to have alienated the land permanently (Table 2.7).

Another interesting finding is that in recent years, the non-tribal money lender is giving way to tribal money lenders primarily rich tribal in the villages to which the land is getting alienated.

The land alienation in the post-1970 period has been classified in time intervals and certain interesting facts have come out of it. Table 2.8 gives alienation in the form of mortgage, Table 2.9 in the form of encroachment and Table 2.10 in the form of sale. The analysis of the table reveals the following major trends:

1. During all the period intervals 1971–1980, 1981–1985, 1980–1990 and 1991–1996, the mortgage had been continuously rising. This mortgage had been increasing to both tribals and non-tribals, the trend was almost identical in Ranchi and Dumka. In Ranchi, there had been increasing trend over the successive time periods under question. During 1970–1980, the total mortgage was 3.25 which increased to 22.45 acres in 1981–1985, 45.41 during 1986–1990 and 37.04 acres during 1990–1996. Similarly, the alienation to

Table 2.8 Mortgage Mode of Land Alienation by Sample Households Year-wise

Alienation by mortgage	Dumka			Ranchi			Total		
	T	NT	Total	T	NT	Total	T	NT	Total
Up to 1970	–	2.00	2.00	15.87	18.40	34.27	15.87	20.40	36.27
1971–1980	–	0.26	0.26	14.43	3.25	17.68	14.43	3.51	17.94
1981–1985	–	–	–	4.00	22.45	26.45	4.00	22.45	26.45
1986–1990	2.46	0.82	3.28	11.52	45.41	56.93	13.98	46.23	60.21
1991–1996	4.59	7.14	11.73	25.28	37.04	62.32	29.87	44.18	74.05
1971–1996 (2+3+4+5)	7.05	8.22	15.27	55.23	108.15	163.38	62.28	116.37	178.65
Overall (1+6)	7.05	10.22	17.27	71.10	126.55	197.65	78.15	136.77	214.92

Note: T = Tribal and NT = Non-tribal.

Table 2.9 Land Alienation of Sample Households by Encroachment

Year	Dumka			Ranchi			Overall		
	T	NT	Total	T	NT	Total	T	NT	Total
Up to 1970	6.38	19.60	25.98	83.99	77.46	161.45	90.37	97.06	187.43
1971–1980	–	2.42	2.42	3.66	1.32	4.98	3.66	3.74	7.40
1981–1985	13.67	1.38	15.05	3.00	1.50	4.50	16.67	2.88	19.55
1986–1990	4.42	3.80	8.22	0.56	0.18	0.74	4.98	3.98	8.96
1991–1996	4.37	1.37	5.74	0.92	3.00	3.92	5.29	4.37	9.66
1971–1996 (2+3+4+5)	22.46	8.97	31.43	8.14	6.00	14.14	30.60	14.97	45.57
Overall (1+6)	28.84	28.57	57.41	92.13	83.46	175.57	120.97	112.03	233.00

Note: T = Tribal and NT = Non-tribal.

Table 2.10 Land Alienation of Sample Households by Sale

Year	Dumka			Ranchi			Overall		
	T	NT	Total	T	NT	Total	T	NT	Total
Up to 1970	1.78	10.54	12.32	85.49	326.93	412.42	87.27	337.47	424.74
1971–1980	3.52	7.76	11.28	15.22	26.79	42.01	18.74	34.55	53.29
1981–1985	0.98	2.03	3.01	0.50	10.74	11.24	1.48	12.77	14.25
1986–1990	5.10	4.34	9.44	–	–	–	5.10	4.34	9.44
1991–1996	1.90	3.18	5.08	2.06	–	2.06	3.96	3.18	7.14
1971–1996 (2+3+4+5)	11.50	17.31	28.81	17.78	37.53	55.31	29.28	54.84	84.12
Overall (1+6)	13.28	27.85	41.13	103.27	364.46	467.73	116.55	392.31	508.86

Note: T = Tribal and NT = Non-tribal.

tribals in the form of mortgage had also been rising. Although the area of mortgage happened to be 14.43 acres during 1971–1980, it declined to 4.00 acres in 1981–1985, increased to 11.52 acres during 1986–1990 and to 25.28 acres during 1991–1996. In Dumka, the quantum of mortgage had been rising as reported by the households. One of the important things is that once a land is alienated in the form of mortgage, the tribal is unable to get it back, and it is almost permanent alienation.
2. The sample households also reported fall in the volume of alienation through encroachment over successive periods in both Ranchi and Dumka.
3. The quantum of land alienated through sales had been declining during the period under study. During 1971–1980, around 53.29 acres had been reported by sample households, which decreased to 14.25 acres during 1981–1985, 9.44 acres during 1986–1990 and only 7.14 acres during 1991–1996. Out of 54.84 acres alienated to non-tribals, 34.55 acres had been reported to be alienated during 1971–1980, while it was 12.77 acres during 1981–1985, 4.34 acres during 1986–1990 and 3.18 acres during 1991–1996.

While in the case of alienation to tribals, 18.74 acres had been between 1971 and 1980, 1.48 acres between 1981 and 1985, 5.10 acres between 1986 and 1990 and 3.96 acres between 1991 and 1996. If one sees the data from Ranchi samples, there had been no land alienation to non-tribals by way of sale after 1985. All the 37.53 acres had been alienated up to 1985. While out of 17.78 acres alienated to tribals, only 2.06 acres had been during 1991–1996.

In Dumka, however, the trends are quite different in the sense that there had been continued alienation from the sample households in the form of sale though the magnitude has not been very big. However, in Santhal Pargana, the SAR Act, 1969, which had provisions of validating the transfer if either the transferee makes available equivalent land or pays compensation if substantial structure had been erected before 1969. There were no such provisions in the SPT Act, 1947. The new provision under the SAR Act, 1969, has, to some extent, legitimized the earlier illegal land alienation.

Reasons for Land Alienation by Sample Households
Through Mortgage

The enquiries were made to ascertain the purpose for which the sample households had alienated land in form of mortgage or sale. The reasons stated for mortgage had been for household expenditure agricultural purpose, education of children, medical expenses, marriages and rituals, litigation and other purpose. Table 2.11 gives the proportion of households specifying the reasons for mortgaging the land in Ranchi and Dumka.

A considerable number of households were unable to recall correctly the purpose of mortgage as in many cases the land was mortgaged by their parents or grandparents, and in some cases, it was done 15–20 years back. However, out of 39 households, who could precisely recall the reasons for mortgage in Dumka, 30.8 per cent reported to have mortgaged if for household expenditure, 48.7 per cent for treatment (medical purpose), 10.2 per cent for marriages and rituals, around 5.1 per cent for agricultural purpose and 2.6 per cent for litigation. The pattern was slightly different in Ranchi. Although 30.8 per cent of the 104 households recalling the reasons reported to have mortgaged land for household's expenditure, 31.7 per cent had mortgaged for

Table 2.11 *Reasons for Mortgaging the Land (Proportion of the Total Sample Households)*

Reasons	Dumka	Ranchi
Household expenditure	30.8	30.8
Agricultural purpose	5.1	3.8
Education	2.5	1.9
Medical purpose	48.7	11.6
Marriage rituals	10.3	31.7
Litigation	2.6	15.3
Miscellaneous	–	4.9
Total	100.0	99.8
Number of households who could recall	39	104

marriage and performance of rituals. In Ranchi, around 15.3 per cent households reported to have mortgaged land for defraying expenses on litigation, primarily SAR cases, while 11.5 per cent on medical expenses, only 1.9 per cent for education purpose and others include 4.9 per cent. Thus, three items dominate the reasons for mortgage, namely household expenditure, which can be termed as consumption gap, medical expenses and litigation. The other causes do not seem to be very important.

Reasons for Alienation Due to Sale

Out of 304 sample households in Ranchi and 300 households in Dumka district, 150 reported selling their land in Ranchi and 119 in Dumka and except for 2 households in Dumka and 7 in Ranchi, all the households have given some reasons for the sale. Table 2.12 gives the proportion of households giving various reasons for selling their land.

From the perusal of the table, it is quite clear except for minor differences, the reasons given for mortgage and sale are almost identical. In Dumka, 36.97 per cent of the households reported to have alienated

Table 2.12 *Reasons for Selling the Land by Sample Households (% Households)*

Reasons	Dumka	Ranchi
Household expenditure	36.97	58.00
Marriage/ceremony	13.45	15.33
Agricultural purpose	22.69	2.00
Education	–	2.00
Medical expenses	15.97	6.00
Litigation expenses	0.84	0.67
Both household and marriage	6.72	11.33
Both agriculture and medicine	–	4.90
Unable to tell	1.68	4.67
Total	100.00	100.00
Total households	119	105

land to bridge their consumption gap, the same was 58 per cent in Ranchi. Similarly, marriages and other ceremonies hold the second most important causative factor for land alienation. This is followed by medical expenses. The other reasons were not reported to be very important in Dumka. Around 22.69 per cent of the households reported that they sold their land for improving agriculture, this percentage was only 2 per cent in Ranchi. In Ranchi, only three households reported to have alienated land for higher education of their children and only one household each in Ranchi and Dumka reported to have alienated land to meet the litigation expenses.

As stated earlier, the sale was the most preferred form of obtaining money by the tribal households, when in need, either for consumption or meeting expenses on marriages, ceremonies, death rites, medical expenses and other exigencies. However, in later years, especially after the 1980s, when a number of SAR cases were initiated, and many decrees went in favour of tribals for restoration, the mode of alienation changed to mortgage and though the *bhugat bandha* mortgage could not continue beyond seven years legally. There are cases that are unaware of this legislation or even when aware, due to local compulsions the mortgage, have become a most popular form of alienation, especially in rural areas of Ranchi.

The land alienation to individual, thus, has a mixed typology. Some of the alienation has been demand induced in the sense that due to industrialization and urbanization in post-Independence India, there has been increase in migration to urban centres such as Ranchi and Dumka. The migrants required land for housing purpose/business in these towns. Such demands have been also from a number of educated tribals who got employment not only in the industry but also in government offices, banks and so on.

This tribal political and administrative elite also wish to settle in the urban centres. A city like Ranchi with a good network of educational institutions and infrastructure facilities has been, therefore, a natural choice for settlement of a considerable section of middle class and lower middle class, business and small industrial groups. Other urban centres also show broadly the same trend. The other type of demand generated for land has been for setting up small industries and business, especially in the town and in the periphery and in the adjoining areas where growth centres emerged over the years.

In the rural sector, much of the alienation has been supply-induced in the sense that tribals in need approached the non-tribals or richer tribals for loans which ultimately led to alienation in the past. The needs, as stated earlier, to bridge the consumption gap, in some cases addiction to alcohol and a natural weakness of tribals for drinking, have also been a cause of alienation.

Methods of Land Alienation by Sale to Individuals

The methods adopted for tribal land alienation have been varied and have changed over the years. From the enquiries of and scanning earlier studies, the following methods of land alienation have been identified in the Ranchi district. The form of sale of land as reported by households is given in Table 2.13.

Out of 40.13 acres of land alienated by sale, the sample households could provide information regarding form of sale for 39.48 acres which happens to be 98.38 per cent, while in Ranchi out of reported sale of 467.73 acres, the respondents could state the form of sale about 401.21 acres (85.77%). This was primarily because some of the sale

Table 2.13 *Form of Sale of the Land*

Form	Dumka	Ranchi (in acres)
Dan patra (Gift)	20.82	14.00
	(52.7)	(3.5)
Badalnama	3.48	–
	(8.8)	
Land sold to tribals after DC's permission	–	23.10
	–	(5.7)
Title suit	–	10.43
	–	(2.7)
Antedated hukumnama	–	1.25
	–	(0.31)
		(Continued)

(Continued)

Form	Dumka	Ranchi (in acres)
Registration (collusive)	0.66	46.66
Titles	(1.7)	(11.6)
Sada patta	14.52	305.77
	(36.8)	(76.2)
	39.48	401.21
	(100.00)	(100.00)
Reported sale by households	41.13	467.73
	(98.38)	(85.77)

Note: Figures in bracket are in per cent.

deeds had been executed and carried on many years back and the respondents were not in knowledge of form of sale of land.

Collusive Title Suits

In the initial phases, this happened to be the most popular way of alienating the tribal land both in urban and rural areas. The method was to get a compromise decree from the civil suits to circumvent the provisions of the CNT Act which prohibited alienation of tribal land to non-tribals. The law of adverse possession was applied during the suit. The process was that a non-tribal filed a suit in civil court saying that he had lent money to tribal, and the money was to be returned in specified period of time for which the tribal had given him possession of land more than 12 years ago, which was the statutory period for limitation then. In the court, the tribal would accept this and the decree would be given. By this way, a considerable amount of tribal land was alienated. However, such decrees had problems in the revenue courts which refused to grant mutation on such land, saying that what cannot be done lawfully and directly cannot be obviously allowed to be done in indirect and ingenious method of getting a decree from the civil courts. This form of alienation has almost stopped, especially after the SAR Act, 1969, which increased the limitation period to 30 years, and the compromise decrees also declared illegal by the honourable high court.

Chaparbandi Transactions

The CNT Act does not apply to holdings of non-agricultural nature. This in past and even in present time has given enough space for non-tribals for alienating tribal land. It may be mentioned that the *raiyats* having agricultural land applied for getting the land converted into *chaparbandi* on the grounds that land in question has become unfit for cultivation, the residential buildings have been constructed near the land, and no cultivation is being carried on the land. The land is being used for dumping garbage or children play on it and though the *ryot* was paying the rent, he was not getting benefit and after conversion he would sell a part of land and would construct building or will use the receipt for business or for enhancing his income.

On receipt of such application, the enquiry was to be made by *karmacharis*, the circle inspector or gazetted officer was appointed, and a recommendation was made. The investigations were to be carried on to ascertain whether the land was within municipal area or there has been considerable a growth of population. The commissioner was empowered to declare *chaparbandi* in case of occupancy ryots, while for original *raiyats*, the same was to be decided by the government.

As soon as the land was converted into *chaparbandi* under the orders of the commissioner or the government, it becomes free for the sale under different Acts, and Section 46 did not apply as regards the transfers. This became an important way of getting the land transferred by the co-operative societies. It may be mentioned that the *chaparbandi* right on a particular land can be declared:

1. If in the *khatiyan* records it is mentioned that the land or a part was *chaparbandi*.
2. The landlord had declared the land *chaparbandi* before the Zamindari Abolition Act.
3. The *chaparbandi* has been declared by the commissioner or the government.

However, from the enquiries, it has been revealed that most of the transfers have been through illegal chaparbandi transactions in which certified copies of chaparbandi written on the copies of Register-II has been produced in the registration office. The word *chaparbandi* is written on Register-II by *karamcharis* in connivance with circle officers, deputy collector of land reforms and such other officials. The transferees immediately after the registration in the registration office get the mutation done at the circle office. The certified copies are then illegally given. Another way has been simply inserting the word *chaparbandi* on the rent receipts issued by the circle office which is used for registration and mutation in connivance with various levels of officers.

Antedated *Hukumnama*

The third way had been getting antedated *hukumnamas* of the old zamindars. This has been done in connivance of zamindars with the help of old papers and stamps. It may be mentioned that 60–70 years old stamp papers are sold at a high premium which are used for such *hukumnamas*. Some of the old zamindars have gained from such transactions, especially in Ranchi town. Although this method has not been major factor but still some land has been transferred, the process is to get a fraudulent antedated surrender by the tribal tenant and show through antedated *hukumnama* that the said land was taken over by zamindar before 1947, as per such *hukumnama*, old papers with the zamindars are fraudulently used. As this is mostly in connivance with the tribal tenants, the tenant normally does not go in appeal.

Through Institution or SAR Cases and Fixation of Compensation

In recent times, the provisions of Section 71 (A) of the CNT Act inserted by the SAR Act, 1969, have come in handy for regularization of already illegally alienated land of tribals. It has already been noted that sale had been a very important mode of alienation in the pre-1970 phase. The provision of Section 71 (A) which empowers DC to validate the illegal transfers if substantial structure or building has been constructed before 1969. The transfer has either to make available to the transfer an alternative holding or give equivalent value.

This provision has been widely used and misused to regularize the earlier illegal transfers. There have been many cases in which SAR cases have fixed the compensation even without getting the conclusive proof that the same was alienated before 1969 (or 30 year back) or transferee is unable to give equivalent land to the tribal. Another novel way which came to notice was that the transferee themselves asking the tribal transfer to file SAR cases and get the transfer regularized through the SAR courts. A group of brokers and lawyers have combined together have acted together in legitimizing the earlier illegally transferred land. In recent times, there has been almost a flood of such collusive SAR cases and compensation compromises.

Sada Patta: Sale on Plain Paper

There have been many cases both in urban and rural areas in Ranchi district when the tribals have alienated their land without execution of any registered deed; in this type of alienation, there has been element of encroachment also. These transactions are primarily oral transactions. There have been many instances in the past when houses were constructed by the non-tribals on such lands. In such transactions, prices paid are considerably lower, and in many cases, the tribals are paid only partially. Such transactions have been conducted by industries in the periphery. In some instances, the enquiries revealed that the alienations have been cautious enough to destroy all the papers which the tribals were having regarding such lands. In some cases, the land was alienated during the period of their forefathers and the tribals are unable to file cases for restoration for want of papers. In some cases, such transactions had been in connivance with close relatives or known agents of the family.

Certain interesting modus operandi of such transactions came to notice during investigation. In some cases, the tribals have been carefully chosen who are most susceptible to such pressure who are given money for satisfying their daily needs including drinking. Slowly, the debt (read advances) burden increased and the tribals are coerced into surrendering the land. Although this form of alienation has declined considerably over the years, still it continues to some extent in the certain rural areas. In the initial years, just after Independence, it was the most popular mode of land alienation.

Gift

In Ranchi district, 14 acres have been reported to have been alienated as gift, but in fact, it is in the form of sale. This mode of alienation is only to the tribals. Gift has not been a very popular form in Ranchi district.

Land Sold to Tribal after DC'S Permission

Around 23.10 acres of land have been reported by households to have been sold to tribals after due permission from DC, which happens to be legal transfer under the provisions of the CNT Act. However, the extent of such a transfer is quite limited.

Form of Land Alienation through Sale in Dumka District

The form of sale of land is quite different in Santhal Pargana because of the operation of the SPT Act, which has certain dissimilarities as compared to the CNT Act. The land of even non-tribals cannot be alienated if in the records of rights it is classified as non-transferable. It may be mentioned that in Dumka district where the SPT Act is in operation the guiding principle is that the agricultural and some such type of land are non-transferable, and land, especially *ghairahi* (homestead), is transferable. The transfer of tribal land is permitted in three ways, namely:

1. *Gift or danpatra to sister, daughter, adopted son, adopted daughter permissible under Santal law with permission of DC:* A tribal ryot may, with written permission of DC, make a grant in respect of their lands not exceeding one half of the area of their holding to their widowed mother or to their wife for maintenance after death.
2. *Badlanama: Badlanama* is exchange of the land with permission of DC. This exchange is to be only between *jamabandi ryots* for the land to be exchanged, and the land should be situated in the same village or contiguous village; the transaction is not a concealed sale but a bona fide exchange. The lands proposed to be exchanged are of the same value.

3. *Temporary alienation on trust for cultivation:* This is the case of temporary absence of the villager, their sickness or physical incapacity, loss of plough cattle due to any cause beyond their control or a widow or minor. The land Santhal Pargana by informing SDO, village headman or *mulraiyat*.
4. *Land may be temporarily transferred by bhugut bandha:* This or complete usufructuary mortgage to a non-tribal by registered deed the rights in their holdings up to the fourth of their paddy and first class Bari land to a *raiyat* of Santhal Pargana, land mortgage bank, grain *gola* recognized by DC and a society registered under the Societies Registration Act.

The following modes of sale were identified in Dumka district during the sample study:

1. *Danpatra:* Out of 39.48 acres alienated as sale, 20.82 acres had been by the way of *dan patra* or as gift. The lands alienated through gift in most of the cases had been in contravention to the SPT Act because in the Act, the persons or relations to whom the gift can be legally given is clearly defined. However, in most of the cases the *dan patras* (gift of land) has been given even to non-tribals and tribals who are not even remotely related to the transferrer. This has been done in connivance with the village Pradhans and circle office in most of the cases. This has been popular way of alienation in both urban areas and rural areas.
2. *Badlanama: Badlanama* or exchange of land has been an important way in which the land sale has been affected in Dumka district. Although, in the sample, only 3.48 acres have been transferred by the method, the extent is quite large. In *badla nama*, the land in urban areas is exchanged for land in rural or remote areas for consideration. This is primarily done in two ways, first by simply exchanging land in rural areas with the land in urban areas, and second, first getting possession of spare land first in rural areas with the connivance of village Pradhan and circle office and then registering badla nama with a tribal in urban areas for considerations. Such exchanges are illegal as per the SPT Act.

3. *Through illegal conversion of jamabandi land into homestead plot:* Another way in which a sale is affected by converting *ryoti jamabandi* land as *bari* (land near homestead), a land which is transferable. This is kin to *chaparbandi* in Ranchi district. Many such incidence have been reported in which educational institution including those run by Church have alienated *jamabandi* non-transferable land. Besides, many small industries have alienated *jamabandi* land by getting it entered as *bari* land. It may be mentioned that *jamabandi* land can be converted into form of *ghairahi* or *basawri* land (homestead plot) only through land acquisition proceedings. Although the *ryot* is permitted to construct houses on *jamabandi* land for their own use, in no case they are allowed to change the nature of the land into *basawri* land. Section 13 of the SPT Act even makes the *ryots* liable for eviction. However, they have been given option to pay higher rent for such conversion. In many cases, even mutation orders have been passed on such land. Thus, in a considerable number of cases, especially in cities like Dumka, such alienation has occurred to both tribals and non-tribals.
4. *Sada patta, that is, transfer on plain paper:* There have been several cases of sale through *sada patta* or transferred to non-tribals permanently. Although in the records it continues to be in the name of original owners, de facto in possession of the alienator. In the sample collected, 14.52 acres have been alienated through this process. In the mode, there are element of encroachment as well as forcible evictions also, but in the majority of cases, it happens to be with the consent of tribals themselves.
5. *Regularization under the SAR Act, 1969:* After the SAR Act, 1969, which inserted Section 71 (A) in the CNT Act, there has been regularization of the earlier illegally alienated land. The process has already been explained for Ranchi district. Almost identical process is being repeated in Dumka district, and process of regularization of such alienated land continues even in Dumka district. It seems that land alienation of *jamabandi ryots* was legally almost impossible under the SPT Act, 1947. Now, the amendments in SAR have enabled alienation of tribal land illegally alienated earlier. It has also opened the flood gate for legalizing the earlier illegal acts of transfer.
6. *Kurfanama:* One of the ingenious methods of alienation has been getting a *kurfanama* signed from the tribal *ryoti*. This *kurfanama* is

not authenticated by the concerned officials. In many cases, this is antedated, much before 1949. This transaction is also illegal.
7. *Bhoodan land:* There have been cases in which the tribal land given to Bhoodan Yagna Committee has been transferred to the non-tribal *ryots*. This is in contravention to the SPT Act. The land could have been settled to the tribal *ryots*.
8. *Land settled by Pradhans:* Under the SPT Act, the Pradhans are empowered to settle land in the village under their jurisdiction. There are cases in which the Pradhan have settled land to non-tribals and to those who are not *ryots* from the same village for very small considerations. In many cases, this settlement has been in violation to the SPT Act. This has been done both by tribal and non-tribal Pradhans.

CONCLUSION

The tribal land alienation has been one of the most important issues in the Jharkhand. It is evident from the study that the rapid pace of tribal land alienation has considerably declined. There have been distinct changes in the process and pattern of land alienation after the 1970s, especially with the enactment of the SAR Act. But this act also helped in regularizing the earlier illegally alienated land. The threats of alienation of tribal land, both for public purpose and to the individuals, are still looming large over the tribals. The tribal land alienation can only be arrested with proper implementation of the Act as well as by having the social security measures for the tribals in general. Various ingenious methods have been adopted to circumvent the Act in the past. The silver lining, however, is that the tribals have become more conscious and are lighting against all such land alienation. It is also worth noting that Gram Sabhas under the new Panchayati Raj Act can play an important role in arresting alienation.

REFERENCES

Gupta, K. L. (1977). Bihar. In S. N. Dubey & R. Murdia (Eds.), *Land alienation and restoration in tribal Communities in India* (pp. 181–184). Himalaya Publishing House.

Iyer, G. R. (1993). Tribal land and forest question in Bihar. *The Administrator, 38*(2), 73–101.

Sinha, B. K. (1993). Alienation of land in Chotanagpur, Santhal Pargana areas. *The Administrator, 38*(2), 103–124.

Sinha, S. P. (1968). *The problem of land alienation of the tribals in and around Ranchi (1955–1965).* Bihar Tribal Welfare Research Institute.

Sinha, S. P. (1990). *Final survey report on problem, extent and remedies of land alienation of tribals in Chotanagpur and Santhal Pargana.* Bihar Tribal Welfare Research Institute.

Thakur, I. N. (1977). Bihar. In S. N. Dubey & R. Murdia (Eds.), *Land alienation and restoration in tribal communities in India.* Himalaya Publishing House.

Chapter 3

Triple Exclusion of Dalits in Landownership in Kerala*

C. R. Yadu and C. K. Vijayasuryan

INTRODUCTION

The current pattern of landownership in Kerala is a blot on the progressive image of the state. The struggling masses of Dalits and Adivasis in different parts of the state present a dismal picture of land inequality and exclusion. The struggles for owning a piece of land by Dalits in Changara, Arippa and many other micro-conflicts in the state speak volumes about the continuing 'land hunger'[1] that this community has been facing from the pre-Independence period. Land inequality in the state is neither sudden nor accidental but has been the result of different exclusionary processes. Understanding this dynamics of exclusion becomes essential for analysing the current land inequality scenario in the state. An attempt is made here to examine the different exclusionary processes at work that perpetuate land deprivation faced by Dalits in the state.

The contours of the Dalit land question can be better understood from the fact that 60 per cent of the Scheduled Caste (SC) population in Kerala lives in 26,109 Dalit colonies spread across the state (Rights, n.d.): all in abysmally poor living conditions. The pathetic state of landownership among the Dalits seriously impinges their mobility options. While other communities have opportunities of migrating to West Asia, Dalits lack this mobility option because of their landlessness (Scaria,

---

* *Social Change*, 46(3), 2016.

2010). Omvedt (2006) notes that the situation of Kerala's Dalits with respect to landownership at the turn of the 21st century was not much different from what is shown in the Travancore Census of 1931. In this context, a study of Dalit landownership in comparison with other social groups becomes important.

The data presented in this chapter are based on 68th round of the NSSO Employment and Unemployment Survey, apart from historical surveys. The chapter is organized in three sections. The first section examines the 'triple exclusion' thesis in detail. The second discusses the current status of landownership in the state using tables derived from NSSO unit-level data. The final section concludes the chapter.

DALITS IN 'TRIPLE EXCLUSION'

As regards the land question in Kerala, Dalits have to bear the brunt of 'triple exclusions'. The very first exclusion is their historical exclusion. They were denied landownership in the feudal caste-based agrarian set-up. The second exclusion is their exclusion from land reforms during the post-Independence period under democratic governance. Dalits had to be satisfied with tiny pieces of homestead lands, so small that they were inadequate for putting up a house. The third exclusion is the ongoing process of their exclusion from the land market. The real estate boom and high land prices in the state totally exclude this historically marginalized group. It has become highly difficult for them to own land through any market mechanism. This section discusses the three exclusionary processes that exist in Kerala denying the opportunities for landownership to Dalits and their current dismal status.

Historical Exclusion

Sangham literature gives valuable accounts of the early history and society of Kerala. Untouchability and caste differences were unheard of during the Sangham period[2] (Pillai, 1970). The historian Ilamkulam Kunjan Pillai (1970) noted that private ownership of land began in Kerala long before the Sangham Age. The landlords and local chieftains of this period were the Pulayas, Idayas, Vedas and other agriculturalists.

There is no evidence of a landowning Brahmin–Namboodiri class or Devaswoms[3] and Brahmaswoms.[4] It was with the Aryan invasion starting from the 9th century that landownership was passed to the present class of landowners. Kunjan Pillai suggested that the process of transfer of ownership of land to the upper castes largely happened between the 9th and 13th centuries.

Kerala in the 7th and 8th centuries CE witnessed a heavy influx of Aryans from the North. The Brahmins who had come to dominate in the region by spreading *chaturvarnya* (four castes) began to influence the Kerala society in different spheres. Their culture spread rapidly. This gave rise to a new culture based on a synthesis of Aryan and Dravidian cultures. This new system under the Brahmin dominance is inextricably bound with the matrilineal system, the rise of the Nairs and, above all, the feudal system (Pillai, 1970). It was during this period that the temples, the spiritual strength of Brahmins, became the cornerstone of the social and economic structure in Kerala.

Temples sprang up in the length and breadth of the region, many of them supported schools, hospitals, Agraharams and rest houses for Brahmins. When a temple was built, it was usual to endow it with large tracts of land, the revenue from which was essential to meet the expenses of daily worship, festivals, schools and feeding Brahmins. During early times, there is evidence to show that these lands were donated by the indigenous people, the Kuravas, Pulayas and so on (Pillai cited in Oommen, 1971). The management of temple property was vested in a board of trustees known as *ooralar*. As temples grew in number, landed property came to be accumulated under these trustees. Both landlords and ordinary men continued to hand over large tracts of land to temples.

The imposition of land tax that was hitherto non-existent, following the 'Hundred Year's War' between the Chera and the Chola kings, reinforced donating land to the temples by landlords and ordinary men. To finance the war, the Chera rulers imposed land tax on all lands other than those owned by the temples. As a result, many people handed over their land to the temples to escape from land tax obligations but continued to cultivate their own. The Brahmins later legalized this surrender and usurped ownership of land, thus reducing the legal owners to the status of *kudiayans* or tenants.

As managers of temple wealth, the power and influence of *ooralars* increased considerably. Temple land was gradually taken over by Brahmins as their private property. Going with this trend, various tenure rights were created to suit their interests. From the 12th century onwards, the Namboodiris became the 'monopolists of wealth, power, education and divine will' (Pillai, 1970). They became more powerful than the kings. The priests and *tantris* amassed large amounts of wealth. It is these developments that caused the evolution of the *janmi* system in Kerala.

The rise of the *janmi* system is an important precursor of Kerala society in the medieval times. *Janmam* means birthright claim. It denotes the right of a person to hold on to land in their lifetime, transfer it to future generations and the right over a part of the produce from land (Ganesh, 1990). In this way, the lands that were the property of the indigenous inhabitants of Kerala were passed on to the Brahmins and temples who later claimed *janmam* rights over this land. This heralded the evolution of a new landlord class in Kerala society known as *janmies*.

The period between 12th and 19th centuries is considered as the feudal period in the history of Kerala. It was with the advent of feudalism that the caste system evolved in Kerala (Gopalakrishnan, 1974). Caste became the dominant reality in the social, economic and political spheres. Kerala after the rise of the *janmi* system presents a complex case of land relations where caste and class tend to coincide with the agrarian hierarchy to produce the most bewildering social structure. The Marxist scholar, E. M. S. Namboodirippad (1981), rightly termed this system as *jati–janmi–naduvazhi Medhavitvam* which means upper caste–landlord–chieftain hegemony. This translates to a situation where social relations are dominated by Brahmins and upper castes, production relations are dominated by landlords and the administration is controlled by chieftains in the medieval Kerala society.

Dalits, descendants of the erstwhile landholding indigenous social groups and who later happened to be at the bottom end of agrarian hierarchy, were subjected to brutal and subhuman conditions. The most draconian form of the discrimination in this period was the prevalence of slavery. The 'moral and religious codes articulated through the ideology and practice of Hinduism and caste' legitimized the system of slavery (Mohan, 2015). The untouchable castes, Pulaya,

Paraya, Cheruma, Vettuva and Ullador, filled the position of agrestic slaves in the paddy fields of kings, chieftains and upper-caste landlords. There were other slaves from other castes such as Ezhavas, Muslims and Arayas as well. These slaves were be bought and sold like cattle. Gopalakrishnan (1974) pointed out that a considerable section of the population in Kerala during the feudal period consisted of slaves and they kept on increasing over time. At the beginning of the 19th century, almost 10 per cent and 15 per cent of the population of Travancore and Cochin, respectively, consisted of slaves (Gopalakrishnan, 1974).

Even after the legal abolition of slavery in the three political units of the state, namely Travancore, Cochin and Malabar, the system continued to be practised in different forms. Dalits were completely denied of ownership rights over land and reduced to the status of agricultural labourers either attached or casual. Untouchability and other forms of 'unfreedoms' were imposed on them. Different gradations of distant pollution decreed that 'a Nair cannot touch a Namboodiri, a Tiyya had to keep at least 32 feet distance from them, and a Cheruman or Pulaya had to keep at least 64 feet' (Mayer cited in Ramakumar, 2014). As Herring (1983) rightly noted, 'landlordism in Kerala was inextricably tied to a social system that imposed disabilities and indignities on the lowest orders which were extreme, severe and rigid even by the Indian standards'.

The Brahmins who became the new owners of lands were neither able to cultivate land nor able to supervise cultivation by others. They considered cultivating land themselves akin to a sin. This meant that a new system of land relations had to evolve, whereby cultivation could go on but the landownership right remained with the landlords. When control of lands was transferred to Brahmin temples or chieftains by indigenous owners under coercion, cultivators were given to understand that they were to till the land as a token of allegiance or respect (Varghese, 1970). This is how one of the most important tenures of Kerala called *kanam* originated. The lands thus attained were given on *kanam*, a 12-year fixed rent lease with a provision of renewal at a higher rent rate, to the Nairs in the south and Nambiars in the north. As they saw direct cultivation something that lowered their social status, the Nairs and Nambiars leased out these *kanam* and *janmam* lands on *pattom* and other inferior kinds of tenures to castes and religions just below them in the hierarchy except the Dalits. The main beneficiaries were Christians and Ezhavas in the south and Muslims in the north. There was another form of inferior tenure, *kuzhikanam*, which was intended to put waste lands into cultivation. But, in this case also, the main beneficiaries were Ezhavas and Muslims (Varghese, 1970). Many lower castes and communities, including Dalits, were pushed to the status of agricultural labourers. Thus, the whole structure of agrarian hierarchy came to be determined and governed by the caste hierarchy, both reinforcing each other, producing one of the most rigid social structures in the country. Keeping in mind the intricacy of this kind of a bewildering land tenure system, Daniel Thorner (1956) offered a useful simplification: 'A many-tiered edifice of interests in land—*janmies, kanamdars, verumpattamdars*—rests on a mass of landless labourers known as the Cherumas, Pulayas or Poliyars' (cited in Herring, 1983).

The coming of the British added insult to injury to Kerala's land relations. Some historians hold the British administrators responsible for the worsening of the feudal land relations in Kerala (see Gopalakrishnan, 1974, p. 431). Panikkar (2006) noted that the coming of the British helped the *janmies* reassert their *janmam* rights on land. Moreover, the British judges and administrators ruled that the *janmies* had all the rights to evict *kanakudiayans* from their lands. The judiciary, interpreting property rights according to the English law bestowed absolute ownership rights of land on the *janmies*. The application of English law by the courts had turned traditional customary land laws upside down.

The historical exclusion of Dalits by the caste ideology ensured that they would never own economic resources that would release them from permanent penury. This was why even after the abolition of slavery, they could not gain upward mobility. In the words of Logan (n.d.), 'The slaves, however as a caste, will never understand what real freedom means until measures are adopted to give them indefeasible rights in small orchards occupied by them as house-sites' (cited in Nair, 1986, p. 58). All through in this phase, it can be seen that the Dalits' landless status was preventing them from attaining citizenship. Their poor economic resources even limited their social movements. Mohan (2015) noted that in none of the social mobilizations in this period were Dalits present in large numbers. It also should be noted that even in the social movements Dalits could not attain the economic and political strength as that of the Ezhavas. This is because they lacked economic power that could be translated into political power (Pramod, 2004). While the Ezhavas had trade surplus and landownership, the Dalits had very little resources to draw upon.

Exclusion from Land Reforms

As Kerala was divided into three political entities, Travancore, Cochin and Malabar, the land legislations implemented in these regions differed in terms of their nature, scope and impact. It is said that the progressive state policies in Travancore ushered in an era favourable to the peasantry. The Travancore government passed major laws to grant full ownership rights to cultivators and to control the power of *janmies*. Towards this end, the government came up with significant legislations including the Royal Proclamations of 1865 and 1867, the Janmi-Kudiyan Act of 1896 and the Janmi-Kudiyan (Amendment) Act of 1932.

In the case of Cochin, the important legislations in this period were the Cochin Tenancy Act of 1914, the Cochin Tenancy Act of 1938, the Cochin Verumpattomdars Act of 1943 and the Devaswom Verumpattom Settlement Proclamation of 1943. In the course of the first half of the 20th century, Cochin accomplished more than what Travancore and Malabar could achieve with regard to tenancy reform (Varghese, 1970).

In Malabar, the British land policy was faulty and actually distorted. Although the Malabar Tenancy Act was passed in 1930, it was not adequate enough to bring about a radical change in the tenancy system. But the constraints that the Act brought on the supreme powers of the *janmies* did provide some slight relief to actual cultivators.

After the formation of Kerala state, three major land reform legislations were put into place. Soon after coming to power, the first Communist ministry passed the Agrarian Relations Bill which was a radical attempt in overhauling the prevailing agrarian structure. But as the Bill invited ire from the landed aristocracy, they took to opposing it, leading ultimately to the dismissal of the first Communist government in the country by the president. The next government, a coalition of the Congress–Praja Socialist Party, passed a watered down version of the Kerala Agrarian Relations Bill in 1961. Meanwhile, extensive land transfers were taking place among owners and their heirs during this time. Heavy transfers took place, both by transfer of ownership and transfer of possession, covering more than 0.4 million acres in the decade 1957–1966 (Raj & Tharakan, 1983). These land transfers constituted a substantial proportion of the area that was intended to be transferred as surplus under the provisions of the Agrarian Relations Bill (Raj & Tharakan, 1983). However, this government too fell due to differences among the coalition partners. With this, the state again came under president's rule with the prospect of implementation of this landmark Act becoming bleak.

The formation of the third ministry in 1967 by the CPI (M) saw a drastic amendment to the Kerala Land Reforms Act of 1964. Thus, the Kerala Land Reforms (Amendment) Act of 1969 was passed in the assembly in October 1969 and brought into force from 1 January 1970. The Kerala Land Reforms (Amendment) Act of 1969 broadly contained three schemes. The first was the conferment of ownership rights to the cultivating tenants of lands leased by them. The government ordered that the ownership rights of all tenanted lands would be vested in the state for subsequent transfer to cultivating tenants. The tenants had to pay a nominal amount as purchase price. They were also exempted from paying any rent to either the government or the landlords. The creation of new tenancies was banned with retrospective effect from April 1964.

The second element of the Act was the provision of homestead lands to homestead tenants or *kudikidappukars*. Under this, they could purchase from their landowners three cents of their homestead in a city or major municipality, five cents in a municipality or ten cents in a panchayat area. The *kudikidappukars* were expected to pay only 25 per cent of the market value of the land for such lands and only half of it if the landowner was found to be holding on to lands in excess of the ceiling limit. One half of this purchase price had to be subsidised by the government. The tenants had to pay the other half in 12 equal annual installments. Under this provision, more than 300,000 agricultural labourers got hutment dwellings (Oommen, 1994).

The third scheme of the Act was to take possession of surplus land above the imposed ceiling and redistribute it among landless labourers and landless poor peasants. The Act had scaled down the ceiling limit to 20 acres for a family of five. The ceiling exemption was confined to rubber, tea and coffee plantations, private forests and other such non-agricultural land and land belonging to religious, charitable and educational institutions of public nature.

Of the three schemes of the Kerala Land Reforms Act of 1969, the first two were implemented successfully, whereas the implementation of the last scheme failed miserably (Krishnaji, 2007; Radhakrishnan, 1981). Only one-tenth of the estimated surplus land could be ordered for surrender as on 1988 (Oommen, 1993). Only a little over 1 per cent of the cultivated area could be redistributed consequent to the imposition of the ceiling. This amounted to an area of 66,984 acres to be distributed over 157,841 households, thus making the average plot size a tiny 0.63 acres: mostly barren and uncultivable, this land was not even adequate enough for a subsistence living.

Studies have found that land concentration did significant reduce consequent to the land reforms (Oommen, 1993; Radhakrishnan, 1981). The landowning power of the upper castes, especially the Brahmins, considerably weakened. But significantly, this legislation was more beneficial to the tenants than the agricultural labourers. Available evidences suggest that it was the rich peasants who were the primary beneficiaries of the land reform of 1970 (Herring, 1980). Rich peasants who constituted 13.3 per cent of the total households could gain 38.7 per cent of the total redistributed area. While Ezhavas, Muslims and Christians gained full benefits of the land reforms, the benefits that accrued to Dalits were confined to small pieces of hutment dwellings. They were completely denied of cultivable land despite being the actual tillers of the soil. The land reforms of 1969 affected the land distribution in such a way that redistribution took place from the upper echelons to the middle level, while the lowest end of the agrarian hierarchy continued to remain landless and poor with very little gains.

Thus, the land reform measures implemented before and after Independence excluded the Dalits in Kerala. Critiques of the homestead land provision in the land reforms of 1970 have emphasized that tiny plots of land received under the scheme were completely inadequate and not enough to even build a house (Radhakrishnan, 1981). Mencher (1980) pointed out that in Tamil Nadu, the Dalit quarter, known as *cheri,* was always the property of Dalits, and thus it was impossible for the landowner to throw them out from here. She argued, 'What the legislation in Kerala gave to the landless labourers was something that the Tamil agricultural labourers had all along. And though some have claimed that the land around the house was cultivable, for the majority of the labourers this is not possible' (Mencher, 1980). Thus the '... legal denial of ownership and access to land meant that dalits would never evolve as land-owning peasants despite their continued role in agrarian society' (Mohan, 2011).

Exclusion from the Land Market

The land market also became exclusionary for Dalits given their poor resource endowments. Historical experience also gave testimony to this fact. In the 19th century, the land market in the state became vibrant after the break-up of joint families and the consequent partitioning of family property. For non-traditional landowning communities, this was an opportunity to attain landed property. However, the available evidence has shown that Dalits could not become beneficiaries of land transactions occurred during this period. It was Christians and Ezhavas who gained access to land through market mechanism in this period. The material deprivation of Dalits prevented them from becoming landowners through market mechanism in the same period, while their traditional non-landowning counterparts could gain from owning landed property.

In Table 3.1, the share of different communities in the land transactions in the princely state of Travancore is shown. It is clear from Table 3.1 that due to the break-up of the joint family system, the upper castes, the Brahmins and the Nairs were selling their land far more than they were buying. And it was the Christians and Ezhavas who were the prime beneficiaries of these sales.

A recent study by the Kerala Sasthra Sahithya Parishad based on the data on land transaction for five years shows that the richest class had gained access to land at the cost of the lower economic classes in the society (Aravindan, 2006). The study categorized households into four economic groups based on a composite index comprising the condition of houses they lived in, per capita income, the educational status of members and landownership. While the first three classes witnessed a

Table 3.1 Share of Different Communities in the Land Transactions in Travancore (in Percentage)

Name of Community	1926 Sellers	1926 Buyers	1930 Sellers	1930 Buyers	1935 Sellers	1935 Buyers	1940 Sellers	1940 Buyers
Brahmin	4.5	2.7	4.3	2.7	3.4	3.2	3	2.4
Nair	38.6	29.2	41.6	36.1	44.4	36.2	47.2	27.7
Ezhava	10.2	12.7	13.3	15.8	14.7	17.2	14.2	13.1
Vellala	6.4	5.8	6.9	5.2	5.1	5.2	4.6	4.3
Other Hindus	9.4	6.9	8.5	8.6	9.1	6.2	6.2	7.1
Backward Hindus	1.9	1.6	1.6	1.9	1.5	0	2	2.1
Christian	23.8	33.9	19.5	25.5	17.7	22.2	18.3	28
Muslim	5.2	4.7	4.3	4.2	4.1	3.8	4.4	5.2

Source: Varghese (1970).

negative accumulation, the highest class had accumulated landed wealth to the tune of 33,023 hectares of land in a period of five years. The findings of the study are summarized in Table 3.2.

If the revenue collected from land transactions could be an indicator of real estate activities, notwithstanding the underestimation in value and all, it can be said that real estate activities rapidly increased in the state. In Figure 3.1, it can be seen that the graph rises all over the period. The fall in revenue between 2007–2008 and 2009–2010 may be due to the effect of the global economic crisis. After this short period of downfall, the revenue shows a steep increase in recent years. In the era of high real estate activities and ever-rising prices, it becomes difficult

Table 3.2 *Net Accumulation of Land (in Five Years)*

Economic Class	Net Accumulation of Land (hectares)
I	–275.8
II	–2110.0
III	–3681.5
IV	33,023.5

Source: Aravindan (2006).

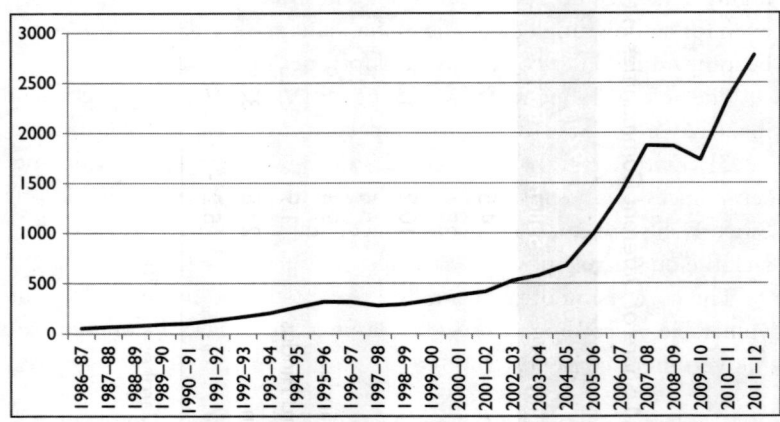

Figure 3.1 *Revenue Generated from Land Transactions in Kerala (in Crores)*
Source: Department of Registration, Government of Kerala (2014).

for Dalits to own land through a market mechanism. While they can easily sell their land, they may be unable to buy a piece of land.

As land is increasingly becoming a real estate asset, it is not only the physical extent of land under possession that matters, the value of land is also very important. The difference in the market value of land can be an indicator of inequality in the society. As Morrison (1997, pp. 86–87) observed:

> ... there is a widening economic gap between those who have marketable land and those who do not... Those with valuable land have the capability to use that resource to advance the family's fortunes. Those who can finance education, underwrite the job search, invest in off-farm income sources will accumulate yet more resources which will be used to advance the family's social and economic standing. The gap between the wealthier, better educated and more capitalist families and the others will increase generation by generation. Those with lower-value land holdings will fall behind and, of course, those without land will fall even farther behind in their income-generating capacity and so in social status.

As most of the Dalit settlements and colonies fall in the peripheral regions, their land commands less value. This is also because of the societal attitude and social stigma attached to the Dalit colonies. So it is highly likely that the real estate boom will also bypass Dalits. Therefore, even for landowning Dalits, the lower value of their landholdings may become a hindrance to advance the fortunes of their families.

The role of remittances in fuelling real estate boom and thus land inequality in the state has long been speculated (Harilal, 2008; Oommen, 1993). Evidence from micro-level studies also shows that migrants' remittances are being invested to buy land (Osella & Osella, 2000). Since Dalits are not a remittance-receiving community as such, they lack the purchasing power which accrues by virtue of being a migrant.

The conversion of farmland into real estate has further made Dalits vulnerable. According to a report submitted to the State Planning Board (Government of Kerala, 2008),

> ... when the area under cultivation, particularly paddy cultivation in the state started depleting in the last more than a quarter of the century, its first casualties where the SCs and STs who lost their livelihood as petty producers or agricultural labourers on these lands.

Here was another dimension of exclusion.

In this way, the three exclusion processes discussed earlier perpetuate the dismal status of Dalits' landownership in the state. As landownership is considered to be vital for the social mobility of marginalized communities, the landlessness of Dalit blocks their upward mobility. They are trapped in a vicious circle—landlessness preventing social mobility and social and economic backwardness preventing landownership. Contemporary land struggles in Kerala by Dalits are nothing but struggles for upward social mobility. It must also be mentioned that the odds working against the Dalit 'land hunger' are multiple and were very much visible during the height of the Chengara land struggle. The agitation had to confront state, political parties and trade unions. What kind of political action could successfully quench the Dalit land hunger is the penultimate question.

LAND INEQUALITY IN KERALA: DALITS VERSUS OTHERS

Conventional literature on land inequality in Kerala turned a blind eye to the social inequality aspect of the land question. The social inequality aspect of land distribution is an important dimension that needs to be focused more. Studies have shown that social inequality in landownership can cause great divergence in the mobility patterns of different social groups (Yadu, 2014).

Table 3.3 shows data collected from different village studies at different time points in Kerala. It clearly shows that the upper castes still dominate landownership in the state. Muslims and Ezhavas come second in terms of their landownership position in the society. Comparing Varghese's (1970) data with other studies can give us a picture of the landownership scenario in the pre- and post-land reform period, though not in a strict sense. It may be seen that the Christians, Muslims and Ezhavas gained considerably from land reforms. All the studies uniformly show that Dalits are at the bottom of landownership and not much has changed even after the land reforms were ushered in. The share of land they owned in relation to their share in the samples was extremely low. In Varghese's (1970) survey, total Dalits constituted 19.43 per cent of the sample, while their share in total landholdings stands was a meager 0.9 per cent. Coming to Scaria's (2010) data which corresponds to the year

Table 3.3 Caste and Landholding in Kerala: Evidence from Village Studies

Caste	Varghese (1958)		Vijayan (1986)		Isaac (1992)		Scaria (2006)	
	Per cent in Sample	Per cent in Total Land Owned	Per cent in Sample	Per cent in Total Land Owned	Per cent in Sample	Per cent in Total Land Owned	Per cent in Sample	Per cent in Total Land Owned
Brahmins	0.43	3.2	1.03	3.45	0.2	0.6	1.61	5.16
Nair	18.47	28.38	1.82	5.27	12.5	18.2	2.26	13.82
Other upper castes	0.87	12.22	3.89	4.91	2.8	2.1	1.61	2.99
Total upper caste Hindus	19.77	43.8	6.74	13.74	15.5	20.9	5.48	21.97
Upper caste Christians	16.63	22.42	–	–	–	–	22.90	34.50
Total upper castes	36.4	66.22	6.74	13.74	15.5	20.9	33.87	78.45
Muslims	11.23	9.75	6.76	7.45	16.1	15.2	11.29	4.68
Ezhava	29.16	19.34	49.62	59.73	43.4	45.4	13.55	16.08
Other backward castes	13.72	2.77	6.75	17.09	19.8	16	15.16	16.82
Dalits	16.41	1.75	30.13	2.18	5	2.3	13.55	3.88
Dalit Christians	3.02	0.15	–	–	–	–	–	–
Total Dalits	19.43	0.9	30.13	2.18	5.4	2.3	13.55	3.88
Tribals	–	–	–	–	–	–	–	–
Total	100	100	100	100	100	100	100	100

Source: Compiled from Kumar (2003) and Scaria (2010).

2006, the same situation almost continues. This clearly shows that the caste–land nexus is not completely broken by the land reforms.

Although there are many village-level studies that shed light on the inequality in land distribution at the micro-level, there is a dearth of studies that have dealt with social inequality in landownership at a pan-Kerala level. In this section, we use the NSSO Employment and Unemployment Survey 68th round (2011–2012) to understand land inequality among different social groups.

In Table 3.4, the mean and median land owned are given along with the standard deviation (SD). It can be seen that the mean is always greater than the median for all social groups, which means that the land distribution is rightly skewed. The mean land owned for all Kerala is 0.15 hectare. It can be seen that Christians have a substantially higher average landownership compared to all Kerala. The same is the case for Hindu upper castes. Compared to all other social groups, especially the upper castes, the Dalits' average landownership is very low. This finding comes in tandem with available village-level studies.

SD gives a picture of dispersion of landholdings within the social groups. It can be seen that SCs have the lowest SD compared to other social groups. While the Christians' SD is as high as 0.60, the corresponding value for SCs stands at 0.08. This means that the landownership of Dalits is homogeneous in nature. There are no significant differences in

Table 3.4 Mean and Median Land Owned across Social Groups (in Hectares)

Social Group	Mean	Median	Standard Deviation
ST	0.13	0.07	0.18
SC	0.05	0.02	0.08
Hindu OBC	0.13	0.05	0.25
Muslim (non-SC and non-ST)	0.11	0.04	0.25
Christian (non-SC and non-ST)	0.28	0.08	0.60
Hindu Others	0.21	0.08	0.41
Total	0.15	0.05	0.36

Source: Authors' calculation based on NSS Employment and Unemployment Survey 2011–2012.

landownership within that social group. The high SD of Christians and Hindu upper castes shows that there are different classes present within these social groups.

Table 3.5 shows the mean and median land cultivated for different social groups. The distribution of land cultivated for all social groups is skewed to the right. The pattern of average land cultivated also shows the same trend as in the case of land owned. While Christians and

Table 3.5 *Mean and Median Land Cultivated across Social Groups*

Social Group	Mean	Median	Standard Deviation
ST	0.10	0.08	0.15
SC	0.04	0.01	0.08
Hindu OBC	0.13	0.03	0.28
Muslim (non-SC and non-ST)	0.09	0.01	0.26
Christian (non-SC and non-ST)	0.32	0.10	0.66
Hindu Others	0.19	0.06	0.85
Total	0.16	0.04	0.50

Source: Authors' calculation based on NSS Employment and Unemployment Survey 2011–2012.

Table 3.6 *Index of Access for Different Social Groups*

Social Group	Index of Access—Land Owned	Index of Access—Land Cultivated
ST	0.80	0.60
SC	0.34	0.22
Hindu OBC	0.84	0.82
Muslim (non-SC and non-ST)	0.71	0.60
Christian (non-SC and non-ST)	1.82	2.19
Hindu Others	1.32	1.22

Source: Authors' calculation based on NSS Employment and Unemployment Survey 2011–2012.

Hindu upper castes dominate the scene, Dalits come at the bottom. The dispersion within social groups follows the same pattern as in the earlier case.

As average land holdings are not a satisfactory measure of a community's control over land, to understand the inequality in access to land, we can use a ratio called index of access (Bakshi, 2008). The index of access is defined as the ratio of the share of total land owned by group j to the share of this group in total number of households. Thus, the index of access for SC, denoted by IA, can be represented as

$$IA = \textit{Percentage of total land owned by SC households} \div \textit{Percentage of SC households to total households}$$

The value of the access index ranges between 0 and ∞. If IA takes the value 1, it represents a situation where SC household's access to land is in proportion to their share in the total population. Where the access index is less than 1, it represents a situation in which the proportion of SC households in the population is greater than the share of total land that they own (Bakshi, 2008).

It may be seen that Christians have highly disproportionate access to land owned and land cultivated. Their index values stand at 1.82 and 2.19, respectively. Hindu upper castes also have index values more than 1, which means that they have higher proportion of land than their proportion in the population. Hindu OBCs have higher index values than Muslims both for land owned and land cultivated. The least index of access happens to be for the SCs. Their index of access for land owned stands at 0.34 and 0.22 for land cultivated. The pathetic state of landownership of Dalits in Kerala is a result of the 'triple exclusion' as we have discussed in this chapter.

CONCLUSION

The triple exclusion processes placed Dalits at the bottom of landownership in the state. The structure of landholding patterns went on drastic changes with the invasion of Aryans in favour of the Brahmins. The land-based caste system completely denied Dalits any landownership rights. All the land reform policies implemented in the pre- and post-land reform period excluded Dalits from their ambit. The land reforms of 1970 did not recognize them as the tillers of the soil. The contemporary exclusion of Dalits from landownership happened by way of their inability to participate in the land market. In an era of sky rocketing land prices, buying a piece of land became very difficult for them.

The analysis shows that social inequality in landownership continues to be high in Kerala. While the Hindu forward castes and the Christians are predominantly landowners, Dalits are at the bottom end of the landownership pyramid followed by Adivasis. It is estimated that compared to SCs, the access to land by forward castes is five times higher in the case of land owned and more than eight times higher in case of land cultivated. The land–caste nexus has not disappeared with the passage of time. Such land deprivation is, in a major way, impeding the presence of Dalits in the mainstream. To ensure their full participation in the development process, landownership becomes a necessary condition.

NOTES

1. Land hunger was the term which missionaries described to denote the Dalits' urge for land (Mohan, 2015).
2. The Sangham period lasted from 5th century BC to 6th century CE.
3. Properties belonging to god.
4. Properties belonging to Brahmins.

REFERENCES

Aravindan, K. P. (Ed.) (2006). *Kerala Padanam* (in Malayalam). Kerala Sastra SahityaParishad.
Bakshi, A. (2008). Social inequality in land ownership in India: A study with particular reference to West Bengal. *Social Scientist, 36*(9–10), 95–116.
Ganesh, K. N. (1990). *Keralathinte Innalekal*. Department of Cultural Publications.
Gopalakrishnan, P. K. (1974). *Keralathinte Samskarika Charitram*. Kerala Bhasha Institute.
Government of Kerala. (2008). *Report of research group on special component plan and tribal sub-plan*. Kerala State Planning Board.
Harilal, K. N. (2008, March 11). Kerala Vikasanam: Bhooprasnam Muthal Bhooprasnam Vare. *Madhyamam*. http://www.madhyamam.com/weekly/
Herring, R. J. (1980, 28 June). Abolition of landlordism in Kerala: A redistribution of privilege. *Economic & Political Weekly, 15*(26), A59–A61+A63–A69.
Herring, R. J. (1983). *Land to the tiller the political economy of agrarian reforms in South Asia*. Oxford University Press.
Krishnaji, N. (2007). Kerala milestones: On the parliamentary road to socialism. *Economic & Political Weekly, 42*(23), 2169–2176.

Kumar, R. K. (2003). *Social and economic mobility of a traditional social group: A case study of Theyyam performing community of North Kerala* (PhD dissertation). Centre for Development Studies, Thiruvananthapuram.

Mencher, J. (1980). The lessons and non-lessons of Kerala: Agricultural labourers and poverty. *Economic & Political Weekly, 15*(41–43), 1781–1802.

Mohan, P. S. (2015). *Modernity of slavery: Struggles against caste inequality in colonial Kerala*. Oxford University Press.

Mohan, P. S. (2011, December 19). Land struggles in contemporary Kerala. *The Hindu Business Line*. http://www.thehindubusinessline.com/opinion/land-struggles-in-contemporary-kerala/article2729300.ece

Morrison, B. M. (1997). The embourgeoisement of the Kerala farmer. *Modern Asian Studies, 31*(1), 61–87.

Nair, A. R. K. K. (1986). *Slavery in Kerala*. Mittal Publications.

Namboodirippad, E. M. S. (1981). *Keralam Malayalikalude Mathrubhumi* (in Malayalam). Kerala Grandhasala Sahakarana Sangham.

Omvedt, G. (2006). Kerala is part of India: The Kerala model of development, dalits and globalization. In J. Tharamangalam (Ed.), *Kerala: The paradoxes of public action and development* (pp. 188–214). Orient Longman.

Oommen, M. A. (1971). *Land reforms and socio-economic change in Kerala: An introductory study*. The Christian Literary Society.

Oommen, M. A. (1993). *Essays on Kerala economy*. Oxford & IBH Publishing.

Oommen, M. A. (1994). *Essays on Kerala economy*. Oxford & IBH Publishing.

Osella, F., & Osella, C. (2000). *Social mobility in Kerala: Modernity and identity in conflict*. Pluto Press.

Panikkar, K. N. (2006). *Malabar Kalapam Prabhuthvathinum Rajavazhchaykkunmethire* (Malayalam). D. C. Books.

Pillai, K. E. (1970). *Studies in Kerala history*. National Book Stall.

Pramod, K. M. (2004). *Spaces of subordination: The making of Dalit colonies in Kerala* (MPhil dissertation). M. G. University, Kottayam.

Radhakrishnan, P. (1981). Land reforms in theory and practice: The Kerala experience. *Economic & Political Weekly, 16*(52), A129–135.

Raj, K. N., & Tharakan, P. K. M. (1983). Agrarian reform in Kerala and its Impact on rural economy—a preliminary assessment. In A. K. Ghose (Ed.), *Agrarian reforms in contemporary developing countries* (pp. 31–90). St. Martin's Press.

Ramakumar, R. (2014). Agrarian change and changes in the socio-economic conditions of dalit households in a Malabar village. In V. K. Ramachandran & M. Swaminathan (Eds), *Dalit households in village economies*. Tulika Books.

Rights (n.d.). *Report of the fact finding mission on Chengara land struggle*.

Scaria, S. (2010). Changes in land relations: The political economy of land reforms in a Kerala village. *Economic & Political Weekly, 45*(26–27), 191–198.

Varghese, T. C. (1970). *Agrarian consequences and economic change*. Alliance Publishers.

Yadu, C. R. (2014). *Land question and mobility of marginalized: A study of land inequality in Kerala* (Unpublished MPhil dissertation). Centre for Development Studies, Thiruvananthapuram.

Chapter 4

Contextualizing Women's Rights and Entitlements to Land*
Insights from Gujarat

Meera Velayudhan

INTRODUCTION

Contextualizing Women's Land Rights

Studies have shown that a key factor linked with rural poverty is land (IFAD, 2001). In the South Asian context, arable land has been analysed as the most valued form of property, for its economic, political and symbolic significance. It is a wealth-creating and livelihood-sustaining asset (Agarwal, 2002). It has also been termed as a metaphor for power, wealth and status (Sud, 2007). Access to land determines the economic status and power relations between/among different social groups (Bakshi, 2008). Studies have shown that in regions where agriculture dominates livelihoods, land is also important for women for reducing the risk of poverty and enhancing food security. Women who own land or control assets are better positioned to improve their lives and cope in the face of crisis. By owing land and homes, women directly gain from the benefits of using land, earning income and also have a secure place to live (Agarwal, 1994a, 1998). Research has shown that individuals who own land generate much higher rural non-farm earnings from self-employment than people without land (Dwyer, 1988). Women

---

* *Social Change*, 42(4), 2012.

can also use the land as collateral for credit during crisis or for investing in other income generating work (UNRISD, 2005).

Studies show that property and asset ownership by mothers has led to better outcomes for survival, education and health of children than assets owned by fathers. A study of marginal farmer households in Kerala showed that the mother's cultivation of a home garden (the output which she controlled) had a consistently positive effect on child's nutrition (Kumar, 1978). Access to and control over productive assets such as land can strengthen women's ability to manage economic shocks and social risks (Addison et al., 2008). Land is a particularly critical resource for women when the household breaks down in cases of male migration, war, abandonment, violence, divorce, polygamous relationships, illness (such as HIV/AIDS) or death (UNRISD, 2005). Secure property rights can also help women avoid or mitigate the impacts of violence, in particular, domestic violence. A study on India pointed out that women with property who experienced violence from their spouses were far more likely to leave their marital home 71% than women without property 19%. Research in Kerala indicated that 49 per cent of women with no property reported domestic violence as compared to 7 per cent of women who owned property.

In regions facing hunger and chronic under-nutrition, women often are the main food growers. Rural women are responsible for half of the world's food production. And in developing countries, they produce 60–80 per cent of the food (FAO, 1996). Studies of developing countries have found a clear link between secure land tenure and increased agricultural productivity and land improvement provided women have access to agricultural credit, market, input supplies and extension (Duncan & Brantz, 2004). Secure property rights for women can have an impact on women's overall role and position in the household and community (Anriquez, 2010). Land titles also serve as collaterals in accessing the benefits of development programmes such as production credits for farmers. In regions with high male migration and where women are the principal farmers, such support is critical for their households. In India, 86 per cent of cultivable land is privately owned (Agarwal, 2002). While all-India data on women's landownership are lacking, sample surveys on inheritance patterns point to low land ownership (with regional variations). Where women were given titles, as daughters and widows, it was mainly joint titles with sons, who effectively controlled the land. Land ownership by women was a mere 2 per cent (Agarwal, 1994b). A study covering 11 districts and 23 villages in Gujarat indicated that only 11.8 per cent of women owned land of which 47.3 per cent were widows, suggesting that it was after widowhood that women held land ownership. Also, 44 per cent were given land ownership to avail of government programmes (WGWLO, 2004).

Entitlements to land are determined by diverse socio political systems that have evolved over time and sometimes exist concurrently. In South Asia, for example, inheritance patterns in land vary within and between countries and further by region, religion, caste, community and ethnicity. The social norms and institutions that constrain women from claiming and controlling land vary region by region. They cause disadvantage to women more in certain region than others. Variations persist, as in India as a whole, in relation to inheritance of agricultural land in the tenurial enactments of different states. These variations have been traced back to the colonial heritage when inheritance and marriage laws were perceived as personal laws of communities. Laws enacted later accommodated customary, religious and pluralistic traditions. Inheritance rights to land, particularly agricultural land, have been most difficult to enact (Agarwal, 1994). In India, it took almost half a century to amend (2005) the Hindu Succession Act (HSA) of 1956. This amendment overriding the varied tenurial laws of different states enables daughters, including those who are married, to become coparceners in joint family property.

Inheritance, transfer from the state and market purchase inform women's access to and ownership of land and, according to several studies, at all of these levels, women face more obstacles than men owing to male preference in inheritance practices, male privilege in marriage, gender inequality in the land market or male bias in state land distribution programmes. Women in many countries may have access to land and other assets through informal arrangements or traditional methods of household or community decision-making. Such practices vary from country to country and community to community. In most of South Asia, women traditionally do not own property since land is inherited through the male family line, since in most cultures, inheritance practices are patrilineal. Customary law in many countries, often related to marriage, bar women from obtaining primary rights to land. Rather, they only have rights of usage through their fathers, husbands and brothers. However, access is not ownership. Women's secondary rights become weaker when norms of social protection diminish.

In most countries, women are legally able to purchase land in the market. However, a weak asset base or a high degree of economic dependency are often the barriers that women have to face. Often a woman must seek permission from her husband or male family members before committing family resources. This hampers effective use of resources and also lowers the motivation of women to invest in the land they use, for example, adding irrigation in land rehabilitation programmes. Where local customs afford women certain entitlements to land, women may be reluctant to demand them for fear of losing social benefits. In India, daughters usually waive their land rights in favour of brothers to avoid being termed as selfish and to avoid losing the support of their natal households. Where women resist forgoing their claims, male relatives forge wills, file court cases, use threats and violence which discourage women from claiming their shares. Studies show that biases also cloud the thinking of land administration officials who refuse to record inheritance shares of daughters (WGWLO, 2004).

One source of land for women is through government laws and policies which involve public land distribution. Be it poverty alleviation, schemes for land distribution or for resettlement, conceptual biases often impact their implementation. In India, agrarian reforms through the 1950s and later took place at a time when gender equality was marginal to the policy agenda and gender issues lacked their current visibility. In most government land reform programmes and land transfers, women's land rights remained marginal since land reforms programmes continue to be premised on the assumption of the household as homogenous or the community as a united collection of households. The household was perceived as the unit of allocation of resources. The Operation Barga Programme in West Bengal in the late 1970s for registering tenants and giving land to the landless carried a strong male bias. A village study in Midnapur district found that 98 per cent of holdings distributed went to men. In 90 per cent female-headed households, the land was given to the women's sons. No married women received joint titles (Gupta, 2002).

Studies on the household have demonstrated significant inequalities within and between households in the distribution of resources and decision-making and brought out the fallacy of the unified household with its income pooling and sharing assumptions. A study on developing countries pointed to into the household as an arena of conflict marked by inequality and negotiation over income and expenditures (Dwyer & Bruce, 1988). Amartya Sen's work challenged the unitary model of the household regarding intra-household gender relations. Referring to the Indian experience, Sen pointed to the conflicts of interest that exist within households. He also held that the household is most usefully represented as a case of 'cooperative conflict'. The solution that is finally adopted is the result of the bargaining ability of the couple. However, the couples do not come to the bargaining table with equal power. In addition to self-worth, there are two important factors that determine a person's bargaining power. These are the actual ability of each member to earn an income or to bring valued resources into the household, and the value given to that contribution by other household members (Sen, 1990). Others like Bina Agarwal have argued that external constraints to women acting on their self-interest, moving beyond intra-household relations to other arenas of power relations within which women are located were significant (Agarwal, 1994a). Grassroots experiences and studies have identified a large number of institutions beyond the household which are also gendered. These include communities, labour markets, property institutions, judicial systems, land administration and local governance (Kabeer, 1994). Recent studies have focused on gender as social relations, on subject positions and subjectivities, on meshing of shared and separate interests within households and on power residing in material assets as well as in discourse. These contexts, it is argued, made women's struggles for land more complex. Another study points to the socially embedded nature of land as resource and the mutuality and interdependence between men and women in the productive use of land (Jackson, 2003). More than gender identity, it was the cross-cutting identities of ethnicity, kinship, education and marital status that motivated women to both stake their claim to land as well as oppose the claims of other women and men. Men too adopt different subject positions depending on their own experiences and context (Rao, 2005). Land was linked with family and kinship relations and structures of social relations in South Asia. It defined identity, hierarchy and status (Dube, 1997).

Since the 1990s, women's engagement with issues of land rights have led to varied land alliances and coalitions in post-colonial developing nations in particular. In several African countries, these have emerged in the context of new legislations or constitutional changes in land tenures. A large number of women have played leadership roles in platforms such as the Uganda Land Alliance, the National Land Forum in Tanzania, the Zambia National Land Alliance, National Land Committee in South Africa, Kenya Land Alliance, Rwanda Land Alliance and the Namibian NGO Federation (NANGOF) for land rights of women, pastoral communities and the landless. Regional networks have been formed across countries, like *Land Net* in East Africa. In countries such as Mali, Senegal and Madagascar, women's organizations have been formed so that women's rights and entitlements to land are incorporated when changes are made in land laws.

The Consult for Women and Land Rights (CWLR), set up in 2004, has evolved as a global forum of local, national and international NGOs and networks, lobbying and advocating for policies, law reform, programmes and administrative mechanisms to increase the resource base for including land rights to the poor, disadvantaged and vulnerable women. These campaigns have led to a recognition of how land rights impact gender relations and have increasingly interlinked with other issue-based networks such as food security, housing, livelihood, property, citizenship, violence against women, starvation, land alienation, migration, dispossession, trafficking, forced eviction and displacement.

LEARNINGS FROM GRASSROOTS FIELD EXPERIENCES: GUJARAT

Popular movements addressing issues of land, apart from the 1930s Adivasi struggles under the Kisan Sabha, were the two main predominantly Gandhian pre-Independence movements, namely the Bardoli and Kheda Satyagrahas led by middle-and upper-caste peasants, though with popular support (Hardiman, 1996). The post-Independence movements in Gujarat were led by varied Gandhian organizations and prominent among these was the Pardi Satyagraha (1953–1963) of

Adivasis on tenancy and the right to grow food crops on grasslands. Other movements involving Adivasis in the eastern forest belt of Gujarat in the 1980s and the 1990s were mainly led by civil society/voluntary organizations on issues such as registration of land in the name of tillers, access to minor forest produce and wages of forest workers (Shah & Sah, 2002). Although a few oral testimonies and narratives point to women's participation in these movements, the environment for focusing on gender issues was clearly lacking. However, for the past 10 years or even earlier, the prevalence of a fairly enabling environment for engendering the development discourse and practices in Gujarat led to the initiation of a Gujarat state level network of 23 organizations in 2003—the Working Group on Women and Land Ownership (WGWLO), perhaps the only state-level network of its kind in India (Velayudhan, 2008).

At the initial meetings of WGWLO in 2003, it was evident that land being a sensitive issue, few civil society organizations had addressed it. Grassroots organizations looked at the significance of land from varied perspectives and examined cases that showed the advantages of women's land ownership. Women, more than men, considered land as key to livelihood security and land ownership provided opportunities for women to enter decision-making processes and gain confidence against heavy odds (Apoorva, 2002). However, several apprehensions persisted. These were:

1. *Land ownership for women will lead to land fragmentation and hence low productivity:* It was argued that the issue of land fragmentation was only raised when women demanded their share in land. If a family had, say, six sons and no daughters, this argument would not be put across. Also, many forms of production such as horticulture and plantation of timber yielding tree are independent of the size of the land. Studies of the pre-Green Revolution period in the 1950s and the 1960s clearly show that small-size farms had a higher value of annual output per unit of cultivated area than large-sized ones. The issue of landholding and economies of scale depended on several factors including nature of crops grown (food crop or cash crop), the quality of land (irrigated, non-irrigated, fertile or infertile). Land consolidation could be undertaken to prevent fragmentation.

For example, four or five plots could share irrigation water from a common source. However, the issue of decision-making and management needed to be addressed.

2. *Daughters married outside the village cannot control land in her maternal place:* There were cases of sons migrating to urban areas for work; their share in the land in their village remains intact. They may receive a share of produce from the land and can also claim and exercise their rights to land at anytime. Hence, daughters residing outside the village can also exercise such rights.
3. *Land ownership by women can lead to family disputes and breakups:* This was a fear expressed by many, including policymakers: Underlying this was the perception of family as a cohesive unit. Brothers too fought with each other for property. The discussion veered towards legal loopholes and the gap between law and reality (Velayudhan, 2008).

There were social, legal and administrative constraints to women's ownership of land. A study (Mandal & Bansal, 2002) commissioned by AKRSP (India) was conducted in field areas—two Adivasi/tribal as well as two caste villages in district Narmada/Surat and Surendranagar.

The main points highlighted were:

- 7.74 per cent women inherited some land in Adivasi areas as compared to 4.63 per cent in caste villages.
- These shares were not recorded formally. Informal ownership was more prominent in a tribal set-up, while in the caste villages only young widows had informal ownership of land.
- The feeling of insecurity among widows from the castes was very high, with the nature of ownership being informal. Even where they had formal ownership, it involved a struggle to gain ownership.

In these meetings, civil society organizations acknowledged the need to make a mental jump as they felt that women's land ownership was not only a rights issue but also key to livelihoods. It was also recognized that this was an issue that needed separate focus as well as strong emphasis. WGWLO (2004) conducted a study. The study pointed to low level of landownership by women in rural Gujarat, and also explored the link between landownership and marital status, rights as daughters, vulnerabilities (such as those faced by widows), ownership and government schemes, perceptions and role of caste leaders and revenue officials. Landownership did increase women's confidence and role in decision-making, including selecting their own cropping patterns. At the same time, women needed support—financial, knowledge inputs as well as inputs on marketing. The study also opened up possibilities on strategies—to focus on private land, take up cases of widows as an entry point and press for changes in the design of government schemes so that families are motivated to transfer land in the name of women.

Sensitization of revenue officials, on the one hand, and leaders of caste/community institutions, on the other, were other possible strategies. A significant aspect that emerged from the study was the need to create wider awareness among rural women and take a fresh look at the broader historical context of changing land relations in Gujarat.

CHANGING LAND RELATIONS IN GUJARAT

Following India's independence in 1947, land reforms were initiated in three phases. In the first phase of the 1950s, abolition of intermediaries was the focus. The next phase was directed at ending tenancy, in particular, sharecropping. The third phase from 1956 aimed at regulating the size of individual holdings through a land ceiling, and then distributing excess land among landless labour and marginal farmers. The central government's role was limited to giving directives and support, the formulation and implementation of land policy being the responsibility of the Indian states. In the case of Gujarat, the populist slogan, *Khedut ni Zamin* (land to the tiller) was played out over the decades as a complex story of the interlinkages of class and caste, state and polity (Sud, 2005). Gujarat state was formed in the 1960s following bifurcation of the erstwhile Bombay state. In terms of historical, sociocultural and physiological background, Gujarat consists of two sub-regions, namely mainland Gujarat and peninsular Gujarat. Gujarat's land tenure systems, as shaped during the colonial era, were distinct.[1] Several legislations largely eliminated intermediaries and zamindars in the 1950s (Shah & Sah, 2002). Tenancy reforms in mainland Gujarat remained partial while the Land Ceiling legislation passed through five amendments before 1976. A 1973 amendment placed a ban on purchase of agricultural land by non-agriculturalists and allowed 'male dependants' of a farmer's household to be independent landowners. Benefiting from the white/dairy co-operative movement and the Green Revolution, the rising urban entrepreneurial class/caste still maintained its *khedut*[2] identity in the 1970s. In the early 1980s, the emphasis shifted from land policy to schemes that periodically leased government land to the poor, some to Dalit/Adivasi co-operatives and not without opposition from landed sections. The move from *khedut ni zamin* to *nana (small) khedut ni zamin* could not make progress. The 1980s also saw changes in the law disallowing purchase or sale of agricultural land beyond the 8 kilometres residential limit, providing opportunity for wealthy farmers and others to buy the land of vulnerable small and middle farmers. This limit was completely done away with in the mid-1990s. Also removed were restrictions on conversion of agricultural land to non-agricultural status for industrial purposes. This was also interspersed with schemes for distribution of government wasteland to the poor. A new land policy was announced by the state government in 1996, where persons holding *navi sharat* (new tenure) would be able to sell it after converting it into *juni sharat* (old tenure). The barrier put earlier on the sale of such land was directed at protecting beneficiaries of land distribution from moneylenders. In 2003, all such tenures were automatically converted as 'old tenures' (Sud, 2005).

Underlying the shifts in policies concerning land is the story of Gujarat's accelerated economic growth, in particular, industrial growth. However, recent studies claim that there has been a steady growth at 9.6 per cent per year in agricultural state domestic product since 1999–2000 owing to the state's agricultural programmes. These were located in liberalizing markets, encouraging private capital, reorganizing agricultural extension, improving infrastructure like roads, improved availability of ground water for irrigation, small water harvesting structures based on community mobilization and well irrigation supported by 8-hour uninterrupted power supply to farmers under the Jyotigram Yojna programme (Shah et al., 2009). Another study (Kumar et al., 2010) has questioned the agricultural growth story, stating that it was more of a good recovery from a dip in the 1999–2000 drought years owing to four consecutive years of good monsoons and bulk water transfer through the Sardar Sarovar Project. The study stressed on the need to consider the interaction among varied actors in the set of interventions, be it policy, institution, market, technology or infrastructure related. Although Gujarat, among the most developed states in India, witnessed an accelerated economic growth in the 1990s, historical legacy (colonial agrarian policy,[3] regional unevenness of natural resource base, climatic conditions) and dynamics of the liberalization process created imbalances between regions and social groups informing adversely, women's livelihood, resource bases and status. This trend is closely linked with the sectoral imbalances in Gujarat's economy that emerged since the 1980s (Bagchi et al., 2005) and the unstable nature of agriculture that tends to leave small farmers and farm labour in poverty. On the one hand, the share of agricultural labour in the rural workforce increased (40.71% in 1991 to 46.97% in 2001) and on the other, about 55.3 per cent operational holdings are with small and marginal farmers who own only 2.13 per cent of the cultivated area (MGLI, 2004) and these areas too are on the decline. Rural women workers predominate the primary sector, in particular, in 'difficult to measure' sectors such as unpaid family work subsistence work and other informal work, and lack occupational diversification. The rural marginal workforce is increasing as are seasonal unemployment and underemployment in agriculture, in tube well and canal dominated areas in particular, increasing the burden on women for whom agriculture remains the main absorber if not the last resort for work (MGLI, 2004.). In terms of work pattern and household groups in rural Gujarat, in 2000, only 8.3 per cent Dalits were self-employed in agriculture, while among Adivasis, 31.2 per cent were self-employed in agriculture. Among Dalits, 58 per cent and among Adivasis 48 per cent of households were involved as agricultural labour. Incidence of poverty is predominant among Adivasis and Dalits and is linked to their low productive asset base, low educational level and lack of access to regular employment outside their villages. In the forest and hilly areas, the poverty of Adivasis is linked with landlessness, limited access to forests, subsistence crops, low input use and lack of diversification. The significant regions of this phenomenon include Sabarkantha, Panchmahal, Dahod, Vadodara, Surat, Bharuch, Narmada and Valsad. Poverty reduction among Adivasis remains the lowest in the state (Mehta, 2006).

Since the 1990s, with the commercialization of agriculture and the shift from cultivation of subsistence food crops to cash crops, there was a marked decline in the share of cereal and food grain production. Voices of rural women and group discussions from Kheda and Banskantha highlight some of the dilemmas that this process posed particularly for small farmers and agricultural labour. Women activists from an NGO, Cohesion, provided the following insights from Kutch district.

> In group discussion with women in Fulpara Vandh (Rapar taluka), the women said that earlier in Kutch most of the farmers opted for food crops. When they cultivated and chose food crops, households had food security for longer term. It reduced the tension of women, as women always seem to be food provider of the family. With cash crop cultivation, women do not have any assurance of food security. Overall income increased, but it automatically does not perpetuate food security. In cash crops, market is a deciding or influencing factor about which crop to sow. In general, women's opinion was not sought or considered since women did not have much idea about market. In food crop production, however, decision making process took place within the household; hence women's views are sought. Another impact of commercialisation is that cash earned always goes to the hands of men folk. Generally they spend it for their own indulgences. We have innumerable cases where earnings from Jira (cumin) is used to redeem debt or could be used for purchase property (which is in the name of men), bikes, jeeps, putting money in banks, purchasing of ornaments, etc. Women felt that commercialisation has increased disparity within the household. Women are no longer involved in the decision making process and are excluded from benefits ultimately.[4]

Such inequities are seen in particular for women working in their own family farms (Jackson & Rao, 2004). A participatory study (WGWLO, 2006) and two mass conferences of rural women held by WGWLO in 2005[5] suggested the need to locate women's land rights and entitlements in the following context.

Entitlement and Usufruct Rights in Common Land
Forest Land

Adivasis, 15 per cent of the state's population, are mainly located in the hilly belt along Gujarat's eastern border, including the predominantly tribal districts of Dangs, Dahod and Panchmahal. About 9.7 per cent of the state's geographical area is under forests though reserve and protected forests now constitute only 6 per cent. Access to land is through owned, shared, traditional cultivable methods. The average landholding in families ranges between 1 and 10 hectares, half of which are not in the revenue category. Land transfer to family inheritors has been very slow and was not considered significant by Adivasis themselves till recent times. Cultivation is mainly for self-consumption, thus subsistence crops are grown, there being little difference between output of owned land and traditional cultivable land. Apart from livestock and poultry, rivers and forests provided additional resources such as fish, fuel and other forest produce, mainly accessed by women.

Following a central government directive, regularization of forestland for cultivation was undertaken by state governments. Experiences of member organizations of WGWLO working in the Adivasi belts in Gujarat showed that even as land cultivated before 1980 by Adivasis was being regularized, several problems persisted. Following the enactment of the new Forest Act in 2005, the Gujarat government imposed some additional conditions for recognizing rights over cultivated forest land. Case studies and RTI information collected by WGWLO suggested that those owning revenue land or who have already received *pattas*[6] to forest land under the 1992 GR will be eligible to rights over a maximum of 10 acres including the land already under their name. The justification is that all land should be required for meeting bona fide livelihood needs. The government also indicated that it was attempting to take a more liberal view of 'reside in forests' requirement. The tribal department issued positive clarifications for government staff, including the forest department, stating that they should not be involved in liaison work in the field as they are 'an interested' party. However, problems persist.

In many areas, *varsai*[7] have not been conducted for up to two or three generations and cases of corruption by revenue officials are evident, depriving widows and other single women in particular of their due share in land. Fewer women participate in gram sabhas[8] and hence there is a lack of awareness about procedures for regularizing forest land. *Van Samitis* (forest committees) do not have sufficient forms. They are also, at times, unaware of procedures for filling up the forms and also do not include the wife's name while applying jointly, violating the provisions of joint titles under the new Act. Also, since *varsai* are pending for generations, it is difficult to get related and other needed documents. Caste certificates are not issued.

In tribal areas, there are innumerable cases of widows being branded as witches (*dakan*) to take away their property. Unmarried daughters are given land by parents but the land given is often less than that given to sons. Increasing conflicts are witnessed within tribal households. Kinship systems and varied cultural notions of 'family' also define vulnerabilities among women. A study (Chauhan, 2007) by AKRSP (I) in 25 villages of Mandvi block, which identified 309 widows in 25 villages, pointed to the impact of changing family structures on Adivasi women's entitlements. While community support systems were on the decline, the perception of male being the head of the family and providing support had yet to take strong roots. The decision on women entitlements to assets (land and other forms of property) were mainly left to the community's traditional decision-making bodies—the *panch* (mainly male) and to local practices. Widows were thus seen to perform labour at both the marital and natal homes and also as wage workers outside. The study also suggested (a) the shift to nuclear families was increasing, (b) the emphasis on monogamous relations had not yet taken roots, (c) on one hand, community support systems that existed in these societies have been declining and, on the other, the system or inclination of the male head providing for security for his wife after his demise had not taken shape, (d) livelihood opportunities for each household are so little that support from sons and brothers was declining and (e) private property rights are not so clearly demarcated, hence, a lot of decisions pertaining to property ownership are left to local traditions and are taken by traditional leaders (*panchs*), mainly men.

A WGWLO[9] conference of Adivasi women in 2007 in Dahod[10] indicated that patrilocality, kinship and position in the marital household—elder or younger daughter-in-law—also defined Adivasi women's work roles. With increasing pressure on land, varied forms of conflicts over land are visible.

Pasture Land

About 300,000 hectares of land is considered as pastureland in Gujarat. Almost in all villages, encroachments are taking place on pastureland.

The government announces reservation of pastureland and yet allows encroachment upon it. According to a study, there was 18 per cent decline in *gauchar* (grazing) land between 1960 and 2003, the highest decline of 35 per cent recorded in south Gujarat, 27 per cent in north Gujarat, 12.9 per cent in central Gujarat, 14.6 per cent in Saurashtra and 3.4 per cent in Kutch. The study questioned the government's role as trustees of common property while transferring these lands to large private interests. The best grasslands and grass species are diminishing in Gujarat (Bharwada & Mahajan, 2006).

Organizations working among Maldharis[11] have estimated a need for 40 acres for 100 cattle in the village.[12] However, as part of its Special Economic Zone (SEZ) policy, in 13 villages in Mundra taluka in Kachchh, 7,686 acres were sold to a private company by the Gujarat government. Where the Gujarat government has offered alternate sites, it was found that no such *gauchar* land is available in the area.

Women from the pastoral communities, Maldharis, are losing many of their traditional skills which not only enabled their control over resources but also contributed towards regeneration of pastures and grasslands. They face the brunt of severe hardships and insecurities owing to migration, debt and lack of livelihood sources. In March 2010, the NHRC issued notice to the Gujarat Chief Secretary, District Magistrate and Collector, Surendranagar, on forced migration of 100 Maldhari families from Zinzinwada village owing to harassment and atrocities by upper-caste Darbars, in particular, sexual and physical abuse of Maldhari women.[13] An increasing number of Maldhari women are working as domestic workers in cities like Ahmedabad. Also, depleting pastureland means lack of fuel and fodder which now have to be purchased from the market and add to the women's domestic burdens.

CHANGING LAND-USE PATTERNS: LAND ACQUISITION AND DEVELOPMENT PROJECTS

A recent study shows that 2.5 million persons, 5 per cent of the population of Gujarat, have since Independence, lost their land and/or habitat, 80 per cent of them from marginalized communities. As many as 60 per cent of the displaced were affected by water-related projects, 23 per cent transport and communication and 7 per cent by industries.

About 18 per cent of 638 villages of Gujarat are affected, partially or totally (Lobo & Kumar, 2009). Gujarat is known for its 'silver corridor', an industrial belt from southern to central Gujarat and 'the Golden Corridor' in western Gujarat. Industries have acquired about 20 per cent of total land and a few thousand hectares more of land are proposed for future expansion. The industries include TATAs for salt making, Ambuja Cement and IPCL and more land is in demand for irrigation schemes, mining and building defence colonies. These have led to displacement of families, changes in land-use pattern impacting livelihoods of women, in particular, and compensation packages that do not give any explicit entitlements to women. The struggles of women's collectives in Bhangadh and Mahadevpura villages in the Bhal region highlight the issues faced by coastal communities. In 1997, the government allotted 6,000 acres of land to Gujarat Heavy Chemicals for salt production. This led to destruction of mangroves and *piloo* forests on thousands of hectares of land. The fishing community lost its livelihood and the decreasing quantity of fodder led to decline in cattle rearing. The company wound up, leaving the land barren. The Tree Growers Co-operative formed by women supported by MAHITI[14] demanded 1,000 hectares of coastal land from government to grow *Piloo* and rejuvenate mangroves. The entire process of filing the application took three years. The application lies with the government and the delay is linked to the KALPASAR project[15] for which land is reserved in the Bay of Khambhatt. The struggle of women continues in Dholera which is now part of Special Investment Region (SIR) spread over an area of 87,933.77 hectares. The trend in industrial development in Gujarat has shifted from industrial clusters to SEZ and SIRs and supported by Dedicated Freight Corridors (DFC), a central government proposal, with its Western Corridor (Integrated Investment-IR-, Industrial Areas-IA-) which will touch 18 of the 26 districts of Gujarat. These are the main drivers of land acquisition in Gujarat today.

Another SEZ has been approved in 2003– 2004 which will extend over 10,000 hectares, over 14 villages in Mundra (Kutch). Dependent on this coastline and ecology are transient villages supporting more than 10,000 fisher folk and their supportive fish-processing industries. In other industrial areas along the same coast, prawn catches have fallen tremendously and the fish that is caught is covered in oil and is not marketable. The fishing community will be tremendous losers in this deal, and are unlikely to get any compensation for the loss of the livelihood enjoyed by their families for generations.

The SEZ has also been given large amounts of common (*gauchar*) grazing land. Dependent on this are the poorest communities in the Mundra tehsil who raise livestock for a living and also make charcoal with a plant found in these lands. The loss of this land is in contravention to a Gujarat Government Order (2002) which states that every village should have a minimum of 40 acres of land for 100 animals. The affected villages have fallen well below this level. Says Vaaljibhai from Jharpara village, where 60 per cent of the families depend completely on livestock rearing, 'We have been protesting against the handover of 1,000 acres of our *gauchar* for the SEZ. We will not let the company set foot on our grazing lands'.[16] On 22 December, the village organized a rally in front of the Mundra tehsil office and warned that they will bring their 8,000-odd cattle and buffaloes into Mundra town and block all the roads if the notices to their panchayats (about the handover of *gauchar* lands) are not withdrawn.

Several women expressed their concern:

> Aminaben: Ever since the plant at Mundra has come up, the fish along that coastline has dried up. Moreover, the Adani Port has displaced many people and the new place that has been allotted has no facility for drinking water, sanitation or education. All that we know is fishing and with the high risk of displacement, we are very worried about our only source of livelihood. Of the people living along the coast, 95 per cent are fisher folk belonging to either the Muslim Wagher community or Pagadia fisher folk. We are waiting for the result of the petition that we have filed in the High Court. If we are not happy with the result we may even go to the Supreme Court. Many of our men have been beaten up and jailed for asking for their rights.[17]

The project is located in an ecologically sensitive area with mangroves, creeks, mudflats and coral reefs. The Maachimaar Adhikar Sangharsh Sangathan,[18] Bhadreshwar in Mundra, Kutch, has been active for the past seven years. A representative said:

> We have been demanding for land so that we can develop our fishery business, but the government has given that land to the Mundra SEZ.

Now, they plan to remove us but we will not leave our land, come what may. Our ancestors have been fishing and even we depend on the same livelihood. But now our children have no access to health facilities or education. We don't even have a road or electricity. Once this land is gone, we will even lose the scope of fishing here. The condition here is so bad that in case of an emergency, if we dial 108, the road is so bad that by the time the woman reaches the hospital, she delivers en route or even dies.

The fishing community which has now lived for nine months in temporary shelters near the coast is demanding that such land be given on lease.

CAMPAIGNS FOR LAND

In Kutch, Zameen Bachao Andolan (the campaign to save land) which included WGWLO members such as Kutch Mahila Vikas Sangathan (KMVS), MARAG and Cohesion emerged in the context of the Gujarat government resolution (17 May 2005) allocating 4.56 million hectares of wasteland to industrial houses and big farmers on lease for 20 years for corporate farming. This land is recognized as wasteland (1.8 million hectares are cultivable waste land) in government records and traditionally the land was tilled by Dalits, backward castes, small and marginal farmers. This forced acquisition of land adversely affected over 5.1 million landless farmers/labourers who depended on wasteland for charcoal making, grazing, fuel wood collection and so on. Meetings, conventions and rallies were held in districts of Kutch, Banaskantha, Sabarkantha, Surendranagar where the state government had identified survey numbers to be allotted to industrial houses. The Zamin Bachao Andolan formed village committees which mobilized people to make applications to government to cancel its order. Alongside, hundreds of applications were filed to demand wasteland for agriculture. Also, using RTI (Right to Information), data on land for allotment to industrial houses was sought. The data revealed that the government had not conducted any study of schemes where such wasteland was being allotted, whether wasteland was being allotted to cooperative societies of the women or self-help groups. They did not even have data to suggest whether these schemes had failed. The information was widely shared in the state, which gave a boost to the movement.

One of the Gujarat government's interventions in this regard was in the form of a GR in 1987, for allocating wasteland to groups of poor on a long-term basis for livelihood. The watershed programme has also built on this by giving preference to only women's user groups for common land (cultivable wasteland) development. While information dissemination on these is an issue, what was significant was that at grassroots level, it involved a long and endless struggle to get land transferred in their names, even as collectives.

The implementation of land reforms in Gujarat in terms of land distribution to the landless has been the weakest, particularly in the face of persistent strong opposition from upper-caste landed sections. A study by a member organization of WGWLO on impact of land reforms in Banaskantha indicated that not more than 35 per cent of households have actual possession and cultivate land while only 2–3 per cent land has been redistributed among single women, mainly widows. They continue to face stiff opposition from upper-caste landed interests and others and in addition lack technical and other support, particularly from the state (Oza, 2007). Another study (Behavioral Science Centre, 2005) on the Land Ceiling Act covering three blocks of Banaskantha District showed that 213 families have been given land. However, these are not in joint names of spouses as per a Government Regulation of 1989. Instead, 'family' was seen as the unit of resource allocation, titles were given to individual men, perceived to be heads of the household (Oza, 2007). Struggles by the landless to take possession of land distributed over two decades ago are still ongoing 18 years after the fact. Since 1987, in Poicha village (Savli taluka), about 56 backward caste villagers (Vankars, Bhois) and Dalits who were allotted reclaimed wasteland by the district collector finally found hope to till their own land. In this village, the upper caste, the Darbars who formed just one-third of the 5,000 strong population, dominate. The area is located in the Mahi ravine and is best for growing trees—lemon or aval—which can fetch up to ₹50,000 a year for the farmer. Under pressure from the Darbars, the revenue officials avoided conducting their survey which is mandatory for formal possession of land. In one case, a man died, and Darbars planted trees on the land allotted to the deceased and claimed that it was disputed land. Many feared paying the survey fees. However, with the support of an NGO, Ghadtar, the issue was taken up and 16 villagers paid the survey fees after ensuring police protection.

The government surveyor accompanied by the police began the formal process of handing over land in June 2006. Upper-caste Darbar women, who are mainly in seclusion, protested, saying that they will not have place to attend nature's call or go to the river. The village sarpanch (elected head), also a Darbar, remains dismissive of the move, saying that they were not fit to till the land. More Dalits subsequently put in applications seeking survey.[19]

RTI has been widely used by organizations, networks, individuals including WGWLO, working on issues of land in Gujarat. According to Valjibhai Patel, a prominent Dalit lawyer, information obtained under RTI revealed that many of the state's so-called Dalit co-operatives or Anusuchit Jati Samudayik Kheti Sahakari Mandalis have been illegally selling agricultural land on a large scale. In many cases, such land has been sold without registering documents and these illegal documents have also been transferred to government records. Many of the members of co-operatives are illiterate and do not even know that their land has been sold. Between 1960 and 1990, about 186,802 acres of land in 25 districts was declared surplus, out of which the government took possession of 114,822 acres. Under the Gujarat Agricultural Land Ceiling Act, 1960, this surplus land was allotted to co-operative societies of SCs, STs, OBCs and landless peasants rather than to landless individuals. For example, in Babra taluka alone about 4,586 acres of land was declared surplus, with government taking possession of 3,815 acres. Of this, 3,751 acres of land was given to the Babra Taluka Anusuchit Jati Samudayik Kheti Sahakari Mandali. Such sales have taken place in Kutch, Amreli, Junagadh, Surendranagar, Bhavnagar, Banaskantha, Mehsana and Sabarkantha.[20]

WGWLO assessments of government programmes indicated that lack of asset bases curtail women's bargaining power, on the one hand, and, on the other, deprives women from the benefits of development programmes. This deprivation is evident when government schemes for development of land are scrutinized. These schemes relate to irrigation, land development (watershed) or agricultural credit where possession of land is mandatory. A study in Ahmedabad of a lift irrigation scheme requiring an average investment of ₹12,000–18,000, revealed that 100 per cent beneficiaries in 6 schemes were men. Since women lacked ownership of land in their names, they were unable to gain benefits from a major part of their expenditure. This is compounded by the fact that a gender-based beneficiary classification is not maintained by government departments. Even where the government promotes a group approach for building and managing assets at village levels such as user groups for check-dam lift irrigation societies and canal irrigation societies, a pre-condition for membership to these groups is ownership of land. Lacking land titles, women are unable to participate in their meetings or cast their votes because land ownership is a prerequisite for the membership of piyat khedut mandali (farmers' irrigation society). Therefore, women are deprived of a role in decision-making processes at village level, in particular, those linked with the government's development programmes (Velayudhan, 2008).

SOCIAL BIASES

Studies[21] conducted by the Gujarat state-level network, WGWLO, point to the following social biases that deprive women of entitlements to land:

1. *Denial of share to daughters:* unequal division of land between legal heirs (sons) or giving land to eldest son or to the one who takes care of parents, giving share of land to adopted sons in cases where parents have daughters and no male heir, a sister who is married off giving away her share of land and receiving instead *kariyawar*[22] at the time of her marriage.
2. *Denial of share to wife:* Not given legal ownership in marital property, denial of share to widow in the property of her husband by removal of the name of the deceased from family tree, denial of share to widow who stays at her parental home fearing her security, denial of share to widow on the pretext that the father-in-law is alive to take care, *varsai* not conducted for 2 or 3 generations, land size is small and there are many claiming shares (*bhagidars*).
3. Land administration biases such as patriarchal mindset of revenue officials and panchayat members, lack of sensitivity shown by revenue officials to women who come forward to claim their share of land, loopholes in the land transfer procedures, demanding bribe (money or feast) from poor women demanding transfer of land in

her name, giving excuses for not handing over relevant revenue documents for land transfer (no electricity, no ink in the printer, computer not working, officials not available and so on).

CONCLUSION

WGWLO's engagements on women's land ownership and field experiences led its adoption of a multi-pronged approach addressing a range of rights and entitlements in the spheres of public land, public land and usufruct rights in common lands, including wasteland, pasture land, forest land and advocacy for policy changes at the state level. A significant achievement was the setting up of a team of para-legal workers during participatory action research processes that addressed live cases at the field/grassroots level through a range of institutional mechanisms such as Nyay Samiti (Justice Committees), Lok Adhikar Kendra (Peoples Rights Centre), Panchayat Information Centre and Mahila Sangathan (women's collectives like federations) which facilitated the mainstreaming of women and land land-related issues within these institutions and wider sections of communities. These institutions also maintain records of the cases filed and document the process. This approach not only made women aware of the land laws and land administration process and gave women protection, but also led to the development of a team of para-legals who guide the specific cases of women, assist in accessing relevant revenue documents, engage in dialogue with family members, revenue officials, elected village-level leaders and seek the help of lawyers wherever necessary. The efforts of poor women to build land-based livelihoods, as in the case of Mahiti cited earlier, highlight the legal/administrative land procedures involved, the lack of political will in the face of large-scale land acquisition for private/corporates and development projects for what is projected as 'public good'. WGWLO's strength has been its process role and its informal structures, with varied grassroots women's collectives, federations and user groups directly represented in the network. A total of 2,463 of the 7,977 women who made claims have received individual titles, 11 of the 46 women's collectives received collective land, 456 of 5,000 who demanded joint titles on land redistributed by government have received the same.

ACKNOWLEDGEMENTS

To grassroots activists, individual members and organizations of the Gujarat state level network, The Working Group on Women and Land Ownership (WGWLO).

NOTES

1. There were three types of land tenure systems during colonial period in Saurashtra—*occupancy, girasdari and barkhali*. Under occupancy tenure, land was held by the cultivator directly from the state. Except in a few principalities, the cultivators did not own the land. In the other tenures, there were mainly intermediaries between cultivators and the states. They were *girasdars* who included *talukdars, bhagdars, mulgirasis and barkhalidars*, the majority being Rajputs. They were landlords with property rights who collected shares of agricultural produce from the cultivators without tilling the land. This system also existed in mainland Gujarat. The Rajput landlords lost their land ownership to the former cultivators, mainly from Kanbi-Patidar middle castes in mainland Gujarat who formed the base of the Indian National Congress during the freedom struggle in this region. They constitute 12 per cent of Gujarat's population today. In contrast to Saurashtra, mainland Gujarat had few zamindaris and the peasant landowners were Brahmins, Banias and Kanbi-Patidars using low-caste tenant tillers.
2. *Khedut*: farmer.
3. In response to domestic and external markets in the late 19 century, not only food crops but also commercial crops—cotton, tobacco—received an impetus along with the beginning of survey and settlement of land on a large scale. In the early 19th century, with the removal of intermediaries and establishment of direct relations with peasants, the Kanbis, elevated later as Patidars (peasant caste in central Gujarat), became the main beneficiaries of these changes in land tenures. With state support, they encroached on lands of Kolis and Adivasis in the northern region; with the Kolis and Adivasis becoming labourers on lands they traditionally occupied. With middle castes gaining control over development inputs through varied channels, distribution of landholdings became highly skewed. See also Shah et al. (2002).
4. Falguni, women leader from NGO, Cohesion, in a personal communication in March, 2008.
5. WGWLO (2005): *Swa Bhoomi: Mahila Ane Jamin Maliki*, reports of two conferences held in Limkheda (Dahod) and Kutch, Gujarat.
6. *Patta*: land deed.
7. *Varsai*: inheritance.
8. The Gram Sabha is a meeting of all adults who live in the area covered by a Panchayat.

9. WGWLO: a Gujarat level network of 23 organizations working on women's land rights since 2003.
10. WGWLO (2005). *Swa Bhoomi: Mahila Ane Jamin Malikin* held in Limkheda (Dahod) on 5–6 May 2005. About 224 rural women and 11 men from 17 blocks of 12 districts attended the event. Additionally, 60 NGO workers from 15 NGOs were closely involved in the event.
11. *Mal* (wealth/domestic animals), *dhari* (possessor): Maldharis include a whole range of pastoral groups, from the existing communities (Charan, Bharwad, Rabari, Sindhi Muslim) to historical communities (Gujjars, Kathis, Yadavas, Ahirs) who were once involved in pastoralism. The traditional grazing resources were *Bets* (islands), grasslands, forests, *Vidis* and *Rakhals* (protected fenced lands), wastelands and village *gauchars*. Grasslands have been cultivated or have deteriorated, forests have been turned into sanctuaries or national parks, with entry prohibited to *bets* for security reasons. Similarly, access is denied to *vidi*, while wasteland and *gauchar* largely have gone to industries.
12. A Gujarat government circular dated 30 December 1988, J.N.M, 1687/7098/01, stated that 40 acres of land should be reserved for 100 livestock and that encroached grazing land should be identified and released. Gujarat government violated its own rules by passing 23 orders in one day to allot 6,582 acres of 23 villages' pastures to the Adanis in July 2005. For all this land, Gautam Adani, the owner of a 250,000 million company and two private jets, paid an average rate of 10 per sq m. Another government resolution dated 16 May 2001 held that protected fencing lands or *Vidis* and *Rakhals*, used by Maldharis to keep their livestock should be registered in their names.
13. *Times of India*, Ahmedabad, 29 March 2008.
14. *Mahiti* is a local community-based organization, organizes rural poor women through cooperatives and facilitates livelihood improvement through collective actions in Ahmedabad and Bhavnagar districts.
15. Experts have questioned the viability of this project aimed at power generation and fresh water supply. The project seeks to build a huge fresh water lake by closing the Gulf of Khambhat across Ghogha in Bhavnagar district and Hansot in Bharuch to harness water from Narmada, Mahi, Sabarmati and Dhadar rivers and generate power with tidal energy. According to P. Shukla (IIM and member, Inter-Governmental Panel on Climate Change), fresh water would depend on amount of surplus water from these rivers draining in Kalpasar. Climate change due to global warming will alter river flows. An IIT-Delhi study pointed to the reduced run-offs from these rivers. While Gujarat has limited alternatives for fresh water supply but, in terms of power supply, there were alternatives. According to Shukla, costs of tidal power from Kalpasar will be more than double that of conventional energy and the required `400,000 million investment will be larger than the total amount invested in all power plants in Gujarat in five decades. Alternatives suggested include the more reliable coal or gas power. The project is at a stage where there is still the possibility of undertaking two environmental assessments: on ecological damage in the command area and damages that future

climate change could cause to the project. See also report in *Times of India*, Ahmedabad, 29 March 2008.
16. Ibid.
17. Ibid.
18. Organization for the rights of fishing community: a union of fishermen, salt pan workers and small and medium farmers.
19. *Indian Express*, 11 June 2006, Vadodara, '18 Years On, Hope Floats in Poicha'.
20. *Times of India* (2 April 2008, Ahmedabad), 'Co-ops selling land using bogus papers'. Valijibhai Patel, Council for Social Justice (CSJ), Ahmedabad, had obtained this data through use of RTI. Data reveals that the Rajkot Taluka Anusuchit Jati Samudayik Kheti Sahakari Mandali sold land in the villages of Gauridal (50–53 acres), Kalipat (300–400 acres) and Khijadia (24 acres). The Lodhika Taluka Anusuchit Samudayik Kheti Sahakari Mandali sold land in the village of Matoda (25 acres). The Babra Taluka Anusuchit Samudayik Kheti Sahakari Mandali sold land in the villages of Lalka (16 hectares) and Kotdapitha (240 acres or more).
21. A study on the *Status of Women and Agriculture Land Ownership in Gujarat*, conducted by WGWLO in 2003–2004 in 23 villages of the state revealed that though there are constitutional rights and other legal provisions for a woman to own land and property equally as men, the status of women's land-ownership in Gujarat was only 11.8 per cent. The 11.8 per cent women got land in their name either due to husband's demise (widowhood) or to avail government scheme/benefits to protect the family land from falling under ceiling limit or to make claim as small farmer for irrigation benefits. Another study by WGWLO, *Paralegal Action Research* (2006) not only brought out the land administrative biases towards women's land ownership but also raised the awareness of staff members of NGOs (who conducted the study) of the land procedures involved in women claiming their rights to land as well as help with women claiming their rights by accessing relevant documents, dialogue with family members, seek help from village leaders/sarpanch, approaching revenue officials, taking the case to court where needed, seeking the help of local women's collectives such as federations or local civil society institutions such as *Nyay Samiti* (justice committees), women and land committees and *Lok Adhikar Kendra* (Peoples Rights Centre), *Panchayat Information Centres*. These institutions have staff that do not see their work as just a 'job' as in government sponsored legal aid centres or multiple counselling centres and have knowledge of both administrative procedures and awareness of social issues.
22. *Kariyavar*: dowry in kind.

REFERENCES

Addison, T., Hulme, D., & Kanbur, R. (2008). *Poverty dynamics: Measurement and understanding from an interdisciplinary perspective* (Working Paper No. 19). Manchester: Brooks World Poverty Institute.

Agarwal, B. (1994a). Gender and command over property: A critical gap in economic analysis and policy in South Asia. *World Development, 22*(10), 1455–1478.

Agarwal, B. (1994b). *A field of one's own: Gender and land rights in South Asia.* Cambridge: Cambridge University Press.

Agarwal, B. (1998). Who sows? Who reaps? Women and land rights in India. *The Journal of Peasant Studies, 15*(4), 531–581.

Agarwal, B. (2002). *Are we not peasants too?* SEEDS Volume. New York, NY: Population Council.

Anríquez, G. (2010). Demystifying the agricultural feminization myth and the gender burden. Background Paper for the State of *Agriculture Report 2010–11: Women in Agriculture: Closing the gender gap for development.* Rome: Food and Agriculture Organization of the United Nations.

Bagchi, A. K., Das, P., & Chattopadhyaya, S. K. (2005). Growth and structural changes in the economy of Gujarat, 1970–2000. *Economic & Political Weekly, 40*(28), 3039–3047.

Bakshi, A. (2008). Social inequality and land ownership in India: A study with particular
reference to West Bengal. *Social Scientist, 39*(9–10), 95–116.

Behavioral Science Centre. (2005). *A study on impact of land reforms in Banaskantha district.* Author.

Bharwada, C., & Mahajan, V. (2006). Changing nature of pastoralists: Development, pastures and maldharis of Gujarat. Unpublished report, Centre for Social Studies, Surat, Gujarat.

Chauhan, D. (2007). *Working with widows: AKRSP(I) experience.* AKRSP (I).

Dube, L. (1997). *Women and kinship—Comparative perspectives on gender in south and south east Asia.* UN University Press.

Duncan, A. B., & Brants, C. (2004). *Access to and control over land from a gender perspective.* FAO.

Dwyer, D., & Bruce, J. (Eds). (1998). *A home divided: Women & income in the third world.* Stanford University Press.

FAO. (1996). *Towards sustainable food security: Women and land tenure.* Prepared by the Women in Development Service (SDWW), FAO Women and Population Division.

Government of Gujarat. (1988). Gujarat government circular dated 30/12 1988, J.N.M, 1687/7098/01.

Gupta, J. (2002). Women second in land agenda. *Economic & Political Weekly, XXXVII*(18), 1746–1754.

Hardiman, D. (1996). *Feeding the baniya—Peasants and usurers in western India.* Oxford University Press.

IFAD. (2001). *Rural poverty report 2001: The challenge of ending rural poverty.* Author.

Indian Express. (2006, June 11). 18 years on, hope floats in Poicha. Author.

Jackson, C. (2003). Gender analysis of land: Beyond land rights for women. *Journal of Agrarian Change, 3*(4), 453–480.
Jackson, C., & Rao, N. (2004). Gender equality: Striving for justice in an unequal world. Background paper prepared for the UNRISD report. UNRISD.
Kabeer, N. (1994). *Reversed realities: Gender hierarchies in development thought.* Verso.
Kumar, D., Narayanamurthy A, Singh, O. P., Sivamohan, M. V. K, Sharma, M., & Bassi N. (2010). *Gujarat's agricultural growth story: Exploding some myths.* Institute for Resource Analysis and Policy (IRAP).
Kumar, S. K. (1978). Role of the household economy in child nutrition at low incomes: A case study in Kerala. Occasional Paper No. 95. Department of Agricultural Economics, Cornell University.
Lobo, L., & Kumar, S. (2009). *Land acquisition, displacement and resettlement in Gujarat (1947–2004).* SAGE Publications.
Mandal, K., & Bansal, R. (2002). *Study of land ownership as livelihood issue for women.* Indian Institute Of Forest Management (IIFM).
Mehta, N. (2006). Imbalances in development between regions and social groups: Evidences from Gujarat. *Anvesak, 36*(1), 1–12.
MGLI. (2004). *Gujarat human development report.* Mahatma Gandhi Labour Institute.
Oza, A. (2002). Opening remarks: Report of the workshop on land ownership as a livelihood issue for women. June 25–26, Ahmedabad, organized by AKRSP (India).
Oza, G. (2007). *Land reforms in Gujarat* [Paper presentation]. Consult on Research, WGWLO, Ahmedabad.
Rao, N. (2005). Questioning women's solidarity: The case of land rights, Santhal Parganas (Jharkhand). *Journal of Development Studies, 3*(41), 353–375.
Report of a Public Hearing. (2010). *Land and livelihood alienation in Gujarat,* February, 2010. Utthan.
Sen, A. (1990). Gender and cooperative conflicts. In Tinker (Ed.), *Persistent inequalities: Women and world development.* Oxford University Press.
Shah, G., Rutten, M., & Streefkerk, H. (Eds.). (2002). *Development & deprivation in Gujarat.* SAGE Publications.
Shah, G., & Sah, D. C. (Eds.). (2002). Introduction. In *Land Reforms in India* (Vol. 8). SAGE Publications.
Shah, T., Gulati, A., Hemant, P., Shreedharan, G., & Jain, R. C. (2009). Secret of Gujarat's agrarian miracle after 2000, review of agriculture. *Economic & Political Weekly, 44*(52), 45–55.
Sud, N. (2005). *Khedut na zamin to land liberalization: The political economy of Gujarat's shifting land policy* [Paper presentation]. BASAS Conference.
Sud, N. (2007). From land to the tiller to land liberalization. *Modern Asian Studies, 41*(3), 603–637.
Times of India, 29 March 2008, Ahmedabad Edition.
Times of India, 2 April 2008, Ahmedabad Edition.
UNRISD. (2005). *Land tenure reform & gender equality.* Research & Policy Brief No. 4, December. UNRISD.

Velayudhan, M. (2008). *Women's rights to land: Voices from the grassroots movement and working women's alliance in Gujarat.* AKRSP (India) Documentation, Ahmedabad.

WGWLO. (2004). *Study on status of women & agriculture land ownership in Gujarat.* Author.

WGWLO. (2005). *Swa bhoomi—Mahila ane jamin maliki.* Reports of two conferences held in Limkheda (Dahod) and Kachchh.

WGWLO. (2006). *Report of paralegal action research.* Author.

Section II
The Agrarian Structure

Sectional Introduction

In the 'Introduction' to this volume, issues of agrarian transition and transformation were referred to in a somewhat sketchy manner. Chapters included in this section, however, have dealt with each one of them in more detail. These chapters have engaged with theoretical propositions of their time, operationalized and validated them in different contexts, contributing richly to conceptual debates. In both these cases, the dialectics of theory and praxis have informed this exercise. In fact, one has noticed that many issues flagged by some of these writings of the 1970s later turned into a full-fledged debate.

The chapter by P. C. Joshi has focused on an issue that would be of everlasting significance for agrarian debates. While dealing with the nature of the interaction between the more dynamic 'capitalist sector' and relatively 'backward' peasant sector, Joshi identified three broad strands in this discourse. During the differentiation of agrarian economy into these two sub-systems, the first perspective identified by the author conceived a harmonious relationship between the two. In this view, the dynamism would percolate down to the peasant sector in due course and the problem of equitable distribution would be taken care of by growth in the agrarian economy.

However, another view believed that though conflict maybe inevitable in the short run but either policy intervention or the forces of development would be in a position to address it. While accepting the imminent instability due to the widening gap between two sub-systems, this perspective seemed to prefer growth even if it was at the cost of social tension over stagnation with stability. The proponents of this view have claimed that income inequality could widen due to some areas benefitting more than others, with gains distributed in proportion to landholding sizes rather than in proportion to labour inputs.

The third view that emerged from the literature on the subject considered the interaction between the two sub-systems as inherently antagonistic and unequal. In this process, the capitalist sector was bound to corner all the fruits of growth at the expense of the peasant sector causing political instability.

Another question that frequently figured in these debates was the role of new technology vis-à-vis privileges and handicaps. Joshi's chapter refers to 'dualism' in the sense of a rigid and enduring division between the privileged and disadvantaged. It has often been argued that the penetration of new technology has 'softened' this divide if not completely obliterated it since technology was scale neutral. It has, if anything, helped reduce the optimum size of a viable farm. Pointing to the fallacies of this argument, another position underlined that these claims were based on possibilities rather than on the reality. Such a viewpoint overlooked the fact that the gains of new technology were monopolized by the privileged ones. In this sense, new technology was not resource neutral and even ended up creating a divide on that basis.

Further, a position that distinguished Joshi from many of his contemporaries was that he doubted the formulation of squeezing out the small producer as a consequence of the penetration of capitalism as socially desirable. He pointed out that economic, political and social implications should also be considered.

While Joshi engaged with these formulations at a theoretical level, Sulabha Brahme drew inferences by investigating the dynamics of change in the three decades after Independence. Published in the 1970s, both these chapters could be fruitfully read together to get an accurate sense of this era's debates. Brahme collected data from a western Maharashtra village in two time frames, between 1942 and 1976. Based on this longitudinal study, Brahme was able to deduce some very interesting observations on the penetration of technology, the ecological crisis, monetization of the agrarian economy and shifting preferences for consumer goods.

Brahme had warned about an impending ecological crisis more than half a century ago when the massive use of chemical fertilizers had just started. This came alongside the time when traditional crop cycles had pushed farmers into a vicious cycle of using more and more chemicals. Earlier, local crops had helped to rejuvenate crop fertility. Added to this ecological disaster was the fact that the village community since the advent of British rule was being pushed aside from its role of conserving pastures, forests and so on. As a result, all these commons now stand degraded.

The increasing usage of fertilizers soon made it the largest cash component of input costs in the 1970s replacing land rent and other government dues from that position in the 1940s. During this period, the practice of paying wages to agricultural labour in kind was also becoming extinct. Changing the cropping patterns also increased the village's dependence on the market for inputs. Due to the increase in sugarcane cultivation, the proportion of sales in gross value of agricultural products also increased. Increasing monetization, dependence on the market for agricultural inputs and implements and shifting preference for industrial consumer goods strengthened linkages of the village with the market economy. The seasonal migration of workers had always been a link to the outside world. Brahme's village now served more as a market for manufactured goods at the expense of its productive base.

Penetration of technology was noticeably slow in Brahme's village. Only three leading families of large landowners owned tractors, the rest remained dependent on bullock-driven ploughs. Family labour was still the mainstay of agriculture with labour hired occasionally for arduous work. Public and private investments in irrigation may have increased water supply but did not increase the irrigated area. Excess water was used for sugarcane cultivation. However, a long gestation period and high input cost did not allow smallholders to grow sugarcane despite a newly set up sugar mill nearby. These three leading families also owned non-agricultural enterprises in the village. They also dominated village institutions, using them to their advantage.

The most significant contribution of Brahme's chapter was to demolish the one linear path of transformation. In her story, monetization of the village economy and crop diversification appeared as leading elements, technology came in later. In some other villages, the story could unfold in some other way. One could only wish if Brahme had taken into account caste and gender elements, her story would have been more interesting.

Prodipto Roy's chapter presented a model for planning at the regional level focusing on agricultural marketing and fertilizer distribution. Both these activities were considered to be concerned with marginal outputs and inputs. The study identified focal points of growth and villages coming in their ambit, unearthing gaps in infrastructure, and plan for an alternative course of action. The radical departure that the growth-centred approach adopted from the original community block perspective was the comprehensive assessment of the total resources of the block such as water, land, manpower, crops, education, health, industries and transportation.

After the turbulent 1970s, there followed a relatively quiet decade. But debates on agrarian change witnessed an upsurge from the 1990s onwards. The remaining two chapters were representatives of this era. B. B. Mohanty's chapter rekindled the old debates on productivity versus equity in his study of a village from the Satara district of Maharashtra. Mohanty's argument was interwoven with three threads. First, agricultural modernization may have enhanced productivity and production but the equity issue was sidelined by design. Second, distribution was skewed in favour of resourceful rich farmers and increasing inequality provided them with means to dominate rural power structure. Third, agricultural modernization was planned to create a market and growth process led by rich farmers.

Mohanty in his contribution studied one 'modern' and one 'traditional' village. They were chosen based on extensive and assured irrigation, mechanization, the prevalence of high-yield variety seeds and infrastructure facilities. The modern village exhibited characteristics such as the shift from food grains to cash crops, higher usage of chemical fertilizers and pesticides, more access to formal credit and deployment of hired labour, while the traditional village relied mainly on family labour and grew cereals. Modernization helped enhance the income of all classes of farmers but levels of inequality were found much higher in a modern village than a traditional village. Village institutions such as the panchayat and cooperatives were completely dominated by rich farmers in the modern village, whereas poor farmers and agricultural labour had relatively better representation in a traditional village.

Swarup Dutta's chapter further extended this line of investigation into India's agriculturally most developed area. Dutta focused on tenancy, labour relations and credit market to narrate an alternative story of the Green Revolution substantiated by ethnographic data collected from a village located in the Malwa region of Punjab. This village had seen a massive upsetting of tenancy relations in the form of the emergence of 'reverse tenancy'. On the one hand, the increasing capital-intensive nature of agriculture forced small farmers out of this sector. Left with no other choice, they had to lease out their land to rich peasants. Simultaneously, to enhance their profits, large landowners had increasingly withdrawn from sharecropping arrangements with poor peasants and resumed their land, either for self-cultivation or leased it out to somebody who could invest in high productivity modern agriculture. Alongside, technological innovations reduced the demand for labour despite an increase in production. Rising input costs, narrowing margins on crop cultivation, stagnant productivity levels and increasing dependence on informal sources of credit, especially commission agents who dominated both credit and produce markets, pushed farmers into a vicious cycle of indebtedness. In this fragile economic condition, a crop loss or volatile prices had the potential to completely ruin farming families. Several farmers' suicides in Punjab's cotton belt reflected this systemic crisis.

Chapters in this section have presented a complete array of positions in spatially and longitudinally different locales. Reading together they have woven a story of changing agrarian relations and have helped us trace the antecedents of the contemporary agrarian crisis that was long in the making. These readings have also clearly outlined how the institutional nature of this distress is apparent and alerted us for disastrous future consequences if it is not arrested immediately.

Chapter 5

Agrarian Structure and the Rural Poor*
Review of Perspectives

P. C. Joshi

Eradication of mass poverty is now becoming the widely accepted normative basis of economic and social thought in underdeveloped countries. In India, for instance, an anti-poverty orientation is no more than the exclusive hallmark of politico-economic radicalism. If an anti-poverty premise is considered to be the dividing line between radicalism and conservatism, then all trends of politico-economic thought have a radical tone in India. The anti-poverty orientation is, however, connected with widely divergent perspectives of technological change and institutional reorganization. The divergence of these perspectives is most marked on questions relating to the agrarian structure and the rural poor. This chapter attempts to review these perspectives which have crystallized in India in the course of a lively debate among economists in recent years.

The background of the recent debate is provided by the differentiation of the rural economy into a dynamic subsystem represented by the large agricultural producer and the backward subsystem represented by small peasant producers and a floating mass of the landless population. The dynamic subsystem is characterized by some economists as the capitalist sector. What is the nature of the interaction between the

---

* *Social Change*, 4(3 & 4), 1974.

two agrarian subsystems in the short-term and the long-term context? This is the basic question posed for scientific thinking and investigations. Even though answers to this question are not yet available on the basis of an intensive investigation in different regions, thinking on this question basically falls into three types:

1. The spread effects from the dynamic sub-sector, which is growing within agriculture are bound to permeate the backward peasant sector. Thus, in conformity to the principle of percolation from the top to the bottom layers, the backward peasant sector will also acquire properties of dynamism. In this conception, the capitalist and the peasant sectors are assumed to be inherently complementary to each other. A rigorous scientific statement of this conception is not available in scientific literature, even though this conception has constituted the unstated assumption of scientific research by a section of scholars in India. These scholars have been concerned with an analysis of trends of growth in the agricultural economy with an implicit view that growth would also take care of the problem of equitable distribution of gains of growth. This conception, therefore, conforms to the 'harmony of interest' rather than to the 'conflict of interest' standpoint.
2. The second type of conception recognizes the existence of conflict between the two sectors. But this conception is based on two important assumptions about the nature of this conflict. First, it is assumed that the conflict between the two sectors is a short-term rather than a long-term phenomenon. And this conflict can be resolved either spontaneously through the forces released by development or through policy intervention. It is believed that the capitalist sector would provide the means for injecting dynamism even into the peasant sector. Second, it is also assumed that there is nothing alarming about such a conflict in as much as it is a necessary and inevitable concomitant of the dynamics of economic growth. Growth with inequality and tensions is to be a preferred to stagnation with stability (Bauer & Yamey, 1957).
3. Unlike 1 and 2, the third conception is based on the following assumptions:

a. That the relationship between the emerging capitalist sector and the traditional peasant sector is inherently antagonistic—being a relationship between two unequal sectors, one strong and the other week.
b. That the dynamics of growth is bound to result in the accumulation of the fruits of growth in the emerging capitalist sector and the impoverishment, if not the disintegration, of the peasant sector.
c. That this economic tendency poses a serious threat to the peasant sector and consequently leads to political tensions and instability.

A paper released by the Research Division, Ministry of Home Affairs, Government of India (Ministry of Home Affairs, 1969) on the causes and nature of current agrarian tension in December 1969 presents a point of view conforming to conception 3. In his Asian Drama and *The Challenge of World Poverty*, Myrdal has provided a coherent theoretical basis for this conception.

In India, when the new agricultural strategy was first introduced, conception 1 seemed to be the implicit, if not the explicit, basis of scientific research and policymaking. Subsequently, however, the widest consensus seems to prevail around conception 2. Conception 3 can be said to constitute a minority trend among social scientists and policymakers.

Conception 2 has been presented with considerable force and lucidity by John W. Mellor in the following passage:

> One of the certainties of a dynamic economy is that relative incomes of various groups in a population will change. Thus the development process, while providing the long-term basis for amelioration of poverty and economic inequality, may in the short run exacerbate it. The dynamics of technological change in the agricultural sector will provide sharp increases in incomes of the peasant farming class in those geographical areas where soil and water resources are favourable to the new technologies. However, the new technologies will, in many areas, provide no basis for improvement at all. Thus inter-regional disparities in income may well be widened. Quite possibly of considerably more importance, the new technologies may provide their benefits

to the peasant farming class roughly in proportion to land holdings rather than in proportion to labour inputs. Already substantial income disparities will thus be widened between the landed peasantry or landlord classes, and the huge, landless labour class. It is likely that income inequities are more tolerable in a static framework than in a dynamic one of widening disparities. (Mellor, 1968, p. 358)

What are the social and political implications of these widening income inequities as between regions and also between classes? Mellor further observes,

> ...We find tremendous regional differences in India not only in the initial division between landowning and labouring classes, but also in the effects of the dynamics of expanding non-farm employment. Widening income gaps and a potentially explosive political situation will be most marked where the relative size of the existing landless labour or subtenant class is greater; where the income-increasing effect of technological change is greater and the effect of that technology in increasing the demand for labour is less; and where the history and opportunity of non-farm jobs is less. Where these conditions appear, it will on the one hand be exceedingly important to take what steps can be taken to mitigate their effects and on the other hand there will be a severe test of the Indian political process as it attempts to relax the resultant tensions.
>
> As great as these tensions can be in some areas, they are unlikely to topple the political structure by themselves. First, the areas of greatest tension tend to be scattered, increasing the difficulty of putting together a cohesive political force. Second, there is a cohesiveness in the Indian rural social structure which will tend to bring to notice and dispel tensions as they arise. (Mellor, 1968, p. 358)

There appear to be major gaps in Mellor's assessment of the agrarian situation. In the first place, Mellor takes note of only the growing conflict between the landed and the landless classes. Even here, he does not distinguish between two types of conflicts, namely (a) those between landlords and tenants and (b) those between employers and employees. Second, Mellor overlooks the numerically largest section of rural society consisting of small producers. They constitute the most vulnerable section which is exposed to great distress and uncertainty with the development of competitive and dynamic agriculture. Third,

Mellor's views regarding the social and political consequences of economic conflict lean towards facile optimism, though the logical or empirical basis of this optimism has not been adequately presented.

In his presidential address to the 53rd Conference of the Indian Economics Association (December 1970), Dantwala (1970) has presented a much more subtle and sophisticated interpretation of conception 2. Professor Dantwala's analysis seems to imply that (a) 'dualism' in the sense of a rigid and stable division between the privileged and the disadvantaged would be more characteristic of static rather than dynamic agriculture and that (b) the new forces of technological change instead of contributing to the emergence of 'dualism' have in fact made a great contribution towards the 'softening of dualism'. Professor Dantwala would not perhaps deny that this contribution so far exists more in the realm of potentiality than in that of actual accomplishment. But his optimistic view seems to be based on three premises:

1. The new technology is not dependent on large size; it has in fact 'reduced the threshold of non-viability to something like three irrigated acres'. Having raised the profit-potential of Indian agriculture in general and of small peasant agriculture in particular, new technology has emerged as a force *against* rather than *in favour of* 'dualism'.
2. Questions of equitable distribution in favour of the small peasants through institutional reforms and so on have assumed a much greater urgency and significance now in a *dynamic* context than they even did in a *static* economic context. Social and political processes against dualism are also likely to gather more strength in a dynamic than in a static economic situation.
3. Last, experience has shown that institutional reforms without technological progress are neither feasible nor capable of leading to any appreciable and sustained improvement in the conditions of the 'vulnerable class of socially and economically disadvantaged persons'. Technological progress in agriculture creates the *possibility* of achieving growth with justice to this vulnerable class. This possibility can be converted into reality in two ways. First, economic and institutional reforms of a 'preventive' type can be initiated with a view to protecting the interests of the poor. Second, from the earlier preoccupation with measures to cope with food shortages,

attention can now be shifted towards planning for the development of the non-agricultural sector of the rural economy. The latter must be given high priority with a view to providing non-farm economic opportunities for marginal groups within agriculture.

Dantwala's address presents one of the most perceptive interpretations of the interaction of institutional and technological factors in Indian agriculture. It offers policy prescriptions also in clear and sharp manner.

One of the major weaknesses of Dantwala's analysis, however, is that, so far, as the equity aspects of growth are concerned, it concentrates more on potentialities than on actualities. Even if one concedes that institutional reforms without technological change would not contribute very much to the uplift of the peasant masses, it is also to be considered that technological progress without institutional reforms has, in reality, led to a situation in which 'the gains of technology have been monopolized by the privileged and the powerful'. In the immediate context, therefore, the impact of new technology has been to accentuate the cleavage between the privileged and the disadvantaged classes. Second, even if one concedes that the new technology creates the possibility of effecting improvement also of the peasant masses, for this possibility to be turned into a reality, the resource availability would have to undergo a tremendous improvement in favour of the weak and the disadvantaged. For such a change in the resource situation in favour of the poor what is the most crucial is a drastic change in the power balance in their favour. One of the crucial gaps in Dantwala's analysis is that the political assumptions and premises underlying his view have not been spelt out and the role of the power balance in determining the allocation of resources to different classes and also the distribution of gains from new technology has neither been explicitly recognized nor given due weight.

Another variant of conception 2 has been presented forcefully by V. M. Dandekar and Nilakantha Rath (Dandekar & Nilakantha, 1971, p. 18) in their recent work *Poverty in India*. The main thesis of Dandekar and Rath is lucidly and candidly stated by them in the following passage:

> The new technological advances have made owner-cultivation in sizeable farms a distinctly profitable proposition. Such farms may be

regulated by registering them as farm businesses and bringing them under suitable labour and taxation laws. But subject to such regulation and within the limits of accepted ceilings they must be allowed to grow. They will grow by absorbing small uneconomic holdings and by mechanization of their operations. This should be recognized as legitimate and desirable because it will lead to an organization of agriculture into not only viable but profitable units with capacity for capital accumulation and development. Undoubtedly this will increase the number of the landless, and though some of them will find more regular and better-paid employment in agriculture, on balance the employment in agriculture will decline. Certainly something will have to be done to these people who will be thrown out of the land and also out of agricultural wage employment. It is important to recognize that their number will grow rather than believe that they can all be settled on land. (Dandekar & Nilakantha, 1971, p. 18)

Dandekar and Rath, thus, consider it futile 'to try to resolve the problem of rural poverty in an overpopulated country by redistribution of land which is in short supply'. In their approach, the land policy has only an extremely limited role to play in solving the problem of poverty; it is to the creation of income opportunities outside agriculture that they attach the greatest importance. Dandekar and Rath have presented a well-reasoned and well-substantiated case for regulated capitalism in Indian' agriculture. Some observations on this contribution may not be out of place here. In the first place, even though it presents data and analysis for different states, the regional patterns of agricultural development do not fully emerge in this work. To put it differently, even though the *direction* in all states may be towards the growth of capitalism, the *stage* of capitalist development and its *features* may vary from region to region. As a result, the scope as well as limitations of land policy in the anti-poverty programme may also vary from region to region. In fact, an all-India perspective should be attempted, along with a regional analysis in depth rather than without it. The second weakness of this work lies in its inadequate exploration of the social and political aspects of the process of agricultural transformation. At a high level of abstraction from reality, it may be easy for an economist to characterize the growth of capitalism, along with the squeezing out of the small producer which goes with capitalism, as a 'socially desirable' development. But what are the economic, political and social concomitants and consequences of such a development in real life? Is there no alternative to capitalism in the Indian context? All these are relevant questions which demand serious thought and research not only by economists but experts from other disciplines.

Before concluding the discussion on conception 2, it is appropriate to refer to the work of two other economists who have sharply brought out the employment dimension of the problem of rural poverty and tried to explore how more employment could be provided within the rural sector itself.

A. M. Khusro, in his work *The Economics of Land Reform and Farm Size in India*, gives an idea of the magnitude of the 'landless labourers, size-disabled and tenure-weary peasants', and also highlights the dismal prospect of shifting them from agriculture to non-agriculture. Khusro observes,

> ... the non-absorption of the many million of small farm population in non-agricultural employment, in the next one or two generations will leave a seething mass of humanity ever growing in numbers, to seek its fortune in agriculture. This, quite apart from considerations of distributive justice and social unrest, will continue to depress agricultural wages. Now, an over-abundance of a depressed wage-seeking mass of population, much in excess of demand, is the greatest drag on the improvement of technique, on inventiveness, on the use of machines and productivity.
>
> ... there is no shortage of convincing historical evidence to support the assertion that the problem of vast numbers in Indian agriculture cannot be forgotten and that failure to absorb it effectively will perhaps be the greatest single stumbling block to progress. Since it cannot just yet be shifted to the non-agricultural sector, it might as well be absorbed more effectively in agriculture. (Khusro, 1972, pp. 112–113)

In Khusro's view land reform measures including a ceiling on large holdings constitute an important part of the strategy for effective absorption of the rural poor within the agricultural sector.

In a paper, 'Rural Poverty, Land Redistribution and Development', B. S. Minhas offers a critique of 'radical' land distribution approach and then suggests a concrete strategy for effectively tackling the problem of the rural poor. He outlines a scheme of compulsory consolidation of landholdings and complementary public works.

The social implications of a large-farmer based agricultural transformation have been explored by non-economists whose contribution to the debate on the land question deserves mention. Guy Hunter, in his book *Modernizing Peasant Societies*, takes note of the emergence of a dynamic sector in agriculture in many developing countries including India but he does not share the optimism of Dantwala or Dandekar. He asks pointedly: 'Is the rich and enterprising farmer a development hero or a social menace?' (Hunter, 1969, p. 18)'.

Hunter shows how the growth of the dynamic sector destroys the economic security which the vast majority of the poor enjoyed in the traditional economy. In the face of technical change, the vast majority of small landholders are 'much more likely to be driven off their land or to sell it to pay debt'.

Hunter warns that this vast majority is 'probably strong enough, even to-day, to rise up and crush beneath its enormous weight a progress which leaves out too many tens of millions of Indian people'.

Hunter's analysis focusses attention on the importance of 'security' in the scheme of life of the peasants and the social and political consequences of the disintegration of this security system unaccompanied by the new mechanisms of security. One of the major weaknesses of this analysis, however, is that it raises the question of security for the majority of the rural population in isolation from the question of economic growth.

Andre Beteille in his paper 'The Social Framework of Agriculture' raises important issues relating to the social context and consequences of agricultural development. His main thesis is as follows:

> There are in rural India two interpenetrating systems, one based on personalities and loyalties and the other on impersonal rules and standards. There is also a small but powerful (and growing) minority of people—progressive farmers, capitalist farmers, rural entrepreneurs—who are successfully using both these systems apparently without being deeply committed to the values on which either is based. The short-run performance of this minority seems to have been good particularly from the economic point of view. But what about its long-run prospects from the view-point of society as a whole?

If it is true that society is more than a mere aggregate of individuals who pursue their respective interests in a kind of market situation, then there may indeed be cause for misgiving if a dominant minority acts in that way, using institutions as instruments and having no fundamental commitment to either rules or personal ties. One might argue, of course, that this is a purely transitional phenomenon, that the transition will lead to a relatively stable social order where public life will be governed by impersonal rules and that this is by and large what happened in the West. But such an argument, besides making too much of historical analogies would appear to leave too many things to chance. (Beteille, 1974, pp. 109–110)

Beteille later identifies 'a general condition of uncertainty' as a major feature of the new social situation and poses the question whether it marks the decline of the old social order without any sign of the new order yet appearing. Andre Beteille has raised a number of issues which open up new areas of enquiry by sociologists and economists.

Although identifying 'the general condition of uncertainty' in the rural areas, Beteille has not explored adequately the causes of this condition. He deals more with the proximate rather than the deeper causes of this 'uncertainty'. He identifies the symptoms without locating the factors lying at the root of the malady. One can refer, in this connexion, to the uncertainty arising out of the loss of security in West Europe in the wake of agrarian reorganization. To quote Schumpeter,

> In principle, mediaeval society provided a berth for everyone whom it recognized as a member; its structural design excluded unemployment and destitution ... This changed in and after the fifteenth century.
> ... The agrarian revolution not only destroyed environments that might have sheltered fugitives from distressed areas but also caused the landless to increase much more rapidly than the effective demand for labour. (Schumpeter, 1954)

Is India now *beginning* to witness similar developments in the rural area? Beteille does not relate the condition of uncertainty to such concrete developments in the economic sphere. 'Uncertainty' appears in Beteille's analysis more as a mystical, psychological state and less rather than as a reflection, at the level of the 'superstructure', of basic changes occurring in the 'economic basis', especially in the character of land relations, under the impact of growing commercialism and technological change. From this point of view, the restructuring of relations between landlords and tenants, employers and employees, the big and the small in Indian villages in a dynamic context requires to study in depth not merely as a reorientation of economic arrangements but as a process of change in the very structure of society at several levels—the economic, the social, the political and the ideological. Further, Beteille's paper does not distinguish between one type of uncertainty which may be inherent in the very process of development from another, which is related to a specific pattern of development. This distinction is important if sociological analysis has to contribute towards enlarging the scope for human intervention for economic and social change in the *desired* direction.

Beteille's paper in this context should logically lead to an important question which needs to be asked but which he has not explicitly raised. Can capitalism provide the economic basis for a stable 'social order' in the Indian context? Can it provide the unifying frame in terms of norms and values which can sustain rural society during the period of 'transition'? Here is one of the problem areas which historically have been the concerns of political economy, institutional economics and Macrosociology. In the Indian context, economists as well sociologists and social anthropologists have in many cases been indifferent to such larger questions.

We now refer to those contributions which can be said to approximate to conception C. It may be repeated again that the main weakness of the critics of the large producer-based strategy of agricultural transformation is that they raise important issues mainly from the standpoint of equity in isolation from the question of economic growth. In other words, there have not been significant attempts in India both on a theoretical and empirical plane to work out an alternative strategy of equity-oriented economic growth. In his two recent papers on 'Ownership and Distribution of Land' and 'Some Questions Concerning Growth, Transformation and Planning of Agriculture in the Developing countries', Raj (1969, 1970) has attempted to provide an alternative perspective on the question of agricultural transformation. Raj's argument is that in countries like India with a relatively abundant supply of labour, and in the absence of economies of scale, the *optimum* size of the farming units may be small. But considering the *actual* size of operating units, one finds that the bulk of the area is concentrated in units not of small but of large size. In fact, 'the size distribution of operational holdings is often not markedly different from that of ownership holdings'. Further, the distribution of credit also tends to be concentrated in large holdings. As a result, the gains of new technology also tend to be concentrated in these large holdings. Raj's analysis implies that the gap between the rates of growth in the large farms sector, on the one hand, and the small farms sector, on the other, would become much wider in a dynamic context of technological change than in a static context.

Raj, however, is not one of those economists who regard this as a 'socially desirable process' deserving to be encouraged and strengthened. And here, his analysis makes a sharp departure from the standpoints of other economists. Raj's argument brings out the conflict between private profit maximization, on the one hand, and social return maximization, on the other, under conditions of large farmer dominance. The large producer tends to economize labour by adopting labour-saving techniques and to 'utilize available land and other inputs only to the extent consistent with these techniques'. The small producers 'have an advantage in so far as the new technology requires intensive application of labour ... but little credit since the risks attached to the new technology also set limits to the application of other inputs'. Under the given pattern of distribution of ownership and operational holdings, there is inefficient utilization of economic resources considered from the standpoint of society as a whole. In other words, Raj's analysis implies that the transfer of land and other resources from the large to the small farmer would contribute not only to equity but also to more efficient utilization of economic resources from the social point of view.

It is pertinent to recall in this connexion C. H. Hanumantha Rao's study on *Agricultural Production Functions, Costs and Returns in India*. Rao's study also suggests that 'with labour-intensive technique, productivity of land and output can be raised best under a more even distribution of the ownership of land which would make for a greater identity between these three factors (i.e., ownership, management and work)' (Rao, 1965).

This question of efficiency of small peasant farms needs to be explored further not only from the point of view of output maximization but also from the point of view of surplus generation for economic development.

We may draw attention to two important contributions in the recent period which have an important bearing on conception 3. Amit Bhaduri (1973), in his recent paper on 'Agricultural Backwardness under Semi-Feudalism', has drawn attention to the in-built structural obstacles to technological change in a small peasant agricultural economy. He has derived empirical support for his thesis from his field visits to selected West Bengal villages. Amit Bhaduri's model of semi-feudalism, however, would apply only to those village economies where the credit structure and the land system are insufficiently differentiated and where the monopolist of land, the landlord, is also the monopolist of credit, the money-lender. The enormous requirement for consumption loans in a perennially deficit peasant economy pushes up the rates of interest to such a high level that the landlord finds it far more lucrative to invest his resources in money lending than in improvement of agriculture. This model of feudalism would not be valid if the peasant has access to independent sources of credit, as in Punjab, or where the cooperative credit comes to the aid of the peasant and reduces his dependence on the landlord-usurer or where the technological improvement promises a much higher return on resources invested in agricultural development than in usury. In other words, Amit Bhaduri's paper corrects the facile view which expects agricultural breakthrough from just transfer of land from landlords to tenants. The narrow concept of structural change implicit in conception C is thus widened so as to include not only land reforms but also credit restructuring, technological innovations, and changes in the power balance.

Attention needs also to be drawn to the J. N. Sinha's paper (1973) on 'Land Reform: A Dissenting View' which offers a critique of conception 3. In Sinha's view, transformation of subsistence into commercial farming is a necessary part of Indian economic development. The breakup of large holdings and the creation of peasant agriculture will contribute to economic development if it transforms subsistence-oriented peasant into a commercial farmer. For this transformation mere breakup of large holdings is not enough: what is required is the creation of an infrastructure for growth and a high level of cultural development of the peasantry. In the absence of the latter, land reforms may retard rather than promote growth.

CONCLUSION

Implicit in the three economic perspectives reviewed in the foregoing pages are three divergent perspectives of agrarian change and also three operational strategies conforming to three agrarian perspectives. Further, conforming to each of these perspectives and strategies is also a specific conception of the balance of political and social forces or class combinations representing a specific power balance. It should be noted, however, that the power balance favourable to conception 3 has not yet emerged in India. The dominant power balance is essentially favourable to conception 2, and even in respect to conception 2, the balance is more favourable to the articulation of programmes than to their effective implementation.

REFERENCES

Bauer, P. T., & Yamey, B. S. (1957). *The economics of underdeveloped countries*. Cambridge University Press.

Beteille, A. (1974). *Studies in agrarian social structure*. Oxford University Press.

Bhaduri, A. (1973). Study in agricultural backwardness under semi-Feudalism. *Economic Journal, 83*(329).

Dandekar, V. M., & Nilakantha, R. (1971). *Poverty in India*. Ford Foundation.

Dantwala, M. L. (1970, December). From stagnation to growth: Relative roles of technology, economic policy and agrarian institutions. Paper presented at Indian Economic Association, 53rd Conference, Gauhati.

Hunter, G. (1969). *Modernising peasant societies: A comparative study in Asia and Africa*. Oxford University Press.

Khusro, A. M. (1972). *The economics of land reform and farm size in India*. Macmillan & Company.

Mellor, J. W. (1968). *Developing rural India: Plan and practice*. Cornell University Press.

Ministry of Home Affairs. (1969). *The causes and nature of current agrarian tensions*. Research Division, Government of India, Mimeographed.

Raj, K. N. (1969). Some questions concerning growth, transformation and planning of agriculture in developing countries. *Journal of Development Planning, 1*.

Raj, K. N. (1970). *Ownership and distribution of land*. Centre for Advanced Studies, Delhi School of Economics.

Rao, C. H. (1965). *Agricultural production functions, costs and returns in India*. Asia Publishing House.

Schumpeter, J. A. (1954). *History of economic analysis*. Oxford University Press.

Sinha, J. N. (1973). Agrarian reforms and employment in density populated agrarian economics: A dissenting view. *International Labour Review, 108*(5).

Chapter 6

Role of Peasant Economy in Capitalist Development*
Case Study of a Maharashtra Village

Sulabha Brahme

INTRODUCTION

Maharashtra state is considered to be one of the most advanced states in India. Industrially, it is highly developed, a third of the state income being contributed by the secondary sector. It stands first among all the states in per capita industrial production, consumption of electricity, bank credit disbursed and such other indicators of economic development. Progressive rich farmers are considered to be a dominant force in the state, and the network of cooperative credit and cooperative sugar factories is quite strong. However, the modern industry in Maharashtra is concentrated mainly in the metropolitan city of Mumbai and a few other centres such as Thane, Nashik and Pune. under the sphere of influence of Mumbai. The cooperative sugar factories are localized only in some of the fortunate parts of the state.

It is important to understand the process by which the investible resources got concentrated in the limited areas of the state. With the beginning of the planning era in 1950, the government assumed the responsibility to extend surface irrigation facilities and to provide credit facilities through an extensive network to land development

---

* *Social Change*, 8(3), 1978.

banks and cooperative banks to support well digging, lift irrigation, well energization programme and to meet the working capital needs. The state government actively helped the setting up of the sugar factories in the cooperative sector. Extension of the road network, marketing facilities, distribution agencies and agricultural extension service under the plan schemes made for effective movement of consumer goods such as vegetables, milk and other primary produce to the major urban centres and ensured delivery of manufactured inputs such as fertilizers and pesticides to the farmer. All the farmers were eligible to receive credit, fertilizers and extension service. However, the distribution of these among the cultivators was closely related to the extent of land that they commanded. In effect, the state support helped growth of capitalist agriculture, which is restricted mainly to the irrigated areas and to a small section of the cultivators. It was mainly the substantial landowner who could use to their advantage the various developmental schemes on the basis of their resource—strength, risk-bearing capacity and creditworthiness.

There was a considerable expansion of the industrial sector in the state. However, most of the newly set up industrial units were highly capital intensive. Consequently, the employment generation in the non-agricultural sphere was far too short of the actual requirement for absorbing the incremental labour force. In this situation, the traditional small-peasant farming economy proved to be a convenient cushion. Measures such as 'Land to the Tiller' and 'Employment Guarantee Scheme' operative only in the rural areas helped maintain the peasant economy and keep up hope among the peasant masses. The development of the capitalist sector in agriculture was possible because of this 'shock absorber' in the form of small-peasant economy to which the majority of the rural population belong, living at the subsistence or below-subsistence level and thus making it possible to channelize the resources for enclave capitalist development.

However, with successive diminution of landholding and only a small change in the productivity level, how does the small peasant family survive? How far can the belts be tightened? In Maharashtra, thanks to the growth of cooperative sugar factories and the giant Mumbai Metropolis, the answer to this problem is provided by migration—seasonal and cyclical or semi-permanent. Thousands of small peasants and agricultural labourers migrate seasonally to sugarcane areas. They work on the sugarcane farms and are employed to cut and transport the sugarcane to the factories. Thus, they manage to make a living for the lean six months. Those near the urban centres get seasonal work in brick kilns, salt pans, construction work or coolie work. If the situation in certain areas turns critical, some sustenance is proved during the lean season on road works or other public works opened up temporarily by the government under the 'Employment Guarantee Scheme'. There is also semi-permanent migration on a large scale. Some of the districts of Maharashtra, notably Ratnagiri and Satara, have been sending out workers in sizeable number mainly to Mumbai.[1] The workers stay in the city for 20–25 years but do not settle in the city. Their family generally stays back in the village cultivating their ancestral piece of land eking out some living, part of the sustenance being provided through the remittances sent by the migrant workers. The land serves as a valuable and the only old-age security. After their return to the village, their sons move on to the city to continue the part support to the family. The small-peasant farming is thus perpetuated.[2]

An attempt is made in this chapter to study this phenomenon drawing upon the information from a Deccan village and on the basis of a case study to briefly indicate the implications of the phenomenon. The data are drawn from the study of village Gulumb[3] from Wai taluka, Satara district of Maharashtra state. The village broadly reflects the economic situation prevailing in the dry agricultural tracts of Western Maharashtra.

VILLAGE GULUMB

The village Gulumb is located at the foot of Mahadeo range of the Sahyadri and is sited on the bank of Chandraganga stream. The village falls in an area classified as having sufficient rainfall for dry agriculture. The village is connected by a two-mile dust road to the Pune–Bangalore national highway and is at a distance of 48 miles from the Pune city. The taluka headquarters and the marketplace, namely the Wai town is 10 miles away from the village, and the village is linked to Wai town by a *kaccha* road.

The geographical area of the village measures 2,691 acres of which 2,175 acres are cultivable. In 1904, about 330 acres of land had been classified[4] as wet. Eight *kaccha* bunds across the nearby streams provided for seasonal storage of irrigation water. This was supplemented in a small way by well irrigation. Bajra and jowar mixed with pulses were the main crops of the village grown in kharif season. Wheat, gram and *shalu* or winter jowar and safflower were grown in *rabi* season. Valuable crops such as sugarcane, chilli, and fruits and vegetables occupied a small area. The food and fuel needs of the village, the non-agricultural producers and service personnel receive their dues mostly in kind. In the off-season, carting provided a supplementary source of income. In the closing decades of the 19th century also seasonal migration to Mumbai to work in the dockyards or in the textile mills was a regular phenomenon.[5]

Gulumb in 1942

The population of the village increased from 1,263 persons in 1901 to 1,558 in 1941 (Table 6.1). In 1942, there were 327 families in the village with 1,621 persons (Table 6.2). Of these, 339 men and 442 women were returned as workers (Table 6.3). Eighty-six per cent of the workers were occupied in agricultural work; most of these were working on their own farms. Only 10 per cent of the total workers served as agricultural labourers mostly on a casual basis. There were

Table 6.1 *Population of Gulumb Village*

Year	Total No. of Persons
1901	1,263
1911	1,323
1921	1,230
1931	1,450
1941	1,558
1951	1,830
1961	2,060
1971	2,604

Source: Author's own.

Table 6.2 Select Demographic Characteristics of the Gulumb Population

	1942	1958	1976
No. of families	327	419	493
Total no. of persons	1,621	2,040	2,583
Average family size	4.95	4.86	5.24
No. of males	729	930	1,160
No. of females	892	1,110	1,423
No. of females per 1,000 males	1,224	1,194	1,226
No. of earners (in the village)	781	1,005	1,295
No. of earners (outside the village)*	203	324	479
Total No. of persons (outside the village)*	271	488	737

Notes: *Persons with definite connection with the village are taken into consideration.

only two permanent farm servants in the village. The non-agricultural occupations in the village were mainly restricted to agriculture-related maintenance and repair work or supply of agricultural implements, leather *mhots* or footwear or personal services to the village families. There were, thus a few carpenters, blacksmiths, cobblers, rope makers, basket makers, barbers, washer men, oil-men in the village. In all, 97 earners were occupied in these agriculture-related work or other services. The artisans were paid mainly in kind for their services. There were only two grocers, two dealers in bangles and three petty traders. Purchases of cloth and other manufactures were made partly at the taluka town of Wai; these articles were mainly brought from Mumbai by the migrant workers working in Mumbai. There was only one group of workers engaged in non-agricultural production, namely Dhangars—the woollen blanket weavers who marketed the *kambals* mainly in the Konkan region. Thirty-three earners were engaged in this craft.

Agriculture

The crop pattern in the village was dominated by food grains production—77 per cent of the cultivated area was under cereals and

Table 6.3 *Occupational Distribution of Earners from Gulumb*

Occupation	1942 Male	1942 Female	1958 Male	1958 Female	1976 Male	1976 Female
			No. of Earners			
Cultivation	238	355	279	483	342	616
Agricultural labour	16	48	40	59	54	140
Cattle herding	11	3	8	1	4	4
Attached farm labour	2	–	5	–	5	–
Sub-total	267	406	332	543	405	760
Production artisan	36	23	35	21	23	19
Service artisan	23	10	21	7	12	8
Trade	5	3	7	3	13	2
Construction	5	–	14	3	9	2
Services	3	–	14	1	28	4
Other occupations	–	–	2	2	7	3
Sub-total	72	36	93	37	92	38
Grand total of earners working in the village	339	442	425	580	497	798
Earners working outside the village	196	7	303	21	468	11

Table 6.4 Changes in the Crop Pattern Adopted by Cultivators from Gulumb

Crop	1942 Per Cent	1958 Area under the Crop	1976
Bajra	42.78	22.54	14.12
Kharif jowar	1.55	1.48	9.41[a] 8.71[b]
Rabi jowar	29.58	45.51	42.35
Paddy	0.31	0.42	0.47
Wheat	2.65	1.69	0.94
Gram	3.75	6.32	0.71
Other pulses	7.95	6.32	2.82
Chevada	0.44	1.69	2.82
Potato	3.09	2.74	1.41
Turmeric	0.97	0.97	0.24
Sugarcane	0.71	2.11	4.71
Groundnut	3.13	4.21	5.64
Safflower and other oilseeds	2.21	3.16	4.24
Other crops	0.88	0.84	1.41
Total	100	100	100
Gross cropped area (acres)	2,265	2,372	2,125

Notes: [a]*Ghagar matki*—a variety of jowar.
[b]Hybrid jowar.

22 per cent under pulses (Table 6.4). The cash crops—groundnut and potato introduced in the early decades of the 20th century—occupied about 3 per cent each of the total cultivated area and sugarcane and turmeric covered nearly one per cent each of the cultivated area. Sugarcane was processed locally into *gur* which was partly exported. Turmeric was also exported after processing. The oilseeds were mainly to meet the domestic requirements of cooking oil, the oil being extracted in the village *ghanis*. Part of the groundnut crop and the bulk of the potato crop was marketed.

Cereals and pulses were used mainly for self-consumption, and for payments in kind to *balutedars*[6] and to the labourers at the harvest time. It was estimated that cash sales accounted for about 35 per cent of the gross value of the total agricultural produce. About 17 per cent of the total produce was used for payments in kind. Almost half of the produce was retained for home-consumption, seed and so on.

The cultivation of land was, thus, oriented primarily towards the consumption requirements of the family. The family farm and the farm animals together supplied cereals, pulses, oilseeds, vegetables, milk, *gur* and so on for family consumption and fodder and manure for farm use. The family farm was operated mainly with the help of family hands. It was noted on the basis of information collected through the farm business survey, that 65 per cent of the workdays put into agricultural operations were contributed by family labour, 15 per cent on a mutual exchange basis and only 20 per cent of the workdays were contributed by hired labour, employed on a casual basis mainly to meet the peak-season workload.

There were 301 families in the village who owned land. The land held by Brahmins and the temple lands were leased out for cultivation. The landholdings of the village functionaries and artisans were small and some of them did not cultivate their land. In all, 228 families reported cultivation as their main occupation, while 35 families reported it as their subsidiary occupation. The average size of landholding was about 7 acres. The land distribution was quite skewed. Six per cent of the landowning families having land above 20 acres each commanded nearly 22 per cent of the cultivated land, while 52 per cent of the families with land less than 5 acres each had a share of only about 18 per cent in the total land cultivated (Table 6.5). In the case of smaller cultivators, food grains production from the family farm could meet the family needs for about 5 to 6 months; the deficit in the budget was partly met by working as an agricultural labourer in the village, by seasonal migration by migrating to Bombay for work but maintaining the link with the village. The village as a whole had a deficit in the production of food grains to the extent of about 30 per cent. Considering the other consumption needs, the deficit was large. The villagers were coping with this deficit situation, not by any agricultural improvement or by taking to non-agricultural production—both of these seemed to be

Table 6.5 Distribution of Gulumb Families by Size of Ownership Holding

Size of Landholding (in Acres)	1942		1976	
	Per Cent Families	Per Cent Land Held	Per Cent Families	Per Cent Land Held
Below 1.00	13.95	1.23	14.79	1.49
1.00–1.99	9.63	2.16	18.55	4.88
2.00–4.99	27.91	14.73	34.59	21.66
5.00–9.99	27.25	29.83	21.55	28.17
10.00–14.99	10.96	19.67	5.26	12.26
15.00–19.99	4.32	10.66	4.26	13.80
20.00 & above	5.98	21.72	1.00	17.74
Total	**100.00**	**100.00**	**100.00**	**100.00**
Total landowning families	301		399	
Landless families	26		94	
Total families	**327**		**493**	

beyond their capacity—but by sending the village workers to work in the city, notably Bombay to augment their income.

Migration

It was noted that more than a third of the male adult earners in the village were working outside the village. The preparation of migrant workers was as high as 50 per cent in the case of landless families and around 40 per cent in the case of families with less than four acres of land per adult male. Even in the case of families with larger holdings about 20 per cent of the adult male workers were working outside the village. Many of these families were large-sized with three to four male workers in the family and found it profitable to send a worker or two to work outside the village; this helped increase the cash earnings of the family. Of the 203 migrant workers (workers with definite connection with the village are taken into account and those who have left the system are not considered here), as many as 196 workers were working in Bombay. Sixty-six per cent of these were employed in textile mills and the others worked as hawkers, domestic or hotel servants, coolies and so on. Workers continued, by and large, to keep their headquarters in the village. Their parents, wife and children would stay on in the village. If they were a *balutedar*, they would come back to the village to serve their turn leaving their outside job. In old age, they would return to the village, and their son would take the turn mainly through the established contact. The remittances from outside contributed to the extent of 25 per cent to the total income of the village.

Gulumb in 1976

The population of the village increased to 2,583 by 1976; there were 493 families in the village, the average family size increased from 4.95 in 1942 to 5.24 in 1966. The number of females per 1,000 males was 1,226. The occupational distribution in the village did not record any significant changes. Out of the total 1,295 earners in the village, nearly 90 per cent were occupied in agricultural work. The number of agricultural labourers increased from 64 in 1942 to 194 in 1976. About 17 per cent of the agricultural workers served as agricultural labourers.

The number of workers in traditional artisan and service occupations declined. The weaning activity has almost totally disappeared. There are now only two looms in the village. The traditional productivity activity, namely manufacture of agricultural implements, earthen pots, woollen blankets could not survive in the face of the onslaught of factory-made products. The *gur*-making activity in the village is under threat, and the units will be soon closed down as a cooperative sugar factory has been set up in the neighbourhood.[7] No new productive activity has come up in the village. Little diversification in the occupational pattern is apparent over the period of the last three decades. A few new occupations that are added to the spectrum are confined mainly to the service sector. There are 10 primary school teachers and 5 secondary school teachers in the village. A cycle repair shop, a loudspeaker hire-cum-pandal decoration service, an electrical repair shop are the new additions; besides four more grocers' shops and two cloth shops have been set up in the village.

Agriculture

There was little margin for the expansion of the area under cultivation in the village. The gross cropped area could increase only through double cropping on the basis of extension of irrigation and changes in the cropping pattern. During the last decade or so, certain investments both on public and private account had been made for improvement of irrigation facility. For examples, in the place of *kaccha bandharas* across the Chandraganga stream *pucca* dams were constructed, thus, saving the annual rebuilding work. However, this did not bring about any addition to the area irrigated. Between 1960 and 1975, work on 11 new private wells and two community wells was started. By 1976, seven private wells were brought into use for irrigation. Even though there was some increase in the water supply, the area irrigated did not increase because of the spread of sugarcane cultivation—a voracious water user. No increase in the double-cropped area is recorded over a period of the last three decades.

The number of irrigation wells in use increased from 39 in 1944–1945 to 50 by 1976. Most of the wells are fitted with electric pump sets. There are in all 45 electric pump sets in the village. Recently, three cultivators have purchased a tractor each; these are mainly used for transport of sugarcane or to reach the village people to the market town of Wai. No other additions to agricultural implements or machinery are noted. The number of bullocks has remained almost unchanged around 260 heads and bullocks still constitute the main source of draught power.

The major change in the cropping pattern is the increase in the area under sugarcane, which now occupies about 100 acres of irrigated land. Turmeric, another valuable cash crop was almost totally uprooted in the 1972 drought. It is quite expensive to re-establish the crop, and hence, today the area under turmeric is quite small. Broad beans a relatively ubiquitous and less demanding crop for which there is a steady market is gaining ground. The cash crop, namely sugarcane, potato, groundnut, chilli, vegetables and so on occupy about 15 per cent of the cultivated land. Nearly 75 per cent of the land is still devoted to production of cereals. Bajra is being replaced partly by *ghagar matki*—an inferior variety of jowar and partly by hybrid jowar. Although the average yield of hybrid jowar is high, because of the higher cost of cultivation and the risk involved if the monsoon is untimely, the spread of hybrid jowar is limited. Rabi jowar, an irrigated cereal crop, continues to be the major cereal crop of the village.

There is a significant decline in the area under pulses, partly because there is no increase in the average yield, and therefore, the per acre returns from the crop are relatively low and also because pulses which are generally grown as a mixed crop with a kharif cereal crop cannot be taken with hybrid jowar, since it is a short-duration crop. Apart from its contribution to a balanced diet cultivation of pulses helps maintain soil fertility through nitrogen fixation. The decline in the cultivation of pulses therefore means an increase in the need for fertilizer application. The supply of organic manure in the village has remained more or less static. Crops such as hybrid jowar and particularly sugarcane need a high dose of fertilizer. For this and other reasons, there is a phenomenal increase in the consumption of fertilizers in the village. A root crop, namely sweet potato which was cultivated mainly to serve as a staple food during the rainy season is no more in vogue. Harvesting of sweet potato involved stirring of the soil up to considerable depth and this ensured proper soil turning. The changes in the crop pattern introduced in the last 20 years have thus upset the traditional soil preservation mechanisms and have increased the dependence of the village on inflow of input from outside in the form of fertilizers to maintain yield levels.

The proportion of sales in the gross value of agricultural produce increased from about 35 per cent in 1942 to nearly 60 per cent in 1976. The increase in the value of marketed produce can be mainly attributed to the increase in the area under sugarcane—a high-value crop. The practice of payments in kind to *balutedars* and to agricultural labourers is almost totally discontinued. The cash component in the total farm expenditure[3] had increased from 45 per cent in 1942 to about 70 per cent in 1976. Thus, the rural economy has been more sharply monetized in comparatively recent decades. The composition of farm expenditure has now changed significantly. Land revenue and other government charges now account for less than 5 per cent of the total farm expenditure. The corresponding percentage was as high as 18 in 1942. Now, fertilizers claim about 25 per cent of the total farm expenditure. Expenditure incurred for the purchase of hybrid seeds, potato seed, pesticides and electricity charges are the other items of outgoings.

The village economy is linked with the outside world to a larger extent both for the purchases of farm inputs and for consumer goods. Fertilizers, agricultural equipment such as pump sets and pesticide are the major factory-produced inputs used on farm. As much as 75 per cent of the total consumer expenditure now involves cash purchases. This is partly because of the increase in the number of families who do not have adequate land and livestock to meet their annual requirements of food grains, milk and vegetables and other requirements of farm production, and partly because of other factors such as shift from village *ghani* oil to mill-produced oil, *gur* to sugar, use of new items such as plastic footwear, soap and allopathic medicine and increase in the consumption of tea, metal ware and tobacco. As a result, it is estimated that the value of manufactured goods purchased in Gulumb had almost doubled (in real terms) between 1942 and 1976. This in effect means that the base which the village economy provided for local productive activity has been shrinking, and the village serves more and more as a market for the products of modern large-scale industry.

Even though there is an increase in the value of agricultural sales and in monetization, the farm households still operate as production-cum-consumption units. No farmer specializes in the production of a specific crop say, sugarcane or potato or oilseeds. They will allocate certain land to meet their requirements of food grains, fodder and so on and try to raise some cash crop to meet part of the cash needs. The farms are still operated mainly with the help of family hands and only at harvest time casual labour is hired. Hired labour is reported for heavy agricultural operations by women cultivators if they do not have any male relative to help.

The average size of landholding has further declined. The land–man ratio had gone down from 1.40 acres in 1942 to .82 acres in 1976. About 68 per cent of the farmers had holdings below 5 acres each. Most of them do not own bullocks. The smaller farmers restrict their production mainly to cultivation of cereals, pulses, safflower for home consumption and put a small area under broad beans or hybrid jowar. Lack of draft power, poor access to credit and low risk-bearing capacity make it difficult for them to experiment with new crops or adopt new cultural practices. It was noted that the water requirements and the cash expenditure requirements of sugarcane are so high that small cultivators find it beyond their means to shift to sugarcane cultivation. Even for the cultivators with farm size between 5 and 10 acres, it is possible to put only half an acre to one acre under sugarcane depending upon the availability of water. Even then, they often face the problem of lack of ready cash to apply fertilizer on time, or inadequacy of water supply. At times, they fail to get a fair price for their crop and as a result the cash earnings hardly provide them with any surplus for investment.

The number of cultivators with more than two acres under sugarcane is quite small and only five cultivators have 4/5 acres under sugarcane. These are the leading families of the village. They have holdings of sizes between 15 and 25 acres each with 5 to 10 acres of irrigated land. Two each of these size-groups own *gur* manufacture-units and flour mills. Three own a tractor each. The village *sarpanch,* the chairman of the village primary cooperative society and the secretary of the cooperative society come from these families. It was reported that the control that these families exercise over the village institutions is used to their advantage.

About 10 per cent of the families in the village reported surplus in farm production and 15 per cent were self-sufficient in an average year. For nearly 75 per cent of the families, farm production is inadequate.

Migration

Larger members of adult men are now moving out primarily to Mumbai or into police service or military service or other jobs. The number of earners working outside the village had increased from 203 in 1942 to 479 in 1976, and now above 50 per cent of the male workers are working outside the village. In addition, about 37 men were returned as unemployed and were looking for gainful employment in Mumbai. Due to the second world war, the workers had to stay in the city on a sustained basis because of the increasing pressure of labour on the job market. However, due to lack of housing, inadequacy of pay and the need for old-age security, the interest in the ancestral land is still retained and the wives and children generally stay on in the village. Between the period 1942 and 1976, 162 men earners returned to the village. Most of them returned after retirement. Some had to get back to the village due to ill-health or to attend to family duties.

In 1976, 283 or 57 per cent of the families reported one or more persons working outside the village. Of these, 209 families were receiving remittances on a regular basis; the average amount sent in a one-year period came to about 1,100 per family reporting remittances. In 112 families there is no working adult male in the village, and it is the women who look after the day-to-day agricultural work. The migrant workers visit the village two–three times a year. They adjust their visits so as to complete the major farm management work, in case there is no other adult male living in the village. Besides the money order which is usually sent every month for the maintenance of the family, the workers bring with them on their home visit consumption goods such as clothing, tea, sugar and spice powder. In the city, the workers live in a chawl or a hutment together with a few other co-villagers and eat out. In one of the chawls, it was noted that three women from the Gulumb village were providing cooked meals on a monthly payment basis for the village workers. The Gulumb migrants form a close-knit group and by and large observed the traditional village mores. The workers try to save some money for contingencies, like family weddings, and if possible for improving the land or the house in the village. However, investments have not been substantial enough to improve the agricultural situation in the case of many. Despite the fact that half the male adults from the village are working in Bombay, the economic position of the villagers, on an average, has not improved. The per capita income in 1976 worked to 620 at current prices. As compared to the 1942 income level, the per capita real income recorded a decline by about 18 per cent.

The problem of ecological imbalance is becoming more acute in the village. Before the advent of the British rule, the use of forest and pasture resources was regulated by customs and the village community held some responsibility in conserving these natural resources It was noted that over the period of last 150 years, pasture land has been reduced in area, the marginal lands being increasingly brought under cultivation. The reduced area of pasture meant over-grazing and deterioration of village pastures. The hills around the village are totally denuded, the trees being used up over time for timber and mainly for fuel. The pasture and the forest resources are being indiscriminately used and no replacement of trees is attempted. This has accentuated the problem of soil erosion and the investments in *bunding* made by individual farmers hardly make up the continual loss at the village level. Successive subdivision of land and the resulting fragmentation of holdings is accentuating the problem. Despite the attempts at land consolidation, nearly 40 per cent of the plots in the village are less than half an acre in size. Unless the land and the water resources of the village are considered as a whole and scientific measures for bunding and levelling, drainage and afforestation are adopted, it is difficult to preserve the resource base of the village.

CONCLUSION

The implications of the development process experienced during the last three decades for the mass of peasant population would be apparent from the case study of Gulumb. There are many villages in a similar situation in Western Maharashtra. For the peasant, it means continuation of farming, by and large, in a traditional way to extract a part of subsistence requirements, depending, for the rest, on non-agricultural manual work in the city, severed from the family and suffering inhuman conditions of living in a city slum. Yet there is a hope to save a certain sum of money and perhaps to improve their lot marginally when they return to the village. The small piece of land and the house in the village at least provide some security for the old age.

The agricultural situation at the village level, as the study of Gulumb village indicates, remains largely static. Despite investments in modern equipment and inputs the returns in terms of increased yields are not substantial. With the majority of the families retaining their interest in land, there is a continuous process of sub-division and fragmentation of holdings so that, ultimately there is little improvement in the farm incomes of small peasants.

Existence of a mass of population at the subsistence or below-subsistence level, however, makes it possible to support the development of *enclaves* of progressive 'rich peasant' agriculture as well as pockets of industrial growth. Peasant farming provides for maintenance of the urban industrial worker's family as well as the reproduction of workers at a considerably lower cost in the village This works to the advantage of the modern industry in the metropolitan centres. The village provides some kind of a social insurance to the village-born, and at the same time, the rural unemployed who work at low wages in the industries or other non-agricultural occupations remain content with their lot. As the growth of the industrial sector is limited, the increase in productivity is experienced only in limited areas in agriculture. The state economy remains crisis-ridden. There is no steady growth in agriculture, the natural resource base deteriorates, the problem of poverty and unemployment deepens; yet the situation does not become explosive, thanks to the persistence of small peasant farming.

NOTES

1. The migrants are concentrated in the metropolitan city of Mumbai—the hub of industrial and commercial activity. In 1961, of the total migrants in Mumbai from rural Maharashtra, half were from Ratnagiri district, the coastal district south of Mumbai and nearly 15 per cent were from the Satara district. The percentage of male workers from Satara working in Mumbai to the male workers working in the Satara district was as high as 25 per cent in 1961.
2. In 1952–1953, the proportion of small holders (those below 5 acres of land) was 47 per cent in the state as a whole. The corresponding proportion was 48.5 per cent in 1969–1970. In this class, 94 per cent holdings were wholly owned. Small-peasant farming is, thus, persisting in Maharashtra.

3. In 1937–1938, Gulumb village was covered in a farm business study carried out by the Gokhale Institute of Politics and Economics, Pune. The institute conducted comprehensive socio-economic survey of the village covering all the families in 1942–1943 and again in 1957–1958. In 1976, the village was resurveyed by Hemalata Dandekar, a research student at the institute. All the families were interviewed with the help of a brief general family schedule.
4. Village records at the Land Records Office, Satara.
5. (i) It was noted that in 1881 about 10 per cent of the population born in Satara district was living outside the district—mainly in Bombay and Pune, Gazetteer of the Bombay Presidency, Satara, 1885, p. 50. (ii) Papers on the Second Revision Survey Settlement of Satara District, Wai taluka and Khandala Mahal, 1929, note that from the Krishna valley villages of the taluka between 10-15 per cent population migrate to Bombay and elsewhere for some months of the year. p. 4.
6. A person who renders agriculture-related and/or other services in the village against a fixed payment in kind or annual basic.
7. The village was electrified in the year 1964.
8. In computing the farm expenditure, the family labour component is not taken into account.

Chapter 7

Micro-regional Planning for the Management of Agriculture*

Prodipto Roy

INTRODUCTION

A large number of studies conducted on agricultural extension (Singh et al., 1970) and agricultural innovation in rural India (Fliegel et al., 1968; Roy & Project on the Diffusion of Innovations in Rural Societies, 1968) typically stop short at identifying who adopts and the characteristics of innovators or studying the process of adoption. They typically do not go further into the changes in the land and water resources, the economics of the amounts of new agricultural technology being bought or sold or the spatial movement of an individual, money and commodities. In short, these studies do not provide guidelines for the total management of the changes due to agricultural technology or the impact on natural and human resources of Indian villages.

Agriculture still dominates the Indian economy, and the husbanding of India's vast resources of land, water, trees, crops and animals should remain the primary concern of planners, politicians and administrators. Unfortunately, the vast array of physical, natural and human assets which is engaged in the agricultural enterprise staggers the imagination and their intelligent comprehension and analysis would be beyond the memory capacity of the most complex computers in India today.

---

* *Social Change*, 3(1 & 2), 1973.

The wheat takeover only illustrates the enormous complexity of the enterprise.

In a provocative book on the dilemma of agriculture in underdeveloped countries, entitled *No Easy Harvest*, Kenneth Boulding wrote a poem of which I quote one verse:

> With facts too many now to list 'em The answer is a General System So what has got to be advised Is, 'get the stuff computerized'. (Millikan & Hapgood, 1968, p. 12)

That book tried to steer a course between the 'Scylla of incomplete single factor solutions and the Charbydis of analytical chaos...' It offered no panaceas or blueprints, and they did not find 'a magic key to unlock the problems of agriculture'.

In two large-scale studies, attempting to cast a wide net on agricultural innovation in India at the village and farmer level, at the National Institute of Community Development, this author wrote a far more optimistic brochure entitled *Two Blades of Grass* predicting 'a vigorous breakthrough...into a modern agricultural era in the next decade or two' (Roy, 1968). Since then, the more optimistic terms such as 'green revolution' or 'white revolution' have been coined. Drought in the past two years (as in 1965–1966) has, however, sobered our optimism and demonstrated that food supplies are perilously close to demand.

In a penetrating article, entitled 'A Charter for Our Land' (Vohra, 1972), B. B. Vohra has argued that 'the neglect of the soil...has contributed to the impoverishment of the land and its people.' He goes on to first describe the 'near-chaotic' state of affairs which exists today in both soil and water resource data and management. He sets down a comprehensive plan for India and works out the cost of a National Department of Land and Water. He sums up by saying 'the cost of looking after our soil, however high it might be, is still less than the price we are paying for neglecting it.'

Vohra decries the lack of accurate soil and groundwater surveys before any systematic programmes can be conducted. He estimates that a 'reconnaissance type survey...can be completed in 10 years at a cost of around "20 crores". Detailed surveys will cost many times this amount'. With the advent of Earth Resources Technical Satellite (ERTS) such a *detailed* survey for our entire nation can be completed in one year at a cost of about ₹1 crore. Discounting the value of ERTS to other users such as the Survey of India or the Minerals Department, just the soil, water, crop and forestry data are of such vital importance for our present agricultural planning that it brooks no delay. Nations beg, borrow or even steal such 'spy in the sky' scientific data, vital for their development.

India is in the peculiar position of literally having hundreds of Indian or ex-Indian scientists working in several nations using some aspects of ERTS data, while our scientific establishment is still debating the utility and the management of such fantastically vital information.

In 1969, the Ministry of Community Development launched a pilot research project to identify the primary growth or service centres (Ministry of Food and Agriculture, 1969) and the villages within their ambit in order to more efficiently service and manage the basic necessities of our agricultural villages. The database at the village level attempted to comprehend the total physical, natural and human resources and gathered information on about 3,800 variables. Even this 'selective' list of variables was obtained after a series of project design meetings of several Indian institutions having experience in this kind of research. The processing and analysis of these data through the Delhi University IBM 360/44 computer continues to plague the project directors. Three planning seminars have been held using these data for 13 of the 20 state field cells, and the remaining 7 field cells will hold a seminar probably in September 1973. However, the more comprehensive sectoral and integrated development systems data, which need to be derived from 20 study area cross-state data, will push back the barriers of both empirical and theoretical analysis of integrated rural development in India.

CONCEPT AND DESIGN OF THE GROWTH CENTRE PROJECT

In a preliminary report, the relevant literature on the growth centre concept was reviewed (Andrade & Roy, 1969). The literature on the subject is voluminous. The theoretical writings began with the Theory of the Location of Industries by Alfred Weber in 1909: Walter Christaller introduced what became known as Central Place Theory, which is based mainly on wholesale commodity distribution (Christaller, 1933, now available in a translation by Baskin, 1966).

August Lösch took these data further and propounded theories on the regional analysis and the economics of location (Lösch, 1941, now available in a translation by Woglom & Stopler, 1954). In geography, Walter Isard, Torsten Hagerstrand and Brian Berry (1967; who has made a number of studies in India) have made contributions to the development of regional science.

Sociological research started with the study of service centres by Galpin (1915). A number of studies were conducted by rural sociologists on trade centres for farmers and rural families in the USA mainly focused around economic activities and were county studies, somewhat similar to our block level studies (Douglas, 1941; Sanders & Doughlas, 1940). In India, the literature and studies in regional planning have been brought together in three volumes published under the guidance of Sen et al. (1971).

The application of Location and Central Place Theory in the total development planning has probably been carried farthest in Eastern Europe. Its use in countries such as Hungary, Bulgaria (Zhivkov, 1969) and Poland (Benku, 1966) which have villages rather than scattered homestead patterns of agricultural settlement is of particular relevance to India. There are two theoretical reasons why the socialist literature has more direct relevance. First, the needs of agricultural sector are not separated from the planning of health, education, transport, groceries or even barber services. Second, the total manpower and commodity management in a marginal sense has been taken into cognizance. That is, as agriculture becomes more mechanized or modern, the 'surpluses' of manpower are carefully planned for in non-agricultural occupations in places near their residence and using their skills as far as possible. This is the basic manpower management differential between a socialist and a capitalist economy. Not only is the transition from agricultural to non-agricultural occupations planned but also the transition from a village to an urban society is planned simultaneously by fixing the target minimum population of a residential village at about 3,000 and providing for all the basic services locally.

RESEARCH DESIGN FOR GROWTH CENTRES

It is just over 20 years since India embarked on its planned strategy of community development (CD) blocks. Each block comprised about 100 villages and a population of 100,000. The nation was, thus, geographically divided into 5,000 CD blocks. The necessary staff were recruited and trained, and blocks started in a phased manner over 10 years to ultimately cover the nation. The basic package of 'felt needs' was reflected in the schematic structure of the budget. The CD programme has had its changes of emphasis: the institution of Panchayati Raj with the 'devolvement' of the programme to locally elected bodies, special programmes in tribal development blocks, special programmes for small-scale industries and rural handicrafts and most recently the strategic change from an integrated approach to a single sector approach by the full time of the village-level worker (VLW) being devoted to agriculture.

The breakthrough caused by the dwarf strains of major cereals and the new strategy of the high-yielding variety programme has resulted in a certain buoyancy in agriculture. In order to ensure that prosperity does not result in increased migration to cities, create rural unemployment and cause social dislocation, the management of development has become urgent.

The radical departure that the growth centre project makes from the original CD programme is that it rests upon a more comprehensive assessment of the total resources of the block—in terms of land, water, crops, trees, manpower, education, health, transportation, cottage industries, industries, commodities movement and consumption—and the planning of selected functions based on this total resource database.

Theoretically, the self-sufficient village republics of India provided nearly all the social necessities for all families. There was very little a village needed to buy or to sell. Agricultural surpluses were stored against lean years. The CD programme has created modern needs for agricultural innovations, schools, health services, transport, recreation and so on and has made village people look outward for these 'felt' needs. In fact, the standards set by a modern state become the basic needs of tomorrow. This study has, therefore, focused a great deal of its data gathering on the marginal inputs and outputs of the village as a social unit. These margins are measured in terms of the various agricultural inputs and crop sales and the movement of people for a variety of activities and the distances of places to which they go, thereby obtaining an approximation of the total mobility of men, money and materials between villages. Thus, a measure of total outflow and inflow between villages could be made. Villages which were dependent on other villages for much of their supplies and services could be classified as non-centres. The 'growth centres' were villages with the largest 'net inflow', which was a manifestation of its surplus institutional capacity to service a hinterland of villages.

There were five specific objectives of the project, the first three of which were:

1. To identify focal points of growth and the villages coming within their ambit and to suggest an optimal hierarchy of growth centres for the most economically efficient provision of goods and services.
2. To specify functional gaps in the physical and institutional infrastructures of these centres and related settlements for present and future needs.
3. Taking cognizance of the resources available and likely trends of spatial and temporal patterns and to plan alternative courses of action for selected functions such as agricultural markets, fertilizer distribution, transportation, health and education.

The remaining objectives dealt with implementation, developing methodologies and the ultimate evaluation of the impact of the project. Operationally, the study concentrated on the felt and emerging economic and social needs symbolized in the basic social institutions of an individual. First, the size of settlements, their major occupational divisions, migration and growth were determined through the census data of 1951, 1961 and 1971. Economically, the volume of crops grown and other goods produced and the markets where they were sold, the agricultural and other inputs bought and all the occupations in which people worked manifest the interdependence of the villages. Data from industries such as cottage industries and shopkeepers were gathered to get information about commodity flows. The physical, personnel, postal and mass communication network was studied: first, in terms of distance from roads and transport facilities and the volume of different kinds of vehicular traffic, second, in terms of contacts of government officials, the travel of village people to outside places and third, the number of radios, newspapers and letters going and coming. All these provided information on the degree of external linkages. Educationally, the number and capacity of different educational institutions in or near the village and the number of pupils attending them indicated the flow of services required to provide educational needs. For *health*, the distance from health facilities, the pattern of diseases, the number of patients attending sub-centres, doctors' visits, medical supplies and where and how many people went for illness, confinement or surgical operations gave indications of present norms. The *political* parties operating in the area, the number of active workers and institutions in each village, where elected representatives come from, the number of government officials who came from the village or visit the village and so on were indications of the state of political growth. For *religious* centres, the major fairs and festivals of various religions, castes and tribes, the number of marriages and size of marriage parties or death ceremonies and expenses incurred showed the pattern of movement for the satisfaction of these social needs. Finally, where did village people go for *recreation*—recreation of traditional kinds or modern cinemas? Where are the pubs? How much investment and services were needed in these different activities?

The study then attempted to define the social, economic and political service areas of different sectors of human activity by gathering both inflow and outflow data to determine how all settlements relate to each other. Consequentially, we deduced how best these systems and the social institutions which they include can be structured and spatially located to effect maximal savings in infrastructure investment and traffic and transport costs and thus to plan for more efficient management of all resources for human life.

The historical development of the present settlements and service institutions sheds light on the pattern of social, economic and political activity under the existing technological conditions. All trend data which could be gathered accurately, particularly during the last decade, show historically the growth of the various sectors of social and material development. These trends have provided data for the realistic appraisal of the potential growth of all sectors of life and permit the design and evaluation of alternative courses of planned action. Specifically, the Growth Centre study has attempted to work out replicable ways to integrate the growth of these sectors and thereby identify and encourage the development of viable rural–urban communities, which can offer a variety of economic opportunities and a range of social services and institutions comparable to those provided by cities which now attract rural immigrants.

In addition to a number of maps and a great deal of descriptive information, seven different questionnaires were designed to gather the data. They are (a) a block questionnaire, (b) a town questionnaire, (c) a village questionnaire, (d) a household questionnaire, (e) a shopkeepers questionnaire, (f) a cottage industries questionnaire, (g) an industries questionnaire. The questionnaires were pre-tested in a number of states, and the format was revised several times until a highly pre-coded version was evolved similar to the National Sample Survey format.

Twenty districts were selected in nearly all states of the union, and a study area consisting usually of one CD block was used for the first round of data collection. Within each study area for the block, town and village, questionnaires data from all units in the block were gathered. For the remaining questionnaires, a sampling procedure was devised in order to get a reasonable estimate for the study area.

The project was managed by a central committee of direction and an executive committee in the Ministry of Community Development. A central research cell sponsored by the Ford Foundation acted as the technical arm for the design and execution of the projects. The state governments appointed the field cell officers who collected all the data, helped with the analysis, prepared the plans in consultation with the central research cell and aided the implementation of the plans.

Since both the theoretical and operational aspects of the project were new, special training courses were organized for approximately 80 officials from the different participating states. The states began to recruit the staff at different times and, therefore, four batches received training of about eight weeks duration: Course I, 15 June–15 August 1970; Course 2, 15 October–15 December 1970; Course 3, 15 January–15 March 1971, and Course 4, 10 December–7 February 1972. The first three courses were organized by the National Institute of Community Development, Hyderabad, and the fourth by the Indian Institute of Public Administration, New Delhi.

On account of this wide phasing of project initiation in different states, (from August 1970 to February 1972) the data gathering and processing have been spread out over a long time span. This has, to some extent, been fortunate because of difficulties experienced in developing the computer programmes to fit the configuration of the Delhi University IBM 360/44 computer. After having designed the software for the Delhi computer, malfunctioning of the computer, power failures and even university strikes caused inordinate delays, which resulted in some strains in the project management.

As the data were processed and tabulated in as convenient a manner as possible for the field cells, batches of staff members from states came to New Delhi for one–two-week planning seminars. Three such seminars have been held so far for 13 of the field cells—September 1972, February 1973 and May 1973. The fourth seminar for the remaining seven cells is scheduled for September 1973. For the purposes of illustration, data from only one field cell are used in this chapter and the problems of analysis and planning are surveyed with reference only to the agricultural sector.

AGRICULTURAL PLANNING

The two foci of *agricultural planning* for this chapter are *agricultural marketing* and *fertilizer distribution*. From the angle of economics, both these activities are concerned with marginal outputs and inputs, which may manifest the increment in the net area sown, the area irrigated, changes in cropping patterns or changes to high-yielding varieties (HYVs) of crops. The logic of selecting the marketing activities and fertilizer distribution activities was that the methodology of planning for the movement, storage and distribution of materials, money or men, in and out of all villages in a given study area could be illustrated. The activities connected with these two foci are neither the only agricultural activities which need to be planned for, nor are they necessarily the primary 'problem' of agriculture needing attention in a particular area.

In addition to these two primary agricultural functions, the principal features of the agricultural situation in all villages will be described along with the existing marketing network for the four or five major crops and the existing fertilizer distribution system. A general spatial analysis of the block will be conducted to partition the block into different levels of spatial reach. Beyond the villages at a maximum travel distance of 4–5 kilometers the primary service villages or *growth centres* and the villages within their ambit are identified, and the block is thereby divided into service areas each with one (or possibly two) growth centres. Each sub-area of the block is analysed for its marketed surplus, fertilizer input and the agricultural facilities available.

The main agricultural problems will be identified out of the analysis of both the agricultural situation and the gaps found in the infrastructure facilities. Spatial planning models to determine the storage or transportation gaps in the infrastructure to ensure a convenient movement of commodities will also be constructed. On account of the recent takeover of wholesale wheat trading, the data bearing on the Punjab study area, Chamkaur Sahib block in Ropar district are used in this chapter because they afford a unique opportunity to fairly accurately gauge the marketable surplus in each sub-region and plan the physical and financial facilities for the smooth 'takeover' of the wheat trade. Except sugarcane, which goes straight to the factories, wheat constitutes the major portion of the marketable surplus, particularly during the spring season.

In short, the methodology of agricultural planning surveyed in this chapter will be illustrative at several levels. *First*, only agricultural marketing for the principal crops and the fertilizer inputs will be selected to illustrate input-output planning problems. *Second*, wheat marketing will be given special attention. *Third*, a general spatial rationale for convenient accessibility and the detailed planning for one sub-area of the block will be worked out to focus attention on the problems of movement out of the village to the primary growth centre. Thus, the final sketch plans for agriculture will demonstrate how the wheat surplus will move within each sub-area and how fertilizer will move into all villages through selected growth centres and what the most logical transportation linkages would be.

Characteristics of the Study Area

The study area, Chamkaur Sahib, forms part of Ropar district which came into existence at the time of the reorganization of Punjab and Haryana states in the year 1966. Ropar district consists of three sub-divisions with six blocks, namely Chamkaur Sahib and Ropar in Ropar sub-division, Kharar and Majri in Kharar sub-division and Anandpur Sahib and Nurpur Bedi in Anandpur Sahib sub-division.

The development block Chamkaur Sahib was started on 1 August 1957 as a pre-extension block. Now, it is in the post-stage two. It is bounded by Majri and Ropar blocks in the East and touches the boundaries of Machhiwara block in Ludhiana district in the West. In the North, the River Sutlej separates it from the district Hoshiarpur, while in the South it meets the boundary of Bassi block of Patiala district.

Chamkaur Sahib is situated at a distance of 15 kilometres from the district headquarters, Ropar. This village has its association with Guru Gobind Singh, the 10th Guru, who left Anandpur Sahib during his fight with the Mughals. He reached Kotla Nihang village and asked the local Pathan residents for shelter. The latter jestingly pointed towards the live kiln as a fit place for him to stay in. The story goes that the moment the Guru took his horse to the kiln, the fire went out instantly. To commemorate this miracle, a big Gurdwara has been constructed where people come from far and near to pay their homage. It is known as 'Bhatha Sahib' which word has been derived from the brick kiln. On being chased by the enemy, Guru Gobind Singh left for Chamkaur Sahib with his retinue where he camped in the garden of Raja Bidhi Chand. The Raja was indifferent, with the result, the Guru established himself in position in the fortress. At this place, Guru Gobind Singh fought his last battle where he sacrificed his two elder sons. The place is now the site of an imposing Gurdwara and is called 'Katalgarh' in Chamkaur Sahib.

The total geographical area of the block is 31,646 hectares. It consists of 185 settlements including one town. Twenty-two villages of the block are uninhabited. There are 100 Panchayats which have administrative units at the village level, under the Punjab Gram Panchayat Act, 1952. There is a three-tier system in the state, namely: zila parishad, Panchayat samiti and Panchayat at the district, block and village level. Chamkaur Sahib has its own Panchayat samiti headed by its elected chairman while the block development and Panchayat officer is the executive officer working under the direction of the Panchayat samiti. They are responsible for the administrative and development work in the block. The Panchayat samiti is answerable both to the zila parishad and the deputy commissioner for their respective functions.

According to 1951 census, the population of the block was 62,045, which rose to 72,065 in 1961 and 86,541 in 1971 showing an increase of 39 per cent in two decades. The density of population of the study area is 273 persons per square kilometre.

The climate of the block is fairly hot in summer and cold in winter with an average temperature ranging from 10°C to 45°C. It has an annual average rainfall of 169 centimetres which starts from the first week of July and continues to the end of September. The soil varies from alluvial in the upper plain to sandy loam in the low-lying region.

'Land' Utilization

Data were collected from each village of the pattern of land utilization as recorded in the revenue categories of use. In order to get some picture of the changes which have taken place over the last decade comparable data were obtained from the 1960 and 1970 land records. Table 7.1 presents the arithmetic sums of the land utilization of all 185 villages (inhabited and uninhabited) in the block.

The net area sown has increased from 79 to 84 per cent and the area irrigated from 48 to 78 per cent, that is, from about 12,000 hectares to over 20,000 hectares. This means that only about 5,000 hectares remain to be irrigated to cover the entire cultivated area. The intensive development of the block is also reflected by the fact that there is no area under forests; cultivable waste had dropped from 1,250 hectares to barely 500 hectares and current fallows from 500 to 200 hectares.

Revenue data in most states do not always reflect the actual situation and furthermore some changes may have occurred between 1970 and 1973. Nevertheless, this block reflects agricultural cropping nearly reaching its full potential of double cropping—47,000 hectares out of a possible 52,000 hectares. It should, however, be stated that this is a traditional Rabi wheat growing area which receives over 160 centimetres of rain in the Kharif season and can grow and has grown, even without irrigation, two crops on nearly all arable land.

The natural endowment of Chamkaur Sahib block is enhanced by the development of its irrigation potential. Not only do two major canals pass through the heart of the block, but it is bordered on the north by the Sutlej River. Canal irrigation, however, covers only 600

Table 7.1 Land Utilization Pattern: Chamkaur Sahib Block, Punjab, 1960 and 1970

Use Category	Area (Hectares) 1960	Area (Hectares) 1970
Forests	0	0
Land put to non-agricultural use	2,928	2,964
Barren & unculturable land	1,141	914
Permanent pastures & common grazing	197	196
Miscellaneous tree crops & groves	6	3
Culturable waste	1,253	496
Fallow land other than current fallows	678	429
Current fallows	480	193
Net area sown	24,852	26,451
Total geographic area	31,535	31,646
Area sown more than once	15,144	20,713
Area irrigated	11,922	20,635
Total cropped area	39,996	47,164

Source: Author's own.

out of its 22,000 hectares of irrigated area in the Rabi (winter) season, 17,500 hectares are irrigated by shallow tube wells, 2 000 hectares by deep tube wells and 2 000 hectares by surface percolation wells. Thus, well irrigation commands and de facto is the primary method of irrigation chosen by the farmers in the block.

The water resources reflect a triple indemnity which merits a commentary.

First, the natural rains of over 160 centimetres in an alluvial plain would traditionally permit 60–70 per cent of the arable area to be double cropped. Second, the older Sutlej canal system passing through the northern half of the block and the new Bhakra canal now passing through the central and the southern parts of the block should have commanded almost the entire block area. In fact, according to our data these canals command less than 600 hectares or less than 2 per cent of the block, and in the northern 'Bet' area of the block have caused problems of salination. Thus, a third system of irrigation wells have come into operation. The farmers' main strategy has been to rely on shallow tube wells, which command virtually the entire arable land. About two-thirds of these tube wells are, however, energized by diesel oil in the hydel energy shadow of the Bhakra dam.

Hydrologically, the farmers have stumbled into probably the most effective ground water management system. Space would not permit a longer commentary, nor has this survey collected any hydrological data of sufficient accuracy to warrant anything beyond intelligent conjecture. In this rich alluvial soil of the upper Indus valley, the old and new canal systems raised the water tables to levels that may have caused salination or proved detrimental to the root growth of trees or even crops. A large number of shallow tube wells (3,700 or about 20 per village) have lowered the water tables sufficiently to permit the healthy growth of plants and perhaps inadvertently prevent salination. In addition, it has provided the farmer with water whenever the needs of exotic dwarfs demanded, freeing him from the capriciousness of the water delivery schedules of the irrigation department.

Chamkaur Sahib block is richly endowed with 'land' in the economic sense. It has greatly enhanced its natural endowment with a man-made system of irrigation canals and wells, which is today capable of providing irrigation to its entire arable land for 12 months. Punjab's extreme climate permits a wide range of crops through the 12 months of the year. Therefore, not only double but also triple cropping is potentially feasible on nearly all the arable land. There is a possibility of bringing another 2,000 hectares of cultivable waste, barren uncultivable waste and fallow land under cultivation, tree crops or permanent pasture crops. There is a critical need that the rich endowment of ground water resources be more accurately surveyed and managed. The block already has a 'Bet' area suffering from salinity problems, and the general movement of salts in rising and declining water tables could spell disaster. These complex problems cannot be left to the 'native' wisdom of the Punjabi farmers who have fortunately managed their water resources extremely well, blissfully ignorant of the rise and fall of their water tables and the movement of salts in their native soil. In short, Chamkaur Sahib block presents a case of rich 'land' resources which if fully and wisely utilized can yield three crops, or if improperly exploited could become a wasteland.

Crop Production and Marketing

The five major crops in the block in terms of acreage are: wheat, maize, sugarcane, groundnut and rice (Table 7.2). All other crops combined do not occupy even 1,000 out of the 36,000 hectares of cropped area. Wheat occupies just over 50 per cent of the total cropped area, maize about 20 per cent and sugarcane about 15 per cent. Groundnut with 3,000 hectares and paddy with 2,000 hectares are relative newcomers. There are problems encountered with groundnut and the real potential of sunflower as an oilseed substitute.

The breakdown of acreages under HYVs and local varieties are given for these five crops (Table 7.2): 27,000 hectares or over 75 per cent of the entire area is under high-yielding strains. This underlines the vigorous innovativeness of the Punjabi farmer. Almost the entire wheat and sugarcane production is under these high-investment and high-yielding strains. The reported yields of wheat are almost double the yields of the local varieties. HYVs maize and groundnut do not show such dramatic differences. Paddy gives about 50 per cent more yield and may become a new crop because on a per hectare basis it has the highest value of production.

There were, 144,000 tonnes of sugarcane produced: about 80 per cent of which was sold to the sugar factory at Morinda. Last year, there were 57,000 tonnes of wheat produced in the block out of which about 35,000 tonnes were marketed. This year's production was reported to be as good if not better, and therefore, the marketed margin would be of a similar order. Later in this chapter, this marketed quantity is broken down to figures for the micro-regions and then for the villages in each micro-region.

The total value of agricultural products at current market rates was estimated at 7.32 crores equivalent to a per capita agricultural income of 850. The value of the wheat produced was 4.4 crores and sugarcane accounted for 1.15 crores.

The pie diagram (Figure 7.1) depicts the relative value of the different crops grown in Chamkaur Sahib block and the hatched proportion shows the proportion sold. The pie shows that just about two-thirds of the agricultural production is marketed, indicating a marked shift from a subsistence to a market economy. About 1 kilogram per head per day of food grains is kept for consumption, which is

Table 7.2 Crops Produced and Marketed in 1971–1972, Chamkaur Sahib Block, Punjab

Crop		Area	Yield/Hectare		Total Production		Total Marketed		Per cent Marketed
			Quantity	Value	Quantity	Value	Quantity	Value	
		(Hectares)	(Quintals)		(Tonnes)	(000)	(Tonnes)	(000)	
Groundnut	HYV	1,484	12	1,572	1,824	2,390	1,674	2,193	92
	Local	1,643	11	1,441	1,770	2,318	1,634	2,141	92
Maize	HYV	1,317	24	1,320	3,097	1,703	1,477	813	48
	Local	5,884	17	935	9,898	5,444	5,109	2,810	52
Paddy	HYV	1,342	45	2,520	6,090	3,411	5,210	2,918	86
	Local	461	29	1,624	1,324	741	1,126	631	85
Sugarcane	HYV	4,630	310	2,408	143,725	11,498	113,062	9,045	79
	Local	10	40	320	40	3	20	2	50
Wheat	HYV	18,026	32	2,464	57,004	438,93	34,862	26,844	61
	Local	383	18	1,386	689	531	516	398	75
Others	HYV	391	—		1,607	849	911	342	—
	Local	445	—		1,113	409	721	218	—
Sub-total	HYV	27,190			213,347	637,44	157,196	4,2155	
	Local	8,826			14,834	9,444	9,126	6,200	
Total		36,016			228,181	731,90	166,322	483,55	

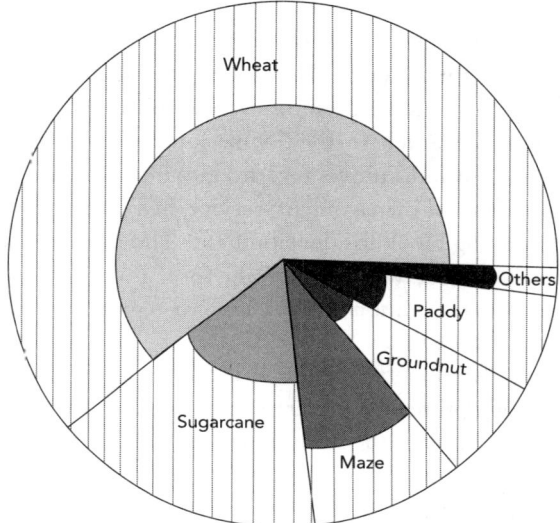

Figure 7.1 *Value of Major Crops Produced and Proportions Sold*

equivalent to about 3,500 calories. (In addition to the principal crops the block has a large number of milch cattle and a great deal of vegetable and fruit production, not shown in Figure 7.1 which provides adequate quantities of protective foods).

While this chapter is concerned mainly with the planning and marketing of wheat, the principal crop, the data show, that the staple *food* in this block is still wheat. Planners should, therefore, be conscious of the basic needs of food for the whole population in the block. The data from Chamkaur Sahib villages indicate that in spite of the large margin marketed, the per capita availability of food would provide, at a conservative estimate, over 4 000 calories and an adequate supply of proteins (the household questionnaires provide data of the relative levels of consumption between the different socio-economic groups, but these results will not be discussed in this chapter).

MICRO-REGIONAL PARTITIONS

What should be the unit of management for effective agricultural planning? The State Planning Board of West Bengal has put forward a

10,000 acre unit, that is, a 4,000 hectare unit. A unit of this size would comprise 10–20 villages which is about the average span of control for a VLW. The third tier of the Panchayat system was often 8-10 villages. Hitherto, none of these units was conceived as having any real standards of the land base, the population base or maximum travel distance in mind. As India moves forward into integrated rural planning, it is this lowest unit of management, service area or micro-region that is the basic building block for development. The primary focus of the growth centre project was 'to identify focal points of growth and the villages within their ambit', that is, a micro-region organized around one viable growth centre.

The project has identified several levels of 'growth centres' and the methods of optimizing either service populations or minimum travel distance. Although the study areas selected are typically for only one block, the methodologies developed can, with modification, be adapted to district or even *state* levels. However, at the higher levels, the location of the growth centres, growth nodes or growth poles is explained by historical and political choice, often by centuries of evolution. 'Rational' erasing of the pages of history is no longer feasible, when the location has turned out to be spatially irrational.

It is at the lowest reaches of political and economic control that effective standards of spatial reach, population base and (for the purposes of this chapter) the agricultural base need to be scientifically devised. The British essentially used the district and ultimately sub-division as the political unit of control. The next lower units were the *tehsil*, *taluk* and the revenue village was the lowest rung of control. The massive cadastral surveys and agricultural crop-cutting surveys based on the aforementioned land use categories (Table 7.1) and conducted from 1910 to 1935 still form the sheet anchor of land classification and form the basis of crop estimates today.

Without entering into any controversies about the virtues of the imperial inheritors of the legacy of a mercantile East India Company, let it be said that the accuracy of the land surveys and the cropping estimates undertaken by the civilian pioneers have hardly been surpassed during the 50 years of agricultural research and management in India. Even in this project, the classical land revenue data were used, supplemented at the village level, with data supplied by the VLW and primary data gathered from functional informants in the village. The levels of inaccuracy that have become evident in going through this exercise of 'validating' the most elementary land, irrigation or crop data, are, to put it mildly, quite alarming.

How can a nation plan the takeover of wheat trade when basic figures like the acres under wheat in any village for 1971–1972 or its yield have a plus or minus error of 10–20 per cent? How much error is compounded when one adds up 185 villages each with errors on area multiplied by errors on yield, and then gives an 'estimate' of the acreage and production of wheat? What are the biases when the revenue department or the irrigation department or the agriculture department record their respective administrative intelligence? On the other hand, this is the fundamental database upon which scientific agricultural planning and management can rest. At the lowest level, our bureaucratic caste system relegates to very poorly paid and poorly trained staff the critical task of data gathering—the foundation of rational agricultural planning.

Turning back to the problem of the unit of planning and management of our agricultural economy, in this project, the block was partitioned at *three levels of spatial reach*. At the first level, there is one centre to serve the entire block—Morinda Town. It serves the entire population of 98,742 and the average travel distance would be 9.3 kilometres. along the existing roads, with a maximum travel distance of 23 kilometres. To the farthest village. At the second level, two centres were chosen which brought all villages within 13 kilometers with five centres—Morinda, Chamkaur Sahib, Bela, Manali and Kainaur—all villages come within 10 kilometers of one or other of these centres.

At the lowest level above the village, with 15 centres, all villages would be within 5 kilometres or 3 miles of a service or growth centre. The number of villages within the ambit of each centre and the total cropped area is shown in Table 7.3. The study area has a network of metalled roads which connects all the growth centres. The connections are typically vertical, that is, lower order centres will have their connections with level II or level I higher order centres, but not necessarily horizontally between the lower order centres. Within each of the micro-regions the connection between villages and the service centres is mainly by *kucha* road. Bullock-carts still seem to be

Table 7.3 Quantities of Wheat Produced and Marketed and Fertilizer Purchased by Micro-regions in Chamkaur Sahib Block, Punjab

Service Centre	No. of Village	Cropped Area (Hectares)		Wheat Produced (Quintals)	Wheat Marketed (Quintals)	Fertilizer (Quintals)	
		Total	Wheat			Recommended	Purchased
Behrampur Bet	22	5,233	1,871	39,650	24,725	6,783	7,250
Dhangrali	4	1,652	650	23,098	13,380	2,231	1,372
Morinda town	20	8,563	3,176	87,727	55,613	11,343	10,983
Chamkaur Sahib	11	2,617	831	26,463	15,685	3,186	3,120
Asarpur	17	1,509	633	13,404	9,299	2,806	1,113
Bela	32	4,214	1,312	35,400	22,485	5,124	7,880
Karanpur	12	4,627	1,408	45,320	28,110	5,913	5,880
Bode Saidpur	9	3,045	1,329	37,705	23,546	3,932	5,975
Bhojha Mehra	6	1,732	524	11,221	7,652	1,822	1,765
Salempur	6	2,884	689	20,539	12,457	2,962	5,241
Hawara	10	4,470	2,109	122,364	68,345	6,544	9,165
Rurki Hiran	12	4,358	1,279	39,156	25,834	5,166	11,349

Ratangarh	9	2,442	1,043	27,440	16,719	3,549	3,817
Khant	8	2,353	871	31,607	19,321	2,965	5221
Debar	7	1 426	525	14,907	9 142	1 936	1 940
Total	185	51,127	18,250	567,001	352,313	66,261*	81,071

Note: *Quintals of nutrients should be multiplied by four to get the rough quantity of fertilizer.

the predominant mode of transporting of agricultural inputs including fertilizers to the village and also of transporting of agricultural outputs including wheat to the marketplaces. Only for the transport of machinery and to some extent to transport sugarcane, are trucks or tractors used as supplementary means of transportation. This information on the modes of transporting agricultural commodities indicates that, in spite of an extremely advanced market-oriented economy, transportation methods are still quite primitive. This is probably because the primary connection from the village to the service centre is a *kucha* road and therefore, farmers continue to use the bullock-carts to go to markets or to purchase agricultural inputs.

Estimated Quantities of Wheat Marketed and Fertilizers Purchased

In order to make a more accurate plan and manage the inputs and outputs of the agricultural sector, one must obtain sufficiently accurate information to make estimates of the quantities of crops marketed and the quantities of agricultural inputs purchased. Hence, the total production of each crop in each partition of the block is sub-totalled along with the quantities of fertilizers purchased in each micro-region. These are presented in Table 7.3.

The quantity marketed in each micro-region varies from 7,000 to 70,000 quintals. Hence, each sub-region will need different sizes of storage facilities to accommodate the market flows. Similarly, the quantity of fertilizer being purchased in each micro-region varies a great deal, from 1,100 quintals to 11,000 quintals. In another column of Table 7.3 the computations of the recommended dosages of fertilizer are shown. Unfortunately, these dosages are in quintals of nitrogen, phosphorus and potassium (NPK) nutrients and not in terms of the quantity of fertilizer. Typically, the nitrogenous fertilizers have a little over 20 per cent of nitrogen; the phosphatic fertilizers have a little below 20 per cent of phosphates and potash fertilizers about 50–60 per cent of potassium. Hence by using a rough figure of 25 per cent nutrient weight to fertilizer weight, the quantity of fertilizer recommended for the entire block would be approximately 260,000 quintals against the present level of utilization of 80,000 quintals. Thus, even in the state that uses the highest doses of fertilizer, we have not yet achieved one-third of the level recommended.

The data was collected on location of the places to which farmers send their wheat and the places from which they buy their fertilizer. The data for wheat marketing shows that there are essentially only three places at which wheat is marketed in this study area—Morinda. Chamkaur Sahib and Bela. About 20 per cent of the wheat goes to five markets outside the study area.

The distribution of fertilizer, however, is very different. Within the block there are 15 distributing centres, but two of these centres essentially dominate more than half the villages. A small amount of fertilizer is also purchased from four centres outside the block. There are theoretically cooperatives in every village of the block. But a number of these cooperatives are inoperative, because previous loans have not been cleared. Thus the villages in the block obtain nearly all their fertilizers from the higher order service centres.

The existing picture of movement suggests that for the purposes of marketing perhaps 15 centres are not necessary for wheat. However, for the convenient distribution of fertilizer 15 service centres would be more efficient.

An assessment of the volume of wheat marketed and fertilizers purchased for each micro-region reveals that if the functions of fertilizer distribution and wheat procurement under the new takeover programme were combined into one institutional structure, the godown capacities would be more fully utilized. During the sowing season of wheat, from November to January, fertilizers would be moving through the godowns to the farmer. After the harvest season for wheat, from March to June, wheat would be stored in these godowns on their way to higher-level markets.

During the sowing period marginal amounts of groundnuts, maize and paddy would be passing into the market, and hence, planning of the quantities of those crops marketed would also be necessary to estimate the warehousing capacities. Sugarcane from all villages moves directly to the factories in Morinda and needs no storage facilities. Thus, wheat is clearly the commodity which accounts for the largest share of the storage requirement: 350,000 tonnes out of 450,000 tonnes of all other crops marketed in the block. Most of the storage capacity would be needed during the spring months from March till June.

Behrampur Bet Micro-Region

Within one micro-region the village by village data are presented in Table 7.4. The data on the total cropped area and the area under wheat are first presented. Based on average yield reported typically by the VLW, the wheat production is estimated. By asking the VLW and selected informants the proportion sold last year, the quantity marketed is computed. If all farmers could have been persuaded to bring all their wheat surplus to one warehouse in Behrampur Bet, about 25,000 quintals would have arrived during April and May of 1972. Actually, most farmers in this sub-region took their wheat to Chamkaur Sahib.

The last two columns give the fertilizer recommendation and the purchases in the previous year. Again, using the 25 per cent thumb rule, about 27,000 quintals were recommended and 7,250 quintals were actually purchased, less than a third of the potential usage.

The wheat marketed from each village is transferred to Behrampur Bet, the hypothetical growth centre. The volume of inputs of fertilizers going to these villages on kacha roads is also assessed. In addition, a number of other crops, and a number of additional agricultural inputs are bought. Some villages have cooperative societies. Unfortunately, no data about cooperatives having godowns and the capacity of these godowns were gathered.

In order to theoretically manage the movement of all crops produced and all inputs purchased, not only has the capacity of all storage to be obtained but the seasonal movement of input and output has also to be planned.

AGRICULTURAL MANAGEMENT

The management of our land, water, crop production and agricultural purchases at present rests with the individual cultivator's family. Each family has reasonably accurate information about these resources. At the village level, the cadastral survey map with the classification of each

Table 7.4 Quantities of Wheat Produced and Marketed and Fertilizer Purchased by Behrampur Bet Micro-region, Chamkaur Sahib Block, Punjab

	Dependent Villages (Place Code)	Cropped Area (Hectares)		Wheat Produced (Quintals)	Wheat Marketed (Quintals)	Fertilizer	
		Total	Wheat			Recommended (Quintals)	Purchased (Quintals)
1	036	10	4	100	66	13	22
2	040	195	100	2,500	1,750	258	25
3	057	212	84	2,100	1,050	280	300
4	071	168	76	1,976	1,581	222	—
5	072	161	38	760	380	212	800
6	087	196	50	750	495	259	140
7	104	336	134	2,948	2,211	444	1,000
8	106	101	26	520	312	133	160
9	108	302	110	2,200	1,540	399	600
10	115	549	215	5,375	2,687	725	308
11	123	389	203	4,060	2,030	514	1,100
12	124	208	72	1,080	540	275	100
13	135	66	23	575	460	87	—

(Continued)

(Continued)

Dependent Villages (Place Code)	Cropped Area (Hectares)		Wheat Produced (Quintals)	Wheat Marketed (Quintals)	Fertilizer	
	Total	Wheat			Recommended (Quintals)	Purchased (Quintals)
14	136	286	60	1,500	750	378	160
15	144	148	66	990	653	196	600
16	155	538	210	4,200	3,360	710	450
17	165	101	48	576	288	133	120
18	176	306	130	2,600	1,300	404	95
19	179	370	142	2,840	2,272	489	500
20	024	473	80	2,000	1,000	625	770
Sub Total		**5,115**	**1,871**	**39,650**	**24,725**	**6,756***	**7,250**

Note: *Quintals of nutrients should be multiplied by four to obtain the rough quantity of fertilizer.

plot, along with annual changes, can yield a reasonable estimate of the land utilization pattern. The Patwari is, however, neither technically nor politically the best person to prepare such a classificatory system indicating the land utilization pattern. Although the VLW attempts to keep a record of acreage and yields of the main crops, no really accurate information is available of the output of all crops, the proportion marketed and the amounts of inputs purchased. Water resources, however, cannot be so easily estimated and no systematic groundwater survey system is in existence for all villages.

Without reasonably accurate information on these basic agricultural facts, the entire management of the agricultural enterprise becomes a probabilistic guessing game for which no reliability or validity checks are built in.

As a follow-through of this growth centre project for which a number of 'plans' are being drawn up there is a need for a technical engineering feasibility study for the package of agro-service plans—soil testing for the fertilizer recommendations, ground water surveys and power needs for irrigation plans, road surveys for approach roads or upgrading of interconnecting *pucca* roads, agro-processing industries, more accurate crop surveys for predicting yields and marketable margins, warehousing capacity surveys for multi-service cooperatives: farm mechanization service centres and so on. It is from such feasibility studies that a 'bank' of viable projects can be designed for being executed over a period of 5–10 years.

The most rational selection of the lowest level 'growth centre' and its tributary villages should not be taken lightly. The present intersectoral necessities and future demands must be weighed and once the decisions are taken on distance and population standards the decision on the plan of linkage between the lower order to higher-order centres is also taken. Once this lowest-order standard is set, the mathematical honeycomb of standards for the higher level centres is mathematically predetermined. The linkage system of a 4 kilometre growth centre will not mesh with a 5 kilometre. Growth centre system. Between districts and states serious interface problems will arise geographically and also socially, and such problems will need the planners' attention.

In five to ten of the 20 pilot 'growth centre' blocks, not only should the feasibility studies be carried out, but even one micro-region should be adopted for experimental execution in order to test the viability of the management structure.

There are a number of blocks like Chamkaur Sahib which are richly endowed and have a potential not only for full employment in the agricultural sector but also for considerable generation of secondary and tertiary employment in agro-industries and agro-services. Case experiments in these micro-regions to demonstrate the costs and benefits of total and integrated agricultural planning and management should claim high priority in the present paradoxical state of uncertainty combined with clear opportunities for progress inherent in Indian agriculture.

ACKNOWLEDGEMENT

The author is indebted to his colleagues in the growth centre project particularly Dr B. R. Patil, Nayan Saini and Bina Aggarwal who co-authored an earlier version of the agricultural sector chapter prepared for a seminar.

REFERENCES

Andrade, C. P., & Roy, P. (1969). *Preliminary report on pilot projects for integrated area development*. The Ford Foundation and the Council for Social Development.
Baskin, C. (1966). *The central places of Southern Germany*. Prentice Hall.
Benku, M. (1966). Rural planning in Poland. In J. C. Fisher (Ed.), *City and regional planning in Poland*. Cornell University Press.
Berry, B. J. L. (1967). *Geography of market centres and retail distribution*. Prentice Hall.
Christaller, W. (1933). *Die Zentralen Orte in Suddeutschland*. Fisher Publishing Company.
Douglas, E. (1941). *Communities and administrative areas of Greene County, Georgia*. US Department of Agriculture.
Fliegel, F. C., Roy, P., Sen, L. K., & Kivlin, J. E. (1968). *Agricultural Innovation in Indian Villages*. National Institute of Community Development.
Galpin, C. J. (1915). *The social anatomy of an agricultural community*. Agricultural Experiment Station of University of Wisconsin.
Losch, A. (1941). *Die Raumliche Ordnung der Wirtschaft*. Fischer Publishing Company.
Millikan, M. F., & Hapgood, D. (1967). *No easy harvest*. Little Brown & Company.
Ministry of Food and Agriculture. (1969). *Pilot research project in growth centre project design*. Department of Community Development.

Roy, P. (1968). *Two blades of grass*. National Institute of Community Development.
Roy, P., & Project on the Diffusion of Innovations in Rural Societies. (1968). *Agricultural innovation among Indian farmers*. National Institute of Community Development.
Sanders, I. T., & Douglas, E. (1940). *Alabama rural communities: A study of Chilton County*. Bulletin of the State College for Women.
Sen, L. K., Wanmali, S., Bose, S., Mishra, G. K., & Ramesh, K. S. (1971). *Planning rural growth centres for integrated area development. A study in Miryalguda Taluka.* National Institute of Community Development.
Singh, K. N., Rao, C. S. S., & Sahay, B. N. (1970). *Research in extension education for accelerating development process*. Indian Society of Agricultural Extension.
Vohra, B. B. (1972). A charter for the land. *Economic & Political Weekly, 8*(3).
Woglom, W. H., & Stolper W. F. (1954). *The economics of location*. Yale University.
Zhivkov, T. (1969). *Problems of the construction of an advanced socialist society in Bulgaria*. Sofia Press.

Chapter 8

Agricultural Modernization in Rural Maharashtra*
Myth and Reality

B. B. Mohanty

In the post-Independence India, systematic attempts have been made to modernize agriculture through a new strategy on the basis of water, seed and fertilizer technology package keeping growth and equity as the prime concern. On the basis of Satara, which is one of the highly agricultural modernized districts of Maharashtra, the study analyses the socio-economic effects of the new measures on various categories of the rural population both at the micro and macro levels. The results of the study indicate that though the collective impact of these measures has substantially enhanced the agricultural production, it has systematically bypassed the equity issue. The conditions of the benefit of the new measures being relative to the resource ownership position, the large farmers have emerged as a class of rich farmers who dominate the socio-economic and political spheres of rural society. Therefore, the chapter concludes that the sole objective of agricultural transformation is to create a market and growth-oriented rich farmer-led agriculture and the question of equality is a myth which constitutes the integral part of the political process of manufacturing consent for a regime of domination and inequality.

---

* *Social Change*, 31(4), 2001.

THE PERSPECTIVE

At the time of Independence, India inherited relatively stagnant and backward agriculture founded on highly inegalitarian rural society. In recognition of this basic proposition, a new normative model was adopted in the post-Independence period for agricultural development in tune with the 'democratic' and 'socialistic' spirit of the new Constitution in which the prime concern was to create a progressive and egalitarian rural society on the one hand and to maximize agricultural production on the other. However, the initial measures introduced in the first two decades of Independence (1947–1967) mainly in the form of the community development programme and land reforms could not lead either to the substantial increase in farm productivity or to the removal of socio-economic inequalities (Dev, 1997; Dhanagare, 1984; Joshi, 1971). Subsequently, since the Fourth Five-Year Plan, efforts have been made to modernize agriculture through a new strategy based on water-seed-fertilizer-technology package keeping growth and distributive justice as the guiding factors. Thus, the policy of growth with equity has been projected as the main thrust of agricultural planning in India, and it has been in operation in all the Five-Year Plans though with varying degrees of emphasis. In fact, for a long run, sustainable agricultural development increased productivity has to be accompanied by a concomitant increase in social justice (Mencher, 1978; Sen, 1997). Moreover, the conventional argument by some of the economists that growth and equity are incompatible has been challenged and proved wrong (Benabou, 1996; Mencher, 1974; Psacharopoulos, 1991). In such a context, how far the agricultural modernizing measures have achieved the claimed objectives draws special attention.

India, like the other Third-World countries, is modernizing its economy and society on the capitalist path. In such a process, the prime concern of the state is to maximize the output, and the question of removal of inequality tends to be undermined. The policy is designed to safeguard and promote the interests of the industrialists, rich farmers and landlords who can pursue a market and profit-oriented productive organization (Byres, 1981; Desai, 1984; Dhanagare, 1987; Kurien, 1981; Parthasarathy, 1970; Rutten, 1995). The state, through its legal repressive machinery, tries to see that any violation of this major framework is prevented and repressed (Desai, 1975, p. 152). Moreover, like other South Asian countries, planning in India which is viewed as 'democratic planning' in the popular notion is fundamentally a political programme through which the state tries to impress the masses in order to get their support without much coercion or regimentation (Myrdal, 1972, p. 362). Therefore, the state representing the industrialists, capitalist or rich farmers, landlords and traders formulates policies that can concede the demands of these propertied classes on the one side and produce an ideological effect which is responsive to 'popular' will on the other. The poor masses are provided with a make-belief world through propaganda and slogan of the welfare state and populist measures. Thus, the main postulate of agrarian transformation is to create conditions and opportunities for the further prosperity of the rich landowning farmers. It can be substantiated by any empirical study.

Against this background, based on the analysis both at the village as well as district levels, the present study attempts to examine the socio-economic effects of agricultural modernization in rural Maharashtra with reference to a highly agricultural modernized district of the state. The chapter has three broad objectives: (a) to examine the nature, extent and trend of agricultural modernization, (b) to analyse the impact of modernizing measures on various sections of the rural population and (c) to assess the changes in the pattern of agricultural production and socio-economic inequalities.

METHODS OF THE STUDY

Keeping in mind the purpose of the study, the highest agricultural modernized district of Maharashtra was identified on the basis of four major parameters: area under irrigation (percentage of net irrigated area to net sown area), mechanization (number of tractors, oil engines and pump sets per 000 hectares of the gross cropped area), per hectare (gross cropped area) consumption of chemical fertilizer and percentage of area under high-yielding varieties (HYV) to the cropped area. Selecting the district ranking method was followed in which each district was given a rank on the basis of its position against each indicator separately and the total rank was obtained by adding all the ranks. However, Greater Bombay was excluded from analysis due to its negligible and even non-appearance in most of the agricultural reports. On the basis of this procedure, of the 29 districts of Maharashtra (excluding Greater Bombay), Satara was selected for the study.

Looking at the agricultural situation of Satara district, it is found that the irrigated belt is more advanced than the unirrigated and dry belt. Therefore, on the basis of taluka-wise available general agricultural information and following the consultation with the agriculture-related officials of the district, two talukas, namely Karad (relatively more advanced) and Khatav (less advanced) were selected, and one village from each taluka was chosen for a comparative analysis. The village (Atke) representing the advanced taluka (Karad) is considered in the study as the modernized village due to its extensive and assured irrigation facilities, a higher degree of mechanization, extensive adoption of HYV and other infrastructural arrangements. On the other hand, the village (Khatval) selected from the less developed taluka (Khatav) is treated as a traditional village because it cultivates its crops mostly on the basis of traditional technology based on a broadcasting method using predominantly bullock and human labour.

For the detailed analysis of the agricultural practices of the two villages and their consequent effects on the socio-economic position of the peasants, 50 households were drawn from each village from various categories in proportion to their number (landless agricultural labourers, marginal farmers, small farmers, medium farmers and large farmers) classified on the basis of land ownership position. The classification of the households 'into various categories were made' on the basis of capacity of holdings for the reproduction of an average household. The classification is shown in the following table:

Categories	Holding Size in Hectares for the Modernized Village (with Extensive and Assured Irrigation Facilities)	Holding Size in Hectares for the Traditional (Un-irrigated) Village
Landless agricultural labourers	–	–
Marginal farmers	< 0.50	< 1.00
Small farmers	0.50–1.00	1.00–2.00
Medium farmers	1.00–2.00	2.00–4.00
Large farmers	> 2.00	> 4.00

It is revealed from group interviews with some senior cultivators of the villages that on average a household of 5–6 members with 3–4 adults and 2–3 children belonging to the first category of holding size (marginal farmers) under no condition can survive without adequate assistance from other sources of income. For the same family which comes under the landowning group of the second category (small farmers), it is also difficult to maintain without additional income, but in exceptional good harvesting years they can manage with some wage incomes. The concerned household belonging to the third category (medium farmers) can manage provided other factors of production and consumption remain unchanged. In contrast, the household of the same type but coming under the holding size of last category (large farmers) can normally generate surplus and can also be able to exercise in expanded production. It is also known from the same source that as regards the productivity one hectare of assured irrigated land is almost equal to two hectares of unirrigated land provided the rainfall and other climatic conditions are usual throughout the year.

For the collection of primary data, a structured interview schedule was administered on sample households. Besides the sampled households, information was collected from persons holding key positions in various institutions at the village level.

AGRICULTURAL MODERNIZATION IN SATARA (A DISTRICT-LEVEL VIEW)

Satara is one of the westernmost districts of Maharashtra. More than 86 per cent of the people of the district live in rural areas and the rural economy of the district agriculture continues to hold a pivotal place both in terms of income and employment. In the post-Independence period, particularly since the late 1960s, the agriculture of the district has experienced profound changes through extensive irrigation, mechanization and adoption of HYV seeds, expansion of credit network and other associated infrastructural development.

The data on the trend of agricultural modernization and its consequent effect on land utilization, cropping pattern, agricultural production and socio-economic conditions of the peasants at the district level have been illustrated in Table 8.1. It reveals that the net sown area and gross cropped area of the district have increased remarkably across

Table 8.1 *Time Series Information on Agriculture of Satara District*

S. No.	Particulars	1970–1971	1980–1981	1990–1991
1	Total population in 000'	1,727 (1971)	2,039 (1981)	2,436 (1991)
2	Percentage of rural population	86.84 (1971)	86.96 (1981)	87.12 (1991)
3	Percentage of scheduled caste population	5.39 (1971)	6.21 (1981)	9.51 (1991)
4	Percentage of scheduled tribe population	0.21 (1971)	0.64 (1981)	0.75 (1991)
5	Cultivated area in 000' hectares	539	590	632
6	Net sown area in 000' hectares	517	630	699
7	Gross cropped area in 000' hectares	557	708	791
8	Cropping intensity	107.85	112.25	113.18
9	Percentage of irrigated area to net sown area	13.47	13.49	22.52
10	Area under food grains (percentage to gross cropped area)	76.50	69.33	70.28
11	Area under oilseeds (percentage to gross cropped area)	12.48	7.91	6.78
12	Area under sugarcane (percentage to gross cropped area)	2.26	3.26	5.70
13	Area under cotton (percentage to gross cropped area)	1.24	0.89	0.12
14	No. of tractors per 00' hectares of gross cropped area	0.060 (1972)	0.145 (1982)	0.378 (1992)
15	No. of electric pumps for irrigation per 00' hectares of gross cropped area	0.889 (1972)	2.689 (1982)	3.641 (1992)
16	No. of oil engines with pumps for irrigation per 00'	1.533 (1972)	1.407 (1982)	1.394 (1992)

(Continued)

(Continued)

S. No.	Particulars	1970–1971	1980–1981	1990–1991
17	Pressure on land	0.36	0.33	0.30
18	Area under HYV (rice, wheat, jowar and bajra)	NA	62.03	74,64
19	Per hectare chemical fertilizer consumption in Kg	14.1	32.6	84.7
20	No. of agricultural co-operative societies	774	752	810
21	Membership of agricultural co-operative societies in 000'	185	248	373
22	Outstanding loan to agricultural co-operative societies (in Rs) in lakhs	1,444	1,236	5,421
23	Production of food grains:			
	1. Total in 00' tones	2,228	3,844	4,747
	2. Per hectare in Kg	502	797	922
24	Production of oilseeds:			
	1. Total in 00' tones	NA	551	975
	2. Per hectare in Kg	NA	814	1,061
25	Production of sugarcane (dressed cane):			
	1. Total in 00' tones	8,671	16,033	31,903
	2. Per hectare in Kg	93,236	91,109	87,167
26	Production of cotton:			
	1. Total in 00' tones	111	142	13
	2. Per hectare in Kg	262	359	300

27	Average holding size of farmers of:			
	< 1 hectare	0.43	0.44	0.41
	1–2 hectares	1.45	1.52	1.44
	2–4 hectares	2.85	2.82	2.75
	4–10 hectares	6.08	5.96	5.76
	> 10 hectares	16.27	17.36	20.61
28	Average holding size of scheduled caste holders in hectares	NA	0.92 (1985–1986)	0.84 (1990–1991)
29	Average holding size of scheduled tribe holders in hectares	NA	1.14 (1985–1986)	1.34 (1990–1991)
30	Percentage of cultivators to main workers:			
	1. Male	55.87	51.10	47.17
	2. Female	56.90	56.73	53.31
	3. Total	56.15	52.90	49.28
31	Percentage of agricultural labourers:			
	1. Male	12.82	12.56	14.50
	2. Female	33.24	30.85	35.09
	3. Total	18.32	18.40	21.58

Source: 1. Report on agricultural census: Maharashtra state, various issues.
2. Statistical abstracts of Maharashtra, various issues.
3. Livestock and farm equipment census: Maharashtra state various issues.
4. District-wise agricultural statistical information of Maharashtra various issues.
5. District Census Handbook of Satara, various issues.

Note: Figures in the parenthesis indicate the exact reference years.

the years along with a sharp rise in cropping intensity. Within 20 years (1970–1971 to 1990–1991), the net sown area and gross cropped area have increased by 35 per cent and 40 per cent respectively. Similarly, the cropping intensity has also gone up to 113.18 in 1990–1991 as against 107.85 in 1970–1971. The most important aspect is that the irrigated land of the district (percentage to the net sown area) has increased significantly (from 13.47% in 1970–1971 to 22.25% in 1991). Following the expansion of irrigation facilities and commercial trend of agriculture, the cropping pattern of the district has witnessed considerable changes. The area under food grains continues to be higher, and it does not show any significant trend. But the area under sugarcane shows a recorded increase across the years and possibly due to this the area under oilseeds and cotton has gone down. Besides, the emphasis has been given on extensive coverage of HYV seeds. More than 74 per cent of the cropped area (major crops) is covered by these varieties. Due to the increasing cultivation of sugarcane along with widespread adoption of HYV, the per hectare chemical fertilizer consumption in the district has tremendously gone up. It increased to 84.7 kg in 1991–1992 as against 32.6 kg in 1981–1982 and 14.1 kg in 1971–1972. Consequent upon the introduction of the new cropping pattern, which is based on improved methods of cultivation, adoption of new technology and implements the rising trend of mechanization has become more prominent. The number of tractors, oil engines, electric pump sets of the district has increased many times over the years. Apart from this, in order to meet the demands of the peasants for more working funds in view of the changing conditions, the credit network has been expanded through the establishment of agricultural cooperative societies. The growth of agricultural co-operative societies has been phenomenal in the district with a noticeable rise in membership and the amount of outstanding loan.

Looking at the analysis of the trend of agricultural production of the district, it is evident that the collective effects of these wide-ranging changes in agriculture have substantially contributed towards the overall growth of total production as well as average yield of the major crops. The total production of food grains, oilseeds, cotton and sugarcane has increased considerably with the march of time. Similarly, the average yield of most of the crops also continues to increase.

On the contrary, the effects of these agricultural modernizing measures have increased the landholding disparity in the district. It is seen that the average holding size of the large holders (>10 hectares) has increased consistently over the years with a corresponding decrease in that of the marginal, small and medium holders. It had increased from 16.27 hectares in 1970–1971 to 17.36 hectares in 1980–1981 and 20.61 hectares in 1990–1991. The perpetual decline of the holding size of lower landowning groups exhibits the trend of marginalization of the peasants in the district in the wake of agricultural modernization. In addition, the average holding size of the scheduled castes holders had also gone down from 1.14 hectares in 1985–1986 to 1.34 hectares in 1990–1991. Although the average holding size of the scheduled tribe farmers has increased, it has a very little impact over the district as their population is very negligible (0.75%). The impact of new agricultural practices on the agrarian population at the district level can also be assessed by analysing the changes in the size of agricultural labourers and cultivators. It is found that the number of cultivators has decreased consistently over the period of time accompanying a steady rise of agricultural labourers. The number of cultivators which was 56.15 per cent in 1971 came down to 52.90 per cent in 1981 and 49.28 per cent in 1991. On the other hand, the number of agricultural labourers increased up to 21.58 per cent in 1991 against 18.40 per cent in 1981 and 18.32 in 1971. From the rising trend of female agricultural labourers, it is also evident that the growing impoverishment of the small and marginal peasants and landless labourers have compelled the women to join as agricultural labourers to supplement their family income.

Thus, it is inferred from the aforementioned analysis at the district level that the agricultural modernizing measures have enhanced the agricultural production of the district, but the contrary effects of these measures have increased the rate of inequalities. The following analysis at the village level will provide more detail picture on the impact of agricultural modernization.

IMPACT OF AGRICULTURAL MODERNIZATION AT THE VILLAGE LEVEL

The comparative analysis of the agricultural practices and socio-economic position of the various categories of farmers of the two villages (modernized and traditional, described earlier) gives ample evidence on the trend of agricultural growth and inequality at the micro level (Table 8.2).

It is found that while in the traditional village, food grains (bajra and jowar) are the principal crops, the agriculture of the modernized village is characterized by the predominant cultivation of cash crops (such as sugarcane and soybeans). The cropping pattern of all categories of farmers of the modernized village is heavily dependent upon HYV seeds. The essential conditions for HYV being the availability of assured irrigation both in terms of quantity and timing, the farmers of the village adopt these varieties extensively for higher productivity and a greater margin of profit. The increasing cultivation of cash crops along with higher coverage of area under HYV in the modernized village has made the application of high doses of fertilizer, pesticides and other inputs as an integral part of cultivation process as a result of which the cost of cultivation of all categories of farmers has increased tremendously as compared to that of the traditional agriculture.

In view of the higher cost of cultivation of modern agriculture, the formal credit agencies have also provided a higher amount of credit facilities to the farmers. The per hectare loan to formal credit agencies among all categories of farmers of the modernized village is many times more than those of the traditional village. However, in the modernized village the major beneficiary of the credit facilities are the large farmers whose per hectare loan is much higher than their cost of cultivation. On the contrary, the per hectare loan of the marginal farmers in the traditional village is higher than their cost of cultivation. It is mainly due to the fact that their cost of cultivation is very low, and they also use a significant portion of these loans mostly to meet the dire necessities other than agriculture. In both the villages the marginal and large farmers have a higher rate of per hectare loan to formal agencies. While the marginal farmers' indebtedness is caused due to their perpetual scarcity of funds, the large farmers indebtedness is attributed to their desire for utilizing the low-cost credit capital in other profit-generating sources. Moreover, the land-based lending policies of the credit agencies help the large farmers to appropriate the lion's share of credit facilities and the share increases further in the modern agriculture due to the abundant flow of credit capital. The average indebtedness of the

Table 8.2 Size Class-wise Distribution of Attributes of Agricultural Production and Inequality among the Selected Households

S. No.	Particulars N=6	Size Classes of the Modernized Village (Atke)						Size Classes of the Traditional (Khatval)					
		Land less N=16	Marginal N=13	Small N=9	Medium N=6	Large N=50	Total N=6	Land less N=15	Marginal N=14	Small N=11	Medium N=4	Large N=50	Total
1	Average family size	5.5	5.06	5.54	5.89	6.67	5.58	6.00	6.07	5.64	5.82	4.75	5.78
2	Average land holding in hectares	–	0.25	0.68	1.27	4.18	1.12	–	0.64	1.50	2.60	5.63	1.85
3	Percentage of irrigated land to total holding	–	93.60	96.60	98.95	98.80	98.01	–	–	–	14.07	14.88	9.02
4	Cropping intensity*	–	109.00	125.00	111.21	105.58	110.63	–	156.90	141.91	131.36	104.18	129.94
5	percentage of area under cash crops to gross cropped area	–	82.35	82.36	82.20	84.92	83.56	–	–	–	0.27	5.41	1.25
6	Percentage of area covered by HYV	–	85.88	96.36	96.85	100.00	97.43	–	33.20	4.71	19.74	15.31	16.46
7	Per hectare ownership of tractors	–	–	0.18	0.47	0.34	0.31	–	–	–	–	0.05	0.01
8	Per hectare ownership of oil engines	–	–	0.18	0.31	0.15	0.18	–	0.13	0.10	–	0.05	0.06

(Continued)

(Continued)

S. No.	Particulars N=6	Size Classes of the Modernized Village (Atke)					Size Classes of the Traditional (Khatval)					
		Land less N=16	Marginal N=13	Small N=9	Medium N=6	Large N=50	Total N=6	Land less N=15	Marginal N=14	Small N=11	Medium N=4	Large N=50	Total
9	Per hectare ownership of electric pump sets	–	0.71	0.36	0.39	0.26	0.35	–	0.20	0.10	0.13	0.27	0.16
10	Per hectare consumption	–	1,948.24	2,054.55	2,005.51	2,043.40	2,029.38	–	63.67	60.88	46.63	110.36	66.68
11	Per hectare use of labour days	–	659.76	369.91	421.97	360.00	399.85	–	78.13	54.25	33.81	56.49	50.81
12	Percentage of family labour days to per hectare labour days	–	75.61	61.05	72.10	28.30	51.30	–	89.76	55.67	70.06	64.11	68.63
13	Per hectare cost of cultivation (in `)	–	25,516.94	24,231.36	26,550.39	25,671.70	25,757.25	–	1,742.00	1,664.98	1,130.03	3,219.82	1,814.28
14	Percentage of total produce sold	–	99.02	99.50	99.80	99.80	99.70	–	40.75	57.21	38.49	89.25	72.06
15	Per hectare net income in (`)	–	42,824.24	43,586.82	47,642.52	47,252.07	46,073.42	–	3,066.00	2,366.30	2,564.35	4,232.43	2,932.75
16	Average household income from all sources in (`)	20,215.00	25,388.00	55,424.31	96,550.00	245,011.67	71,740.68	15,225.00	15,433.27	26,240.00	17,208.20	54,001.50	21,910.10
17	Percentage of agricultural income to total income	–	44.81	66.54	69.63	85.18	70.22	1.81	19.87	19.15	50.84	43.50	28.13

18	Average labour days hired in	–	42.75	121.92	166.11	1140.00	212.08	–	8.00	57.07	34.55	112.50	33.30
19	Average labour days of family members in own land	–	132.50	191.08	428.89	450.0	223.36	–	70.13	64.14	80.82	134.00	72.86
20	Average labour days hired out	466.33	113.19	20.31	23.33	–	101.66	440.00	267.00	121.86	104.55	85.00	196.82
21	Per hectare loan from formal credit agencies (in `)	–	21,082.35	4,227.18	11,401.57	28,490.57	20,437.10	–	2,340.00	945.17	644.82	2,855.86	1,443.61
22	Average amount of loan from credit agencies (in `)	–	5,600.00	9,492.31	16,088.89	125,833.33	22,256.00	–	2,340.00	2,007.14	2,200.00	15,850.00	3,016.00
23	Average transaction cost as percentage of Average loan	–	4.12	1.97	1.12	0.65	1.14	–	1.64	0.43	0.41	0.16	0.60
24	Percentage of literacy	51.52	79.01	81.94	84.91	92.50	79.57	50.00	60.44	73.42	70.31	68.42	64.71
25	Percentage of literate persons having post matric qualification	00.00	3.13	27.12	17.78	29.73	16.67	61.11	52.73	53.57	73.33	69.23	59.90
26	Percentage of household owning pucca houses	00.00	18.75	38.46	55.56	83.33	36.00	–	–	21.43	36.36	75.00	20.00

(Continued)

(Continued)

S. No.	Particulars N=6	Size Classes of the Modernized Village (Atke)						Size Classes of the Traditional (Khatval)					
		Land less N=16	Marginal N=13	Small N=9	Medium N=6	Large N=50	Total N=6	Land less N=15	Marginal N=14	Small N=11	Medium N=4	Large N=50	Total
27	Percentage of household owning television sets	16.67	50.00	76.92	77.78	100.00	64.00	–	20.00	21.43	18.18	50.00	20.00
28	Average ownership of trucks/cars/jeeps	–	–	–	0.11	0.83	0.12	–	–	–	–	–	–
29	Average ownership of mopeds/scooters/motorcycles	–	0.13	0.62	1.11	2.00	0.64	–	–	–	–	0.5	0.04

Source: Field survey.

Note: Per hectare calculation is based on gross cropped area. Although sugarcane is one-year crop, the area under this crop is taken as single cropped area.

* Cropping intensity of the modernized village looks lower as compared to the traditional village due to the extensive cultivation of sugarcane.

large farmers in the modernized village is remarkably higher than that of the other categories of farmers. Besides it, the proportion of transaction cost borne by the farmers of both the villages provides some interesting facts. The percentage of transaction cost to the amount of loan is more in the modernized village as compared to the traditional village. As the cultivation process of the modernized village is highly expensive the farmers in order to get higher amount of loan at the appropriate time are required to entertain the officials of these credit agencies in various ways which makes their transaction cost more. In both the villages the marginal farmers pay a higher percentage of transaction cost and the amount decreases with the increase in holding size. The higher amount of loan of the upper landowning farmers along with their wider political network reduces the proportion of the transaction costs. In addition to this, the availability of a higher amount of low-cost credit facilities helps the large farmers of the modernized village to acquire the high valued income-generating agricultural machinery such as tractors. As most of the agricultural operations of modern agriculture are tractorized, the large farmers get a considerable amount of additional income by hiring out their tractors to the small and marginal farmers. Besides, they also hire out the tractors during lean periods for non-agricultural activities.

The advent of agricultural modernization has altered the pre-existing labour relations. Compared to the traditional village, the demand for hired labour services is quite more in modernized village. The new cropping pattern and the associated water management system of modern agriculture which needs quick completion of all agricultural operations within a short period makes the hiring of labour services inevitable. The small and marginal farmers who were earlier managing mostly with their family labour are compelled to depend upon the hired labour services to a considerable extent. The heavy demand for hired labour services of the modernized village has attracted the migrant labourers from the different parts of the district as well as of the state on a large scale. Now, there are two sets of labourers, namely the migrants and the natives. The migrant labourers mostly work as contract labourers. In contract labour system, the labour service is provided by a group of labourers in which the group is required to complete a definite agricultural operation within a stipulated period of time and the wage is fixed taking into account the nature of the operation, time limit, location of land and bargaining capacity of the group leader and the employer. This type of labour is now widely preferred among the landowners because the agricultural operations are completed with the prescribed time duration. The large-scale cultivation of sugarcane specifically increased the demand for this kind of labour services. Around 80 per cent of labour requirements of modernized village are met by the contract labourers. The farmers who hitherto were earlier dependent upon the native labourers now prefer the migrant labourers because of favourable terms and conditions. Of the total hired labour days of the village, 89.82 per cent is contributed by the migrant labourers. As a result, the native labourers who largely derive their livelihood from agricultural labour services get impoverished and are forced to work as labourers for building and road construction works. The participation of women belonging landless labour category as wage labourer has also become more in view of this reduced employment opportunities. In the traditional agriculture, on the other hand, the use of family labour predominates across the size classes. The marginal, small and medium farmers of the village manage with exchange labour services during peak periods and the large farmers along with their family labour use the casual and attached labour services.

The combined effects of these new measures have tremendously enhanced the overall agricultural production in the modernized village as compared to the traditional one. The per hectare gross return and net income of all categories of farmers of the modernized village are much higher than that of the farmers of the traditional village. Every additional hectare adds to the income stream of a farmer which in turn has increased the household income disparity among the various categories of the rural population due to unequal distribution of land. The household income of the large farmers of the modernized village is many times more than that of the other categories of farmers. In the traditional village, on the other hand, household income disparity is minimal. An analysis of the distribution of resources among the sampled household of both the villages on size class basis reveals that the modernized village exhibits a higher rate of inequality than the traditional one in terms of ownership of land, land-based resources and other high valued household assets. Although the concentration of land is associated with the concentration of resources in both the villages, the magnitude is higher in the modernized village.

A comparative study into the major socio-political institutions of the two villages provides a more detailed picture of the pattern of inequality existing in these villages. The Gram Panchayat, which is the apex sociopolitical body at the village level and through which most of the state-sponsored developmental measures are launched, is completely dominated by the large farmers in the modernized village. Of the 16 positions, 10 (62.5%) positions including the key positions such as sarpanch and deputy sarpanch are occupied by them. Similarly, the cooperative societies through which the state-supported credit facilities for agricultural development and allied activities are supplied to the village are largely under their control. There are two agricultural co-operative societies in the village with 18 various positions. Of these, the large farmers have occupied 12 (66.67%) along with the two chairman and two vice-chairman positions. In addition, in two milk co-operative societies of the village, they hold 11 (61.11%) out of 18 positions with all the key positions. The domination of the large farmers of this kind helps them to corner the benefits of all developmental measures. On the contrary, in the traditional village, the landless labourers and the lower landowning farmers have relatively been well represented in the village level institutions. In the Gram Panchayat of the village, marginal farmers and landless labourers along with the positions of Sarpanch and deputy sarpanch could occupy some other important positions. Of the nine, they occupy six (66.17%) positions. Likewise, in the primary agricultural cooperative society and milk co-operative society, the small and marginal farmers and the landless labourers have relatively better access. Although the key positions of these institutions are held by the large farmers, out of 18 positions of agricultural co-operative society and milk co-operative society (9 each) the marginal, small, and medium farmers and landless labourers have taken 15 positions (83.33%) in their favour. It is inferred from the aforementioned analysis that as modern agriculture is heavily dependent upon the state-sponsored inputs and facilities which largely flow to the village through these institutions the large farmers take an active part in the management for the protection and promotion of their economic interests.

CONCLUSION

It is summarized from the preceding analysis both at the district and village levels that though the process of agricultural modernization has substantially enhanced the agricultural production; it has systematically bypassed the equality issue. The new measures, instead of removing the earlier inequalities have provided an easy outlet for the generation of further inequalities. In fact, in the process of modernizing the agricultural practices, the new forces and conditions have improved the economic position of all categories of farmers by increasing the productivity and per hectare income. But the extent to prosperity being relative to the resource ownership position the large farmers have emerged as a class of rich farmers who dominate the socio-economic and political spheres of rural society. It appears that the abolition of inequality which the existing plan and policy aim should be achieved in a manner that does not fundamentally alter the class inequality. In a state where the process of modernization follows the capitalist axis of the developmental path the measures for the removal of inequality are undertaken only to the extent that it does not act as a disincentive to the main proprietary classes who are accepted as main agents of development (Desai, 1984, p. 28). Thus, in the whole process of agrarian transformation, the sole objective is to create and promote a market and growth-oriented rich farmer-led agriculture and the question of equality is a myth which constitutes, the integral part of political process of manufacturing consent for a regime of domination and inequality.

ACKNOWLEDGEMENT

The chapter constitutes a part of the larger study 'Agricultural Modernization and the Trend of Social Inequality in Rural Maharashtra' conducted by Gokhale Institute of Politics and Economics, Pune, and submitted to the Ministry of Agriculture, Government of India, New Delhi. The earlier draft of the chapter was presented in XXV All India Sociological Conference held at Aligarh Muslim University, Aligarh. The author likes to acknowledge the participants for their useful comments and suggestions. The usual disclaimer applies.

REFERENCES

Benabou, R. (1996). Inequality and growth, *NBER Macroeconomics Annual*, 11. https://www.journals.uchicago.edu/doi/pdfplus/10.1086/654291

Byres, T. J. (1981). The new technology class formation and class action, in the Indian countryside. *Journal of Peasant Studies*, 8(4), 405–454.

Desai, A. R. (1975). *State and society in India: Essays in dissent*. Popular Prakashan.

Desai, A. R. (1984). *India's path of development: A Marxist approach*. Popular Prakashan.

Dev, M. S. (1997). Growth, employment, poverty and human development: An evaluation of change in India since Independence with emphasis on rural areas. *Review of Development and Change*, 2(2), 209–250.

Dhanagare, D. N. (1984). Agrarian reforms and rural development in India: Some observations. *Research in Social Movements: Conflict and Change*, 7(1), 177–201.

Dhanagare, D. N. (1987). Green revolution and social inequalities in rural India. *Economic & Political Weekly*, 22(1), 175–199.

Joshi, P. C. (1971). Land reforms and agrarian change in India and Pakistan since 1947. In P. C. Joshi & R. C. Dutt (Eds.), *Studies in Asian social development*. Tata McGraw Hill.

Kurien, C. T. (1981). *Dynamics of rural transformation: A study of Tamil Nadu 1970–1975*. Orient Longman.

Mencher, J. P. (1974). Conflicts and contradictions in the green revolution: The case of Tamil Nadu. *Economic & Political Weekly*, 9(6, 7 and 8), 309–322.

Mencher, J. P. (1978). *Agriculture and social structure in Tamil Nadu: Past origins, present transformations and future prospects*. Allied Publishers.

Myrdal, G. (1972). *Asian drama: An inquiry into the poverty of nations*. Penguin Books.

Parthasarathy, G. (1970). *Green revolution and weaker sections*. Thacker.

Psacharopoulos, G. (Ed.). (1991). *Essays on poverty, equity and growth*. Pergamon.

Rutten, M. (1995). *Farm and factories: Social profile of large farmers and rural industrialists in West India*. Oxford University Press.

Sen, A. (1997). *What's the point of a development strategy?* DERP No. 3, Economics Research Programme, London School of Economics. http://eprints.lse.ac.uk/6705/1/What%27s_the_Point_of_a_Development_Strategy.pdf

Chapter 9

Green Revolution Revisited*
The Contemporary Agrarian Situation in Punjab

Swarup Dutta

INTRODUCTION

The Green Revolution resulted in a rapid growth of food grain production with the introduction of new packages of mechanical and petrochemical inputs along with the well-developed irrigation infrastructure, especially in developing countries during the 1960s and the 1970s. It was for the first time that modern capital-intensive agriculture was introduced to India, replacing the traditional one. The package consisted of high-yielding grain varieties, mainly rice and wheat, heavy fertilizer and pesticide application and carefully controlled irrigation, leading to more mechanized type of farming systems. The potentiality of new grain varieties, however, could only be obtained through proper supplement of these new inputs. Without proper and controlled application of these inputs, the new varieties yielded no more and sometimes much less than the traditional strains. This new technological paradigm virtually replaced the subsistence farming system. How-ever, the introduction of the Green Revolution was not a part of spontaneous development in rural India, as it was a deliberate attempt of several international donor agencies and the Government of India to initiate new capital-intensive agricultural development only in a few selected areas of the country. These selected areas were strategically

---

* *Social Change, 42*(2), 2012.

chosen on the basis of high level of growth in productivity and higher frequency of large landholders. Punjab, with its suitable climate, soil and pre-existing canal irrigation network in the colonial period, along with a sizeable population of large landholders, was first considered to be a part of this new form of agricultural transformation.

After the introduction of the Green Revolution in the late 1960s and the 1970s, Punjab experienced a remarkable agricultural growth. It had improved the general socio-economic condition of the farmers and catapulted it to the status of being called the 'grain bowl of India' or the 'bread basket of India'. Since then, the agricultural production sectors in Punjab have become highly capital intensive and mechanized. According to the Commission for Agricultural Cost and Prices (CACP) report 1997, the state achieved irrigation coverage of 95 per cent of the net sown area and 98 per cent coverage of improved high-yielding seed varieties. The agricultural growth rate in Punjab was highest among all the states between the 1960s and the mid-1980s. According to Goldman and Smith (1995), the wheat harvest in Punjab between 1964–1965 and 1984–1985 increased more than fourfold, 2.4 million metric tonnes to 10.2 million metric tonnes, contributing 44 per cent of the total wheat harvest in India. The rice cultivation, on the other hand, received marginal importance in the pre-Green Revolution days, which increased up to 75 per cent in the early 1970s and became one of the most important cash crops of the state.

The euphoria, however, was short-lived. The momentum of the Green Revolution did not sustain for a long time, as the so-called 'grain bowl of India' is now facing a huge crisis in its agrarian sector. The elation at this new agro-technological revolution came to be identified with 'disaster', as it brought about a massive socio-economic crisis in the mid-1980s and thereafter. Nadkarni (1988) reported that by the mid-1980s, a wheat grower in Punjab was obtaining lower net returns per hectare even after incurring higher costs per hectare on modern technological inputs. On the other hand, Gandhi (1997) argued that the increase in input costs came largely from over-mechanization, labour and irrigation costs. Because of this high input cost of cultivation, farmers resorted to various formal (banks, cooperatives and so on) and informal (local moneylenders or *arhtiyas*) credit institutions for borrowing money. But after the stagnation in production, the net output and subsequent profit margin reduced drastically. As a result, far-mers could not repay the loan and eventually got trapped into the vicious cycle of debt. To get rid of indebtedness, many farmers across the state committed suicide. Since the mid-1980s, suicide by the farmers in Punjab has became a public issue. The state government itself admitted that 2,116 suicides had taken place since 1986 and this could just be the 'tip of an iceberg', as many more cases might have gone unreported (Tribune, 2005). Gill and Singh (2006) reported that the majority of suicide victims were small and marginal farmers and one of the reasons behind the suicide was indebtedness. Besides the problem of stagnation in production and subsequent indebtedness and suicides, the Green Revolution also brought a massive social inequality in rural Punjab. The major contradiction is directly related to the unequal distribution of benefits among the small and large farmers. The medium and large farmers strengthened their economic and social position, acquiring more and more land, whereas the resource-poor small and marginal farmers started leasing out their tiny agricultural land to the large farmers due to high input cost of cultivation.

Thus, Punjab, being the 'showcase' of Indian agriculture, is now facing severe socio-economic crisis that is largely unforeseen and overlooked by the architects of the Green Revolution. The present study has been conducted to evaluate the contemporary agrarian situation in rural Punjab, and that eventually helps us understand the consequences of India's first agricultural revolution.

STUDY AREA

The research was conducted in the Malwa zone of southern Punjab. Punjab has traditionally been divided into four eco-cultural zones, namely Doaba, Majha, Malwa and Powadh. Over time, each region has metamorphosed into distinct regions, separate in their physical environment, economic structure, social organization and cultural pattern. Therefore, each region is also called 'folk region'. Altough there exist inter-regional differences, within the region there is uniformity in geography, climate, vegetation, soil, drainage and cultural environment. The study area was located in the village of Chaina (district Faridkot) in Malwa zone. The Malwa zone was chosen as most of the cases of indebtedness and suicides were reported from this region. The district Faridkot is subdivided into three regions based on soil, topography climate and natural vegetation—Hathar-Sadiq plains (sandy plain), Uttar Dhudi plains (sandy loam) and the Jaitu region (sandy loam to loam). Chaina is located in the Jaitu region. The region is famous for cotton cultivation, due to its dry terrain, sandy soil and scanty rainfall. It is also well known for producing the best staple of cotton in North India. The market called Kotkapura Mandi and Jaitu Mandi (in district Faridkot) are considered as Asia's biggest cotton market. The village is largely dominated by Sikhs with a negligible population of Hindus. The dominant caste in the village is the upper caste Jatts. They are mainly agriculturists and possess a large amount of land in the village. Besides Jatts, various artisan castes such as Tarkhan (carpenter), Nai (barber), Sunar (goldsmith), Kumhar (potter), Brahmins (priest) and Scheduled Castes (especially Mazhbhis) also live there. Wheat, paddy and cotton are mainly cultivated as major cash crops. The farmers usually practise monoculture with a single crop rotation (wheat-paddy or wheat-paddy-cotton or wheat-cotton). The main *kharif* crops are paddy and cotton and these are cultivated between April–May and October–November. On the other hand, wheat, being a major *rabi* crop is cultivated between December and April.

METHODOLOGY

The research was primarily based on qualitative methods, especially ethnography. It is a holistic approach that perceives human actions as a part of the whole system. In the light of this approach, I mainly focused on the local's point of view, households and the knowledge of the community to identify significant cate-gories of human experiences. The fieldwork was conducted in the village of Chaina between 2007 and 2010.

During the qualitative data collection, three kinds of non-probability sampling (purposive sampling, quota sampling and snowball sampling) were employed. In purposive sampling, the respondents were chosen purposefully, who were thought to be relevant to the research topic. In case of quota sampling, the respondents were chosen from a specific group. For instance, during the data collection on farmer–labour relation, rural credit institution in pre-Green Revolution Punjab, and so on, only elder farmers were selected as key informants. On the other hand, snowball sampling was also applied in which the respondents were asked to recommend any other persons who met the criteria of the research queries. To minimize the weakness of snowball approach, random sampling was employed, which helped in breaking linkages of snowball methods after a series of five respondents. These respondents provided information on the contemporary socio-economic condition, relationship between small and large farmers, farmers and farm labourers and so on. Besides qualitative sampling, the probability sampling for quantitative analysis was chosen to understand the magnitude of debt among the farmers in Chaina. A survey of 230 farm households was conducted. The samples were selected on the basis of stratified random sampling. The stratification of the farmers was done on the basis of their landholding capacity. I considered the actual amount of land that the farmers possessed and avoided leased-in and leased-out land. After getting the total number of farm households in the village, it was segregated into various classes on the basis of landholding capacity. According to the Director Agriculture, Punjab (1995–1996), farmers having less than 2.5 acres are considered as marginal, 2.5 to 5 acres as small, 5 to 10 acres as semi-medium, 10 to 25 acres as medium and more than 25 acres as large farmers. The percentage of every class of farmers was calculated and the percentage was taken as a sample size of that particular group of farmers. It is known as representative sampling.

THE GREEN REVOLUTION AND THE CONTEMPORARY AGRARIAN SITUATION IN PUNJAB

To assess the contemporary agrarian situation in Punjab, it would be essential to understand the changing pattern of system of cultivation. The system of cultivation is defined as the functioning of relationship that is based on landownership and the factors underlying various agricultural operations. It determines the position of individuals in the production process. There are two types of cultivation: (a) the self-cultivation or *khudkasht* in which farmers undertake all the agricultural operations and occasionally depend on hired labourers and (b) involving others in the cultivation in a form of labourers or sharecroppers. In the former case, workers work for their own family farm and do not hire labourers from outside. However, they seek help from their close relatives (especially from minimal lineage or *Lahna*s) when needed. Most of the small and marginal farmers come under this category. On the other hand, the hired labourers include a variety of contract labourers. The farmers generally employ contract labourers in two ways—the daily-wage labourers or *dehari majdoor* in which the form of work is not permanent in nature as they work on a daily basis and receive payment at the end of the same day; second, the permanent attached labourers who work for farmers on a fixed contract basis (minimum one year). In the latter case, there are two types of employment. First, the landowner may permanently keep *siri* or sharecropper, who works on a fixed payment basis (one-twentieth produce after harvest). Second, the landowner may keep servant or *naukar*, who works on fixed cash rent for one year. Both *siri* and *naukar* generally come from lower castes (especially the Mazhbhi caste). The minimum time period of the contract is one year and the further extension of the contract is largely based on the relationship between the farmer and the labourer.

The *naukar* is given a responsibility to perform major agricultural tasks (e.g., ploughing, sowing, pesticide spraying, harvesting and so on) as well as the rearing of cattle with the payment of ₹25,000–30,000 annually. There are two types of *naukar*s available in the village—the *balig* (adult) and *nabalig* (child labour).[1] The *nabalig* or child labourers receive less money from farmers (12,000–15,000 annually). They mainly do all the household work for farmers, including the rearing of cattle, growing and carrying of fodder from the field and so on. In return, they receive meal. The rate of the *naukar*s varies and largely depends on the availability of the labourers in the village and the market rate of the crop in that particular season. For instance, the labour charges increased from ₹25,000 (2007–2008) to ₹35,000 (2009–2010) as the minimum support price (MSP) of cotton increased from ₹2,500 per quintal to ₹5,000 per quintal in the last three years. On the other hand, the *siri* or sharecroppers are those who do farming on a sharing basis. They receive a share of the crops as their wages. The farmers keep the *siri* when they do not spend much time in the field. Sometimes, they give complete responsibility of the farm operations to the *siri*. The mode of payment is traditional *Jajmani* type of a system[2] in which the relationship between the landowner and labourer plays an important role. The wife and other female members of *siri* work as sweepers in the house of the same landowner. Sometimes, they also do some domestic works for the landowners (such as cleaning utensils and looking after the cattle). To minimize the expenditure of outside labour, the female members of the *siri* family take the responsibility of cotton plucking. Mr Sandeep Singh, a *Jatt* farmer, said that to keep a *siri*, farmers consider the following factors: (a) a *siri* should have a good knowledge of agriculture and skills to manage the whole farm operations on behalf of the farmer, (b) he should maintain a good relationship with daily labourers, ensuring a leadership quality to conduct the field operations peacefully in the absence of the farmer, (c) he should bear the responsibility of any loss in the farm operations and (d) he should be honest and trustworthy. Besides *siri*, tenant farming is also very common nowadays. In this system, the landowner leases out their land to another farmer in the village where the tenant has to pay a fixed rent (annually) to the landowner.

I observed three situations pertaining to the changing pattern of system of cultivation. First, a growing trend of reverse tenancy in which the small and marginal farmers started leasing out their land to the medium and large farmers. Second, a decline in employment of *siri* under the traditional *Jajmani* system. Third, a changing nature of labour employment in which the large farmers have started employing cheap migrant labourers from Bihar and Uttar Pradesh instead of local labourers.

PROBLEM OF REVERSE TENANCY

The crisis in Punjab agriculture started with the declining viability of small and marginal holdings and higher rate of rural indebtedness after the Green Revolution. The development of capital-intensive industrial agricultural technology in the 1960s jeopardized the economic condition of the small and marginal landholders in Punjab. The majority of the small and marginal farmers in Chaina could not mechanize their farming due to lack of capital and many of them leased out their land to the large landholders. This phenomenon is known as reverse tenancy. The system of reverse tenancy changed the existing pattern of system of cultivation in Punjab. In this system, the large landholders started leasing land from the small landholders on a fixed rent basis. Mr Joginder Singh, a medium farmer in the village, has 16 acres of land. In 2005, two small farmers in the village approached him for leasing their land. Due to good production of Bt cotton in 2004, he decided to lease land for cotton cultivation for the next season. Finally, he took it on a fixed rent (₹22,000 per year for each acre). He further mentioned that it has become very difficult for the small farmers to invest in new seed varieties, petrochemical inputs, agro-machineries and so on. Thus, farming has become an expensive option for them. Many small and marginal farmers felt that due to the expensive cost of cultivation, they could not lease land from the large farmers. Moreover, they have to pay a fixed rent for the leased land.

After the initial success of the Green Revolution, the value of land in Punjab has increased. As a result, the landowners do not want to give land for sharecropping, rather they prefer to lease it on an annual rent basis. The rent of the land depends on the rate of the crop, especially on the basis of the MSP of the crop in the market. For instance, in 2007, the MSP of cotton was approximately ₹2,500 per quintal and the rent of per acre of land varied from ₹22,000 to ₹25,000 depending on the quality of the soil. But in 2010–2011, the rent increased to ₹35,000 as the MSP of cotton increased to ₹5,000 per quintal.

Mearns (1999) reported that the percentage of leased-in area in Punjab increased up to 13 per cent in the 1980s as compared to 9 per cent in the 1970s. According to the Human Development Report, Punjab (2004), a rapid decrease in operational holding among the marginal farmers is noticed from 37 per cent to 26 per cent between 1970–1971 and 1990–1991, which further declined to 12 per cent in 2000–2001. Simultaneously, operational landholding among the medium, large and extra-large farmers (Table 9.1) has also increased. Hence, there is a clear indication of reverse tenancy. The small and marginal farmers mentioned that after the Green Revolution, farming no longer remained as primary source of income. In the pre-Green Revolution period, they were dependent on traditional agricultural practices.[3] However, the production was not sufficient in the traditional technology, but it did not put any economic burden because of

Table 9.1 Distribution of Operational Landholdings in Punjab

Size-class (in Hectares)	1970–1971 (in %)	1980–1981 (in %)	1990–1991 (in %)	1995–1996 (in %)	2000–2001 (in %)
Marginal (0–1)	37.63	19.21	26.50	18.65	12.34
Small (1–2)	18.91	19.41	18.24	16.78	17.35
Medium (2–4)	20.44	27.99	25.85	29.31	32.90
Large (4–10)	18.02	26.20	23.40	27.98	30.19
Extra-large (10+)	5.00	7.19	6.01	7.28	7.22
Total	100	100	100	100	100

Source: Human Development Report (Punjab) (2004, p.41).

low input cost of cultivation. After the introduction of the Green Revolution technology, they purchased expensive farm inputs (mainly fertilizers, pesticides and so on) to intensify the production. It eventually increased the cost of cultivation. In the pre-Green Revolution period (mainly the 1940s and the 1950s), the practice of sharecropping or the employment of *siri* by the large landholders used to be a common phenomenon in the village. Moreover, to get the benefits of new technology, many small farmers in the village leased land from the large farmers. But it proved to be successful only after the proper supplement of expensive chemical inputs with assured irrigation. Due to lack of capital, they could not purchase the expensive farm inputs. Thus, it was very difficult for them to survive in this mechanization and commercialization of agriculture, as they could not reap the benefits out of it. Thus, without having any option, they not only returned the land but also leased out their own land to the large farmers.

DECLINE IN THE EMPLOYMENT OF *SIRI*

In the era of post-Green Revolution the system of tenancy has been commercialized. The mechanization of agriculture enhanced the ability of the large landholders to operate the whole land with minimum labour employment. The large landholders have started withdrawing themselves from sharecropping. After the application of chemical inputs and irrigation, there was a significant increase in the yield and in return; the farmers also received a good price from the government. Hence, unlike small and marginal farmers and landless labourers, the large farmers could afford the high cost of cultivation and they benefited a lot. Many large farmers in Chaina mentioned that the sharecropping with poverty-stricken landless labourers or small farmers seemed to be a huge loss for them, as the commercial value of land increased invariably. To reap the benefits of modern capital-intensive farming technology, most of the large farmers in the village stopped sharecropping with the resource-poor small and marginal farmers and gave their land to those who could afford to use capital-intensive mode of production. There were very few large and medium landowners in the village who gave land for sharecropping. Interestingly, I found that none of the sharecroppers belonged to the resource-poor Mazhbhi but to the upper caste Jatt who could afford a huge investment in modern technology. Mr Sarabjit Singh, another Jatt landholder and a government officer, shared his experience regarding the employment of a *siri* in his land. He wanted to keep a *siri*, as he could not look after his land due to his government job. He owned 12 acres of land in the village. In 1995, he employed Gulab Singh, a small farmer from the village who belong to lower caste, Mazhbhi. But during the cultivation, he observed that it was very difficult for Gulab Singh to afford the high input cost of cultivation. Finally, the production was very low. Hence, after this incidence, he decided to give his land to medium and large farmers on rent basis, as they could afford the input cost of cultivation. He mentioned that after the advent of the Green Revolution, the practice of sharecropping was no longer a lucrative option for the farmers. Thus, instead of crop sharing, the farmers now prefer to give land on a fixed rent basis.

CHANGING NATURE OF LABOUR EMPLOYMENT

Due to new technological innovation of various agro-machineries (such as tractors, threshers, grinders, seed planters and harvesters), chemicals (such as pesticides, fertilizers, weedicides and fungicides) and mechanized irrigation systems (electric tubewell and diesel pumps), a drastic reduction in the manual farm operations was noticed. Although these chemical inputs assured irrigation, and high- yielding seeds increased the food grain production manifolds, these declined the labour intensity abruptly. It reduced the task of the agricultural labourers and forced them to move out of agriculture. As a result, the local farm labourers adopted some low-investment, low-earning and self-employment ventures such as working in a flourmill, repair shop, construction work and grocery shop. In a report titled 'Status of farmers Who Left Farming in Punjab', Singh et al. (2007) argued that in the last few decades, a large proportion of lower caste people were pushed out of their traditional occupation as agricultural labourer and allied activities, and dissociated themselves from the upper caste Jatt landholders.

Thus, it is important to understand the present relationship status between the landowners and the local agricultural labourers. I conducted interviews with various classes of farmers as well as local agricultural labourers. My key informants, Mr Pritpal Singh and Mr Jattha Singh, explained how the trend of employment of labour has changed since the last two decades. Mr Pritpal said that due to dry and sandy terrain, almost all the farmers in the village cultivated American cotton as a major *kharif* crop. They mostly employed the local labourers for various agricultural operations related to cotton and wheat cultivation. But after the massive attack of American bollworm in the 1990s, many farmers (especially the medium and large) left cotton and forcefully adopted paddy cultivation. Mr Jattha Singh mentioned that a majority of the farmers in the village did not have proper skills in paddy cultivation, as they had never cultivated it before. Thus, both the farmers and local labourers are not well equipped with paddy cultivation. Many farmers started employing migrant labourers from the states of Uttar Pradesh and Bihar.[4] The migrant labourers are locally known as *bhayya* labour and their continuous presence became a common feature of the village, especially after the adoption of paddy in the late 1990s.

Mr Sakattar Singh, owner of 32 acres of land, mainly employs migrant labourers for both paddy and wheat cultivation. He said that the migrant labourers live on the farm and are in regular contact with the landlord, giving him detailed information pertaining to farm operations. But the local labourers live in the village and spend working hours in the farm. During irrigation, farmers need proper supervision to ensure that the amount of water he receives from the government should come to his land only. Sometimes, farmers receive water at night which needs proper surveillance. The migrant labourers are given the responsibility to supervise this operation at night on behalf of the farmers. Unlike migrant labourers, the local labourers are very reluctant to work at night. Unlike them, the migrant labourers are increasingly entrusted with many different jobs with a diversity of skills and varying levels of responsibility. Besides agricultural tasks, they also help their landlord in various household works. For a time being, they tend to become all-purpose farm and household hand for farmers. In this way, over a period of time, a regular migrant labourer moves into supervisory roles, especially in handling of farm machinery, loading and unloading of the produce, harvesting and sowing of crops and, even at times, helping with the marketing of the produce. After employing the migrant labourers, the farmers not only started withdrawing themselves from most of the tasks requiring hard physical labour but also getting more specialized even in performing supervisory function.

Hence, there has been a demand for migrant labourers instead of local labourers. As a result, many local agricultural labourers started dissociating themselves from their traditional occupations and moved to the local town/city for better jobs. Thus, the unintentional adverse impact of migrant labourers created a rapid disjunction between the landowning Jatts and local Mazhbhi labourers. The farmers argued that leaving agricultural jobs could not be a good option for the local labourers, as the competition is much high in the industries. The labourers rush to the nearby town where thousands of labourers throng to get a job. Moreover, they also complained that a few debt and poverty-stricken labourers tend to display kleptomaniac tendencies and, thus, nowadays they often prefer to keep contract labourers, especially the *naukars* who are trustworthy and reliable. However, after interviewing many local labourers in the village, I came across a very different situation. Mr Goggi Singh, a contract labourer in the village, said that the Jatt landholders behave like a commission agent or *arhtiya* with the Mazbhi labourers. He said that the poor labourers do not have the option to go to the *arhtiyas* or the local banks for borrowing money. For any urgent need, they immediately rush to the farmers. The farmers give money to the labourers on the conditions that they do all the agricultural works free of cost for the next one year. Many labourers said that they could borrow money but not more than ₹20,000–25,000 at a time. If the labourer agrees to work for the farmer (both domestic and agricultural works), soon they become a servant rather than a labourer. Besides the agricultural tasks, they are given all the domestic chores such as rearing of cattle, growing and carrying of fodder, and maintenance of house. If they take leave even for one day, they have to work extra time. These, according to the labourers, are the conditions for borrowing money from the farmers. Goggi Singh also mentioned that if a labourer refuses to work, farmers put an additional interest of 4–5 per cent. That is why many labourers mockingly remarked that the farmers are nowadays turning into *arhtiyas*.

Thus, the system of cultivation has completely changed in rural Punjab since after the advent of the Green Revolution. Now, the question is how the changing nature of system of cultivation is responsible for an ongoing agrarian crisis. I will discuss it in the latter part this chapter. However, the condition became worse, especially after the new economic policy of globalization and liberalization in the 1990s, which not only suffocated the agrarian economy but also left it to the logic of market forces. Every section of farmers, irrespective of class and caste, was badly affected by this new economic policy. The late 1990s witnessed an emergency of debt-driven suicides and rapid indebtedness that had taken hold across the countryside of Punjab and elsewhere in India.

IMPACT OF GLOBALIZATION AND LIBERALIZATION

In the new economic policy of the 1990s, science, technology and business enterprises (perhaps the combination of these three) were projected as a new paradigm of development. This new economic reform, however, paved the way for many multinational companies to enter into the Indian agricultural sector. This multinational interference eventually led to corporate control over agricultural production and the trade sector of our country. On the one hand, free trade and open market are considered the backbone of a 'new economy' with reduced state intervention and, on the other hand, agriculture and rural people received marginal importance. It was brought to the notice of the government and policymakers by many social scientists after the drastic reduction of agricultural growth in the share of national income, mainly in the mid-1990s. The economy of the Indian farmers is largely based on the MSP provided by the government. But due to improper public distribution mechanism, the farmers were deprived of proper remunerative prices. The farmers (both small and large) found it very difficult to survive in the open market system, as they were forced to sell their entire production to the market. Moreover, those in debt and the illiterate small and marginal farmers found it more difficult to bargain with the government and private procurement agents to sell their crop. Therefore, they have been suffering enormously from this new liberalized economic system, which largely undermined and marginalized the interest of the poor farmers.

After the harvest of paddy at the end of year 2000, when millions of people were in starvation across the country, the granaries in Punjab were flooded with unwanted surplus of paddy. The farmers mentioned that the government procurement agents rejected to procure their crops, calling it inferior quality. They were unwilling to purchase it and not even ready to pay the MSP to the farmers. Meanwhile, the private traders and rice millers were ready to procure the crop at a very low cost (even much lesser than the MSP). The farmers still kept on waiting for the official agencies, but they never turned up for further procurement of the crop. The grains were stored wherever the farmers could find place—in school grounds, public parks and so on. Hence, the unintended withdrawal of state support from the economic sphere, especially in agriculture, leaving it to the vagaries of free market forces, proved to be deleterious and disastrous during the liberalization stage and aftermath.

INDEBTEDNESS AND SUICIDE IN PUNJAB

Hence, due to the declining growth rates, severely weakened public distribution system (PDS), heavy farm investments, low level of savings and extensive crop failure, agriculture no longer remained a profitable source of income, especially for the small and marginal farmers in Punjab. As a result, many of them left agriculture due to the low income from farming, fragmentation of land and repayment of old debts. After leaving farming in distress, these farm families generally adopted lower level of activities and most of them joined the labour market.

Several studies have already been conducted by a number of agricultural economists in Punjab to estimate the extent and magnitude of indebtedness among different categories of farmers. On the recommendation of Punjab State Farmer's Commission, three economic experts[5] from Punjab Agricultural University (PAU) conducted a survey titled 'Flow of Funds to Farmers and Indebtedness in Punjab'. It has argued that 89 per cent of the farmers in the state are indebted and 12.8 per cent are those who have committed suicide. The worst affected area is cotton-growing southern Punjab (i.e., Malwa), where 93.5 per cent cotton farmers were under debt. They also estimated that the average debt of marginal and small farmers in the cotton belt was ₹80,000. Few years back, the crisis became worse when the whole village was declared for sale by the *gram panchayats* (village head council) due to an outstanding debt.

To understand the magnitude of debt among various classes of farmers in Punjab, I conducted a survey in Chaina. A large number of small and marginal farmers were found to be indebted. Out of the total 230 farm households in Chaina, 189 households were highly indebted in which 100 household belonged to small and marginal farmers. However, the magnitude of debt of more than ₹20,000 was substantially higher among the semi-medium sell off its property spread over medium, and large farmers. According to National Sample Survey Organisation (NSSO, 2005), the total amount of rural debt of Punjab was ₹24,000 crores in 2003. The report also estimated that each farmer in Punjab has an outstanding debt of ₹45,576 against the national average of ₹12,505.

During my informal visit to Malsinghwala village, Mansa district in January 2007, Mr Jasbir Singh, the *sarpanch* (the head) of the village revealed that each of the 290 households had an outstanding debt of ₹13,000. With a severe cotton crop failure, they had no other hope of repaying this outstanding debt and, therefore, the village had decided to sell off its property spread over 1,800 acres. It did not happen only with Malsinghwala as there were several other villages in southern Punjab, who put themselves in the queue of auction such as Harkishanpura in Bhatinda district and Bhuattal Kalan in Sangrur district.

Thus, the high input cost, practice of monoculture and stagnation in yield with low output have led farmers to borrow money from various formal and informal sources. Overborrowing of money has become a regular task that increases rural indebtedness. But Satish (2006) argued that the indebtedness is a function of availability of credit in relation to its demand, as also the ability of the recipient to service it. If properly serviced through income generated from farm operations, debt would not turn into burden.

Moreover, the commercialization of agriculture has created a cultural link of rural population with towns and cities. This has resulted in the acquiring of all modern luxury machines, appliances and facilities which are seen as basic necessities nowadays. To compete with the city dwellers, the farmers started spending a huge amount of money in house construction and other modern facilities. Mr Gurdarshan Singh

(54), a medium farmer in Chaina, invested more than ₹15 lakhs for his house construction. He built a two-storied building furnished with modern furniture and accompanied by modern facilities, including an air conditioner, washing machine and several other expensive household appliances. And for this, he took a loan of ₹15 lakhs from the local Punjab National Bank (PNB). I also observed that the farmers, especially the Jatts, were extremely fascinated with tractors. To enhance the social status in the village, unnecessary purchasing of new farm machineries (mainly tractors) has become a regular trend. The tractor is seen as a status symbol for many Punjabi farmers. It serves as a car but is more useful than a car. The primary use of a tractor is ploughing, and it also helps carry the agricultural produce to the local market. Thus, to the farmers, the best way to assert higher status in the village is to buy tractors as well as modern agricultural implements. Even the farmers with less than five acres of land also purchased tractors to enhance their social position and status. Mr Amarjeet Sharma (59) stated that he was not eager to buy a tractor unlike his friends who bought it by taking a huge loan from the local bank. He also said that it would be matter of prestige if one does not have tractor. To buy a tractor, a farmer would always resort to local banks and cooperatives for credit. To sanction the loan quickly, many of them pay bribes to the bank officers. The cost of the tractor lies between ₹75,000 and ₹400,000. After buying a tractor, the farmer usually throws a party for friends and relatives. After this celebration, he would proudly go around the village in his tractor. It becomes very difficult for the small farmers to spend such huge amounts of money.

After the Green Revolution, there was a growing trend of overborrowing, especially from the informal sources, and use it for other purposes rather than in agriculture. Moreover, the farmers are not earning enough to meet their needs and to repay the loans due to low yields. Professor Succha Singh Gill, an economist from Punjabi University, Patiala, rightly pointed out that 'when a farmer is unable to pay bank or cooperative loans, he resorts to borrowing from the moneylenders at an exorbitant rate of interest'.[6] It has been found that the *arhtiyas* or commission agents in the grain markets are playing a dominant role to control the local credit market in Punjab. Singh et al. (2005) have argued that more than 50 per cent of all outstanding debts held by the farmers were accounted for by the *arhtiyas*. Several other studies, like those by Gill (2000) and Kaur (2002) also argued on similar aspect confirming the dominance of *arhtiyas* in the local credit market. Gill (2004) also noted that the *arhtiyas* not only dominate the local credit market, but also filled the gap between the availability of credit from institutional sources and total demand for credit in rural Punjab. Despite all efforts at making institutional credit available by the government, the farmers still rely on this non-institutional credit market of short-term borrowing only because of lesser paper work and other hassles.

However, in the pre-Green Revolution Punjab, the '*taccavi*' loan was one of the major sources of rural credit institutions. It was functional until the bank and cooperatives actively participated in the rural credit market. With the help of revenue agencies, the government spent money on the farmers for purchasing seeds, fertiliz, and so on, in the form of short-term loans. These loans were also given in the case of severe crop failure due to flood and drought. Mr Manjit Singh, an old farmer in Chaina, shared his experiences regarding the *taccavi* loans. He said that unlike the modern commercial banks and cooperatives, the *taccavi* loans never became a burden, because in case of delayed repayment, the penal interest was also waived. Even a micro-level relief was also available in the case of the farmers who were unable to repay the loan. Sometimes, the government also extended the time of repayment.

In the latter part of the 1970s, cooperatives and commercial banks progressively entered the rural credit market and flourished after the liberalization and globalization in the early part of the 1990s. As per the Reserve Bank of India (RBI) guidelines, the commercial bank has to reserve 40 per cent of their total lending to the priority sector, in which 18 per cent should go to agriculture. Mr Neeraj Kumar Singh, a probationary officer in the State Bank of Patiala, Jaitu, told me that the majority of agricultural loans are given to farmers to purchase agricultural machineries and only a few of them give crop loan as such. On the other hand, the cooperatives provide crop loan to farmers.

After talking to the farmers, I found that there is a lack of proper mechanism to recover the loan. Unlike with the *taccavi* loan system, the waiving of interest, penal interest or rescheduling of payment and so on are absent. In the absence of these, the lending agencies start punitive actions for recovery of loans and drive farmers to suicide. Profesor Gill informed me that the lending agents used to recover their loans by taking away animals, agricultural implements and so on in full public view. It is the worst kind of insult that the farmer has to bear. Some scholars were of the opinion that this social stigma could be a reason for farmer suicides in Punjab.

Hence, economic factors such as declining productivity and viability of land holdings, low MSP and heavy investment on agro-machineries and social factors such as fragmentation of farming classes, lack of interest in agriculture and a huge expenditure on non-agricultural purposes pushed farmers into a debt trap and forced some of them to commit suicide, especially in the view of dishonour suffered by them in the debt-recovery process. According to a report by the Institute of Development and Communication (IDC), the number of suicides in Punjab experienced a sharp increase in 1992–1993, estimated 51.97 per cent, while the comparable figure for the country as a whole was only 5.11 per cent. In 1993–1994, the increase was 14 per cent in Punjab as against 5.88 per cent for the country. While there was a decline in the reported cases at an all-India level, Punjab once again reported an increase in 57 per cent in 1994–1995. The IDC report also recognized the fact that there was always a possibility of underreporting of suicides (IDC, 1998). In the mid-1980s, the state government itself admitted that 2,116 suicides had taken place since 1986. Apart from the study by IDC, Iyer and Manick (2000) and an NGO called the Association for Democratic Rights (AFDR, 2000) also conducted an in-depth study on farmer suicides in Punjab (Table 9.2). Recently in 2006, a report on farmer suicides prepared for Punjab State Farmer's Commission by IDC, Chandigarh, estimated the rate of farmer suicide in Punjab. The report shows that the suicide rate of Punjab was 0.57 per cent in 1988 and rose up to 2.04 per cent in 2001 and further declined to 1.38 per cent in 2005. However, Mr Umendra Dutt, an environmental activist in Punjab, criticized the report saying that the data did not support the true picture of suicide deaths in Punjab, as the actual suicide rate is much higher. He pointed out that most of the suicide cases in rural Punjab are not registered by the local police and shown as cases of natural death or death due to disease. The report also confirmed that higher number of suicide cases could be found in six districts, namely

Table 9.2 *The Profile of Suicide Victims in Punjab*

Study by Characteristics	IDC (1998)	Iyer and Manick (2000)	AFDR (2000)
Districts Surveyed	Gurdaspur Sangrur Mansa Ludhiana	Sangrur	Patiala Mansa Sangrur Bhatinda
Village covered	14	11	29
Households covered with confirmed cased of suicides	53	75	79
Percentage of cultivators who committed suicide	55	66.66	84.80
Percentage of agriculture labour households	45	33.33	15.20
Percentage of small and marginal farmers	25	84	65.70
Percentage of illiterates	58.50	66.25	27.40
Percentage of married victims	81.10	–	76
Percentage of debt exclusively from commission agents	36.72	65.50	27.40
Percentage of debt from commission agents and other services		81.25	73.60
Percentage of unproductive use of loan	68.20	51.61	20.00
Percentage (causes of suicides)			
1. multiple of which indebtedness is one	38	78.75	62
2. crop failure	1.05	10	5.10

Source: Gill and Singh (2006).

Faridkot, Bhatinda, Ferozepur, Ludhina, Amritsar and Hosiarpur. It also mentioned that a vast majority of suicide victims belonged to a category of small and marginal farmers with minimum literacy rate. Interestingly, all the studies concluded that indebtedness is one of the key factors for farmer suicides in Punjab. However, in my study village, I did not come across any suicide case but the problem of indebtedness was highly prevalent.

On 2 March 2009, the Government of Punjab announced a relief package for the families of suicide victims. The government decided to pay ₹2 lakhs to the families of farmers who had committed suicide since the previous year. A debate has already ensued on the sudden step of the government before the assembly poll, as the critics have argued that a new provision might actually prompt more suicides. They also blamed that these kinds of short-term policies of the government are neither preventive nor curative. I think that this kind of an announcement may even lead to more suicides, as farmers will start taking their lives, which would be an option for further repayment of loans by their families. Instead of paying the price of suicide to the farmers, the government should sort out the MSP issue and bring down the input cost of cultivation. Agriculture has become an expensive proposition in Punjab, as the farmer has to spend ₹5,000–8,000 per acre on hybrid seeds, fertilizers, pesticide, diesel and labour (both migrant and local). The PAU economist, Dr Sukhpal Singh, rightly pointed out that 'since the Punjab government can't seem to deal with the prospect of farmers killing themselves, it has done the next best thing: offer compensation for the suicides'.[7]

CONCLUSION

The introduction of the Green Revolution in India was a 'Western' endeavour and this radically new technological paradigm was promoted as a prototype and measure of social progress. True, it altered the pattern of farming technology and organization, but equally true, none of these transformations were the part of spontaneous development in rural India. The contemporary agrarian crisis across Punjab is an adverse impact of both the Green Revolution and globalization. This 'agrarian crisis' is not only about the problem of indebtedness among various classes of farmers or about those who committed suicide, but it subsequently maximized social inequality in rural Punjab. The landed classes found their economic position to be more strengthened, whereas the poor farmers and landless classes became more marginalized and proletarianized. The unusual phenomenon of reverse tenancy is the one of the adverse consequences of the Green Revolution. Therefore, the Green Revolution largely benefited the large farmers and squeezed the small and marginal farmers and landless agricultural labourers. It changed the existing pattern of system of cultivation. Cleaver (1972) rightly pointed out that there has been a growing effort by the landlords to acquire more land and convert their tenants into hired labourers in order to reduce their costs, thus, creating a class-based society in the Green Revolution-dominated area. With the incorporation of industrial farming, the capitalist farmers accumulated more capital in the form of mechanical equipment, whereas the small and marginal farmers who wanted to participate in the Green Revolution could not do so because of lack of capital.

In a true sense, the relative success and failure of the Green Revolution is a fiercely debated issue. It involves a wide circle of actors—from small holders and agricultural labourers to large farmers, planners, policymakers and politicians to environmentalists and activists to economists and so on. These actors, however, have taken radically different positions to explain the pattern of progress and crisis and success and failure of the Green Revolution. However, in recent years, both the advocates and the critics of the Green Revolution have shared less polarized views recognizing the problem of rapid market penetration and biased development and application of petrochemical inputs and high-yielding varieties. Many analysts have questioned the sustainability of the Green Revolution technology. The sustainable yield-enhancing potential of these mechanical and petrochemical inputs of food production are now seen sceptically.

Thus, the contemporary farm enterprises are mainly dealt with the interconnections between different sets of actors. Within this multiplicity of local–global interconnectedness, the restructuring of agriculture from small landholders to large-scale transnational and multinational companies posed new research challenges for social scientists. Thus, they ought to explore these new research challenges in relation to the larger context and changes being experienced at the village and regional as well as local and global levels. This would probably help us raise more meaningful questions about what is happening to contemporary rural India.

NOTES

1. The *nabalig* females do not go to the field except during the harvesting time when they assist their mother.
2. The Jajmani system is a kind of caste-based economic system in India that largely de-pends on the relationship between upper and lower castes.
3. The input cost of cultivation was very low. Farmers mostly used bullock-driven plough for tilling the land, local seed varieties for plantation, farm yard manure as fertilizer, and so on. Although the cultivation was largely based on rain-fed irrigation, ill-developed irrigation facility was available to them.
4. In Bihar and Uttar Pradesh, paddy is the staple of cultivation.
5. Dr Sukhpal Singh, Dr Manjit Kaur and Dr H. S. Kingra
6. Personal communication, Punjabi University, Patiala, Punjab.
7. Personal communication, Punjab Agricultural University, Ludhiana, Punjab, India.

REFERENCES

Association for Democratic Rights (2000). *Suicides in rural area of Punjab*. Author.
Cleaver, H. M. (1972). The contradictions in the Green Revolution. *The American Economic Review*, *62*(2), 177–186.
Commission for Agricultural Costs and Prices. (1997). Report on price policy for rabi crops 1996/97. Department of Agriculture and Cooperation, Ministry of Agriculture, Government of India.
Gandhi, V. P. (1997). Technology, cost reduction and returns in agriculture: A study of wheat and rice in Punjab. *Vikalpa*, *22*(2, April–June), 35–43.
Gill, A. (2000). *Rural credit markets—financial sector reforms and the informal lenders*. Deep and Deep Publication.
Gill, A. (2004). Interlinked agrarian credit markets: Case study in Punjab. *Economic & Political Weekly*, *39*(83), 3741–3751.
Gill, A. & Singh, L. (2006). Farmer's suicides and response of public policy: Evidence diagnosis and alternatives from Punjab. *Economic & Political Weekly*, *41*(26), 2762–2768.
Goldman, A., & Smith, J. (1995). Agricultural transformation in India and Northern Nigeria: Exploring the nature of Green Revolution. *World Development*, *23*(2), 243–263.

Government of Punjab. (2004). *Human development report Punjab.* Author. Institute for Development and Communication. (1998). *Suicide in rural Punjab.* Author.

Iyer, K. G., & Manick, G. S. (2000). *Indebtedness, impoverishment and suicides in rural Punjab.* India Publisher.

Kaur, G. (2002). *Role of rural financial market in Punjab: A case study* (Working Paper 1). NBRAD, Department of Economic Analysis and Research.

Mearns, R. (1999). *Access to land in rural India—policy issues and options* (Policy Research Working Paper Series No. 2123). World Bank.

Nadkarni, M. V. (1988). Crisis of increasing costs in agriculture: Is there a way out? *Economic & Political Weekly, 23*(29), A114–A119.

National Sample Survey Organisation (NSSO). (2005). *Indebtedness of farmer's household 2003* (NSSO Report No. 498). Ministry of Statistics and Programme Implementation, Government of India.

Satish, P. (2006). Institutional credit: Indebtedness and suicides in Punjab. *Economic & Political Weekly, 41*(26), 2754–2761.

Singh, K., Singh, S., & Kangra, H. S. (2007). *Status of farmers left farming in Punjab.* A report by Punjab State Farmer's Commission in collaboration with Punjab Agricultural University, Ludhiana. Government of Punjab.

Singh, S., Toor, M. S., & Sharma, V. K. (2005). *Magnitude and determinants of indebtedness in Punjab agriculture* (unpublished seminar paper). Punjabi University.

The Tribune News Service. (2005, August 10). Suicides by farmers being underplayed: Report. *The Tribune.* http://www.tribuneindia.com/2005/20050810/punjab1.htm

Section III
The Globalization Era

Sectional Introduction

For agriculture as a sector and groups of people dependent on it, the policies adopted by Indian state since the mid- 1980s and more specifically from 1991 onwards represented a major break on several counts. Agriculture was de-prioritized in favour of the service sector that was considered the engine of growth during the last three decades. It resulted in the reallocation of resources in favour of other sectors of the economy consequently creating a deficit in credit supply, technological innovations, infrastructure development, input subsidies and procurement of the produce.

All of this had a bearing for the relatively higher escalation in input costs as compared to output prices squeezing out profits of crop production to the extent of negative income for marginal farmers from cultivation in some areas. Added to this were rising costs of education and health in the absence of required public investment which left the agriculture sector and people dependent in a situation of crisis. It was quite well known that income from cultivation contributed only a minor portion of the total income of farm households, especially smallholdings.

The four chapters that have constituted this section narrate the story of agriculture riddled with cyclical downturns. Sukhpal Singh's chapter has addressed one of the most crucial problems of contemporary agricultural scene, that is, the survival of small farms. The importance of smallholdings in ensuring food security and livelihood in an agriculturally dependent country like India does not need further elaboration. But this lifeline of the majority of Indian households is under existential threat, not because the small size itself cannot survive but because agriculture is not getting sufficient support from the state in terms of capital financing and incentive structure. Singh believed that small farms facing a crisis in both backward and developed areas could be rescued by promoting diversification towards high-value crops and commercialization. However, this would require a risk mitigation structure and efficient supply lines but the market did not seem interested in dealing with small farmers, while the state was unwilling to go beyond symbolic gestures.

One of the myths that Singh blasted was that small farms were a liability in the agrarian sector. Their higher cropping intensity, capacity to combine cultivation with animal farming, producers of an increasingly large share of food grains and more than three-fifths share in total holdings actually made them indispensable. But small farms were fragmented which raised transportation cost, lowered productivity and negative externalities from land quality improvement. Faced with a higher extent of interlocking, they were deprived of remunerative prices for their produce. Small farmers were also cheated in the input supply market. They were dependent on informal sources of credit in the absence of access to adequate institutional credit, often relied on costly water supplies, bypassed by extension services for commercial crops and lacked non-farm income. In the Green Revolution areas, they also suffered from over-capitalization and under-utilization of capacities.

It has often been suggested that the way out from the current impasse passes through commercial farming and tapping of international markets. However, Singh has argued that while doing commercial cropping, small farms could not pay higher input prices in the face of declining public investment and costlier private sector credit; additionally, they also lost out in terms of price realization due to the opening up of the domestic economy. Consequently, instead of accessing international markets, they ended up losing the domestic market, often forcing them to quit farming and lease out their land to rich farmers.

Contract farming was another 'quick-fix' solution offered to the problems of the agrarian sector, in general, and small farms, in particular. When a deepening ecological crisis, stagnant income from cultivation and saturating productivity rise turned out to be the defining features of the agrarian scene in Punjab, contract farming emerged as one alternative to break the impasse. This was experimented in different parts of the country, especially Punjab. Mahesh Pratap Singh's chapter has critically investigated the institutional framework of contract farming, mainly the role of the state as an arbitrator between farmers and agri-business firms.

The assumption underlying contract farming was the distribution of risk between farmer and agri-business firms, the former on production and the latter on marketing. Another feature that distinguished this arrangement from other forms of transactions in agricultural commodities was its demand-driven nature. But contract farming turned out to far removed from the initial suppositions about it. Agro-business firms did not show any interest in the minimum support price protected commodities citing price rigidity. They mainly dealt with basmati rice that had an export market. They also avoided entering into contracts with small farmers. In a nutshell, Singh argues that contract farming had little impact on non-cash crops and their growers.

In all the previous chapters, the impact of the agrarian crisis on farmers was discussed in details. In other places too literature on farmers has been abundant. But scholarship on agricultural labour as a class has skipped the attention of economists, political scientists and sociologists alike. The major changes in agriculture such as land reforms, the Green Revolution and new economic policies were examined but they concerned only farmers. Gurmanpreet Singh and Kamaljit Singh in their chapters have identified and filled this deficit in social science research. Based on a thorough probe into the socio-economic conditions of the second-largest class of workers in Punjab, they have argued that agricultural labourers have been economically exploited, politically dominated and socially discriminated. A vast majority of them have been Dalits, and their proportion to total workers was rising since the 1970s. Traditional systems of debt bondage have survived even today and most people caught in its vice have belonged to one single Dalit caste—the Mazhabi Sikh.

While agricultural labourers were completely shunned by redistributive land reforms, worse was to follow. When gains from the Green Revolution started accruing to rich farmers, they started employing cheaper migrant labourers from Uttar Pradesh and Bihar to forestall demands for wage hike by the local labour. Rich peasantry also deployed more and more machines to reduce the demands for labour after the 1980s. These measures, alongside the socio-economic conditions of agricultural labourers, denied them their due share in Punjab's new-found agricultural prosperity. However, when it came to sharing the burden of the ensuing crisis, agricultural labourers found themselves equal if not more vulnerable. Stagnant wages, increasingly shrinking number of employment days and rampant indebtedness forced many agricultural labourers to commit suicide, at times, in larger numbers than those committed by farmers.

The last chapter occupies this important space and is completely devoted to finding a way out of the current impasse facing the agriculture sector and millions of families dependent on it. P. M. Bhargava's approach of looking at agriculture security as virtually synonymous with farmers' security, food security and security of rural economy and national security has made his chapter even more interesting. He has made wide-ranging recommendations within this integrated and comprehensive framework.

P. M. Bhargava has argued convincingly that seed companies had a vested interest in not propagating true-breeder seed varieties of which a number have been developed by the Indian Council for Agricultural Research. Besides, strong fertilizer and pesticide lobbies have been pushing for the excessive usage of these chemicals that are harmful to the soil's health, plants and humans. Integrated pest management and organic farming practices must be encouraged as an alternative, which have a huge demand in the national as well as international market. Further, the agriculture sector does not need free power that has an ecological cost. Instead, assured and quality power supply must be ensured. He also recommended locating and resurrecting traditional water bodies to deal with the acute water crisis.

Soil health has occupied an important place in Bhargava's schema of agricultural security. For this, a publicly available soil map of the country that would include information on damage done to soil health by excessive usage of fertilizers and pesticides along with micro-nutrient deficiency should be prepared, he suggested. Further, while the rural sector should remain open to modern agricultural practices, their blind acceptance should be discouraged. For instance, genetically modified crops should be released only after rigorous testing and risk assessment procedure. Alternatively, validated and cross-validated traditional agricultural practices should be popularized.

P. M. Bhargava's schema emphasized remunerative prices for agricultural products through a commensurate hike in minimum support prices and restrictions on cheap and subsidized imports. Further, the contract farming model should be tweaked to ensure that farmers receive a share in profits of the company. Farmers' income should be augmented by the cultivation of medicinal plants, uncommon vegetables, marine products and so on. Further, knowledge empowerment of rural areas by imparting free and quality education and vocational training, and strengthening of the panchayat system should be taken up. Besides, Bhargava also recommended important steps in the areas of loans to farmers, rural–urban integration, land records and agricultural policy. He also warned against external threats, bioterrorism and climate change.

The chapters in this section have presented clinching evidences on ensuring distress in the agrarian sector and indicated a way out. They all urged that a focus on small farmers and agricultural labour, most hit by this crisis, was essential. Equally critical, enhanced public investment in agriculture that would ensure support to the peasantry at the points of credit, marketing, technological support and crop losses due to natural calamities would go a long way in addressing concerns of farming communities.

Chapter 10

Changing Structure and Organization of Agriculture and Small Farmers in India*

Sukhpal Singh

Agriculture in India still engages about 58 per cent of the workforce and contributes about a quarter of the gross domestic product. Majority of the farmers/cultivators are in the category of small and marginal farmers. The number and proportion of such farmers has been growing over time. They constituted 69.07 per cent of the total holdings in 1970–1971 but their proportion increased to 77.96 per cent in 1990–1991. The area cultivated by them has grown from 20.86 per cent of the total in 1970–1971 to 32.31 per cent in 1990–1991 (Gill, 2004). Further, 59.4 per cent of the total holdings were marginal, that is, below 1 hectare (ha), 18.8 per cent small (1–2 ha), 13.1 per cent semi-medium (2–4 ha), 7.1 per cent medium (4–10 ha) and 1.6 per cent large holdings (above 10 ha). The share of marginal and small holdings increased to 61.6 per cent and 18.7 per cent, respectively, by 1995–1996, together accounting for 80.3 per cent of all holdings. The number of farms in the largest category declined and the average size of the largest category was falling. In 1990–1991, there were 1.654 million large holdings averaging 17.33 ha, which had dropped to 1.404 million holdings averaging 17.21 ha in 1995–1996. Given this general picture,

---

* *Social Change*, 35(4), 2005.

it is not surprising that the average holding size has been declining since the 1960s and was only 1.49 ha in the late 1990s (GoP, 2005).

Small farms produce 41 per cent of India's total grain (49% of rice, 40% of wheat, 29% of coarse cereals and 27% of pulses), and over half of the total fruit and vegetable production despite being in rainfed areas, resource constrained and assuming that they are as productive as large farms (Muller & Patel, 2004; Singh et al., 2002). Their contribution to incremental wheat and rice production during 1971–1991 was even higher (62% and 48%, respectively). The marginal holdings also had higher cropping intensity (143) compared with that of the small, medium and large farmers (129.9, 119.6, and 111.6, respectively) in the mid-1980s and a higher irrigated area as percentage of net sown area, with more of it being irrigated by tube wells and canals (one-third each) and even that with tanks being quite important (8–11%; Agrawal, 2000; Singh et al., 2002).

This chapter examines the nature, problems and significance of small farms in India, particularly those under commercial agriculture. It profiles the state of small farms in India, highlights the difficulties faced by small farmers in dealing with commercial and diversified farming and deals with the changing structure of the sector in terms of contract farming (CF) and its implications for small farmers. It also focuses on mechanisms for facilitating small farmer participation in commercialized agriculture and outlines some important policy and institutional measures to that end.

NATURE OF SMALL FARMS AND FARMERS IN INDIA

Small farmers (with holdings of <2 ha) were estimated to account for 81 per cent of all operational holdings by 2000–2001 and projected to rise to 83 per cent by 2010–2011, with the area being only 39 per cent and 45 per cent of all holdings, respectively. Large holdings (>4 ha) were estimated to decline to only 7 per cent by 2000–2001 and 5 per cent by 2010–2011 and account for only 36 per cent and 28 per cent of the area, respectively. Only medium-size holdings (2–4 ha) were estimated to remain somewhat stable (12%) in their share and gain in area operated (25% and 27%, respectively, over the two time periods from only 23% in 1990–1991). Also, small farmers (including landless) had higher livestock ownership (60–80% of all livestock population) including cross-bred cattle where 12–20% small farm and landless households owned these animals, compared with only 8–15% in the case of larger farm households (Jha, 2001).

Dairying accounts for more than 50 per cent of the household income of the landless and 30 per cent of that of the marginal and small landholders. In fact, at the lower end of marginal and small farmer category were those who were 'near landless', that is, they owned land between 0.002 ha and 0.200 ha only and accounted for more than 31 per cent of rural households in 1991–1992. These were households besides the landless (owning <0.002 ha) who accounted for 11.3 per cent of the total rural households. The 'near landless' category showed a steady increase since the late 1960s. Thus, more than 42 per cent of the rural households were landless or near landless (Rao & Hanumappa, 1999).

The average size of marginal holdings was only 0.39 ha and of smallholdings 1.43 ha in 1990–1991, compared with 2.76 ha and 5.90 ha, respectively, of semi-medium and medium-category holdings and 17.33 ha in the case of large-category holdings. In the case of rural labour households which were landless or near landless, the average size of holding varied from 0.04 ha in Punjab to 0.74 ha in Rajasthan in 1993–1994 (ETKS, 2003). Further, small farms were highly fragmented. Land transactions led to further fragmentation, making them non-viable in terms of resource use as well as family sustenance. The costs of fragmentation included increased travel time between farms and, hence, lower labour productivity, higher transportation cost of inputs and outputs, negative externalities for land quality improvement like irrigation, loss of land on boundaries and greater potential for disputes (Mani & Pandey, 1995). A study of a Tamil Nadu village found that of all the farmers in the village, small farmers (60%) owned less than 3 ha of land each, of whom 35 per cent had 3–5 plots and 25 per cent had 5–10 plots and the remaining had less than 3 plots. Only 20 per cent of all farmers in the village had more than 5 plots, another 40 per cent had 3–5 plots each and remaining had less than 3 plots each. Thus, small farms were more fragmented. Further, the study showed that fragmentation had an adverse impact on the technical efficiency and production of most crops, and consolidation led to large gains in technical efficiency. Still, markets had not led farmers to consolidate their operational holdings, if not owned holdings (Parikh & Nagarajan, 2004).

Similarly, in Punjab, where the average size of the operational holding was 37 and 22 acres, respectively, for contract and non-contract growers, each holding had 4.45 plots on an average in the case of contract growers and 2.67 plots in the case of non-contract growers. The number of plots ranged from 1.36 for small farmers to 5.15 for larger farmers in CF households and 1.46 and 5.13, respectively, in the case of non-CF households. The larger number of plots per holding was also partly due to leased land owing to the practice of reverse tenancy in the state, especially by contract growers (Kumar, 2005).

In India, the cropping pattern on small farms is dominated by food grains (75%) compared with large farms (67%) and medium farms (72%). However, small farms devote more area to fruit and vegetable production (3.7%), compared to only 1.7 per cent large farmers and 2.4 per cent medium farmers, as these crops are more labour intensive (Jha, 2001). Even the diversification option in terms of change of crop sequence was exercised more by smallholders than by large holders, both in irrigated and non-irrigated areas (Singh et al., 2002). Also, relatively more marginal and small holdings than medium or large holdings were irrigated and used higher amount of inputs such as fertilizers and farmyard manure (ETKS, 2003; Singh et al., 2002), human labour, bullock power (Reddy, 1993; Sharma, 2000), pump sets and tractor power, though not owned (Sharma & Sharma, 2000; Singh et al., 2002).

The extent of interlocking of markets was more in the case of marginal and small farmers, more so in irrigated areas since agriculture there requires modern inputs (Swain, 2000). The input market constraints include lack of information about markets, of business and negotiating experience and of a collective organization. These deprive small farmers of interaction on equal terms with other market participants or intermediaries. Worse, they receive lower prices than those obtained by larger farmers due to their weak bargaining power and holding capacity (Agrawal, 2000). Major problems of small and marginal farmers in India include spurious input supply, inadequate and costly institutional credit, lack of water and costly access to it, lack of extension services for commercial crops, exploitation in marketing of produce, high health expenditure and lack of alternative (non-farm) sources of income. Small and marginal farmers also form bulk (more than half) of the rural poor and the undernourished (Agrawal, 2000; Muller & Patel, 2004; Singh et al., 2002; Vyas, 1996). The low employment elasticity of output due to increasing mechanization and the kind of crops being grown lower the potential for these farmers to supplement their incomes. The size of the farm alone does not influence poverty and nutrition, but how much of it is irrigated also influences them (Muller & Patel, 2004).

SMALL FARMERS IN A GREEN REVOLUTION REGION

In Punjab, the average landholding of a small farmer is 0.9 ha. The state has a cropping intensity of 192, 83.5 per cent net sown area, 96 per cent irrigated area—that too 75 per cent with tube wells—tractor intensity of 68 tractors per 1,000 ha of net sown area and 66 per cent holdings being below 4 ha (GoP, 2005).

Yet there is a crisis of sustainability (economic and environmental) of farming since the late 1980s due to higher costs of cultivation. By the early 1990s, the income of the holder of a seven acre, two-crop irrigated farm in Punjab was less than the annual income of an assistant in a government office (Johl, 1995). In 2001–2002, small farm households had only 20 per cent surplus family labour (unutilized) compared to 32 per cent and 49 per cent in the case of medium and large farmers, respectively, and they had more of family labour (50%) being used in the crop sector; but tractors were being under-utilized at a much larger scale in small farms (77%) against only 50 per cent and 32 per cent in medium and large farms, respectively, with the overall idle tractor power being 43 per cent for the region (Bathinda district). This indicates over-capitalization of small farms in the state that has led to higher costs of cultivation due to the fixed-cost component. Even electric motors and diesel pumps, which number more than 11 lakh in the state (GoP, 2005), were being grossly under-utilized on small farms (16% and 84%, respectively) against overuse of electric motors—11 per cent on both medium and large farms—and under-utilization of diesel pumps—67 per cent and 38 per cent, respectively (Singh & Sharma, 2004). In fact, by 1991–1992, machinery costs on small farms in Punjab were higher than those on large farms, whereas in 1981–1982, they were the lowest. Also, machinery costs accounted for 23 per cent of all operating costs in 1991–1992 and were no different from those on large farms (Jha, 2001). In the early 1990s, economists suggested that a small farmer holding less than 10 acres in a Green Revolution region had no future in growing rice and wheat and should have exited farming as it was not going to yield a reasonable living for the family.

The benefits of input subsidies in Punjab are also skewed towards larger farmers. Small and marginal farmers constitute 36 per cent of the farming community and cultivate 9 per cent of the land but receive only 6 per cent of the power subsidy, 7 per cent of fertilizer subsidy and 5 per cent of canal water subsidy. Small farmers generally do not own tube wells and get water from tube well owners who, though receiving free electricity for running tube wells, charge them under the pretext of recovering maintenance costs and part of the capital cost incurred on installing tube wells. Small and marginal farmers, who constituted about 54 per cent of farmers growing rice and wheat in Punjab, obtained only 21 per cent of the financial benefits of the minimum support price for rice and wheat. This distribution of benefits was roughly in line with the rice and wheat area (22%) that was cultivated by small and marginal farmers. Marginal farmers received just over one-tenth of the various subsidies disbursed to large farmers. Although not unexpected, since these subsidies are universal and not targeted by design, this result is a serious indictment of the subsidy regime. Politically, continuation of these subsidies is often justified in view of the inability of small and marginal farmers to pay higher user charges, but in reality the larger farmers obtain most of the benefits (WB, 2003).

COMMERCIAL AGRICULTURE, DIVERSIFICATION AND SMALL FARMERS

Commercial farming means risks in addition to the natural phenomena that are intrinsic risks of farming everywhere: the risk of output prices that fluctuate, of input prices that may not be commensurate with increased output, of increased vulnerability to pests and so forth (Payer, 1980). A sudden drop in international prices can drive already poor and indebted farmers off the land over the short term. So small farmers not only lose in terms of lower price realization but also pay higher prices for inputs due to opening up of the domestic economies in the presence of declining public investment in agriculture and high-interest private sector credit (Muller & Patel, 2004). Instead of access to lucrative markets, they end up losing their domestic markets to imported goods in the absence of proper mechanisms. Thus, the cost to poor people of adjusting to globalization and trade liberalization is substantial when markets do not work well. Market failure can happen due to many reasons, such as lack of basic information, dominance of markets by a few key players, weak economic governance or poor enforcement of the law. The declining viability of small farms in such situations leads small farmers to sell or lease out land to larger farmers (Payer, 1980). This is known as 'reverse tenancy' in India. CF has increased the incidence of reverse tenancy recently (Singh, 2002). The leased-in area in Punjab was 19 per cent and, in Haryana, as high as 34 per cent of the total area cultivated in 1992. In India as a whole, marginal and small farmers leased only 35 per cent of the total leased area, the rest being with large farmers (43%) and medium farmers (22%). Although reverse tenancy seems to be a win-win situation for both the small farmers leasing out and the large farmers leasing in as they maximize their incomes, in agriculturally backward areas this practice may alienate marginal and small farmers from land altogether, leaving them without alternative sources of employment (Haque, 2000). In fact, due to reverse tenancy, the number of operational holdings in Punjab declined from 13.75 lakh in 1970–1971 to 10.88 lakh in 1985–1986 and 10.93 lakh by 1995–1996 (GoP, 2005). This decline in number of holdings occurred largely in the category of small land marginal holdings, which declined by over two lakh between 1990–1991 and 2000-2001 and accounted for only 29.66 per cent of the total in 2000–2001, compared to 44.74 per cent in 1990–1991 (Gill, 2005).

Widespread distress among farmers in both agriculturally grown and backward regions is manifested in farmer suicides. A large number of suicide cases are reported from marginal and small farmers, mostly in Andhra Pradesh, Karnataka, Maharashtra, Haryana and Punjab (Ahlawat, 2002; Deshpande, 2002; Iyer & Manick, 2000; Mohanty, 2001; Shiva et al., 2000). Areas which have achieved a greater level of modernization and commercialization of agriculture have also witnessed suicides by farmers and agricultural labourers (Gill, 2004). In the absence of any support, the costs of coping with commercial modern farming are too high for marginal and small farmers. For example, motor burn-out costs for marginal farmers were 10 per cent of their gross farm income in Haryana and 7.7 per cent in Andhra Pradesh. This figure for large farmers was only 1.6 per cent and 2.3 per cent, respectively (WB, 2004). Further, since marginal farm households are net buyers of food, the increasing and fluctuating prices can hit them hard (Singh et al., 2002).

Viability of smallholdings is an important issue and it is argued that promoting agricultural diversification towards high-value crops is one of the means through which this can be achieved (Sen & Raju, 2005; Vyâs, 1996). Also, the seasonality of employment induced by specialization could, to a large extent, be mitigated by introducing a larger number of crops in the cropping pattern that would offer fuller employment to agricultural labour round the year (Sen & Raju, 2005). Small farmers in irrigated areas tend to specialize in a few crops. This is more of a forced specialization, for the larger farmers in dry (water-scarce) regions are found to have diversified their crop and livestock patterns. Thus, there is a positive relationship between farm size and crop or livestock diversification, but a negative relationship so far as employment and income diversification are concerned (Saleth, 1997).

Crop diversification can be viewed as a strategy for profit maximization or risk minimization. Profitability would depend on yield, price and cost of cultivation (Sen & Raju, 2005). Farmers adopt or do not adopt a technology/crop depending on the economic sense it makes and other risks and environmental factors associated with it, besides awareness and persuasion that do help to an extent. However, they do not easily switch from field crops to horticultural or other high-value crops as these are much more labour and other input intensive and require more post-harvest handling. Further, profitability depends much more on meeting market requirements of freshness and quality. Thus, while farmers can expect to earn more from these crops, they are required to work harder, learn new skills and risk more capital (Benziger, 1996).

Therefore, to adopt a new crop or technology, farmers need more than just technology. Diversification towards high-value crops would involve a higher level of investment per unit area, both direct and indirect. The former is in terms of higher cost of production, and the latter due to infrastructural and institutional changes required for producing and marketing many of these products—that are mostly perishable or semi-perishable. Many high-value products such as fruits, vegetables and flowers are characterized by highly volatile and speculative pricing structures owing to the 'small volume' of trade. Diversification and risk are, thus, closely linked as diversification exposes producers to the greater volatility of both domestic and world prices. Risk aversion has been identified as a significant impediment to what would otherwise seem to be a rational diversification on the basis of average profitability of alternative crops which, in turn, is affected by the attitudes of individual farmers and the nature of technology (Sen & Raju, 2005).

However, concerns have been raised about certain in-built constraints facing marginal and small farmers, particularly while diversifying towards high-value profitable crops. The primary constraints to successful diversification by small farmers include non-availability of sufficient and timely irrigation, relatively higher costs of cultivation, lack of capital and credit availability, lack of knowledge about markets, lack of access to new technologies, relatively shorter shelf life of produce, price fluctuations, pests and disease proneness of improved varieties of these commodities (fruits and vegetables) and high risks (Pingali & Khwaja, 2004; Sen & Raju, 2005). However, the nature of the product/crop in favour of which diversification is taking place would, to a large extent, influence the motivation for diversification for small farmers. Diversification by its very nature favours large farmers (Pingali & Khwaja, 2004). Even those small farmers who can be encouraged to go for the crop switch cannot be immune from the problem of 'double exploitation', where they receive lower prices for their horticultural output but pay higher prices for food grains obtained from the open market. In fact, it is this phenomenon emerging from the existing system of agricultural marketing that explains why small farmers lack the incentive to switch easily to non-food crops (Sen & Raju, 2005).

A study of cut flowers for the Delhi market by growers in an Uttar Pradesh village indicated that the net returns from flower cultivation were many times higher than those from traditional crops of sugarcane or wheat. Further, flower-cultivating households had much higher gross and net returns than the others. However, small farmers received lower prices and incurred higher costs due to smaller volumes. The variability in prices received by small farmers was also above average and higher than those for other categories of farmers for all categories of flowers. As for the risk, the proportion of households making losses was very high in flower cultivation (12–38%) and almost negligible (1–2%) in wheat and sugarcane, mainly because of yield fluctuations and, to some extent, price fluctuations. This risk dimension makes it difficult for small and resource-constrained farmers to diversify into high-value crops like flowers. Further, the proportion of small farmers among flower cultivators was only 20 per cent, though they accounted for 80 per cent of the non-flower cultivating households and 29 per cent of the total households in the village. In the case of medium and large farmers, more than half were involved in flower cultivation. Also, the small farmers were relatively late entrants to this crop, and it seemed they could not stay in it for long due to the high risk and cost of cultivation involved (Sen & Raju, 2005).

CF AND SMALL FARMERS

Among the various institutional mechanisms available for agricultural development, India has so far relied mainly on state and public sector led growth and development of the farm sector, with micro-level operations, that is, farming *per se* (with or without controls) being with individual farmers. But since most of the operators have been small and marginal farmers, growth in the farm sector was mainly determined by the role of the state—both in capital financing and in regulation of activities in terms of the incentive structure created. With liberalization of the farm sector policy, the other two modes—private industrial capital directly entering into the farm sector with large resources (corporate farming) that is still not legalized (Singh, 1998) and industrial capital aligning with farming interests to bring about improvement in productivity and value addition (CF)—are evolving in almost all parts of the country, especially CF in the more developed regions. Various experiences of CF in other situations across the world and in India are analysed further.

CF can be defined as a system for the production and supply of agricultural and horticultural produce by farmers/primary producers under advance contracts, the essence of such arrangements being a commitment to provide an agricultural commodity of a type, at a specified time, price and in specified quantity to a known buyer. In fact,

CF can be described as a half-way house between independent farm production and corporate/captive farming and can be a case of a step towards complete vertical integration or disintegration, depending on the given context. It basically involves four aspects—pre-agreed price, quality, quantity or acreage (minimum/maximum) and time (Singh, 2002). Some others recommend CF as the only way to make small-scale farming competitive as the services provided by contracting agencies cannot be provided by any other agencies (Eaton & Shepherd, 2001). CF also lowers transaction costs for farmers as many transactions are internalized by the procuring firm (IFPRI, 2005). It is also an alternative to corporate farming which may be costly, risky, difficult to manage and still not viable (Payer, 1980). CF has various models/variants being practised in India at present (Appendices 1, 2 and 3).

There have been some quick studies of the CF system in India recently, but most of them look at the economics of the CF system in specific crops compared with that of the non-contract situation and/or competing traditional crops of a given region, for example, gherkins (hybrid cucumber) in Tamil Nadu (Chidambaram, 1997) and Andhra Pradesh (Dev & Rao, 2004; Haque, 2000) and tomato in Punjab (Bhalla & Singh, 1996; Haque, 2000; Rangi & Sidhu, 2000) and Haryana (Dileep et al., 2002). It is found that contract production fetched much higher (almost three times) gross returns compared with those from the traditional crops of wheat, paddy and potato in the case of tomato (Bhalla & Singh, 1996; Rangi & Sidhu, 2000), and tomato and onion in the case of gherkin (Chidambaram, 1997) due to higher yield and assured price under contracts. Studies of tomato contract production in Punjab and Haryana (Dileep et al., 2002; Haque, 2000) and of cucumber in Andhra Pradesh (Haque, 2000) also found that the net returns from these crops under contracts were much higher than those under non-contract situations, though the production cost was higher under the contract system (Dileep et al., 2002). A more recent study across crops, companies and locations in Punjab also confirms this (Kumar, 2005). The Punjab and Haryana study also showed that contract growers faced many problems, such as undue quality cuts on produce by firms, delayed deliveries at the factory, delayed payments, low price and pest attacks on the crop (Bhalla & Singh, 1996; Dileep et al., 2002; Rangi & Sidhu, 2000; Satish, 2003; Singh, 2002).

Also, all the studies found that most companies work mostly with large and medium farmers (Bhalla & Singh, 1996; Dev & Rao, 2004; Haque, 2003; Kumar, 2005; Singh 2002; Singh and Asokan, 2005), except firms in Andhra Pradesh, which worked with small and marginal farmers due to the nature of the crop (cucumber/gherkin) itself. This bias in favour of large/medium farmers is perpetuating the practice of reverse tenancy in regions like Punjab, where these farmers lease in land from marginal and small farmers for contract production (Haque, 2003; Singh, 2002). Breach of contracts by farmers as well as firms has also been reported (Bhalla & Singh, 1996; Haque, 2003; Singh, 2002). Some studies recommended further expansion and promotion of the CF system due to its benefits (Bhalla & Singh, 1996; Chidambaram, 1997; Dileep et al., 2002; Rangi & Sidhu, 2000). In fact, the eligibility criteria for participation in CF projects/schemes such as irrigated land, suitable land, land near main road and literacy level of the farmer are themselves discriminatory in terms of who can be a contract grower. CF of trees is not attractive to marginal and small farmers mainly because it is not labour intensive, involves a long gestation period, requires large initial capital and provides no regular income flow (Baumann, 2000).

The more recent models of CF like franchising (Appendix 3) being practised by the Tatas (Tata Kisan Sansar) for wheat in states such as Uttar Pradesh, Haryana and Punjab and by Mahindra Shubhlabh Services (Mahindra Krishi Vihar) for paddy in Tamil Nadu, Andhra Pradesh and Karnataka and basmati and maize in Punjab and Haryana are also not delivering results as expected. Mahindra and Mahindra's recent involvement in Punjab agriculture has not worked to the advantage of farmers. In fact, this model creates a monopsony where a single buyer buys produce of hundreds and thousands of farmers. It works to the disadvantage of farmers who lack adequate information about the market; this is termed asymmetry of information. This model increases the buyer's power disproportionately and puts the seller entirely at its mercy. Small and marginal farmers have not gained from these experiments. Wherever any gain has been reported, it is for farmers in general and does not reflect in any way a distinction between big/rich and small/poor farmers' gains. The interests of the poor farmers are not synonymous with those of large/rich farmers (Gill, 2004).

Even the state-sponsored programme of CF did not deliver in Punjab. The contracted winter maize and hyola crops failed almost completely due to inclement weather and poor-quality seeds. In the case of green peas, contract growers were forced to dump their produce in the open market after it was rejected by PAIC on grounds of quality as per the contract specification; there had been fungus infection due to inclement weather marked by heavy rains in winter and then a sudden rise in temperature. An area of 500 acres under contract production of green peas in the Patiala and Fatehgarh Sahib districts had been affected. Some farmers found fault with the fungicide supplied by the contracting company in this regard. The dumping of contract-produced crop in the open market led to a fall in local market prices and it was being sold at ₹3 per kg now against a promised price of ₹5 per kg (Rangi & Sidhu, 2003; Singh, 2003). In general, across crops and regions, the CF programme could not achieve the stated area goal. Not only did it fall short in terms of contracted area being less than that stated by the agency, but farmers too did not plant the entire contracted area with the contract crops. The gap was much larger in the latter case, even as high as 50 per cent in winter maize in Ludhiana and 20 per cent in hyola in both Ludhiana and Patiala. There was a different private seed company for each crop and they only provided seed and no other extension service. Finally, none of the companies procured the produce and instead advised the farmers to sell in the open market, either because open market prices were higher than the contract price or the quality was not as desired. Except the oilseed crops (hyola and sunflower), the net returns from contract crops were found to be lower than the possible yield from wheat crop. Most problems that farmers faced related to production and quality (like quality of seed and extension), not marketing of produce (except peas), since the open market could take care of the contract produce. A large majority (60%) were not willing to enter into a CF arrangement again after this experience (Dhaliwal et al., 2003). There have also been instances of corruption and malpractice in the PAIC-run CF programme due to conflicts of interest among implementing agencies and lack of monitoring (Ramachandran & Dogra, 2006).

Recent World Bank reports also point to the deficiencies in the CF programme launched by the state government. It states that for the programme to be successful, it should take into account the aspects of selection of crops for contracting, develop a quick and effective contract enforcement and dispute resolution system, limit fiscal risks to the state government, limit the number of parties in a contractual arrangement and develop farmers' organizations capable of contracting with sponsors, with a view to reducing transaction costs, increasing information flow and improving farmers' negotiation position (WB, 2003, 2004). Some of the coping strategies/innovations adopted by farmers in CF situations included labour–water exchange, share cropping and group leasing of land by marginal and landless farmers (Deshingkar et al., 2003; Singh, 2002).

At the same time, vast areas of the country such as Bihar, Jharkhand, Chhattisgarh, Odisha, West Bengal, the entire Northeast India and areas of Uttarakhand, Himachal Pradesh, Kerala and Jammu and Kashmir have been bypassed by these companies. Does it mean that these areas and farmers would not benefit from commercialization and vertical integration of agriculture? These are areas with highest concentration of small and marginal farmers (Gill, 2004). This essentially means that contracting companies do not in any way encourage those who need to be helped to participate, since risk preference and innovativeness require not just attitude but also resources and risk-taking capability. The aspects of contracting which contribute to the exclusion of small farmers from CF are enforcement of contracts, high transaction costs, quality standards, business attitude and ethics such as non-/delayed/reduced payment, high rate of product rejection and the weak bargaining power of small growers (Kirsten & Sartorius, 2002).

SMALL FARMERS AND GLOBALIZED COMMERCIAL AGRICULTURE

Market access for small producers depends on:

- Understanding the markets
- Organization of the firm or operations
- Communication and transport links
- An appropriate policy environment

There are a large number of interventions which attempt market access for small producers, ranging from integrated foreign investment (by multinationals) to large private buyers in the First World, developing country producers, alternative trading companies, export and import promotion agencies, aid programmes, technical research projects and agencies promoting alternative trade. On various parameters of ensuring market access, multinational corporations and alternative trading companies and large direct private buyers seem to be better placed (Page & Slater, 2003). Further, there are a large number of institutional arrangements to co-ordinate with small producers, which should be assessed for their relevance and effectiveness in a given context (Table 10.1), though *a priori*, it seems that cooperatives and other similar forms of farmer organizations are more relevant and sustainable, especially the new generation cooperatives (NGCs) which are more market-oriented and avoid free-riding and horizon problems because of their contractual equity-based transaction with grower members (Singh, 2004). In India, Amul has been able to successfully link up/integrate small and marginal milk producers with the national and international milk markets. It is estimated that 21 per cent of its nine million members are landless and another 66 per cent are small and marginal farmers (Gandhi et al., 2001; Pingali & Khwaja, 2004). Some cooperatives, like those dealing with sapota (chikoo) in south Gujarat, have also attempted a quality-based grading and pooling system and contractual relations with members for procurement, along with market-orientation strategies such as multiple outlets and efficient use of market information to achieve better business performance (Singh, 1997). In fact, the cooperative form of organization of even farm production activity by resource-constrained farmers has been found to be more efficient than private farms in Romania (Sabates-Wheeler, 2002).

With the right policy environment, small farms can not only survive but can also make a developmental contribution to poverty reduction. There have been cases of success when public or private assistance to growers in terms of technical assistance and supply of input credit was made available. In some places in Brazil, small farmers have gone in for collective tanks to meet the scale requirement, though the large farmers will have an advantage as they do not face the transaction cost involved in collective use of physical assets. Dairy companies and cooperatives encourage the use of collective tanks, even by financing or facilitating credit for milk producers in some cases (Farina, 2002). Many attempts including offering differentiated contracts under CF

Table 10.1 Relative Benefits of Alternative Marketing Structures for Small Farmers

Structure	Sales Position of SFs vis-à-vis LFs	Sales Position of SF vis-à-vis Buyer	Input Facilities/ Technical Assistance	Government Support Required
Private local firms	Can be against SFs due to bargaining power	Advantage of access to alternative outlets	May be available/ based on local experience	Provision of market infrastructure, information, ensuring competition, price stabilization
MNCs/large firms	Equitable prices through contract	Dependent but secure if supplies quality	Direct supply on credit/direct and intensive	Should negotiate prices and participation for SFs
Cooperatives/ new generation cooperatives	Equal if successful	Favourable if efficient cooperative	May arrange	Financial support
State boards/bodies	Equal prices if can reach official buying position	May be exploited	Rare/left to other govt. agencies	Insist on reaching small farmers
Development agency	— do —	Protected if meets quality	Direct supply on credit	Financial support required

Source: Abbott (1993).
Note: SFs, small farmers; LFs, large farmers.

schemes to include small farmers failed in Mexico, though companies had no option but to contract with small vegetable growers. A few firms succeeded in including small farmers in their CF projects only when they also employed the farmers' family members in their processing units, used local intermediaries to supervise small growers and/or limited the small grower contracts only to areas close to the highway, besides other reasons such as the small growers being lower cost and more efficient than the firms' own farms, their poor access to alternative outlets for produce and source of credit and having low labour and land opportunity cost. These measures reduced the information asymmetry between the growers and the firm and the transaction cost of dealing with small growers (Warning et al., 2003).

Development agencies and projects need to internalize the fact that product markets will increasingly mean supermarkets. Therefore, market-oriented programmes and policies will indeed be supermarket oriented. If, in a given country, a few chains command majority of the food sector, then development policies and programmes need to learn how to deal with this handful of big companies. The agencies also need to realize that small farmers and entrepreneurs have to gear up quickly to compete in the new markets spreading over most of the food economy. Local market niches are disappearing and the distinction between global and domestic markets is getting blurred. Governments and donors will have to focus their programmes not just on exports but also on the growing market of local supermarkets. It is important to promote good business practices that optimize retailer–supplier relations, protecting both sides. This can be initiated by establishing or improving contract regulations and business rules of practice, some of which are already available in the form of legislation in the USA and Argentina. These practices can also be enforced by private sector codes of practice.

However, regulations do not ultimately change the economic forces under which supermarkets operate. Changes in procurement systems are driven by these forces. These changes and the basic requirements they impose on growers are conditions which will have to be met if growers are to be able to tap that powerful market. Therefore, small farmers and entrepreneurs ought to be helped to make investments in equipment, management, technology, commercial practices, etc., and strong and efficient organizations need to be developed to meet those requirements. There have been such attempts in Brazil and Guatemala (Reardon & Berdegue, 2002). In organic produce chains as well, group certification by public or development agencies can provide a chance for small farmers to take up organic cultivation.

Fair trade is another route to help link small producers with global markets profitably (Warning et al., 2003). It involves partnership with producers and consumers for improving the position of disempowered members through trade. It aims at poverty alleviation through fair price to producers, supporting producers in social/environmental projects, gender equality, product development for market access and long-term relationship for stability and security of livelihoods. The logic of fair trade is that terms of trade are unfavourable to the developing world in terms of unfair prices, which need to be corrected through intervention. Also, it aims to serve as a cushioning mechanism during the transition of producers to high-value products. Partnership involves fusion of market and ethics in the supply chain links from producer to consumer. There are two approaches to fair trade—labelling and branding. The core of fair-trade partnership is the branding approach adopted by alternative trading organizations and the producer organizations/self-help groups/cooperatives. Fair trade aims at bridging the North–South divide in development through trade (Tallontire, 2001).

CONSTRAINTS OF ACCESS

The main requirements of small farmers in this changing environment are better access to capital and education. Management capacity is as important as physical capital and the most difficult thing to provide. Further, collective action to deal with scale requirements needs to be designed to satisfy new product and process standards or to avoid exclusion from the supply chain. Collective action through cooperatives or associations is important not only to be able to buy and sell at a better price but also to help small farmers adapt to new patterns and much greater levels of competition (Farina, 2002). Small farmers require professional training in marketing and in technical aspects of production. There is also need to strengthen small farmer organizations and provide them technical assistance to increase productivity for the cost-competitive market, provide help in improving quality of produce and to encourage them to participate more actively in the marketing of their produce in order to capture value added from the supply chain. Finally, the problem of financing small producers needs to be tackled through innovative ways (Schwentesium & Gomez, 2002).

Although there are concerns about the ability of small farms and firms to survive in the changing environment of agribusiness, still there are opportunities for them to exploit, for instance, in product differentiation with origin of product or organic products and other niche markets. But the major route has to be through exploitation of other factors like external economies of scale through networking or clustering and such other alliances like CF (Kirsten & Sartorius, 2002). The experience of CF across the globe suggests that it is not the contract per se which is harmful as a system but how it is practised in a given context. If there are enough mechanisms to monitor and use the contract for developmental purposes, it can certainly lead to a betterment of all the parties involved, especially small and marginal farmers.

Viewed in the light of experience, potential problems of CF point to the policy steps required to reduce the ill effects of such a system, like regulation and monitoring of contracts. Legal protection to contract growers as a group must be considered to protect them from malpractices in contracting by supply chain drivers. There are cases of legal protection being given to subcontracting industries in Japan in their relations with large firms. These laws specify the duties (to undertake written and clearly termed contracts with subcontractors) and forbidden acts for the large parent firm. The latter include refusal to receive delivery of commissioned goods, delaying payment beyond agreed period, discounting of payment, returning commissioned goods without good reason, forcing price reduction, compelling subcontractors to purchase the parent firm's products and forcing them to pay in advance for materials supplied by it. These provisions are monitored by the Fair Trade Commission. Interestingly, most violations by parent firms were committed on the written form and clear terms of contract (Sako, 1992).

If CF is the only flexible production system prevalent in industry applied to farm production, it is logical to extend such legal provisions with necessary modifications to farming contracts. In the farming sector *per se*, there is the Model Producer Protection Act, 2000, of Iowa state in the USA, which requires contracts to be in plain language and disclose material risks, provides a three-day cancellation period for the producer to review and discuss production contracts with advisors, provides producers to be first-priority lien for payments due under a contract in case the contracting company goes bankrupt, protects against undue cancellation of contracts by companies and prohibits 'tournaments' (contracts where compensation to grower is determined by their performance relative to others; www.flaginc.org/pubs/poultry/poultrypts).

Contracts need to be transparent and require frequent and independent scrutiny so that they remain competitive, both with similar contracts and with open market transactions. Wide publicity of contract terms can help stimulate competition. Second, vigorous bargaining by cooperatives or other agricultural producer organizations is needed to negotiate equitable contracts. In the USA, such organizations have been able to secure standardization of contracts and their scrutiny by a government agency (Wilson, 1986). In Japan, too, farmers have managed their relationships with companies well through cooperatives (Asano-Tamanoi, 1988). Producers' organizations amplify the political voice of smallholder producers, reduce the costs of marketing of inputs and outputs and provide a forum for members to share information, coordinate activities and make collective decisions. Producers' organizations create opportunities for producers to get more involved in value-adding activities such as input supply, credit, processing, marketing and distribution.

The practice of contracts needs to be monitored by farmer organizations or non-governmental organizations (NGOs). In fact, the companies should proactively involve NGOs in their CF operations and even organize farmer cooperatives or groups for more sustainable CF programmes (Mayers & Vermeulen, 2002; Pingali & Khwaja, 2004). Groups or farmers' organizations like cooperatives not only lower transaction costs but also lower input costs for farmers and give them better bargaining power. In contract arrangements with small producers in west African countries, the cotton companies started transferring some of the operational or functional responsibilities such as distribution of inputs, equipment orders and credit repayment management to the village associations in the 1970s itself. They provided these associations with management skills for these tasks. The companies relied on traditional village authority structures for organizing the associations but limited the associations to one per village for simpler company purchasing, delivery and marketing procedures. This arrangement accounted for a significant part of each cotton company's success (Bingen et al., 2003). Unfortunately, agri-business companies have not been very keen to organize or support cooperatives. Rather, they have tried to fail cooperatives whenever they emerged (Konings, 1998).

Finally, it is the trust between farmers and processors that is important for realignment of the chain (Heron, 2003). Trust has been defined as the willingness to rely on an exchange partner in whom one has confidence. It is the function of relationship-specific investments, satisfaction with product quality, prior experience and importance of input. Trust is developed by a constant and detailed exchange of information that reduces the uncertainty of performance. In the case of farmers, a reciprocal purchase agreement has positive relationship with the farmer's trust in the buyer. Commitment is thought to be closely related to mutuality, loyalty and the forsaking of alternatives (Batt & Rexha, 1999). Regulation of supermarket chains to control or mitigate their market power can be an effective tool to ensure the presence of small growers in value chains as seen in the case of the banana trade regime in pre-WTO period in the EU policy, single-channel (monopoly) exports by producer bodies in some exporting countries like South Africa and regulation of domestic import markets in France (Gibbon, 2003).

CONCLUSION

Small farmers are certainly going to be around for a long time in India, though they will face a number of challenges. Therefore, what happens to small and marginal farmers has implications for the entire economy and people's livelihoods. But they can adequately respond to these challenges only if the policy environment is right. Otherwise, they will only be losers in the process of globalization and liberalization.

Major conditions for successful interlocking between agri-business firms and small producers include increased competition for procurement instead of monopsony, guaranteed market for farm produce, effective repayment mechanism, market information for farmers to effectively bargain with companies, large volumes of transactions through groups of farmers for lower costs, cooperation among genuine agri-business firms in the area and no alternative source of raw material for companies (Kirsten & Sartorius, 2002). Further, for the sustainability of company–farmer partnership schemes, it is important that the company is able to successfully market its products so that farmers do not suffer from lack of market (Baumann, 2000; Haque, 2000). Building of relationships of trust with farmers through company reputation rather than marketing gimmicks is crucial. This requires mutual respect, a fair and transparent negotiation process, realistic assessment of benefits, long-term commitment, equitable sharing of risk and sound business plans (Mayers & Vermeulen, 2002).

In India, the legal reform process has been accelerated by the union government with the enactment of the Model State Agricultural Produce Marketing (Development and Regulation) Act, 2003, which deals with setting up of private markets, selling of produce by growers outside the Agricultural Produce Marketing Committee (APMCs) (regulated markets), setting up of direct markets, specialized commodity-specific markets, regulation and promotion of CF, provision for agencies and measures to promote quality, standards and alternative markets and public–private partnerships to facilitate more and better linkage between firms and farmers (GoI, 2004). The amended Agricultural Produce Marketing (Development and Regulation) Act has certain mandatory and optional provisions wherein mandatory ones include aspects such as who can undertake CF, contract specifications, liabilities, farmer asset indemnity and dispute resolution. The optional features include those relating to farm practices, insurance, monitoring, role of farmer bodies and support from the sponsor. Under this Act, registration for contract operations with local authority is a must and the model contract agreement is quite fair in terms of sharing of costs and risks between the sponsor and the grower (GoI, 2003). But, here again, there are state-level variations in the amended Acts and the spirit has been diluted. For example, in Gujarat, the amended Act makes the APMC party to the contract, which is totally unnecessary and will only create problems as that is not the best way to protect farmers' interests, if that at all is the logic. Further, there cannot be a single CF model suitable for all situations.

It is also important to note that farm-sector problems, such as high cost of farming, lower returns and environmental sustainability require different kinds of institutions (collectives instead of individual enterprise), for which institutional innovations are a must. The legal system made available a new organizational option, that is, producer (cooperative) companies under the Companies Act, which farmers in many states have gone ahead with in various existing and new projects. A large number of institutional innovations in agriculture in India have taken place at the local level recently. These include the non-pesticidal management of crops, for instance, cotton in Punnukula village in Andhra Pradesh which had suffered from use of pesticides on cotton, both in terms of economic and physical health of the farmers who have now decided to make a total switch to organic management of the cotton and other local crops (CSA, 2004). Farmers in Kerala have come together in the form of producer companies undertaking organic production and marketing.

In Uttarakhand, they have organized themselves into farmers' groups. The regulation of private tube well water prices by village councils in West Bengal is another case of non-market-based, local-level institutions managing a local, private, market-driven resource (groundwater). Also, in other villages of West Bengal, cooperative tube wells by small and marginal farmers have improved efficiency (lower cost) and equity in water access and reduced reverse tenancy (Rawal, 2002). In Punjab, the local-level, people's initiative is happening on a significant scale in the case of tractor markets in the Malwa region and, more specifically, the cotton belt of Punjab. There are daily, weekly and fortnightly markets for the sale and purchase of second-hand as well as new tractors in various market towns of the state where thousands of farmers participate and sell or buy tractors. In a state which today has more than 3.87 lakh tractors accounting for one-fourth of the total population of tractors in the country with just 2.5 per cent of cultivated area, this phenomenon is both encouraging and disturbing. With only about 11.17 lakh operational holdings in the state, it means that every third holding in the state is equipped with a tractor. Added to this is the fact that more than 70 per cent of the farms are below 10 acres each (Singh, 1999).

This kind of market development points to the hidden local potential for robust local institutions in such a crucial area of economy, that is, marketing. There is need to allow and encourage such informal arrangements, provided there are no irregularities and practices detrimental to the interests of market participants. The role of the state in such situations should be supportive and somewhat supervisory in order to ensure the most efficient functioning of these institutions which can deliver objectives of growth, equity and sustainability. Another important aspect of these institutions is that they function fairly competitively, which is beneficial to the users of these markets as they get a fair deal in their transactions.

Given the nature of modern farming involving tremendous amount of technological input and market orientation which require capital resources, involvement of private corporate business interests in agricultural development through the CF system is inevitable. Marketing extension is needed in terms of better product planning at the farmer level, provision of market information, securing/accessing markets for farmers, provision of alternative markets and market orientation in terms of improved marketing practices at the farmer level (Patnaik, 2003). Diversification has to be beyond crops and include allied activities. The agri-business sector is much larger than just farm production and other allied activities. This approach can help examine many possibilities in the off-farm parts of the agri-business chains to involve poor people gainfully. This is also important from the point of view of value addition.

Although there has been ample, successful intermediation in primary production by the state and NGOs, much more is needed in agro-processing, credit, market access, information and technology to enable small farmers to reap enhanced competitive benefits offered by freer markets. Although land reforms are needed, the poor need access to markets as well as assets to get out of poverty. In this, land reforms should be part of the overall reform agenda, but these alone will not help make a dent on poverty if unaccompanied by marketing links for small farmers who are more efficient and more valuable as they are labour intensive. Intermediation is required for small farmers to link them up with global markets in processing and marketing (Lipton, 2002).

In India, due to the small-farm domination of the agricultural sector, the delivery systems require to be attuned to the demands and needs of small farmers, being small in scale and of sporadic nature (Vyas, 1996). Therefore, new institutional mechanisms such as groups, associations, cooperatives, NGOs and other collectivities or networks are needed to reach small and marginal producers more effectively. State agencies and NGOs need to intervene in contract situations as intermediaries to protect farmers and broader local community interests. NGOs can also play a role in providing information and in monitoring and regulating the working of contracts. Better cooperation and coordination between companies and cooperatives for agricultural development also need to be encouraged.

Further, both companies and state should promote group contracts with the intermediation of local NGOs and other institutions so that contractual relationships can be more durable, enforceable and fair. An insurance component in farming interventions is a must to protect farmer interest. Some companies are already doing it, but it is important to ensure a market for farm produce at better prices under these agribusiness projects. The government should also play an enabling role through legal provisions and institutional mechanisms, like helping farmer cooperatives and groups to facilitate smooth functioning of the contract system.

APPENDIX 1

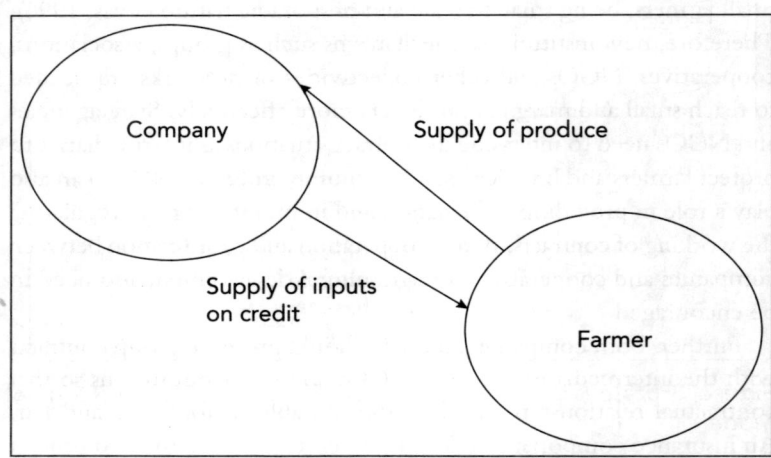

Figure 1 *Bipartite CF Model*
Source: Author's own.

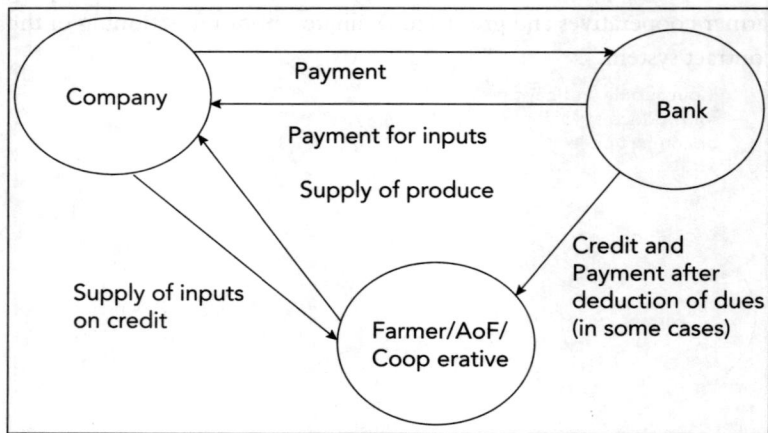

Figure 2 *Tripartite CF Model*
Source: Author's own.

Changing Structure and Organization of Agriculture and Small Farmers in India | 245

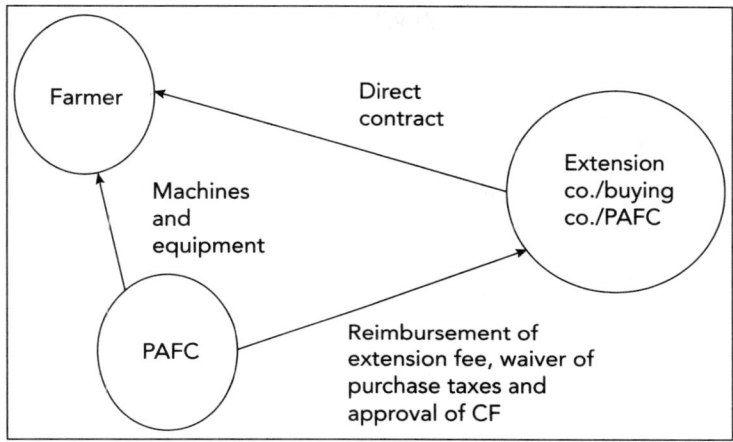

Figure 3 State-led Contract Farming System in Punjab (Original Model)

Source: Author's own.

APPENDIX 2

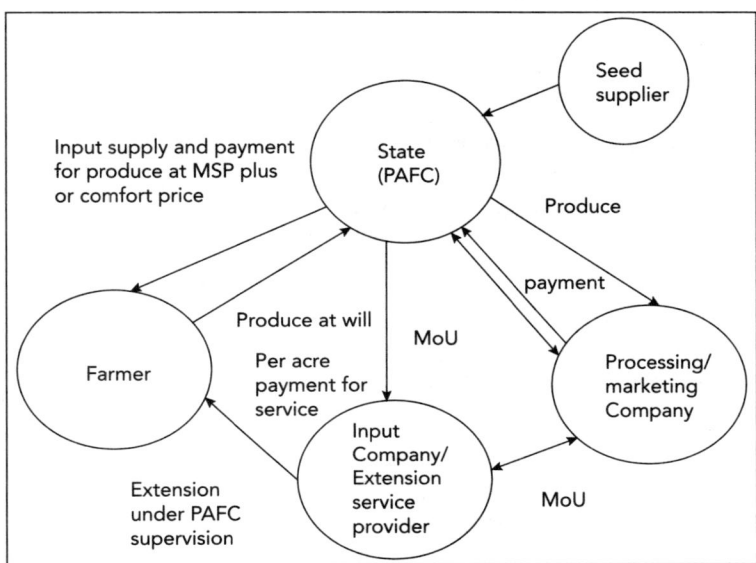

Figure 4 State-led Contract Farming System in Punjab (Revised Model)

Source: Author's own.

APPENDIX 3

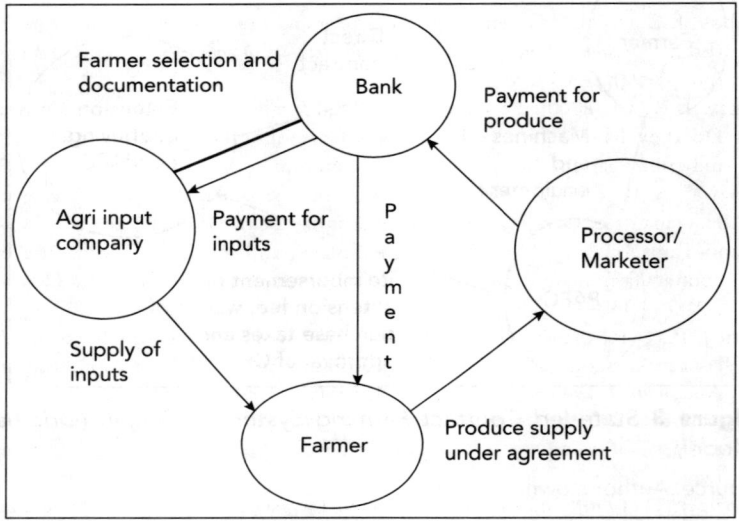

Figure 5 *The Quadpartite CF Model*
Source: Author's own.

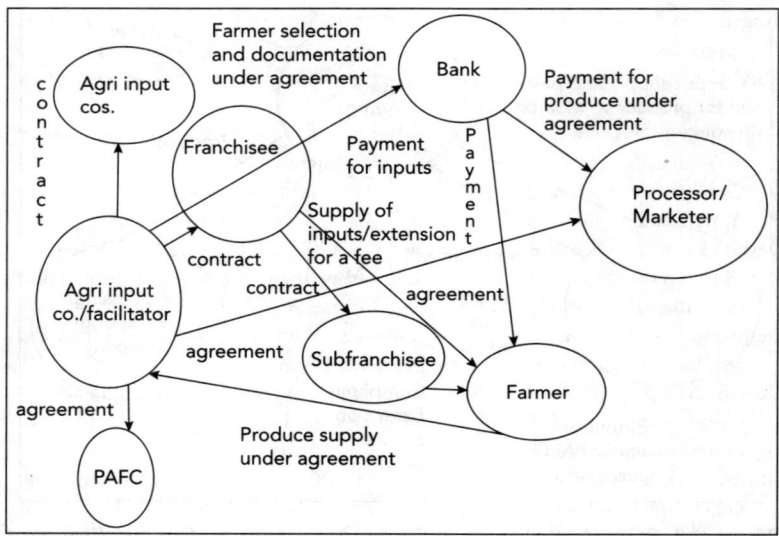

Figure 6 *The Sixpartite (Networking) CF Model*
Source: Author's own.

REFERENCES

Abbott, J. C. (1993). Marketing, the rural poor and sustainability. In J. C. Abbott (Ed.), *Agricultural and food marketing in developing countries—selected readings* (pp. 65–92). CAB International.

Agrawal, R. C. (2000). Perspectives for small farmers in developing countries: Do they have a future? Forum zur Gartenkonferenz. http://userpage.fu.berlin/~garten/Buch/Agrawal(englisch).htm

Ahlawat, S. R. (2002). Political economy and the peasant suicide—A case of Haryana state. *Guru Nanak Journal of Sociology, XXIII*(1), 1–17.

Asano-Tamanoi, M. (1988). Farmers, industries, and the state: The culture of contract farming in Spain and Japan. *Comparative Studies in Society and History, XXX*(3), 432–452.

Batt, J. P., & Rexha, N. (1999). Building trust in agribusiness supply chains: A conceptual model of buyer-seller relationships in the seed potato industry in Asia. *Journal of International Food & Agribusiness Marketing, XI*(1), 1–17.

Baumann, P. (2000, October). *Equity and efficiency in contract farming schemes: The experience of agricultural tree crops* (ODI Working Paper No. 139). Overseas Development Institute.

Benziger, V. (1996). Small fields, big money: Two successful programs in helping small farmers make the transition to high value-added crops. *World Development, XXIV*(11), 1681–1693.

Bhalla, G. S., & Singh, G. (1996). *Impact of GATT on Punjab agriculture.* Ajanta Publications.

Bingen, J., Serrano, A., & Howard, J. (2003). Linking farmers to markets: Different approaches to human capital development. *Food Policy, XXVIII*, 405–419.

CSA. (2004, October). *No pesticides, no pests—The remarkable story of how a village in AP rid itself of pesticides.* The Author.

Chidambaram, M. (1997). *A study of export potentials for gherkins (hybrid cucumber) in Tamilnadu* (Unpublished paper). Department of Agricultural Economics, Centre for Agriculture and Rural Development Studies, Tamilnadu Agricultural University, Coimbatore.

Deshingkar, P., Kulkarni, Rao, U., & Rao, S. (2003). Changing food systems in India: Resource sharing and marketing arrangements for vegetable production in Andhra Pradesh. *Development Policy Review, XXI*(5–6), 627–639.

Deshpande, R. S. (2002). Suicide by farmers in Karnataka: Agrarian distress and possible alleviatory steps. *Economic & Political Weekly, XXXVII*(26), 2601–2610.

Dev, S. M., & Rao, N. C. (2004, June). *Food processing in Andhra Pradesh—Opportunities and challenges* (CESS Working Paper No. 57). Centre for Economic and Social Studies.

Dhaliwal, H. S., Kaur, M., & Singh, J. (2003). *Evaluation of contract farming scheme in the Punjab state.* Department of Economics, Punjab Agricultural University.

Dileep, B. K., Grover, R. K., & Rai, K. N. (2002). Contract farming in tomato: An economic analysis. *Indian Journal of Agricultural Economics, DVII*(2), 197–210.

Eaton, C., & Shepherd, A. W. (2001). *Contract farming: Partnerships for growth*. FAO.
ETKS. (2003). Rural economy 2002–2003. *The Economic Times*.
Farina, E. M. M. Q. (2002). Consolidation, multinationalisation, and competition in Brazil: Impacts on horticulture and dairy products systems. *Development Policy Review, XX*(4), 441–457.
Gandhi, V., Kumar, G., & Marsh, R. (2001). Agroindustry for rural and small farmer development: Issues and lessons from India. *International Food and Agribusiness Management Review, II*(3–4), 331–344.
Gibbon, P. (2003). Value chain governance, public regulation and entry barriers in the global fresh fruit and vegetable chain into the EU. *Development Policy Review, XXI*(5–6), 615–625.
Gill, S. S. (2004). Small farmers and markets. *Economic & Political Weekly, XXXIX*(23), 2356–2358.
Gill, S. S. (2005). *Diversification of Punjab agriculture: A faulty design and bureaucratic apathy* (Unpublished paper).
GoI. (2003). *Contract farming agreement and its model specifications*. Ministry of Agriculture, Department of Agriculture and Cooperation, Krishi Bhawan.
GoI. (2004). *Economic survey 2003–04*. Ministry of Finance.
GoP. (2005, February). *Statistical abstract of Punjab, 2004*. Publication No. 905. Economic Adviser to GoP, Economic and Statistical Organisation.
Haque, T. (2000). Contractual arrangements in land and labour markets in rural India. *International Journal of Agricultural Economics, DV*(3), 233–252.
Haque, T. (2003). Land reforms and agricultural development: Retrospect and prospect. In S. Pal, Mruthyunjaya, P. K. Joshi, & R. Saxena (Ed.), *Institutional change in Indian agriculture* (pp. 267–284). National Centre for Agricultural Economics and Policy Research.
Heron, L. R. (2003). Creating food futures: Reflections on food governance issues in New Zealand's agri-food sector. *Journal of Rural Studies, XIX*(1), 111–125.
IFPRI. (2005). *High value agriculture and vertical co-ordination in India—Will the smallholders participate?* (Draft research report). International Food Policy Research Institute.
Iyer, K. G., & Manick, M. S. (2000). *Indebtedness, impoverishment and suicides in rural Punjab*. Indian Publishers and Distributors.
Jha, D. (2001, January 22–24). *Agricultural research and small farms*. Presidential Address at 60th Annual Convocation of the Indian Society of Agricultural Economics (ISAE), Kalyani, West Bengal.
Johl, S. S. (1995). Agricultural sector and new economic policy. *International Journal of Agricultural Economics, D*(3), 473–487.
Kirsten, J., & Sartorius, K. (2002). Linking agribusiness and small-scale farmers in developing countries: Is there a new role for contract farming? *Development Southern Africa, XIX*(4), 503–529.
Konings, P. (1998). Unilever, contract farmers and co-operatives in Cameroon: Crisis and response. *The Journal of Peasant Studies, XXVI*(1), 112–138.

Kumar, P. (2005, May 4–5). *Commercialisation of Indian agriculture and its implications for small and large farmers: A case study of Punjab* (Paper presentation). FAO Symposium on Agricultural Commercialisation and the Small Farmer, Rome.

Lipton, M. (2002, June 3–6). *Access to assets and land in the context of poverty reduction and economic development in Asia* (Paper presentation). Global Distance Learning Course of the World Bank Institute on Reaching the Rural Poor: Strategies for Rural Development for the East Asia Region, Chulalongkorn University, Bangkok.

Mani, G., & Pandey, V. K. (1995). Agrarian structure under the new economic policy. *International Journal of Agricultural Economics, D*(3), 524–530.

Mayers, J., & Vermeulen, S. (2002). *Company–community forestry partnerships: From raw deals to mutual gains?* International Institute for Environment and Development.

Mohanty, B. B. (2001). Suicides of farmers in Maharashtra: A socio-economic analysis. *Review of Development and Change, VI*(2), 146–189.

Muller, A. R., & Patel, R. (2004, May). *Shining India? Economic liberalisation and rural poverty in the 1990s* (Food First Policy Brief No. 10). Food First/Institute for Food and Development Policy.

Page, S., & Slater, R. (2003). Small producer participation in global food systems: Policy opportunities and constraints. *Development Policy Review, XXI*(5–6), 641–654.

Parikh, K., & Nagarajan, H. K. (2004). *How important is land consolidation? Land fragmentation and implications for productivity: Case study of village Nelpathur in Tamil Nadu* (National Bank for Agriculture and Rural Development [NABARD] Occasional Paper No. 31). NABARD.

Patnaik, G. (2003). Marketing, storage, and extension services: State of agriculture in India. In B. Debroy & A. U. Khan (Ed.), *Enabling agricultural markets for the small Indian farmer* (pp. 81–120). Bookwell.

Payer, C. (1980). The World Bank and the small farmer. *Monthly Review, 1*, 30–46.

Pingali, P., & Khwaja, Y. (2004). Globalisation of Indian diets and the transformation of food supply systems. *Indian Journal of Agricultural Marketing, XVIII*(1), 26–49.

Ramachandran, R., & Dogra, C. S. (2006, January 23). Punjab—Caught in a contract. *Outlook*, 24–26.

Rangi, P. S., & Sidhu, M. S. (2003). Contract farming in Punjab. *Productivity, XXXXIV*(3), 484–491.

Rao, V. M., & Hanumappa, H. G. (1999). Marginalisation process in agriculture— Indicators, outlook and policy implications., *Economic & Political Weekly, XXXIV*(52), A133–A138.

Rawal, V. (2002). Non-market interventions in water-Sharing: Case studies from West Bengal, India. *Journal of Agrarian Change, II*(4), 545–569.

Reardon, T., & Berdegue J. A. (2002). The rapid rise of supermarkets in Latin America: Challenges and opportunities for development. *Development Policy Review, XX*(4), 371–388.

Sabates-Wheeler, R. (2002). Farm strategy, self selection and productivity: Can small farming groups offer production benefits to farmers in post-socialist Romania? *World Development, XXX*(10), 1737–1753.

Sako, M. (1992). *Prices, quality and trust—Inter-firm relations in Britain and Japan.* Cambridge University Press.

Saleth, R. M. (1997). Diversification strategy for small farmers and landless: Some evidence from Tamil Nadu. *International Journal of Agricultural Economics, DII*(1), 73–86.

Satish, P. (2003). *Contract farming as a backward linkage for agro processing—Experiences from Punjab* (Paper presentation). 63rd Annual Conference of ISAE, Bhubaneswar.

Schwentesium, R., & Gomez, M. A. (2002). Supermarkets in Mexico: Impacts on horticulture systems. *Development Policy Review, XX*(4), 487–502.

Sen, S., & Raju, S. (2005). *Globalisation and expanding markets for cut-flowers: Who benefits?* (Paper presentation). South Asia Regional Conference on Globalisation of Agriculture in South Asia: Has It Made Difference to Rural Livelihoods? Centre for Economic and Social Studies, Hyderabad; International Food Policy Research Institute, Washington; International Association of Agricultural Economists; Indian Society of Agricultural Economics, Mumbai; Indian Society of Agricultural Marketing, Nagpur; Acharya N G Ranga Agricultural University, Hyderabad.

Shiva, V., Jafri, A. H., Emani A., & Pande, M. (2000). *Seeds of suicide: The ecological and human costs of globalisation of agriculture.* Research Foundation for Science, Technology & Ecology.

Singh, G., & Asokan, S. R. (2005). *Contract farming in India—Text and cases.* Oxford & IBH.

Singh, J. (2003, March 28). Contracted green peas dumped in open market. *The Tribune*, 15.

Singh, R. B., Kumar, P., & Woodhead, T. (2002, March). *Smallholder farmers in India: Food security and agricultural policy.* FAO, Regional Office for Asia and the Pacific.

Singh, S. (1997). Managing marketing: Co-operatives in horticultural business in South Gujarat. *Indian Journal of Agricultural Marketing, XI*(1–2), 73–82.

Singh, S. (1998, August 24–September 6). Should Indian farming go corporate? *Business India*, 122–123.

Singh, S. (1999). Institutional innovations in Indian agriculture: A case of input markets. *Institutional Development, VI*(2), 3–10.

Singh, S. (2002). Contracting out solutions: Political economy of contract farming in the Indian Punjab. *World Development, XXX*(9), 1621–1638.

Singh, S. (2004). The new generation co-operative: Theory, practice and relevance. *The Co-operator, XXXXII*(5), 229–230.

Singh, T., & Sharma V. K. (2004). Employment of farm resources in Punjab agriculture. *Productivity, XXXXV*(1), 140–144.

Swain, M. (2000). Agricultural development and interlocked markets. *Indian Journal of Agricultural Economics, DV*(3), 308–316.

Tallontire, A. (2001, November). Fair trade and development (Draft paper). Natural Resources and Ethical Trade Programme, Natural Resources Institute, University of Greenwich, Chatham.

Vyas, V. S. (1996). Diversification in agriculture: Concept, rationale and approaches. *International Journal of Agricultural Economics, DI*(4), 636–643.

Warning, M., Key, N., & Hoo, W. S. (2003). Small farmer participation in contract farming (Draft paper).

Wilson, J. (1986). The political economy of contract farming. *Review of Radical Political Economics, XVIII*(4), 47–70.

WB. (2003). *India: Revitalising Punjab's agriculture.* Rural Development Unit, South Asia Region, WB.

WB. (2004). *Resuming Punjab's prosperity—The opportunities and challenges ahead.* Author.

Chapter 11

Shifting Pattern of Agricultural Space*
Evolution of Contract Farming in Punjab

Mahesh Pratap Singh

A conscious policy shift relying heavily on the private sector participation for a boost to agriculture through contract farming has failed to produce the desired results on the ground. There is now a move to reverse the trend and check the harm suffered by the farming sector in Punjab.

Policy changes do not occur suddenly or in isolation and often have a gestation period. Responses to various push and pull factors can be innumerable, but actual results indicate the dominant current of thought. The changes that have started taking place in the production system of Indian agriculture since the 1980s are not only a result of the demands coming from within this sector but are also representative of the changing 'development paradigm'. The new paradigm that has come to dominate development thought since the 1990s has three main drivers—'neoliberalism', 'consumerism' and 'environmentalism'. Although the resurgence of each of these thought processes took place independent of each other and in a different historical milieu, with the advent of neoliberalism, these have been co-opted as part

---

* *Social Change*, 35(4), 2005.

of a new paradigm that has redefined sociopolitical and economic thought. The resurgence of environmentalism as a theme of thought has started a perceptive change towards resources and production systems. Agriculture no longer has to just provide food for consumption or raw materials for other sectors; it also has to be environmentally sustainable (Bowers, 1995). It cannot be regarded as a dumping ground for environmentally harmful chemicals or an extractor of precious resources (Clnies-Ross & Cox, 1994; Zimmerer, 1993). There must be an end to contamination of the food chain that has taken place in the past, and the food chain has to be made safer and healthier for consumers (Goodman & Redclift, 1991).

The spread of consumerism has further heralded a move towards the supremacy of the consumer. Consumer choices, often 'manufactured through complicated system of identity creation' (Williams, 2002, p. 533), have to be heeded and consumers provided with the best of alternatives. The growing hold of consumerism on the lives of people is evident from the changing patterns of consumption. Consumption is no longer merely a need-satisfying phenomenon; it has become a style statement, a status symbol and an aspirational mode of living. An individual's worth depends on their capacity for consumption, and new categories of consumers are created by new values reflected in terms such as environment-friendly consumption, healthy consumption and ethical consumption (Luke, 1998; A. Veeck & Veeck, 2000). Myriad ways of consumption have created a web of production dynamics where 'demand runs supreme' and which have to be met by creating a product or by importing it, and laws and governance structure need to be devised in a manner so as to fulfil this demand. The dawn of neoliberal thought—that laws cannot be contrary to profits and policies of profit maximization can take care of demands, both consumer and environmental—has introduced a culture in which everything has to be environment-friendly, consumer-oriented and profit-making.

The agreement over formation and implementation of agendas of supranational agencies like the World Trade Organization (WTO) has also made it amply clear that trade and environment are going to be internationally deliberated and will no longer be dealt with within the confines of national laws. That flows and networks having global dimensions are going to shape the priorities of local governance is more than evident. The predominance of this mode of thinking has led to the rewriting of the development agenda. This involves the modification of policies considered crucial in the earlier developmental framework. Policies aimed at increasing agricultural production with the assistance of a price support policy, subsidies and credit facilities are no longer regarded as desirable (Burmeister, 2000). The changed meaning of development has highlighted the drawbacks of previous policies. This change is visible in all the sectors of the economy but is more vivid in the case of Punjab—an agriculturally developed state.

OBJECTIVES

The aim of the study is to trace the changing paradigms of development in the context of agriculture in Punjab. The state has initiated a crop diversification programme with the help of contract farming. This study tries to critically analyse the evolving institutional framework of contract farming with particular reference to the role of government agencies in devising a level-playing field and protecting the interests of farmers and contracting firms.

METHODOLOGY

A multi-pronged methodology has been adopted to analyse various issues. Secondary data collected from various Punjab Agro Foodgrains Corporation (PAFC) reports have been analysed using simple statistical techniques. Further, reports of the PAFC have been studied and non-directed interviews have been conducted with various PAFC officials to understand policies for regulating and guiding contract farming in the state.

EMERGENCE OF NEW DEVELOPMENT AGENDA IN AGRICULTURE

Punjab was considered the success story of the green revolution strategy during the late 1960s and the early 1970s. However, this success story could not continue for long as the fault lines of the green revolution paradigm started appearing from the late 1970s. The appearance of a productivity plateau and rapidly increasing soil salinity were the first signals of the forthcoming, bigger malice. These trigger signals did not, however, attract attention as farm incomes were still increasing and macro-economic policy, preoccupied with food shortages, relied on the policy of subsidy and minimum support prices (MSP) to boost agricultural production. As agriculture became more intensive, returns started diminishing and problems became acute. Higher yields and production were achieved but through greater application of external inputs and mechanization, thereby removing any cost advantage (Gill & Brar, 1996). Growing intra- and inter-regional differences, falling water table, increase in salinity, diminishing crop and genetic diversity and decreasing profitability—all became too apparent (Chand, 1999). The cropping pattern in the state, being heavily skewed in favour of the wheat–paddy monoculture, has severely degraded soil fertility and caused a fall in the underground water table. The water table in Punjab has been declining at an alarming rate of 1 foot per annum, due to which 84 out of 138 blocks in the state have come under the 'grey category' (Aulakh & Bahl, 2001). Domination of the wheat–paddy monoculture, besides creating environmental problems, has also created serious market distortions. A continuous upward revision of MSP has made wheat and paddy non-competitive in the international market, while excessive production and added costs of handling, packaging, transport and storage have overburdened state finances with food subsidy. Many of the practices that manifested the 'intensive agriculture' policy, including excessive use of fertilizers, poor irrigation management, ignorance of fallow periods and improper use of heavy machinery, have threatened the overall sustainability of agro-ecosystem in the state (Johl, 1988). The turnaround in Punjab's agriculture has been so unsettling that it has earned the name of 'crisis' from the mid-eighties (Chand, 1999; Siddhu, 2002; Singh, 2000b, 2004). Dubbing the situation as 'crisis' marked the turning point in the history of agricultural development in Punjab. The state, which till late was cited as a case study for the reduction of rural poverty, has become an example of waste and inefficiency (Aulakh & Bahl, 2001; Shergill & Singh, 1995; Sidhu & Dhillon, 1997).

The crisis prevailing in agriculture has compelled a search for solutions. Diversification from the wheat–paddy monoculture is not only a desirable option but also an inescapable requirement. Changes in agriculture have coincided with broader changes in the macro-economic scenario. The structural adjustment programme and liberalization of the economy have charted out a territory for reforms in agriculture too. Crop diversification, proposed as a solution to the problems of Punjab's agriculture, has now to be implemented in the new 'liberal' framework (Singh, 2000). There is need to experiment with private and public partnership, the core of the new policy initiative, in agriculture as well, in the form of contract farming. This partnership has got a further fillip with the introduction of the WTO agenda in the economic policymaking.

CONTRACT FARMING AS CROP DIVERSIFICATION INITIATIVE

Contract farming is fundamentally a way of allocating risk between farmer and contractor; the former taking the risk of production, and the latter the risk of marketing. It allows for establishing direct relations between growers and agri-business firms as a substitute for open-market exchanges by linking 'independent family farmers' with central processing, export or purchasing unit (Glover, 1984; Glover & Kusterer, 1990; Goldsmith, 1985; Key & Runsten, 1999; Watts, 1992). It is a flexible way of regulating price and production practices, arranged in advance under contract. Contract farming is essentially demand- or market-driven, unlike traditional farming where the farmer first produces a commodity and then searches for its market. The contracts can be formulated in a variety of ways, depending upon the objectives and resources of a sponsor(s), the experience of the farmers, number of participants, number and variety of crops, the stated and unstated objectives of participants, the scale of operations, government support and sociocultural factors (Singh, 2000).

Historically, the conception of contracting agricultural production started in the colonial period and was mainly associated with plantation crops (Dev & Rao, 2005). The produce was meant for the market situated in the colonial countries, and therefore, the demand originating in these countries determined the nature and amount of the produce. Later, the contractual mode of production was adopted in the developed countries and was mainly concentrated in cash crops (Leckie, 1958). With the adoption of export-oriented policies, this mode of production was also adopted by the newly independent countries, with capital for starting such ventures coming from big corporations headquartered in the developed countries (Glover, 1984; Morrissy, 1974). The dominant theme of most of these projects was to enhance the income of the nation (Runsten & Key, 1996). The benefits also accrued to the farmers but were not comparable to the profits made by the investing agencies. During the financial breakdown in the Latin American countries, the world lending institutions and financing agencies recommended contract farming for reforming their respective farm sectors (Little & Watts, 1994). As the reform wave gathered pace, some independent countries also adopted contract farming to selectively deal with the problems faced by their agricultural sectors (Baumann, 2000; Ellman, 1986; Glover, 1987; Goldsmith, 1985). For example, in Thailand and Taiwan, contract farming was adopted to help small rice farmers make a transition to high-value-added horticultural crops (Benziger, 1996).

In Punjab, contract farming has been adopted to bring about crop diversification, but in actual practice, it represents a broader transformation in agricultural production involving a radical departure from earlier practices. Hence, the level of state engagement in the formulation and execution of contract farming is also of an unprecedented level (Singh, 2000). This is not only because a large number of people depend on agriculture for their sustenance, but also because agriculture is a culture and has a tradition. Introduction of a new mode of agricultural production does not simply involve modification of earlier policies but also the culture of people, which is a highly complicated process. The various intertwining issues such as food security of a large number of the poor, constitutional commitment for distributive justice, environmental degradation, fast-growing urban population and their demands, WTO norms and international competition have all made it difficult to chart out of a clear-cut trajectory for policy changes in agriculture. The cautious adoption of contract farming in India also reflects its history, where several cases of exploitation of farmers and bypassing small farmers have been reported (Carney, 1988; Clapp, 1988; Glover, 1990; Glover & Kusterer, 1990; Goodman & Watts, 1994; Porter & Phillips-Howard, 1997; Singh, 2004).

Therefore, the model of contract farming that has been chosen for experimentation in India has to take care of all these concerns. In

Punjab, where crop diversification has been proposed as the solution to most ills in the agricultural economy, contract farming is being used to popularize alternative crops and cropping systems. There are three crucial elements which have to be taken care of to achieve crop diversification. They are:

- Existence of a market providing sustained demand for the product
- A price structure that is competitive vis-à-vis existing crops
- Providing good quality seed and extension technology to farmers in order to achieve a stable and high yield (Johl, 1988).

Establishment of a framework of the evolution of contract farming, where it can fulfil these three requirements, has been a critical element of the crop diversification initiative in Punjab. Various incentives and concessions are being provided to the players, and government machinery has been organized to meet the challenges and provide them support. Evolution of contract farming in Punjab and the trajectory followed by it demonstrate the process of transformation of agriculture in the state.

ROLE OF GOVERNMENT INSTITUTIONS

The overall responsibility of devising and implementing contract farming has been mandated to a separate government corporation—PAFC. Its role encompasses the entire gamut of farm activities directed towards crop diversification, ranging from providing/arranging high-yielding varieties of seeds for farmers from reputed companies, technical and machinery support, supervision and follow-up on agronomic practices to buy back of the entire production with returns comparable to or better than wheat and paddy. PAFC has also taken on the role of fixing quality specification of crops in consultation with buyers/processors and specifying a contract price to buy the quality crop. The most important role, however, has been to devise buffers to secure the interests of the contracting parties. Of all the available models of contract farming, PAFC has adopted the 'multipartite model'. This model involves three sets of players—the farmer, the government or PAFC in this case and the 'private firm'. The 'private firm' itself is a large group and includes a number of players such as buyers, extension service providers and seed providers.

The contract is a tripartite agreement signed by the three parties and forms the core of contract farming. Other agreements that form the periphery of the multi-partite model are agreements between the government and the seed provider, between the government and the buyer, between the extension service provider and buyer and between the extension service provider and seed provider. These agreements vary, depending upon a variety of factors, for example, nature of the crop, nature of the market (international or domestic) and the government's policy thrust. The multipartite model is also a multi-crop, multi-year model thought to be more suitable for achieving objectives like crop diversification. In this model, agencies are selected to undertake contract farming in a number of crops and over a period of time. A single agency can be allowed to contract in a number of crops, and multiple agencies can also be employed to undertake contracting in one crop.

The straightening of the food chain, one of the essential prerequisites for the success of any crop diversification, has been attempted by putting in place players and organizing chains of the network so that demand can be organized first and supply be generated accordingly. The demand in this case is not just to be organized locally but also internationally. Therefore, the players incorporated in the network are also the ones who serve international markets. One of the major benefits in inviting international players is that, since they have well-identified and segmented consumer markets, they can provide more stable demand and, therefore, a better price for alternative crops (Benziger, 1996). Since previous experience showed that any attempt towards crop diversification would not succeed in the absence of a stable demand and remunerative prices for the proposed crops, a receptive atmosphere has been created for local as well as international players.

The high fluctuations and low yields of the proposed crops, other crucial elements in the crop diversification programme are being addressed by bringing in suitable technology at appropriate rates. This is being done by placing another chain in the form of seed and agriculture technology providers. The main link between seed and technology providers and buyers and farmers is being formed by extension service providers. Their primary task is to provide seed and technology and extension services to farmers, help in growing the desirable quality of crop and, finally, arrange for buyers of the crop at predetermined rates. For their services, the extension service providers are paid by PAFC according to the acreage brought under contract farming. Integration of the functional links of contract farming is managed by PAFC.

Another important dimension of crop diversification, that is, remunerative prices, is managed by prescribing minimum purchase rates for each crop in which diversification is being attempted. In the case of crops where MSP is declared by the Government of India, PAFC declares some premium over the MSP. However, in the case of crops where MSP does not exist, for example, basmati rice, PAFC declares a 'comfort price'. This is the average market price of the previous three years of the traditional variety of basmati. Contracts cannot be signed below this price. If companies are not interested in the traditional variety, and want to introduce a special variety, they are free to do so, but they are required to disclose their price structure to the PAFC beforehand, and can enter into a contractual agreement only after it approves their price structure. In any case, the contract price cannot go below the comfort price, which acts as a benchmark. This is a mechanism to ensure the farmer of government support in case of crop failure, and also to minimize the hassles of price negotiation between the farmers and firms, who are supposedly unequal partners in the contract farming network (Singh, 2004). Providing incentives to produce more eco-friendly crops and putting in place buffers to prevent any loss to the farmers, who grow these crops, is the starting point for crop diversification.

The main aim of policymakers is to devise a model and practices of contract farming that meaningfully incorporate the concerns of various stakeholders. PAFC has also tried to evolve various modes of intervention not only to achieve its objective of crop diversification but also to help in developing agriculture to tackle multiple challenges.

MODES OF INTERVENTION

Being the nodal agency for implementation of contract farming, PAFC has attempted to frame different modes of intervention. Interventions can be direct or indirect, depending on the crop and the experiences of PAFC with agencies regarding the implementation of contracts. The most direct intervention by PAFC is with respect to the selection of crops. Contract farming under the crop diversification programme can be done in a few selected crops for which it has listed the following important criteria:

- Crops for each district/area should be chosen taking into account local agro-climatic conditions so that crop potential is achieved to the maximum extent.
- The crops and cropping system should be chosen in such a way that they not only save natural resources, especially underground water, but also lead to balanced production of food grains, pulses, oilseeds, vegetables, industrial crops and so on.
- The crops and cropping system should ensure higher returns compared to wheat and paddy even at low volumes of production.
- Low but profitable volumes of production of these crops should also result in a significant saving in costs of handling, cleaning, grading, packaging, transport, storage and so on.

The all-inclusive criteria proposed by PAFC were not only desirable but also necessary to guide contract farming towards crop diversification. This also represents efforts on the part of a state agency to regulate the development process in accordance with specific production and consumption priorities (Murdoch & Marsden, 1995). Adoption of criteria for selection of crops is considered necessary to minimize environmental vulnerabilities and regulate international food networks, which are 'in (the) habit of acting at a distance' (Marsden, 1997, p. 323). This also has been a desirable step in preventing contract farming from becoming just a profitable venture for a select few (Singh, 2004). The aim of quick profits and absence of any substantial investment for resource augmentation on the part of companies participating in contract farming has been held responsible for the long-term resource degradation (Morvaridi, 1995, 1997). A review of the targets (Tables 11.1 and 11.2) set by PAFC for crop diversification through contract farming gives an indication of the approach towards a balanced cropping pattern.

There is a fair mix of cash crops such as basmati, durum wheat and cotton as well as oilseeds such as hyola, sunflower and groundnut.

Table 11.1 PAFC Targets and Achievement for Contract Farming ('000 Acres)

Crop	Achieved Rabi 2002–2003	Target 2003	Achieved Kharif 2003	Target Rabi 2003–2004	Achieved 2004	Target Kharif 2004	Revised target Rabi 2004–2005	Target 2005	Target Kharif 2005	2006	2007
Hyola	9.798	50		19.111	200		64	300		400	450
Barley	0.82	5		5.341	15		3.822	25		40	70
Winter Maize	1.92	3			5			11		12.5	15
Durum wheat		50		11.362	200		6.404	300		400	450
Sunflower	8.541	9		22.014	40		31.5	100		150	225
Spring corn	1.233	5			15		1.022	15		40	80
Basmati		85	90.529		100	100		150	102	150	150
Kharif maize		50	28.089		300	31.857		400	55	500	600
Guar gum		5	4.65		6			7.5		10	14.5
Castor		3	1.667		10	.2		20		40	50
Groundnut		1			1.5			15		20	25

Organic basmati	5		3		5		7	15
Vegetables		2		4		6		
Cotton		15		50.5		120		
							10	20
							150	200
Moong		12	2.081	50.5	2.1	25.5	3	135.5
			2.412				70.5	
Total	22.312	300	59.909	1000	108.848	1500	161.5	2500
			127.347				2000	
				136.461				
Grand total	22.312	187.256		245.309				

Source: Punjab Agro Foodgrain Corporation (PAFC) Reports.

Table 11.2 Distribution of Year-wise Targets (%)

S. No.	Crop	2003	2004	2005	2006	2007
1.	Hyola	16.67	20.00	20.00	20.00	18.00
2.	Barley	1.67	1.50	1.67	2.00	2.80
3.	Winter maize	1.00	0.50	0.73	0.63	0.60
4.	Durum wheat	16.67	20.00	20.00	20.00	18.00
5.	Sunflower	3.00	4.00	6.67	7.50	9.00
6.	Spring corn	1.67	1.50	1.00	2.00	3.20
7.	Basmati	28.33	10.00	10.00	7.50	6.00
8.	Kharif maize	16.67	30.00	26.67	25.00	24.00
9.	Guargum	1.67	0.60	0.50	0.50	0.58
10.	Castor	1.00	1.00	1.33	2.00	2.00
11.	Groundnut	0.33	0.15	1.00	1.00	1.00
12.	Organic basmati	1.67	0.30	0.33	0.35	0.60
13.	Vegetables	0.67	0.40	0.40	0.50	0.80
14.	Cotton	5.00	5.05	8.00	7.50	8.00
15.	Moong	4.00	5.05	1.70	3.52	5.42
16.	Total	100.00	100.00	100.00	100.00	100.00

Source: PAFC Reports.

Percentage distribution shows that hyola, durum wheat and kharif maize are the main crops adopted for crop diversification and consistently enjoy more than 60 per cent weightage in the proposed plan for diversification. The selection of oilseeds (hyola, sunflower, castor and groundnut), coarse cereals (barley and maize) and moong is important as acreage and share in the production of oilseeds, coarse cereals and pulses have been persistently falling in Punjab (Singh & Sidhu, 2004). Maize enjoys the highest preference among all crops because of low water requirements and farmers' familiarity with the crop. In most districts, increase of paddy and wheat acreage has been at the expense of maize, and it could be relatively easy for farmers to revert to the old crop if the price structure and yield are increased through suitable interventions.

Another important form of direct intervention by PAFC is the purchase price (PP) of the produce. The PP is declared in advance and has to be mandatorily mentioned in the written contract between the extension service provider and the farmer. This seems to be an extension of the mechanism of MSP devised to motivate farmers to increase food production by ensuring them remunerative returns. The PP mechanism has been incorporated to protect farmers from price fluctuations by ensuring buyback at the declared price and motivating them by providing a premium over MSP. However, farmers are in no way bound to sell to the buyer or the extension service provider. In case the market price rises above the proposed PP, they are free to sell in the open market. To deal with such unforeseen circumstances, a clause is mentioned in the contract indicating a certain amount of premium to be given to the farmer in case the market price rises above the proposed PP.

This system seems to be unfairly biased against the buyers, as farmers are protected by PP and are also free to sell in the open market when the market price breaches the proposed PP on the higher side; buyers have no such protection. It is necessary to attract farmers by fixing the PP to guarantee an income comparable to that from wheat and paddy. However, a constant upward revision of the MSP and the policy of open-ended procurement of wheat and rice have created a situation where the prices of wheat and rice are considerably higher than the international market rates (Gill & Brar, 1996). This situation cannot be maintained in the case of export crops or non-public distribution system crops. This may be partly responsible for the low participation of private buyers in the case of oilseeds and millet crops, as they find it more attractive to import rather than procure them through contract farming. This also explains the low acreage of these crops under the diversification programme, as PAFC remains the single largest buyer for some of these crops. In the case of basmati, which is an export crop and does not come under the purview of MSP, there are large numbers of buyers and exporters willing to foray into contract farming. This is one reason why contract farming has been quite successful in basmati and the acreage target for basmati was nearly achieved in 2003 and met in 2004.

PAFC also intervenes in the distribution of seed and farm technology. Availability of good quality and high-yielding variety of seeds is essential for undertaking cultivation of the proposed crops. In order to ensure that sufficient amount of high-yielding variety seeds are available and are provided to farmers at appropriate rates, PAFC has collaborated with the Punjab Agricultural University and private seed providers such as Pro Agro, Advanta India Ltd, Syngenta India Ltd, Pioneer India Ltd and Monsanto. It is also experimenting with the involvement of private extension service providers as a separate category in a bid to strengthen the distribution chain network. They are being engaged to provide the whole gamut of consultancy services related to agronomic practices. However, this arena of consultancy services has been widened to create a middle-level structure that appears to be the most important, albeit controversial, part of the contract farming model devised by PAFC. Extension services include the organization of camps for popularizing contract farming, identifying the contract farmer and signing of agreements with them, arrangement of seed from seed providers, distribution of seeds to farmers, imparting knowledge about agronomic practices to farmers, collaboration with buyers to study the nature of demand in international and national markets, conducting feasibility studies of crops and their price structure, and finally entering into agreements with buyers to purchase the crop at pre-determined rates. Creation of a new class of extension service providers seems more like a political act rather than a commercial decision. Most of the work transferred to private service providers was earlier mandated to government departments and their affiliated agencies. This represents a policy shift in consonance with the liberalization paradigm. An interview in October 2005 with a senior PAFC manager highlighted this policy shift:

Every government has its own agenda of governance, and it fixes its priorities accordingly. This government has put agriculture as its priority and has been taking various policy decisions to promote agriculture. Contract farming was one such decision, and the government since then has made a lot of effort to promote it. The aim was to achieve the goal of crop diversification by utilizing every possible means, even if it required going beyond the existing mechanism. The available government machinery was not only ill-equipped and lacking in expertise, but also highly fragmented. In the past, numerous departments were established by various governments to carry out different activities but none yielded satisfactory results. This government conceived crop diversification on such a grand level that it required a well-knit structure that was incomprehensible with the existing structural mechanism, where coordination between various departments is almost non-existent. Therefore, the involvement of private players to achieve crop diversification was a kind of necessity for the programme to be successful. Sometimes, motivation for the involvement of private players in the agriculture extension is attributed to corruption and questions are raised as to why the government, despite having its own extension machinery, is keen to involve private players. The point is that when the government takes a momentous policy decision and feels committed to implement it, at times it becomes necessary to go beyond the existing establishment which is known for being less efficient and lacking in professional competency.

Private expertise seems to have been deployed extensively at the cost of public sector enterprises. However, in order to lend a semblance of overall government supervisory authority, district and regional-level managers have been appointed to monitor the progress of diversification efforts. Districts have been subdivided into blocks that are being allocated to private players to prevent spurious competition and help maximize their efficiency. Blocks are being assigned on the basis of the infrastructure set-up of the providers. However, all this has been done very informally and there is no ground mechanism to ascertain the professed level of infrastructure. In the blocks allocated to a particular extension service provider, all crop diversification efforts have been implemented by that player. In the beginning, PAFC also kept some blocks for itself. Later, it adopted a monitoring and supervisory role and allocated those as well to private parties. Table 11.3 lists the allocation of blocks to various extension service providers.

Private players are being given a free hand in the operation, and government machinery has been mobilized to provide all support to them. The success of private players is being treated as synonymous with the success of contract farming. However, complete reliance on private players and blind faith in their organizational efficiency has not yielded the desired results, maybe due to over-ambitious targets

Table 11.3 Allocation of Areas to Various Extension Agencies for Undertaking Contract Farming: 2003

S. No.	Name of District	Name of Tehsil/Area	Name of Extension Agency
1.	Amritsar	Amritsar—2, Ajnala, Tarn Taran, Patti	Rallis
		Amritsar—1, Khadoor Sahib,	PAFC
		Baba Bakala	Mahindra Shubh Labh
2.	Kapurthala	Bhulath	PAFC
		Rest of blocks	Mahindra Shubh Labh
3.	Jalandhar	Phillaur	PAFC**
		Rest of blocks	Mahindra Shubh Labh
4.	Nawanshahr		Mahindra Shubh Labh
5.	Ropar	Morinda block	PAFC
		Rest of blocks	Mahindra Shubh Labh
6.	Fatehgarh Sahib	Bassi Pathana, Khamano	PAFC
		Rest of blocks	Mahindra Shubh Labh
7.	Patiala	Patiala & Samana Tehsil	Rallis
		Rajpura, Nabha	Mahindra Shubh Labh
		Dera Bassi	PAFC
8.	Ludhiana	Samrala	PAFC
		Khanna, Jagraon	Mahindra Shubh Labh
		Rest of blocks	Escorts

9.	Faridkot		Escorts
10.	Moga	Moga Tehsil	Mahindra Shubh Labh
		Bagha Purana, Nihalsighwala	Escorts
		Dharamkot	PAFC
11.	Ferozpur	Zira Tehsil	PAFC
		Rest of blocks	DCM Shriram
12.	Muktsar	Muktsar, Gidderbaha	Escorts
		Malout	PAFC
13.	Bhatinda	Rampura Phul	Mahindra Shubh Labh
		Bhatinda Tehsil	Escorts
		Talwandi Sabo	PAFC
14.	Mansa		PAFC
15.	Sangrur	Malerkotla	Mahindra Shubh Labh
		Barnala	PAFC
		Rest of blocks	Escorts
16.	Gurdaspur	Pathankot	PAFC
		Rest of blocks	Rallis
17.	Hoshiarpur	Mukerian	PAFC
		Rest of blocks	Mahindra Shubh Labh

Source: PAFC Reports.

without taking into account the ground realities or conducting any feasibility study. Lacunae in the programme have started showing up, making PAFC adopt a more cautious and proactive approach. This is how PAFC officials put it.

Contract farming started in a very informal manner, with no fixed procedure or rule book to follow. Private firms came with their proposals to undertake contract farming in certain crops, for which the government gave its approval. Later, as the concept gathered steam, guidelines evolved and some procedures were formulated. Lack of clear guidelines and experience in the initial phase was responsible for some deficiencies in the functioning. Some companies were more interested in making quick money and adopted corrupt procedures. For example, an already standing crop was registered as a result of the diversification effort, and money was claimed for extension services not provided; false accounting was done to exaggerate the area brought under diversified crop; improved seeds were not provided to farmers and; unemployed and unqualified youths were hired as extension workers who were unable to provide any value addition to farmers' agronomic practices. These actions created a lot of distrust about extension service providers and misconceptions about the contract farming programme. Therefore, for a long time, the results of the programme were visible only on paper, while on the ground, little crop diversification was taking place.

Alarmed by the ground results, PAFC has decided on amending the crop diversification programme. It has adopted a more segmented and crop-differentiated approach. In the case of basmati, a 'seed to seed'[†] approach has been adopted, where private exporters have been allowed to operate independently of extension service providers. They are also free to select the area, farmer, seed and package of practices and declare their own purchase price which, however, cannot go below the comfort price. They are also required to submit a copy of the contracts with farmers to the PAFC and maintain a 'farmer diary' for entitlement to reimbursement for the services provided to each beneficiary. They are reimbursed after field verification by PAFC officials.

Norms have been tightened for extension service providers, too. They are required to indicate the name of the high-yielding variety

---

[†] A terminology used by extension service providers.

of seed which they are providing to farmers, its manufacturer and amount of seed obtained. Further, a list has been drawn up of seed manufacturers from whom extension service providers can obtain seeds. In the case of hyola, PAFC has decided to take the responsibility of purchasing seed and its distribution. Extension service providers are required to support the district regional managers in seed distribution and follow-up activities. PAFC has started purchasing seed directly from the seed manufacturer, Advanta. The support structure of farmers' cooperative societies and other agencies has been mobilized to help PAFC managers achieve targets. To motivate and cover the expenditure of helping agencies, a margin has been built into the prices at which seeds are issued to them and at which they are to be distributed to the farmers.

At the secretary-level meeting held in June 2005, guidelines were issued to the district administration to help achieve the acreage targets of the crop diversification programme. Such a level of mobilization of government machinery to achieve contract farming targets is indicative of a policy reversal and reminiscent of the 'mixed economy' approach. This trend has been further consolidated by extending forward linkages in the form of processing of contracted products. PAFC has launched its own brand of hyola oil and has decided on greater involvement of its own distribution mechanism for extension services. While PAFC has decided to venture alone in hyola, in other crops it has liberalized the norms for seed distribution. Now, private extension agencies can purchase and package the seed and sell it to farmers in their own brand name, but seeds must conform to quality norms and must carry the name of its manufacturer. This represents a conflicting movement in the contract farming and has led to some discontent among district-level PAFC staff.

The district-level staff feels that policy formulation at the PAFC headquarters in Chandigarh is unduly biased in favour of private extension agencies. These agencies are being paid for work that PAFC staff, too, do but for which they get no extra remuneration. While achieving crop diversification is considered the duty of the PAFC official, private extension agencies are rewarded for the same work. This disquiet has also resulted in some corrupt practices among PAFC officials, which came to light recently and reflected adversely on the government's intentions. High-yielding variety seeds given to district managers under the programme were sold at higher margins in neighbouring Haryana and Rajasthan, where they were in great demand, and in the records, it was shown that targets had been achieved.

It seems that contract farming policy formulation for the rest of the crops is slower than it was in the case of basmati. However, other crops have not been able to evoke similar interest among processors and exporters. The greatest limiting factor seems to be the MSP, which is beyond the control of buyers and exporters and introduces price rigidity. This acts unfavourably for the buyers and exporters. Basmati being out of the MSP purview, the mode of operation is quite flexible and favourable. Also, being an export crop, it enjoys a well-established, high-value market which, in turn, has created a lot of room for exporters. In the case of oilseeds and pulses, India has been a net importer, and therefore, any increase in production is easily consumed in the domestic market, leaving little room for exports. Therefore, exporters are hardly interested in these crops, and any sustained demand can only be created by organizing demand from domestic processors and distributors. If international prices of these crops continue to rule weak and MSP continues to be higher than international prices, private players will remain reluctant in entering contract farming. Therefore, it seems that contract farming in oilseeds and pulses or, more specifically, non-cash crops will have very limited impact.

Another important factor which has received little attention so far in the evaluation of the programme is the preparatory measures taken at the policy level to reorient agriculture and make it more WTO compliant. PAFC has listed as one of the reasons behind introduction of contract farming the WTO norms for international marketing in agricultural products, which require maintenance of complete records for the 'traceability of the product origin'. Under these norms, exporters of food products are required to maintain history sheets and records, right from seed sourcing till packaging and marketing for five years or more, through computerization to enable easy access for overseas buyers. This listing of 'Traceability' demonstrates long-term planning for the transformation of agriculture in Punjab. While the WTO norms came into force from 1 April 2005, PAFC started preparatory measures from 2002. This is in consonance with the overall policy shift in the Indian economic and political structure, which started from the late 1980s and has been gathering momentum with the liberalization phase in the 1990s.

The aim of policy measures is to reform every sector and make it more investor and business friendly. In the case of agriculture, this means not merely transforming an economic activity but also a culture. This implies transforming agriculture from a cultural and social activity to an entrepreneurial one, whose overwhelming concern is to generate profits and business opportunities for the people involved in it. Agriculture has since come out from the 'field' and become more of a 'boardroom activity', wherein international demands and profit margins determine which crop is to be cultivated and where. The farmer's role has been altered from an independent and knowledgeable producer to that of a mere recipient of decisions taken off-field, and of which he is not a part. They have to just respond to the demand generated in some urban centre or overseas market and conveyed to them by some conglomerate with all the specifications and technology. They are not required to concern themselves with any issue except their labour. They are provided seed, technology and machines, and the production is purchased at the predetermined rate. The only aspect they have to be concerned about is the weather and acts of nature, to which they are most vulnerable and against which they have no security.

CREDIT AND MECHANIZATION EFFORTS

Bringing institutionalized credit to farmers has been a long-standing goal of the agriculture and credit policy. It was proposed that with the help of contract farming, farmers would be brought within the ambit of institutionalized lending. Tie-ups were entered into with private sector banks and public lending institutions for providing credit. Extension service providers were also required to help farmers in need of credit by liaising with these institutions. A PAFC manager described the situation thus: for timely and cheap distribution of credit to farmers, PAFC has collaborated with private and public sector banks. Its role is that of a facilitator, and the rates and norms of lending are decided by the institutions. PAFC is also trying to launch the Kisan Credit Card Scheme in collaboration with Punjab National Bank and UTI Bank. Under this programme, block-level identification of farmers will be done for issuing them credit cards. The aim is to bring more farmers under the formal credit mechanism and free them from the clutches of local moneylenders. But progress in this direction is very slow, as farmers are not willing to depart from the old system. They are so attuned to informal mechanisms that it is a part of their lifestyle and socialization process. Changing to new and formal mechanisms involves totally abandoning one's lifestyle and adopting a completely new style, which the older generation of farmers find difficult to adopt. Therefore, the adoption of a new formal mechanism involves a kind of generational change, which will become popular when the new generation, which is more aware of modern-day mechanisms, takes over.

PAFC, along with the Punjab Mandi Board, has also been trying to develop and purchase new crop-specific machinery to be distributed under the crop diversification programme. This project is being financed by the Rural Development Fund. A proposal known as 'demonstration scheme for crop specific mechanization' (DSCSM) in Punjab has been prepared under the Central sector scheme. There are seven categories of implements that will be developed by various agencies and distributed by PAFC under the scheme:

- Common-use implements
- Maize and sunflower implements
- Paddy implements
- Groundnut implements
- Cotton implements
- Rapeseed and mustard implements
- Implements for vegetable crops

New equipment for the following crops developed/purchased for use by the farmers/extension agencies are:

- *Maize:* Subsoiler (soil chisler), maize planters, Mahindra mouldboard plough, dehusker-cum-thresher, maize and sunflower combine harvester, maize ear Dehusker, maize driers.
- *Paddy:* Paddy disc puddler, paddy seedling marker, paddy pre-cleaner, paddy transplanter, combine harvester.

- *Castor:* Threshers 30 × 14 drum and 30 × 30 drum, motorized-cum-pedal spinners.

Equipment has been provided/recommended as part of the extension service under the contract farming programme.

Other facilitating steps taken by PAFC include setting up *mandis* and warehousing facilities for procurement of produce from contract farmers. In order to make the procurement of agri-produce competitive for processors, the state government has reduced taxes and levies like market fees and rural development cess from 2 to 0.25 per cent each, thus leading to a reduction by 3.5 per cent in the aggregate.

CONCLUSION

Contract farming represents a paradigm shift in Indian policymaking. Engagement of corporate players to bring about crop diversification and achievement of more sustainable agricultural practices has been a novel experiment, unparalleled in the history of independent India. In the initial phase, the crop diversification programme in Punjab seemed more like an effort to give space to private players to venture into the agriculture sector. There was a high degree of eagerness to involve private players in a misplaced belief that all problems will be taken care of by the private entrepreneurial system. Tardy progress in oilseeds and pulses and the failure of contract farming to take off in vegetables and other crops indicate that crop diversification will remain a far-removed target in the years to come. Private players, with local and international operations, may help in increasing farm incomes and broadening the acreage of export crops, but expectations that they would bring about crop diversification in non-export and non-cash crops will be misplaced. While targeting international markets, the highly imperfect and volatile nature of these markets should not be overlooked. Caution is required while preparing a platform for the international players. While they can help in increasing earnings and bringing foreign markets within the reach of farmers, it will be far-fetched to hope that they will continue with the programme when international markets become unremunerative, or a shift in consumption patterns takes place. A case of wilful policy negligence has been noted with respect to engagement of small farmers in contract farming. Despite several studies highlighting high transaction costs that prevent firms from contracting with small farmers, there has been no express provision to remedy matters. On the contrary, the clause for paying extension service providers on the basis of acreage brought under contract farming has virtually justified contracting only with big farmers. If left unaddressed, the perception of contract farming as a tool for social marginalization will only grow. There is need to broad-base the programme by incorporating other structures of government machinery and society to achieve the desired targets.

It will not do to involve a few corporate players in outsourcing of farm activities. A total overhaul of agriculture and food policies is needed. Continuous upward revision of MSP in the case of wheat and paddy is a severe restraint on the spread of contract farming in oilseeds and pulses. The experiences of PAFC show that Indian institutions are evolving, and contract farming can be considered only a step in the evolution of a competitive marketing system and not the only option. Vigilant and proactive regulatory institutions will become more important in a liberalized economy to guide market forces towards achieving various goals.

REFERENCES

Aulakh, M. S., & Bahl, G. S. (2001). Nutrient mining in agro-climatic zones of Punjab. *Fertilizer News*, *46(4)*, 47–61.

Baumann, P. (2000, October). Equity and efficiency in contract farming schemes: The experience of agricultural tree crops (Working Paper No. 139). Overseas Development Institute. http://www.fao.org/forestry/42695-0287ef8599d65a70616fe5bc900382cb5.pdf (accessed on 19 September 2020).

Benziger, V. (1996). Small fields, big money: Two successful programs in helping small farmers make transition to high value added crops. *World Development*, *24*(11), 1681–1693.

Bowers, J. (1995). Sustainability, agriculture and agricultural policy. *Environment and Planning A*, *27*(8), 1231–1243.

Burmeister, L. L. (2000). Dismantling statist East Asian agricultures? Global pressures and national responses. *World Development*, *28*(3), 443–455.

Carney, J. A. (1988). Struggles over crop rights and labour within contract farming households in a Gambian irrigated rice project. *The Journal of Peasant Studies*, *15*(3), 334–349.

Chand, R. (1999). Emerging crisis in Punjab agriculture: Severity and options for future. *Economic & Political Weekly*, *34*(13), A2–A10.

Clapp, R. A. J. (1988). Representing reciprocity, reproducing domination: Ideology and the labour process in Latin America contract farming. *The Journal of Peasant Studies*, 16(1), 5–39.

Clnies-Ross, T., & Cox, G. (1994). Challenging the productivist paradigm: Organic farming and the politics of agricultural change. In P. Lowe, T. Marsden, & S. Whatmore (Eds.), *Regulating agriculture* (pp. 53–74). David Fulton.

Dev, S. M., & Rao, N. C. (2005). Food processing and contract farming in Andhra Pradesh: A small farmer perspective. *Economic & Political Weekly*, 40(26), 2705–2713.

Ellman, A. (1986). Nucleus Estates and Smallholder Outgrower Schemes'. *Overseas Development*, 105.

Gill, S. S., & Brar, J. S. (1996). Global market and competitiveness of Indian agriculture: Some issues. *Economic & Political Weekly*, 31(32), 2175.

Glover, D. J. (1984). Contract farming and smallholder outgrower schemes in less developed countries. *World Development*, 12(11–12), 1143–1157.

Glover, D. J. (1987). Increasing the benefits to smallholders from contract farming: Problems for farmers organizations and policy makers. *World Development*, 15(4), 441–448.

Glover, D. J. (1990). Contract farming and outgrower schemes in East and Southern Africa. *Journal of Agricultural Economics*, 41(3), 303–315.

Glover, D., & Kusterer, K. (1990). *Small farmers, big business: Contract farming and rural development*. St. Martin's Press.

Goldsmith, A. (1985). The private sector and rural development: Can agribusiness help the small farmer? *World Development*, 18(10–11), 1125–1138.

Goodman, D., & Redclift, M. (1991). *Refashioning nature: Food, ecology and culture*. Routledge.

Goodman, D., & Watts, M. (1994). Reconfiguring the rural or fording the divide? Capitalist restructuring and the global agro-food system. *The Journal of Peasant Studies*, 22(1), 1–49.

Johl, S. S. (1988). Future of agriculture in Punjab (Discussion Paper No. 5). Centre for Research in Rural and Industrial Development, Chandigarh.

Key, N., & Runsten, D. (1999). Contract farming, smallholders and rural development in Latin America: The organization of agroprocessing firms and the scale of operation. *World Development*, 27(2), 381–401.

Leckie, H. H. (1958). Dynamics of integration of agricultural production and marketing. *Journal of Farm Economics*, 40(5), 1356–1367.

Little, P., & Watts, M. (1994). *Living under contract: Contract farming and agrarian transformation in Sub-Saharan Africa*. University of Wisconsin Press.

Luke, T. W. (1998). The un(wise) and (ab)use of nature: Environmentalism as globalised consumerism. *Alternatives*, 23(2), 175–212.

Marsden, T. K. (1997). Reshaping environments: Agriculture and water interactions and creation of vulnerability. *Transactions of the Institute of the British Geographers*, 22(3), 321–337.

Morrissy, J. D. (1974). *Agricultural modernization through production contracting.* Praeger.

Morvaridi, B. (1995). Contract farming and environment risks: The case of Cyprus. *The Journal of Peasant Studies, 23*(1), 30–45.

Morvaridi, B. (1997). Environmental and social impact assessment: Methodological issues (DPPC Discussion Paper No. 1). DPPC.

Murdoch, J., & Marsden, T. K. (1995). The Spatialization of politics: Local and national actor-spaces in environmental conflict. *Transactions of the Institute of the British Geographers, 20*, 368–380.

Porter, G., & Phillips-Howard, K. (1997). Comparing contracts: An evaluation of contract farming schemes in Africa. *World Development, 25*, 227–238.

Shergill, H. S., & Singh, G. (1995). Poverty in rural Punjab: Trend over green revolution decades. *Economic & Political Weekly, 30*(25).

Sidhu, H. S. (2002). Crisis in agrarian economy in Punjab: Some urgent steps. *Economic & Political Weekly, 37*(30), 3132–3138.

Sidhu, R. S., & Dhillon, M. S. (1997). Land and water resources in Punjab: Their degradation and technologies for sustainable use. *Indian Journal of Agricultural Economics, 52*(3), 508–518.

Singh, J., & Sidhu, R. S. (2004). Factors in declining crop diversification: Case study of Punjab. *Economic & Political Weekly, 39*(52), 5607–5610.

Singh, S. (2000a). Contract farming for agricultural diversification in the Indian Punjab: A study of performance and problems. *Indian Journal of Agriculture Economics, 56*(3), 283–294.

Singh, S. (2000b). Crisis in Punjab agriculture. *Economic and Political Weekly, 35*(23), 1889–1892.

Singh, S. (2004). Crisis and diversification in Punjab agriculture: Role of state and agribusiness. *Economic & Political Weekly, 39*(52), 5583–5590.

Veeck, A., & Veeck, G. (2000). Consumer segmentation and changing food purchase patterns in Nanjing, PRC. *World Development, 28*(3), 457–471.

Watts, M. (1992). Peasants and flexible accumulation in the Third World: Producing under contract. *Economic & Political Weekly, 27*(30), 90–97.

Williams, C. C. (2002). A critical evaluation of commodification thesis. *The Sociological Review, 50*(4), 525–541

Zimmerer, K. S. (1993). Soil erosion and social (dis)courses in Cochabamba, Bolivia: Perceiving the nature of environmental degradation. *Economic Geography, 69*(3), 312–327.

Chapter 12

Employment Patterns among Agricultural Labourers in Rural Punjab*

Gurmanpreet Singh and Kamaljit Singh

INTRODUCTION

Punjab with its predominantly agricultural economy was one of the states of India which adopted the New Agricultural Model in the 1960s. After that, the northern Indian state made tremendous progress in the production of food grains leading to increased levels of self-sufficiency. Today, agriculture still plays a dominant role in Punjab's economy providing employment to 39 per cent of the state's working population, indicating their high level of dependence on agriculture for their income (Government of India (GoI), 2001). Despite this fact, however, agricultural labourers still receive the lowest share of the national income, living often in impoverished conditions.

Since Independence, the state has been aware of the challenges being faced by agricultural labourers. Even though the primary aim of the planned economy in India, initiated in 1951, was to raise standards of living among the weaker sections of society, especially agricultural labourers, who constituted socially and economically the weakest sections of society, their impoverished conditions continued. Various surveys were conducted to assess this issue but the basic problems were not properly studied, analysed or understood (Ghosh, 1969).

---

* *Social Change*, 46(3), 2016.

Agricultural labour forms the second largest category of workers in Punjab. The share of this category in the total workforce of the state, as well as its number, has consistently increased from 20.10 per cent in 1971 to 22.16 per cent in 1981 and 23.81 per cent in 1991 (Government of Punjab (GoP), 2004). According to the Census of India 2001, a majority of the agricultural labourers belong to the Scheduled Castes category constituting 66.97 per cent of the total of 14.90 lakhs of agricultural labourers in Punjab state. With land reforms not being implemented efficiently, land remains in the hands of a few, with the majority of the working population being completely dependent on agriculture, remaining as agricultural labourers. Even though the much touted Green Revolution's technological leaps in the 1960s ushered in prosperity and fortune for some, agricultural labourers remained excluded from this new found well-being.

The expected hike in wages due to an increase in demand also did not take place because of the migration of labour from Uttar Pradesh and Bihar to Punjab, increasing supply and effectively suppressing levels of wages. Despite their significant contribution to the Green Revolution, Punjab's agricultural labour did not reap any benefits or see an improvement in their living conditions (Bharti, 2011). There were other setbacks too. Due to the increased use of farm machinery like combine harvesters, and the use of weedicides, the demand for human labour in the farm sector decreased significantly since the late 1980s (Sidhu & Singh, 2004). Unorganized and mostly illiterate, agricultural labourers were not in a position to partake in a just share in Punjab's agricultural prosperity (GoP, 2004). Unemployment among agricultural labour households constitutes 60 per cent of the total rural unemployment (Parthasarathy, 1991). The debt trap is so vicious that more than 70 per cent of agricultural labourers of Punjab are in debt.

The farming community in Punjab, however, is not the sole bearer of the current agrarian crisis. With reduced workdays, stagnant wages and a constant state of indebtedness, the lower caste and landless agricultural labourers too are committing suicides along with the farmers. But their plight has hardly been studied or noticed by the media, academicians and rural activists and has unfortunately never become the stuff of headlines. In Bathinda and Sangrur district alone, 2,890 suicides were committed by farmers and agricultural labourers during 2000–2008, out of which 1,133 (39.20%) were agricultural labourers (Singh, 2009).

While the impact of the agrarian crisis on the peasants in Punjab is comparatively more widely known, less well known is the grievous impact it has had on agricultural labourers as well. The bulk of local labourers are able to get work in agriculture for only 8–10 days a month. About 64 per cent labourers have to work between 8 and 12 hours in a day, only 0.48 per cent earn more than ₹100 a day and nearly 52 per cent labourers have a family income below ₹1,000 per month. In the Malwa region, due to the high cost of tap water, labourers are left with only two options: either drink contaminated land water and most probably get cancer or take loans from the rich who charge 4–5 times more interest than banks to install water taps (Ghuman et al., 2007). It is by using labour-saving machinery, pesticides and shifting from grain production to cash crops reducing jobs and increasing the workload that landlords have been able to squeeze out a higher profit. In the process, they are squeezing the already miserable income of agricultural labour and attacking their subsistence levels (Chopra, 2005).

Although agricultural labourers form a large section of the Indian workforce, they are least protected and uncared for. Ironically, this situation exists despite rising agricultural trade and labour productivity worldwide. They are assigned the lowest place in the social ladder: belonging to the depressed classes, socially handicapped they never have the courage to assert themselves. Exploited because of their caste, economically subservient because of their low wages and indebtedness, struggling with long hours of work their penury is evident (GoI, 1956–1957). Generally conservative, tradition-bound, resigned to the insufferable lot to which, according to them, fate has condemned them, the level of bondage among local agricultural labour is high in Punjab.

The labourers in debt bondage in Punjab are known as *siri*. They generally belong to the Scheduled Castes. Besides enduring long working hours, they have no freedom to choose employment, the right of movement, use the village commons and so on. Cattle shed cleaners are usually the wives of the *siris* and they, too, suffer from indirect bondage.

Sepi, sanjhi and *siri* are some of the traditional forms of bondage which have received legitimacy from the dominant social structure and which survive even today. Punjab has nearly 100,000 bonded agricultural labourers and nearly three-fourths of them hail from a single caste, namely the Mazhabi Sikh (Singh, 2006). Working for negligible wages, they sometimes wash dishes, clean cattle sheds of rich farmers in the hope of getting two meals a day and some used clothes. The agricultural labourers have to undertake all kinds of menial work, farm and domestic, at the bidding of the landlord. Their life is unimaginable, a form of hell (Barst, 2009). With lower wages being paid to them than male labourers, the conditions of female agricultural labourers are much worse than their male counterparts. The difference between the average wages of male and female agricultural labourers has widened over the years. Protests from this community, including attempts to release them from bondage, have been met with physical violence and social boycotts in a number of cases (Srivastva, 2005, p. 13).

OBJECTIVES

The present study is an empirical analysis of the employment pattern among agricultural labourers in rural Punjab. The study relates to 2008–2009. To fulfil the most important objective of study, we have mainly concentrated on economic and demographic features, levels and pattern of income and consumption, nature and pattern of employment, incidence and magnitude of poverty and indebtedness among agricultural labourers and to estimate their wealth by examining the assets structure of agricultural labourers.

METHODOLOGY

For the purpose of study, following a random sampling method, one village each from all the development blocks of Patiala District, was selected. Thus, in all, eight villages, that is, Lang (Patiala block), Takhtu Majra (Rajpura), Jand Mangholi (Ghanaur), Gunike (Nabha), Atalan (Patran), Rajgarh Saundhewal (Samana), Bhankhar (Bhunerheri) and Karhali (Sanaur) were selected for study. In total, there are 143 households of agricultural labourers, including 38 agricultural labour households in Lang, 7 in Takhtu Majra, 14 in Jand Mangholi, 8 in Gunike, 21 in Atalan, 9 in Rajgarh Saundhewal, 17 in Bhankhar and 29 in Karhali, respectively. All agricultural labour households were selected for the study. A detailed schedule was prepared for collecting data from sampled households through personal interviews.

The whole study contains nine sections. The first section introduces the problem, indicates the relevance of the present study, highlights its main objectives and gives a database and methodology. The second section outlines the profile of agricultural labourers in terms of characteristics. The third section is devoted to the analysis of levels and pattern of income and consumption. The fourth section deals with the nature and pattern of employment. The next fifth and sixth sections bring under focus the incidence and magnitude of poverty and indebtedness, respectively. The seventh section estimates the assets owned by agricultural labour households. The next section describes in detail the social conditions, that is, their position and rank in society. The last section sums up main findings, makes some suggestions emerging from our findings and draws attention to further areas of research.

OVERVIEW OF SOCIAL AND ECONOMIC FEATURES

This section presents an overview of social and economic features. In this section, gender, age, size of the family, caste and basic provision for subsistence level of living are taken as the indicators of social features. There are 705 persons in total, in 143 sampled agricultural labour households, out of this 51.77 per cent are male and 48.23 per cent are female. Overall the sex ratio is found to be 931.51. The average family size is 4.93 constituting 51.72 per cent male and 48.28 per cent female. 59.29 per cent of the total population falls in the working age group of 15–59 years. The main source of drinking water is tap water and 53.15 per cent households have water taps. For drinking water about one-third households depend upon neighbours and relatives as they do not possess any source of water. Around 85.31 per cent of the households have the facility of electricity and 82.52 per cent belong to Scheduled Castes category.

Further, the education level, conditions of house and number of earners in the family are taken as indicators of economic features. Around 42.98 per cent of the total population is illiterate and among the literates only one person has been educated up to graduation. 23.55 per cent of the total population come under the category of earners and 47.09 per cent as dependents. Further, 89.16, 9.04 and 1.81 per cent, males, females and children, respectively, constitute total wage earners. It is very interesting to find out that only 14.69 per cent households have *pucca* houses. A majority of them belong to the Scheduled Castes, less than half of the population is literate and far away from basic provisions for decent living such as drinking water, electricity, *pucca* houses and sanitation.

ANALYSIS OF INCOME AND CONSUMPTION

In this section, levels, patterns and per capita income and consumption of agricultural labour households are analysed. On an average, an agricultural labour household earns ₹47,154.49 annually, of which 88.70 per cent comes from the agriculture sector and remaining 11.30 per cent from the non-agricultural sources as shown in Table 12.1: there are considerable variations in the income earned from different components of income sources. The income is 67.82 per cent and 20.88 per cent from hiring out permanent and casual labour in agriculture, respectively. The average annual income from hiring out casual labour is further classified into *rabi* (10.17%) and *kharif* (10.70%) seasons. Non-agricultural sources such as hiring out labour in the non-agriculture sector, income from dairying, piggery and poultry, salaries, pensions, sale of manure and other activities also contribute to the average annual income with their meagre share of 11.30 per cent. Further, the annual average per capita income is ₹9,564.68, comprising ₹8,483.45 from the agriculture sector (i.e., ₹6,485.60 and ₹1,997.85 from hiring permanent and casual labour) and the remaining ₹1,081.23 is from non-agricultural sources.

Consumption is an important economic variable that determines and shows the living conditions of any section in society. For the purpose of analysis, the consumption basket is presumed to constitute consumer non-durables, consumer durables, services and for social-religious ceremonies. The average annual consumption of an agricultural labour household is ₹56,895.44. However, there are considerable differences in the level of consumption expenditure on different items. A sizeable chunk (76.21%) of overall average consumption expenditure is spent on non-durables, followed by social-religious ceremonies (12.83%), services (7.67%) and durables (3.29%). Among non-durables, food grains (33.09%) account for the largest proportion of total consumption expenditure, followed by milk and milk products (15.40%). The per capita consumption expenditure is ₹11,540.49 which is the maximum

Table 12.1 Levels and Pattern of Household Income

Source of Income	Income (Per cent)	Per Capita Income
Permanent labour		
1. Cash	40.79	3901.20
2. Kind	0.20	18.88
a. Corn	21.73	2078.07
b. Meals	5.10	487.45
c. Tea and milk		
Sub-total	67.82	6485.60
Casual labour		
1. *Rabi*		
a. Cash	8.05	770.32
b. Kind	0.14	13.82
i. Corn	1.36	130.49
ii. Meals	0.63	60.55
iii. Tea and milk	8.63	825.15
2. *Kharif*		
a. Cash	0.12	11.09
b. Kind	1.30	124.51
i. Corn	0.65	61.92
ii. Meals		
iii. Tea and milk		
Sub-total	20.88	1997.85
Non-agricultural sources	11.30	1081.23
Total	100.00	9564.68

Source: Field Survey, 2008–2009.

for non-durables items amounting to ₹8,794.63 followed by social-religious ceremonies, services and durable items amounting to ₹1,479.87, ₹883.90 and ₹382.09, respectively.

Average propensity to consume comes to 1.21 per cent which shows an annual deficit of ₹9,740.95 incurred by them. It appears that they have tried to maintain a minimum level of consumption whether they can afford it or not with their present income which means that they end up borrowing from different agencies.

The levels of earning in this community are too low to meet their basic needs. The main reasons being the seasonal employment nature of agriculture and a lack of alternative employment opportunities in rural areas. They spend a major share of their income on non-durables, especially on food grains, not on luxuries. It should be emphasized that even after the back-hard work, they are not able to fulfil their daily consumption needs. The reason for this deficit is the unequal distribution of gains in agriculture. Landlords keep a major share of the gains as they claim their ownership on the means of production, while labourers get a meagre share for their physical labour.

PATTERN OF EMPLOYMENT

This section is devoted to the analysis of the nature and pattern of employment of agricultural labourers. The nature and pattern of employment of agricultural labourers depend upon many factors, that is, the economic status of the agricultural labour households, the average family size, the average number of wage earners, the number of persons in the working age group (15–59 years), the distribution pattern of male, female and child labour used in agriculture, the average man-days of hiring out labour in agriculture and the pattern of prevailing wage rate according to male, female and child labour used in agriculture.

The economic status of the agricultural labour households, the average family size, the average number of wage earners, the number of persons in the working age group (15–59 years) have already been discussed in the previous sections. Table 12.2 exhibits the number of persons employed as agricultural labourers (i.e., both as permanent and casual labourers) and also depicts the distribution pattern of male, female and child labour used in agriculture. It reveals that 31.07 per cent are male, 33.33 per cent are female and 35.60 per cent are children (below 14 years), constituting the total population of agricultural labour households. Out of the total of 197 agricultural labourers, 62.44 per cent are employed as permanent and 37.56 per cent as casual agricultural labourers. It further reveals that 60.41, 1.52 and 0.51 per cent male, female and child, respectively, constitute the permanent agricultural labourers. In only one village, Gunike, child labour is used as permanent agricultural labour. The use of casual labour is further divided into the *rabi* and *kharif* seasons. The number of casual agricultural labour is the same for these two seasons. Out of it, 20.30 per cent are male,

Table 12.2 Pattern of Male, Female and Child Labour Use in Agriculture

Children				Permanent Labour				Casual Labour			
Male	Female	(below 14 years)	Total	Male	Female	Child	Total	Male	Female	Child	Total
219 (31.07)	235 (33.33)	251 (35.60)	705 (100.00)	119 (60.41)	3 (1.52)	1 (0.51)	123 (62.44)	40 (20.30)	32 (16.24)	2 (1.02)	74 (37.56)	197 (100.00)

Source: Field Survey, 2008–2009.
Note: Figures in parentheses are showing percentage.

16.24 per cent are female and 1.02 per cent are children. Only in two villages, Lang and Karhali, child labour is used as casual agricultural labour and the proportion of female casual agricultural labour is close to male casual agricultural labourers.

On an average, a permanent and casual labourer got work for 354.49 and 178.80 man-days annually (88.15 and 90.65 man-days in the *rabi* and *kharif* seasons, respectively) as shown in Table 12.3. Whereas, on an average, a permanent male, female and child agricultural labourer in the entire sampled villages got work for 355.03, 342.33 and 338.00 man-days, respectively, a casual male, female and child agricultural labourer hired out labour for 217.00, 135.41 and 109.00 man-days, respectively. The share of male, female and child casual agricultural labourers for *rabi* and *kharif* seasons is 49.59, 48.72 and 49.54 per cent, and 50.41, 51.28 and 50.46 per cent, respectively.

It is important to note here that the number of man-days comes close to the number of days in a year for agricultural labourers because here we take the man-day to be eight hours a day, even though they end up working more than eight hours a day. Most of the permanent agricultural labourers reported that they have to work almost 12 hours in a day.

Wages constitute an important component for determining the material conditions of agricultural labourers. In the case of permanent agricultural labourers, on an average, an agricultural labourer gets a wage rate of ₹104.92 which consists of 60.09 per cent cash and 39.91 per cent kind wages (i.e., 0.38, 32.01 and 7.51 per cent as corn, meals and tea and milk, respectively) as shown in Table 12.4. Almost 40 per cent of the total wage rate paid to permanent agricultural labour comes in the form of kind wages and out of it almost one-third is occupied by meals only.

The prevailing wage rates for casual agricultural labour are different for the *rabi* and *kharif* seasons. In the *rabi* season, on an average, a casual agricultural labourer gets ₹105.38 which consists of 79.00 per cent cash and 21.00 per cent kind wages (i.e., 1.41, 13.38 and 6.21 per cent as corn, meals and tea and milk, respectively). In the *kharif* season, on an average, a casual agricultural labourer gets a wage rate of ₹107.63 which consists of 80.68 per cent cash and 19.32 per cent kind wages which consist of 1.09 per cent corn, 12.17 per cent meals and 6.06 per cent tea and milk.

Table 12.4 also further exhibits the pattern of prevailing wage rate for permanent and casual agricultural labourers according to the male,

Table 12.3 Average Labour Man-days Hired Out by Per Man, Woman and Child Labourer

Description	Permanent Agricultural Labour	Casual Agricultural Labour		
		Rabi	Kharif	Total
Male	355.03	107.60	109.40	217.00
		(49.59)	(50.41)	(100.00)
Female	342.33	65.97	69.44	135.41
		(48.72)	(51.28)	(100.00)
Child	338.00	54.00	55.00	109.00
		(49.54)	(50.46)	(100.00)
Total	354.59	88.15	90.65	178.80
		(49.30)	(50.70)	(100.00)

Source: Field Survey, 2008–2009.
Note: Figures in parentheses are showing percentage.

female and child labour use in agriculture. On an average, a male permanent agricultural labourer gets ₹105.87 per day which consists of 60.55 per cent cash and 39.45 per cent kind wages, whereas a female permanent agricultural labourer gets a wage rate of ₹74.84 which consists of 42.17 per cent cash and 57.83 per cent kind wages. Only in three villages, females are used as permanent agricultural labourers and more than half of their income comes in form of kind. A child permanent agricultural labour gets a wage rate of ₹78.26, which comprises 36.51 per cent cash and 63.49 per cent kind wages.

Further in the *rabi* season, on an average, a male casual agricultural labourer gets ₹114.57 per day which consists of 80.79 per cent cash and 19.21 per cent kind wages and a female casual agricultural labour gets a wage rate of ₹66.47 which consists of 65.32 per cent in cash and 34.68 per cent in kind. A child casual labourer gets a wage rate of ₹46.54 which consists of 60.06 per cent in cash and 39.94 per cent in kind.

In the *kharif* season, 83.71 per cent in cash and 16.28 per cent in kind wages constitute the total wages for the male casual agricultural labourer, whereas a female casual agricultural labourer gets a wage rate of ₹67.31 consisting of 70.02 per cent in cash and 29.98 per cent

Table 12.4 Pattern of Prevailing Wage Rates

Description	Permanent Labour					Casual Labour								
	Cash	Kind			Total	Rabi					Kharif			
		Corn	Meals	Tea and Milk		Cash	Kind			Total	Cash	Kind			Total
							Corn	Meals	Tea and Milk			Corn	Meals	Tea and Milk	
Male	64.10 (60.55)	0.41 (0.39)	33.51 (31.65)	7.85 (7.41)	105.87 (100.00)	92.56 (80.79)	1.05 (0.92)	14.23 (12.42)	6.73 (5.87)	114.57 (100.00)	108.53 (83.71)	0.66 (0.51)	13.34 (10.29)	7.11 (5.48)	129.64 (100.00)
Female	31.56 (42.17)	0.00 (0.00)	34.76 (46.45)	8.52 (11.38)	74.84 (100.00)	43.42 (65.32)	2.48 (3.73)	14.30 (21.51)	6.27 (9.43)	66.47 (100.00)	47.13 (70.02)	2.23 (3.31)	12.53 (18.62)	5.42 (8.05)	67.31 (100.00)
Child	28.57 (36.51)	0.00 (0.00)	40.43 (51.66)	9.26 (11.83)	78.26 (100.00)	27.95 (60.06)	0.00 (0.00)	13.96 (30.00)	4.63 (9.95)	46.54 (100.00)	26.78 (56.91)	0.00 (0.00)	15.37 (32.66)	4.91 (10.43)	47.06 (100.00)
Total	63.05 (60.09)	0.40 (0.38)	33.59 (32.01)	7.88 (7.51)	104.92 (100.00)	83.25 (79.00)	1.49 (1.41)	14.10 (13.38)	6.54 (6.21)	105.38 (100.00)	86.84 (80.68)	1.17 (1.09)	13.10 (12.17)	6.52 (6.06)	107.63 (100.00)

Source: Field Survey, 2008–2009.
Note: Figures in parentheses are showing percentage.

in kind wages. A child casual agricultural labourer gets a wage rate of ₹47.06 consisting of 56.91 per cent cash and 43.09 per cent kind wages.

The employment in agriculture is seasonal, the demand for labour increases in the peak season and decreases during the lean season. Permanent labourers are employed throughout the year because they are on a contract with landlords. The contract is valid for a year, but agricultural labourers generally attach themselves to a particular landlord for years.

INCIDENCE OF POVERTY AMONG AGRICULTURAL LABOURERS

One of the primary aims of the nation's economic planning is to raise standards of living of the weaker sections of the population, both absolutely and relatively, to that of other sections. However, poverty continues to persist in India, even after almost six decades of planned economic development. And much of the poverty is located in rural areas. The term 'poverty' is defined as the inability of an individual to meet certain minimum desirable levels in living conditions. All those people who live below this minimum desirable level are said to be living below the poverty line. In this analysis, we have used the state-specific poverty line given by the Planning Commission of India in 2004–2005, that is, ₹4,924.56 per capita, per annum for the rural areas of Punjab (GoP, Planning Commission, 2004). All the agricultural labour households with a per capita income or per capita consumption below this are considered poor households. The commonest measure of overall poverty is the head count measure, given by the proportion of the total population that happens to be identified as poor, that is, falling below the specified poverty line income. In the most recent literature on the incidence of poverty, by following World Bank methodology of $1 per day, we have worked out a poverty line of ₹17,680.60 per year per person ($1 = 48.44) (Reserve Bank of India, 2009). Another method to define poverty is the nutrition norms in calories by using the NSSO(—) 61th Round Data, that is, the inability to access 2,400 calories per day per capita in the rural areas. The state-specific, official poverty line given by the Planning Commission for Punjab is just sufficient to access only 1,700 calories per month per capita. The required monthly and annual per capita expenditure to access a nutrition level of 2,400 calories is ₹795.00 and ₹9,540.00, respectively. People with an expenditure below this benchmark are considered poor (Patnaik, 2007).

INCIDENCE OF POVERTY

As per the Head Count Measure, 38.58 per cent and 13.90 per cent of the agricultural labour households' population live below the poverty line on the basis of a per capita income and expenditure level, respectively, as shown in Table 12.5. According to the World Bank's definition of the poverty line, that is $1/day/person, as many as 98.60 per cent and 97.20 per cent of households live below the poverty line on the basis of per capita income and consumption level, respectively.

SEN'S 'P' MEASURE OF POVERTY

Sen's 'P' measure of poverty is a measure which is akin to the Gini measure (Sen, 1976). It uses rank order weight in a manner which is sensitive to the gap between the below the poverty line income of the poor and the poverty line itself. Thus, it gives more weight per unit to the incomes farthest below the poverty line. To overcome the problems of

Table 12.5 Different Measures for Measuring Poverty

Description	Per Capita Income Level	Per Capita Consumption Level
Head Count Measure		
Proportion of persons below the poverty line	38.58	13.90
International Standard of Poverty, i.e., $1 method		
No. of households below the poverty line	141	139
Proportion of households below the poverty line	98.60	97.20

Source: Field Survey, 2008–2009.

the head count procedure, Sen made two changes: first, the 'P' measure of poverty is concerned not merely with the number of people below the poverty line but also with the amount by which the incomes of the poor fall short of the specified poverty level, and second, the bigger the shortfall from the poverty level, the greater should be the weight per unit of that shortfall in the poverty measure (Sen, 1973). For estimating the 'P' income, differences are calculated from the poverty line and not from the mean income of the distribution. The 'P' measure of poverty is given by:

$$P = \frac{2}{(q+1)nZ} \sum_{i=1}^{q} (Z - yi)(q + 1 - i)$$

where 'P' is the measure of poverty, q is the number of the people at or below the poverty line, n is the population size, Z is the poverty level and yi is the income of the individuals arranged in an ascending order of magnitude. The poverty measure 'P' for the agricultural labourers is given in Table 12.6 and this is depicted through Figures 12.1 and 12.2.

It is clear from Table 12.6 that on the basis of a per capita income level, the proportion of poor persons is 38.58 and the average per capita income of persons below the poverty line is ₹4,317.27. The value of the 'P' measure of poverty is 0.05926 for all the agricultural labour households. On the basis of the per capita consumption level, the proportion of poor persons is 13.90 and the average per capita consumption of persons below the poverty line is ₹4,494.09. The value of 'P' measure of poverty is 0.01543. A comparison of 'P' measure of poverty on the basis of income and consumption expenditure reveals

Table 12.6 Sen's 'P' Measure of Poverty

Description	Per Capita Income Level	Per Capita Consumption Level
Proportion of persons below the poverty line	38.58	13.90
Per capita income of the persons below the poverty line	4317.27	4494.09
'P' measure of poverty	0.05926	0.01543

Source: Field Survey, 2008–2009.

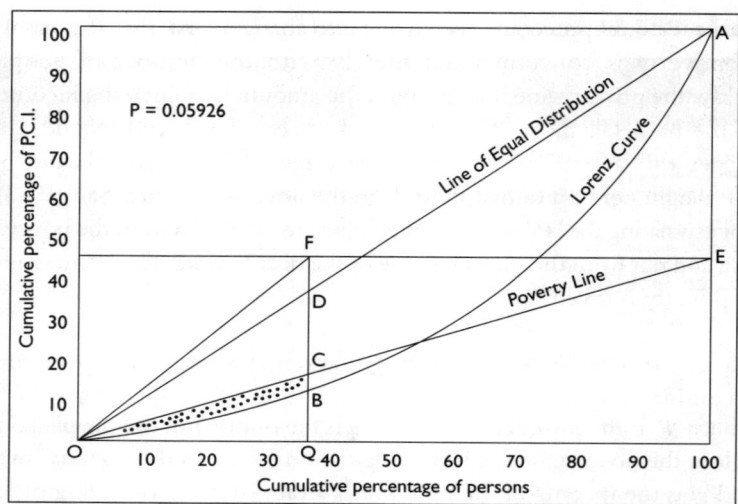

Figure 12.1 *Poverty among Agricultural Labourers: Per Capita Income Level*

Source: Field Survey, 2008–2009.

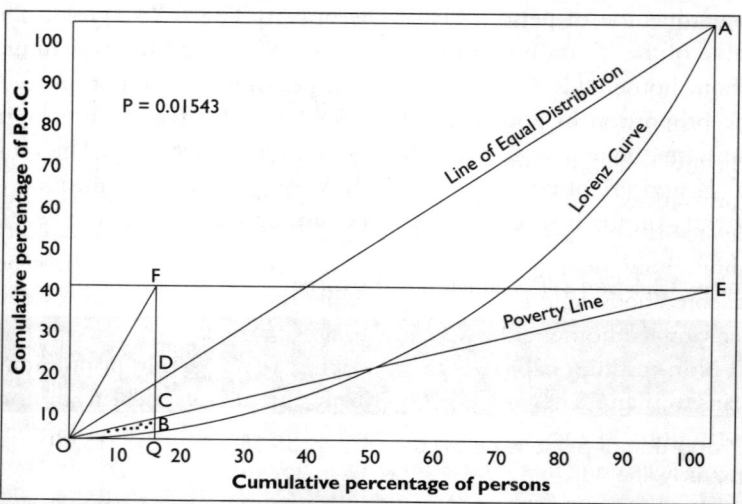

Figure 12.2 *Poverty among Agricultural Labourers: Per Capita Consumption Level*

Source: Field Survey, 2008–2009.

Table 12.7 Measuring Poverty by Nutrition Method

Description	Agricultural Labourers
No. of households below the poverty line	102
Proportion of households below the poverty line	71.33

Source: Field Survey, 2008–2009.

that the 'P' measure of poverty on the basis of consumption expenditure is considerably lower than that of the income-based poverty.

Table 12.7 shows that as many as 71.33 per cent of agricultural labour house-holds live below the poverty line on the basis of a nutrition method, that is, 2,400 calories per day, per capita.

Despite the government's claims of initiating a number of employment programmes and aids to the agricultural labourers for uplifting their levels of living, a large proportion of agricultural labourers still remain poor, both in absolute and relative terms, and continue to demand a better implementation of these schemes.

THE DEBT TRAP

The low level of income coerced agricultural labourers to borrow loans from various institutional and non-institutional agencies to meet their day-to-day expenses. About three-fourths (74.83%) of agricultural labour households are under debt. The average amount of debt per indebted household is ₹33,581.08, while the average amount of debt per sampled household is ₹25,127.10.

Non-institutional agencies are playing a greater role in providing loans to them. They get 84.90 per cent of their total debt from non-institutional agencies and remaining 15.10 per cent from institutional agencies. Among non-institutional agencies, they are found to be more indebted to large farmers and landlords who represent 68.06 per cent of the total loan and among institutional agencies, commercial banks provide 10.62 per cent of the total loans. They find it easy to get loans from non-institutional agencies and hesitate to take loans from institutional agencies because of the time-consuming formalities and cumbersome procedures. Moreover, generally institutional agencies do not advance loans to them because of lack of security.

The purpose for which a loan is taken is an important indication of its potential to be repaid. Agricultural labourers spent 40.26 per cent of their total credit on marriage and other social-religious ceremonies followed by the purchase of livestock (18.36%) with the least share being attributed to education (1.07%). Agricultural labourers take the maximum amount, that is, 49.47 per cent of the total debt at a rate of interest ranging between 24 per cent and 36 per cent. They get 6.86 per cent of their total debt from large farmers and landlords without any interest. Except from relatives and friends, non-institutional agencies charge very high rates of interest, ranging from 0 per cent to 40 per cent and above, whereas institutional agencies provide loans at relatively low rates of interest, ranging from 8 per cent to 16 per cent. The maximum number of indebted households (14.95%) fell in the debt range of ₹35,001–₹40,000. Agricultural labour households have to take loans at a high rate of interest from non-institutional agencies because they are not able to give adequate security or surety for getting loans from institutional agencies.

OWNERSHIP OF ASSETS

Ownership of assets plays an important role in determining levels of living conditions in any section of the society. The possession of productive assets directly affects their income, consumption and place and position in society. The share of different components that constitute total assets is shown in Table 12.8. The value of household assets is ₹157,552.41 and per capita value of assets is assessed at ₹31,957.41. Table 12.8 depicts that the dwelling house accounts for 73.38 per cent of the value of total assets followed by cattle (10.03%). The least share is occupied by means of communication accounting for 0.12 per cent of the total assets. The average value of assets does not show the actual economic status of the respondents because of the variations in the family size, so it becomes relevant to examine the per capita value of

Table 12.8 Components-wise Distribution of Household Assets

Component	Mean Value	Per Cent	Per Capita
Livestock	15808.17	10.03	3206.48
Dwelling house	115618.48	73.38	23451.67
Electronic gadgets	2492.06	1.58	505.48
Wooden goods	3400.97	2.16	689.84
Financial assets a Cash saving	1159.03	0.73	235.10
b Ornaments	1492.64	0.95	302.76
Means of conveyance	1259.26	0.80	255.42
Means of communication	189.20	0.12	38.38
Non-agricultural land	6947.08	4.41	1409.12
Others	9185.52	5.83	1863.16
Total	157552.41	100.00	31957.41

Source: Field Survey, 2008–2009.

household assets. The per capita value of household assets for dwelling house is ₹23,451.67 followed by cattle assets (₹32,06.48).

Further, the total number of cattle possessed by all the agricultural labour households is 143. Out of this 62.94 per cent are milch animals. Buffaloes (43.36%) prove to be the most preferred cattle as compared to other any other cattle. Among these cattle, 46.85 per cent have a value up to ₹15,000, followed by 24.48 per cent with a value ranging between ₹15,001 and ₹25,000 and further followed by 28.67 per cent having the value ranging between ₹25,001 and above. On an average, an agricultural labour household possesses cattle worth ₹15,808.17 and 2.38, 4.71, 0.64 and 0.037 numbers of electronic gadgets, wooden goods, means of conveyance and communication, respectively.

Dwelling houses constitute a major share that accounts almost three-fourths of total assets value and the remaining assets account only one-fourth. Dwelling house and livestock combined claim about 84 per cent of the total assets of agricultural labourers representing a degrading condition of them as they posses hardly any asset for a better life such as motorcycle, gas, TV, refrigerator, furniture and bedding.

SOCIAL CONDITIONS OF AGRICULTURAL LABOURERS

In this section, an attempt has been made to throw light on the social conditions of the agricultural labourers, on their position and rank in the society. In any social system, the ownership of means of production determines one's position in society. One, who dominates the means of production, acquires the higher position in the society. In Punjab, land is the most important means of production. As they are landless, agricultural labourers are assigned the lowest position in society. They depend on land for their earnings, but they get nothing from it because of the unfavourable distribution of gains in agriculture. A major share of the gains is kept by the landlords/farmers themselves because of the ownership of means of production. This study also reveals some important facts about the social condition of agricultural labourers which is not explained in figures nor neglected as these represent the clearcut picture of their position in the society. In the society, the lowest place is assigned to them. Agricultural labourers live in one corner of the village. Their homes are located on the banks of the ponds in the villages. The streets to their homes are narrow and are always full of water as there is no drainage facility. Their homes generally constitute single room, or in some cases a couple of rooms with no facility of bathroom, toilet, kitchen, water or electricity, all essential for a decent standard of living. Even the number of beds in the house is not adequate for number of family members. The utensils in the houses hardly meet their needs. They tie their cattle as well as keep the fodder in the same house where they live. The size of the households of all agricultural labourers in a village is equivalent to the area of houses owned by three or four big landlords. Even government housing schemes have tended to reinforce caste segregation as most of these housing schemes are located at a distance from the village and houses under these schemes are allotted exclusively to Dalits. The question of housing is very important to the Dalit agricultural labourers, and it is tied up with issues of their dignity as well as their practical needs (Ghuman et al., 2007).

The situation of agricultural labourers, employed as permanent labourers, is much worse. Victims of economic-bondedness as they have taken credit from their employers they cannot leave their job until they repay the full debt. Should they change their employer, then the new employer has to pay the entire debt of the permanent agricultural labourer to the old one. This never improves the situation for the labour because it is only a mutual transfer of the employer, they still remain economically bonded. Famers treat the labour badly, typically being rude and using filthy language while talking to permanent agricultural labourers, as well as their children. The utensils in which the labourers take their meals and tea are kept separate from the family utensils of a farmer's.

Normally, a permanent agricultural labourer has to perform two tasks simultaneously, one as agricultural labourer and the other as a house servant. Young female agricultural labourers are inevitably sexually exploited, the brunt of vulgarities spouted by the landowners. Should they dare to demand a minimum humane treatment, they can be forbidden to use village fields to defecate and urinate in. The class of agricultural labourers is the most exploited and oppressed class in the rural hierarchy. Being Scheduled Castes contributes to their degrading condition even further because Scheduled Castes population is already a victim of social discrimination in our society.

CONCLUSION AND POLICY RECOMMENDATIONS

This study has attempted to examine the employment pattern among agricultural labourers in rural Punjab from 2008 to 2009. After more than six decades of planned economic development, the class of agricultural labourers remains the most exploited and oppressed class in the rural hierarchy. Some land reforms, the Green Revolution and the New Economic Policy in India may have contributed to the improvement of sections of society, the conditions of agricultural labourers remain abysmal. They are victims of social discrimination and economic exploitation.

The study has concluded that almost 43 per cent of the total population of agricultural labour households is illiterate and 82.52 per cent belong to Scheduled Castes category. Almost one-third households do not have any source of drinking water. Their income is too low to meet even the basic requirements for decent living. To meet their basic needs or to bridge the consumption–income gap, they fell into a vicious debt trap leading to about three-fourths of the households are indebted. More than 62 per cent of agricultural labourers are employed as permanent agricultural labourers. On an average, a permanent and casual agricultural labourer gets work for 354.59 and 178.80 mandays, respectively. Almost one-third of the total wage rate paid to permanent agricultural labour is taken up by meals only. In case of woman permanent labourers, the share of kind wages is more than half of their earnings. The majority of them are living below poverty line. Dwelling houses and livestock make up about 84 per cent of the total assets representing a degrading condition of them.

In words of Alfred Marshall (1919, p. 199), 'Every agricultural problem has peculiarities of its own; and some side of it can be mastered by shrewd, experienced, alert, instinctive judgement better than by systematic reasoning based on ordered knowledge.'

To overcome these problems, effective measures should be taken by government and its institutions, such as agricultural growth is one of the important components for productive inclusion. The global experience has shown that GDP growth originating in agriculture is at least twice as effective in reducing poverty as GDP growth originating outside agriculture. Discrimination on the basis of caste still exists in society and because of the fact that this job is simply assigned to the lower castes by the prevailing social system, proper legislation and ensured penalty on any type of caste-based discrimination is needed. For providing them land for houses and cultivation, government should use village common land as well as provide financial at low rate of interests and technical assistance. With the development of subsidiary occupations such as dairying, poultry, fishery, piggery and repairing and other shops, employment will generate and it will lead to an increase in their earnings. Establishment of agro-based industries in rural areas must be given top priority to provide them employment opportunities at the village level itself. Government should launch more employment generation programmes such as MGNREGA and *Atta-Dal* schemes to provide them daily consumption items on very nominal rates to fulfil their consumption needs in the existing income level. Adequate steps towards a revision and implementation of a minimum wage act will prove helpful in improving their conditions. The most important suggestion comes in the form of cooperative farming, which definitely will improve the conditions of agricultural labourers and the abolition of forces of discrimination on the basis of caste, class, gender is necessary to provide conditions for dignified living.

In the given socio-economic and political structure of the Punjab economy, some of these policy measures can help in minimizing problems faced by the agricultural labour households.

REFERENCES

Barst, K. (2009, May). *Agrarian and nationality question in Punjab*. Takht Bharti Parkashan.
Bharti, V. (2011). Indebtedness and suicides: Field notes on agricultural labourers of Punjab. *Economic & Political Weekly, 46*(14), 35–40.
Chopra, S. (2005). The problems of agricultural labour and neo-liberal reforms. *People's Democracy, 29*(15). http://archives.peoplesdemocracy.in/2005/0410/04102005_suneet.htm
Ghosh, K. K. (1969). *Agricultural labourers in India*. Indian Publications.
Ghuman, R. S., Singh, I., & Singh, L. (2007). *Status of local agricultural labour in Punjab*. The Punjab State Farmers Commission, Government of Punjab.
Government of India (GoI). (1956–1957). *Report on the second agricultural labour enquiry* (p. 104). Ministry of Labour and Employment.
Government of India. (2001). *Census of India*. Ministry of Home Affairs, Office of the Registrar General and Census Commissioner.
Government of Punjab (GoP). (2004). *Human development report*. Economic and Statistical Organisation.
Government of Punjab. (2009). *Statistical abstract of Punjab*. Economic and Statistical Organisation.
Ishikawa, S. (1978). *Labour absorption in Asian agriculture, ILO-Artep Publication* (p. v). Wah Printing.
Marshall, A. (1919). *Industry and trade*. Cosimo Classics.
Parthasarathy, G. (1991). Agricultural wages and rural wages: National policy for agricultural labour. *IASSI Quarterly, 9*(3), 19–56.
Patnaik, U. (2007). Neoliberalism and rural poverty in India. *Economic & Political Weekly, 42*(30), 3132–3150.
Reserve Bank of India. (2009). India's Central Bank, Government of India. https://www.rbi.org.in/
Sen, A. (1973). Poverty, inequality and unemployment in: Some conceptual issues in measurement. *Economic & Political Weekly, 8*(31/32/33), 1457–1459, 1461, 1463–1464.
Sen, A. (1976). Poverty: An ordinal approach to measurement. *Econometrica, 44*(2), 219–231.

Sidhu, R. S., & Singh, S. (2004). Agricultural wages and employment. *Economic & Political Weekly, 39*(37), 4132–4135.

Singh, S. (2009). Survival of agricultural labour in Punjab: A burning question. *Economic & Political Weekly, 44*(29), 18–24.

Singh, M. (2006). *Analysing the effectiveness of the programmes for the eradication of the bonded labour system in Punjab* (Working Paper V). Centre for Education and Communication.

Srivastva, R. S. (2005). *Bonded labour in India: Its incidence and pattern.* International Labour Office.

Chapter 13
Agriculture Security*
How to Attain It

Pushpa M. Bhargava

I. THE CRISIS

Food security, important for every country, means ensuring availability of enough food for the people of a country at affordable prices that would take care of the basic nutritional requirements of the population on a sustainable basis. There are two ways of ensuring food security:

1. Dependence primarily on indigenous production
2. Dependence primarily on imports against exports of other indigenous products to countries that cannot do without receiving such exports.

For India, the first alternative is clearly the one of choice as a vast majority of our population (over 60%) is engaged in agriculture, and some 70 per cent of our people derive their total income from agriculture or agriculture-related activities such as animal husbandry and fisheries, or activities in the rural sector that support our agriculturists. Therefore, agriculture security in our country should be considered functionally synonymous with food security, and with the security of our farmers and of the rural sector where they live and work.

Given this perspective, India's agriculture security is facing a serious crisis as is clear from the following:

---

* *Social Change,* 38(1), 2008.

1. From a situation of self-sufficiency in food following the Green Revolution in the 1960s, we now need to import five million tons of wheat alone this year, besides other food items like vegetable oil, without a corresponding increase in the export of agro-products; and this is not the first year we would be doing so.
2. Virtually no attention has been paid to the plight of small farmers (with holdings of 2–4 hectares) and marginal farmers (with less than 2 hectares who account for 84% of our farmers).
3. Suicides of farmers continue unabated. Some 40 per cent of farmers, even though in love with their land, want to opt out of farming as a profession. There has been, thus, a substantial migration from the villages to the cities which have been ill-equipped to handle this migration in any civilized manner.
4. Following liberalization beginning with the last decade of the last century, the gap between the rich (mostly urban) and the poor (mostly rural, including a vast majority of the farmers) and thus between the urban and the rural sectors has increased. The vastly increased consumption in the country has been almost exclusively confined to the middle and the upper classes, living largely in the urban sector. Thus, 78 per cent of our population (which, according to the last census, includes 84% of all Dalits, 82% of OBCs, 80% of Muslims and 85–88% of the unorganized sector including the small and marginal farmers) lives in less than ₹20 (equivalent to two dollars in terms of price parity) per day. One out of every five Indians is hungry, and 46 per cent of children under three years of age are malnourished according to the latest National Family Health Survey. The dramatic rise of consumerism in India in the present decade has not touched above 78 per cent of our people.
5. While the infrastructure in many of the urban areas (e.g., parts of Hyderabad) has undergone an unprecedented and dramatic change (making these areas, perhaps, among the best residential or business districts anywhere), it would be probably impossible to find any rural area in the country where a comparatively similar change has occurred during the last 15 years or so.
6. Our soil has, in many places, become badly contaminated/eroded, and its productivity substantially decreased on account of excessive use of fertilizers, pesticides and water, even though water

is becoming a scarce commodity, with groundwater levels falling drastically year after year in many parts of the country, both rural and urban.
7. Our overall agricultural productivity has, in most cases, either decreased or increased only marginally.
8. Our procurement, pricing and public distribution policies, instead of helping people, have created, on the whole, havoc on account of both corruption and intrinsic systemic faults.
9. Our rural sector comprising over 600,000 villages, inhabited mostly by small and marginal farmers, has inherited a vast repertoire of traditional knowledge and skills (including traditional arts and crafts) which, if commercialized ethically, have the potential of employing at least 100 million people and generating a gross income of over ₹600,000 crores per year (Annexure 1). A vast proportion of this income and employment will be in rural families with a stake in agriculture, thereby empowering the countryside economically and reducing, if not preventing, the drift of population to our bursting cities. It will also help maintain a healthy rate of the agriculture sector's contribution to India's GDP, which has come down from over 40 per cent to below 20 per cent. The effort in the country today to use our traditional knowledge and skills for optimal social and economic gain is highly fragmented and largely ineffective, and the condition of a vast majority of those engaged in traditional arts and crafts is pitiful, partly on account of unbridled exploitation by middlemen.

The list mentioned earlier is by no means exhaustive. In spite of a few but notable exceptions to many, if not all, of what has been said earlier, the present policies, taken all together, cannot be the driver for sustainable food security, farmer security, agriculture security and the security of our rural sector.

All this calls for drastic changes in our policies concerning agriculture, food production, farmers and the rural sector in general. The increasing population and rising consumption due to the rising purchasing power of people, and the widening gap between the requirement of food and domestic production with the consequent import dependence, could seriously affect the country's autonomy in policymaking and imperil internal calm and security by breeding hunger and by aggravating poverty and discontent on a vast scale. And all this could happen earlier than we imagine—say, in a few years.

Our future, therefore, lies in ensuring as soon as possible that our 600,000 villages become places where, on certain counts like advantage of open space, some people may prefer to live rather than live in cities, as has happened in many other countries. This can only happen when the basic general standard of living in our villages improves; this can, in turn, happen only when the survival, health and growth of our rural sector (which would include farmers and, therefore, agriculture) are secured on a sustainable basis.

This chapter attempts to define the aforementioned crisis in detail and suggest means to defuse it.

II. THE IMMEDIATE OBJECTIVES OF AGRICULTURAL SECURITY

These would be:

1. Higher productivity, especially of small/marginal farmers, and sufficient production leading to food security.
2. Larger per capita income in the rural sector that would be in the direction of closing the gap between the rich and the poor in the country.
3. Substantial increase in employment in the rural sector, with optimum utilization of knowledge and expertise already existing in the sector.
4. Connectivity with the urban sector through roads and communication channels.
5. Education facilities that would enable every child in the rural sector to receive high-quality education up to Class X to begin with and eventually up to Class XII, comparable to that obtained in the urban sector.
6. Basic, affordable and approachable health facilities with linkages with specialized health and medicare facilities in the urbanized areas which cannot be replicated in the rural sector.
7. Environmental security in the rural sector (clean air and water and uncontaminated soil).
8. Some advantages over those in the urban sector.

III. THE COMPONENTS OF AGRICULTURE SECURITY

These are listed in Figure 13.1.
The problems in regard to most of the items in Figure 13.1 are mentioned in Section IV, and their possible solutions in Section V.

IV. THE PROBLEMS

(The Arabic numerals in parenthesis refer to item numbers in Figure 13.1)

(i) Seeds (1)

- We often have inadequate availability of certified, quality hybrid seeds that have to be supplied by seed companies (Annexure 2).
- Our farmers do not have easy access to checking seed quality.
- Use of hybrids requires farmers to purchase seeds each time. In fact, there will be no seed companies if there were no hybrid seeds. Seed companies have a vested interest in not propagating true-breeding varieties of which a large number has been developed by the Indian Council of Agricultural Research (ICAR). The extension capabilities of ICAR must, therefore, be strengthened. The Green Revolution pioneered by ICAR in the 1960s would not have been possible but for true-breeding varieties.
- There has been an alarming increase in foreign control of seed production which must be curbed (Annexure 2).
- While our regulatory systems of plant and animal quarantine have worked well, our regulatory system for permitting release of genetically manipulated (GM) crops grown from GM seeds is highly unsatisfactory (Annexure 2).
- We have no effective system of crop insurance to guard against, for example, bad seed or faulty rainfall.

(ii) Agrochemicals and Organic Agriculture (2, 8)

We have a strong fertilizer and pesticide lobby which is partially controlled by foreign interests. This lobby not only recommends but ensures through various means (including bribery), excessive use of

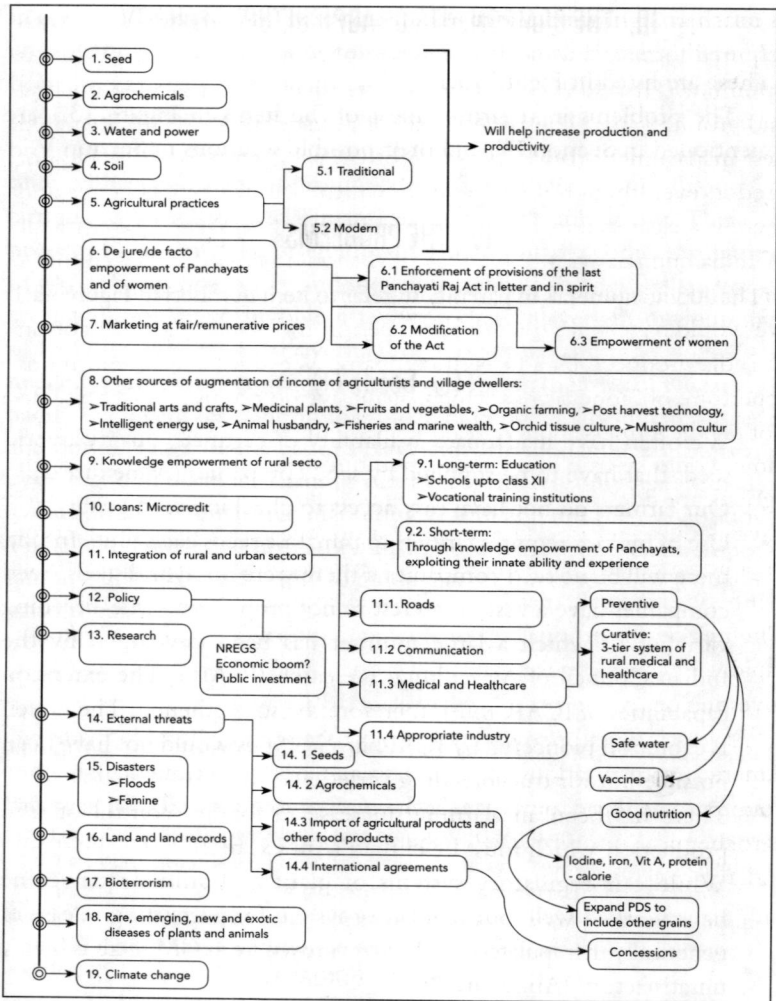

Figure 13.1 *Components of Agriculture Security (with Objectives Mentioned in the Text)*
Source: Author's own.

fertilizers and pesticides, and use of pesticides that should never have been permitted to be used such as chlorpyriphos. We do not make any organized effort to counter this lobby. This inaction has resulted in serious problems in the country. In the case of fertilizer, sometimes as much as 20 times more nitrogen is used when compared to what is required to maintain the nitrogen:phosphorous:potassium ratio that is optimum. This excess nitrogen has extensively contaminated our soil and groundwater. The same is true of pesticides. We have integrated pest management (IPM) available for over 80 crops but we have not used it, even though it has been shown to be extremely effective and there is a clear statement in the agriculture policy of the Government of India enunciated in 2001 that IPM should be used in the country. In fact, if we had used IPM for cotton for which it was first developed, we would have had no rationale to permit the plantation of Bt cotton in India produced by a foreign company. We also have an enormous repertoire of biopesticides which, again, we do not use: in fact, we do not tell the farmers about it or do not give the technology to them. The same would be true of organic agriculture where the future lies. Such agriculture does not use either chemical fertilizers or pesticides. We have all the expertise and resources for organic agriculture. Products of organic agriculture fetch higher prices than products of agriculture using synthetic chemicals. Yet we have not encouraged organic agriculture. The market for products of organic agriculture is growing extremely rapidly—even in India—and if we do not step in, China, which is investing heavily in organic agriculture, will capture it.

At least two efforts (which were fortunately foiled) were made by American organizations (one private and one governmental) in the country to market a spurious agrochemical or to do research on harmful agrochemicals prohibited elsewhere with a view to market them in India (Bhargava, 2003).

(iii) Water and Power (3)

An easy, short-term and effective solution to substantially augment water supply in the rural sector which has been a major bottleneck in increasing productivity and production in many parts of rural India is rainwater harvesting. Wherever this has been done, for example, substantially in Rajasthan and to a small extent in Andhra Pradesh, the results have been revolutionary. The traditional techniques of rainwater harvesting have been well documented by Narayan and Agarwal (2001). Yet we have hardly exploited our potential in this area. Therefore, there is a case for taking appropriate steps for rainwater harvesting in the rural sector to augment current programmes of irrigation schemes.

It is now widely recognized that a large number of traditional water storage tanks have silted over the years or dried up, the land being then illegally occupied. Records of location of these tanks are available in the State Archives, for example, in the Andhra Pradesh State Archives. They can also be located through remote sensing as has been done in and around Hyderabad. Every effort should be made to resurrect these tanks. This could be the responsibility of national/state water harvesting programmes.

It is ironical that while we have shortage of water for agricultural purposes at many places, at many other places, excessive use of (often pumped, underground) water has led to soil damage. This is partly on account of the availability of free power which is neither reliable nor of the right quality. What the farming sector actually needs and desires is *not* free power but *assured and quality* power.

(iv) Soil (4)

The country needs a detailed soil map which must be updated periodically and be accessible to every farmer—at least to every village panchayat. It must record the damage done to the soil in various parts of the country due to excessive use of pesticides and fertilizers and, at times, water. It must also record micronutrient deficiency about which the farmer generally knows very little but the removal of which may be vital for maximizing productivity.

(v) Traditional Agricultural Practices (5.1)

ICAR has recently, in five volumes, compiled over 4,000 traditional agricultural practices. This documentation is unparalleled in the history of any country and has been extremely well done. As of December 2005, over 90 of these practices had been validated and close to 40 cross-validated. These should be popularized. Further, there is clearly a need for setting up a system to validate and cross-validate the other documented traditional agricultural practices which could lead to substantial cost reduction and revolutionize our agriculture.

(vi) Modern Agricultural Practices (5.2)

While our rural sector must be open to modern agricultural practices, their blind acceptance could sow the seeds of disaster. An example would be the use of GM seeds (Annexure 2). Before we use them, we must, at the national level, determine if there are other cheaper and conventional alternatives (this was not done for Bt cotton). We must then go through an appropriate risk assessment; details of such a risk assessment appropriate for our country are available (Bhargava 2002). Such a risk assessment for any GM crop will take between 10 and 15 years. If a GM crop goes through successfully such a risk assessment, there is bound to be still some residual risk left which should then be assessed against probable benefits. It is only after all this has been done that a GM crop should be released. As of today, not a single GM crop anywhere in the world has been released following the above risk assessment procedure.

(vii) De Jure/De Facto Empowerment of Panchayats and of Women (6)

The 73rd Amendment to the Indian Constitution in 1993 on Panchayat Raj which was followed by relevant Acts passed by most of the state governments empowers the panchayats substantially. However, in practice, such empowerment has not always happened. Lok Satta (now an Andhra Pradesh-based political party) had negotiated in 2002–2003 with the Government of Andhra Pradesh for certain powers to be transferred to the panchayats as per the above Act. Unfortunately, even though there is an official record to say that this should be done, such a transfer never took place. A similar exercise must be undertaken by the centre, and the states must be persuaded to empower panchayats appropriately.

The Act as of now vests the financial powers with the secretary of a panchayat who is appointed by the government. While the institution of the panchayat secretary who provides the link between the lowest and the highest tiers of the government is appreciated, it is only appropriate that their appointment should be made in consultation with the panchayats, and that the financial powers be exercised jointly by the secretary and the panchayats, with the panchayats having a veto power.

Today, even the most enterprising women in our villages have difficulty in, for example, getting a loan as there is generally no collateral that they can provide. Their professional inability is also curtailed on account of their having to take care of small children during the day.

(viii) Marketing at Fair/Remunerative Price (7)

The minimum support price for an agricultural product must ensure that the primary producer has a reasonable net profit. Further, we must not permit cheap and highly subsidized imports of agricultural products (unprocessed or processed) except to meet real and crucial shortages.

Contract farming should be encouraged but under the condition that the farmers are given a share of the profit that the contracting company makes; one way would be to provide the farmer shares in the company (like ESOPS) under specific but fair conditions. This step, of course, must be in addition to a fair price to the contract farmer. If the farmer believes this price is not fair in relation to the cost of production, they should be able to take their case up to a commission empowered or set up to handle such cases (like the Monopolies and Restricted Trade Practices Commission).

The non-functioning of and corruption in the Food Corporation of India (FCI) should be a matter of great concern (Cherian, 2007).

(ix) Augmentation of Income of Agriculturists and Village Dwellers (8)

Some of the ways in which this can be done are listed in Figure 13.1.

Organic farming has already been mentioned under Sub-section (ii) above. A mention has been made of traditional arts and crafts in Section I (i).

Post-harvest technologies can save a large proportion of (at least) ₹58,000 crores worth of food that goes to waste in our country every year as stated by the Minister of State for Food Processing in the Rajya Sabha (*Hyderabad Times*, 2002; estimates of such wastage made by the Ministry of Chemicals and ASSOCHAM are 1.5 to more than 2 times higher (*Economic Times*, 2006).

As regards medicinal plants, we have some 40,000 distinct plant-based drug formulations that have come to us through the four documented traditional systems of medicines (Ayurveda, Unani, Siddha and Tibetan) and the undocumented tribal systems of medicine. We have every reason to believe that at least 4,000 (if not several times more) of these formulations would be validated if tested according to current stringent modes of testing of drugs. If we keep in mind the fact that as of today, on an average, only some 20 new chemical entities (drugs) come into the market every year, and the fact that our country has the capacity to test at least 200 new formulations every year, we can see the potential of India virtually capturing the world's drug market in the next 20 years. The medicinal plants are high volume products which can complement or substitute traditional agro-products.

As regards fruits and vegetables, India has many uncommon vegetables and fruits and an unparalleled variety of many of them. Thus, there are some 150 documented vegetables for which nutritional information is available and perhaps some 50 used by tribals which have not been systematically documented so far. The same is true of fruits. Not only that, the variety we have in each vegetable or fruit is staggering: over 400 varieties each of mangoes, ladyfingers and brinjals are there in our National Bureau of Plant Genetic Resources, New Delhi. India has thus the potential of capturing the world's vegetable and fruit market if it could only appropriately publicize its rich heritage in this regard and evolve a marketing strategy involving the hospitality industry (which today serves no more than 10 varieties of vegetables or fruits), as happened with bottled water (which was unknown in the USA and the UK until the 1960s) at France's initiative (so, today, hundreds of millions around the world [including in poor India!] drink bottled water even when tap water is perfectly safe or can be made safe by simple procedures such as the use of an appropriate filter). The price that the vegetables and fruits command in terms of produce per acre is much higher than what other food crops bring to the farmer. This would, therefore, be a good way to increase their income, specially of farmers that have smallholdings.

A word about orchid tissue culture. The second largest foreign exchange earner for Thailand is believed to be the export of orchids worth apparently ₹10,000 crores annually. The technique of plant tissue culture was introduced in Thailand only some 30 years ago, whereas it has been operative in India for more than 55 years. Not only that, the state of Arunachal Pradesh alone has more than 600 varieties of orchids and its State Forest Research Institute has developed technologies for growing them through tissue culture. Some of them can also be grown in temperate climates in India. In fact, Arunachal Pradesh orchids are recognized as being far more beautiful than the Thai orchids which are much more limited in number, and of which the world now seems to be 'tired'. Therefore, Arunachal Pradesh has the potential of capturing the world's orchid market and contributing substantially to its own income as well as to the national GDP. Orchids are being grown currently on a small scale in Sikkim, near Darjeeling, and in the Bangalore region, but are not exported.

With our over 8,000 km coastline, appropriate temperatures and an extremely rich marine wealth, marine biotechnology has the potential of providing to the world a vast range of products of medicinal and industrial use at a fraction of the cost (in some cases, like polyunsaturated fatty acids, at a thousand times less cost) at which they are available now. Thus, the entire Vitamin A requirement of a child (Vitamin A deficiency being one of the most common and important nutritional deficiencies) in the country can be met at a cost of about ₹15 per child by natural beta-carotene produced by the marine algae, *Donalila*.

ICAR has excellent documentation of inefficient energy use in our agriculture.

(x) Knowledge Empowerment of the Rural Sector (9)

All indices of human development relate to knowledge. Therefore, for the rural sector to be a major partner (which it should be in view of its size) in meeting the developmental and societal goals of the country, it must be empowered with knowledge.

The only *long-term* means of such empowerment is compulsory, free and high-quality education up to Class XII to all children in the age group of 6–18 years, and provision of enough vocational training institutes covering rural and traditional art, craft and skill-specific vocations such as weaving and metal work in our villages.

On a short-term basis, the panchayats can be provided information packages covering the following items:

1. General knowledge that would make them reasonably informed citizens of the country and the world.
2. Specialized knowledge, for example, on seeds, optimal use of fertilizers, water and power, management of livestock, output channels, market information, water management like rainwater harvesting, technologies for value addition, time and labour-saving devices, energy plantations, etc. One would also need to establish a system by which one could update this knowledge in real time.
3. Knowledge for immediate use, that is, updated information, for example, on the weather and the movement of fish, which one can obtain using satellite imagery.

Items (1) and (2) can be taken care of in 40 hours (one working week) by carefully selected/trained personnel.

(xi) Loans (10)

The need for a national programme of credit, including micro-credit for the farming and other self-employed rural communities is well-recognized. As of today, less than 3 per cent of the credit available for the agricultural sector goes to marginal farmers who need it the most.

(xii) Integration of Rural and Urban Sectors (11)

The need for roads to and telecommunication facilities in our villages is also widely recognized. Fortunately, the government is acutely aware of this need. The need for giving top priority to this work must be reiterated continuously.

Industrialization is, today, a key factor for rapid development, and could bridge the rural–urban divide, without either sector losing its specific advantages and character. However, for this to happen, the impetus for such industrialization must come from the rural community itself while the technology and the technical expertise may come from elsewhere. In fact, our villages have tremendous scope for locating agriculture-produce-related, environment-friendly industries such as those using post-harvest and food processing technologies, or producing biofuels, sugar, salt or products of aquaculture (in coastal areas). Special economic zones (SEZs) should not be located in existing rural communities. It may be more advantageous to provide concessions to village product-based industries located in or near the villages than to other industries in SEZs.

As regards rural health and medical care, a three-tier system appears to be the most suitable and workable. It would be based on the fact that a vast majority of the population (about 80%) suffers from less than 1 per cent of known diseases, most of which can be diagnosed successfully from symptoms and a cure prescribed. A vast proportion of these diseases is caused by contaminated water, lack of sanitation or lack of adequate nutrition. To diagnose/treat these diseases, one need not be a full-fledged medical doctor or need a laboratory. With an appropriate computer programme such as the one which has been validated by distinguished medical persons like Noshir Antia (one of our country's best-known plastic surgeons), an intelligent high-school-pass person can do the job. This person can be provided by the village and helped by the staff that is already attached to primary healthcare centres. What is important is that the appointment of the aforementioned para medical staff, which is now made by the central administration of the state, should be made by the local self-government, preferably from local people. It should not be difficult to set up training programmes for such staff. The remaining (perhaps, about 20%) patients should be referred to taluka/district hospital which should have all the basic facilities. A system of transporting patients from the village to the taluka/district hospitals and of the stay of the accompanying persons near the hospital should be an integral part of the programme. A small number of the above 20 per cent of the patients (perhaps, not more than 1–2% of the total patient population) would need to be referred to the closest tertiary care unit in a town/city. The primary and secondary healthcare should be provided by the state, while tertiary care could be provided by private/corporate hospitals (in addition to government hospitals where they exist) and covered by insurance which should be paid partly by the government and partly by the community concerned.

(xiii) Policy (12)

1. Continuous review of the National Rural Employment Guarantee Scheme (NREGS) should be made to ensure that (a) payment is adequate, (b) it reaches the intended beneficiaries and (c) the beneficiary carries out work which is a part of the developmental plan of the region.
2. It must be recognized that high GDP growth rate does not necessarily benefit the rural sector in a commensurate manner. For example, a recent article by P. Chatterjee (2007) states that child malnutrition and health risk have increased in India (probably more in rural India than in urban India) in spite of the economic boom. Therefore, our liberalization policies must ensure increase in equity concurrently with a high GDP growth rate. Considering that 70 per cent of India is, population wise, rural and (mostly) agricultural, this means that our liberalization policies must be directed towards making rural India relatively more prosperous, rather than primarily benefiting the affluent urban upper and middle class. This would be perhaps the most important step we can take to ensure agricultural security and prevent major internal strife.
3. There is clearly need for a higher goal and project-directed investment in the agricultural sector.

(xiv) Research (13)

Annexure 3 lists areas where research needs to be done by ICAR and the agricultural university system, and where the existing or new information gained through research should be communicated to our agricultural sector.

We have also failed in optimal commercialization of the products of research in ICAR and agricultural university system. We have not recognized that there are often village or area-specific problems in the rural sector and, therefore, we have not set up a mechanism to handle them.

The value of design, for example, in agro implements and in agricultural practice, has not been recognized.

(xv) External Threats (14)

1. The external threats in regard to seeds and agro-chemicals have already been mentioned in Sub-sections (i) and (ii) and Annexure 2.
2. In view of the 400 billion dollar annual subsidy to agriculture in the USA and Europe which are, in functional terms, orders of magnitude higher than the subsidy we provide to our agriculture, the developed countries are in a position to dump agriculture produce in our country at prices that are lower than our cost of production. Such dumping may have irreversible disastrous effects on our agriculture and must be guarded against. There should, therefore, be a ban on all imports of agriculture produce (unprocessed or processed) except to meet a genuine demand that cannot be locally met. Note must be taken of the recent wheat import which, it appears, did not even satisfy obligatory phytosanitary standards.
3. We need to carefully review the Indo-US CEO agreement and the Indo-US Knowledge Initiative which have the potential of transferring a substantial part of control of our food business into the hands of foreign organizations.

(xvi) Disasters (15)

The inadequacy of our system to deal with disasters that impact our agriculture is exemplified by (a) the recent Orissa famine when we allowed the import of genetically manipulated soya bean flour from the USA, even though we had our FCI's godowns overflowing and (b) the occurrence of floods (with floods and famine occurring in the same area at different times of the year). There is, therefore, a need for setting up an agriculture disaster rapid action force and an effective flood control system for working out means to prevent floods (e.g., by diverting and then collecting flood waters), for which precedents exist in the country.

(xvii) Land Records (16)

Land records are not complete and not maintained in most parts of the country. Further, while we need to bring more land under cultivation, SEZs are alienating valuable agricultural lands.

(xviii) Bioterrorism (17)

We have not adequately recognized the possibility and consequences of biological warfare against or a terrorist attack using biological weapons on our agricultural crops or our animal wealth.

(xix) Rare, Emerging, New and Exotic Diseases of Plants and Animals (18)

One of the outstanding successes (unfortunately not widely known) of ICAR has been the prevention of entry of new and rare diseases of animals that have not existed in the country by the High Security Animal Lab of ICAR at Bhopal which, in spite of its outstanding facilities (it being the only lab in India with the highest (P4) level of containment facility) and performance, is just a unit of the Indian Veterinary Research Institute at Izatnagar. No such facility exists in the country for identification and handling of rare, emerging, new and exotic diseases of plants.

(xx) Effect of Climate Change

There is new awareness that climate change can progressively affect agricultural output like of wheat; this should be factored in our future objectives.

V. RECOMMENDATIONS

(The Arabic numerals in parenthesis at the end of a para refer to item numbers in Figure 13.1. A few other related recommendations are mentioned in the text.)

1. The recommendations made in the report of the National Farmers Commission that was submitted to the Government of India recently by its Chairman, Dr M. S. Swaminathan, which also speaks about agricultural security and emphasizes (among other measures) the need for appropriate credit facilities for farmers, should be accepted in principle and appropriate action taken on it expeditiously.

2. A system needs to be set up to ensure adequate availability of seeds by, perhaps, revamping Seed Corporation of India. Seed production must be in our own hands, with no foreign direct investment (FDI) normally permitted in this sector. In special cases where there is a clear, transparently established benefit to India which cannot be accrued in any other way, up to 25 per cent FDI may be permitted in the seed sector. An appropriate seed bill needs to be passed to ensure this. Seed subsidies (a source of corruption today) should be replaced by provision of quality seeds at the market price (1, 14.1)
3. A set of seed-testing laboratories which can be easily accessed by farmers through seed collection centres should be set up in the public sector. They should be capable of testing GM seeds and establishing seed identity through DNA fingerprinting (the research component of DNA fingerprinting of seeds is being already taken care of by an ICAR set-up in Delhi). An effective, fair, socially relevant, scientifically sound, transparent and professionally managed regulatory and supervisory system should be set up for evaluation and release of genetically modified organisms (the present system does not satisfy these criteria). (1)
4. An appropriate system of crop insurance should be set up, for example, as a safeguard against supply of bad seed. If the seed is supplied by a seed company, the company should pay a part of the premium, such a scheme replacing the system of penalties for supply of bad seed.
5. Integrated pest management (IPM) technologies and biopesticides developed by ICAR must be used as a matter of policy, in preference to synthetic pesticides or the so-called pest-resistant GM crops. Standard operative procedures should be prepared for IPM (which would drastically reduce the use of synthetic pesticides and thus contamination of soil and groundwater) for various crops, in all Schedule VIII languages. An industrial set-up should be put in place, through an initiative of ICAR, to produce various requirements for IPM. ICAR should set up a national quality control laboratory for material used in IPM. A strategy for dissemination of procedures of IPM should be worked out. An appropriate number of ITIs should be set up for training in IPM at various levels, some within the ICAR system itself. (2)

6. The existing subsidy on fertilizers should be reduced or eliminated depending on the size of the agricultural landholding. A micro soil atlas for the country should be prepared (if one is not already available), updated and made available widely to farmers. (2, 4, 14.2)
7. An empowered rainwater harvesting authority should be set up in every state as well as at the centre. The central authority should document and disseminate the success stories in this regard, for example, in Rajasthan, Bengal and Gujarat. The policy of free power should be replaced by a policy of providing quality and assured power at cost. The financial implications of resorting to drip irrigation (to save water and prevent overuse of water) should be investigated on the national scale, and the technique resorted to wherever possible and economically feasible. The government needs to evolve a rational policy for water use and groundwater extraction, treating water as a commodity, which could be charged. (3)
8. A national mission should be set up for validation of our over 4,000 traditional agricultural practices and commercialization of the validated ones. The mission should involve the National Innovation Foundation and ICAR; it could become a model of cooperation between government and civil society in an area which is of the utmost importance to the country. (5.1)
9. ICAR should set up a permanent panel for assessment of new technologies from outside India; the panel should consist of people with high public credibility and established competence, integrity, courage and commitment to our agriculture and the country; it should include scientists, economists, sociologists and farmers. (5.2)
10. A rational policy for farm labour must be evolved. A knowledge-based policy for use of agricultural land should be framed. Farmers with smallholdings should be encouraged to produce high-value crops. (5)
11. Elections to the two lowest levels of local self-government (the panchayats and the panchayat samitis) should be depoliticized de facto, as per constitutional requirements, by the Election Commission. All possible steps must be taken for true empowerment of panchayats in accordance with the provisions of the 1993 Panchayati Raj Act. Panchayats should have a say in the selection of secretaries to the panchayats. There should be greater devolution of financial powers to panchayats. Adult education should

concentrate on rural women who should have a legal right over agricultural lands belonging to their respective husbands. The government, including village administration, should provide crèches in villages to enable women to be mobile. (6.1, 6.2, 6.3)
12. The minimum procurement price and the minimum selling price of a primary agro-product should ensure a fair return to the farmers; they should be determined with the active involvement of the farmer community and should ideally be, especially in the latter case, the market price. FCI should be wound up and replaced by creation of local storage facilities and local buffer staff, procured and managed by the local self-government like the panchayat. Contract farming should be encouraged under conditions specified in Section III (viii). Marginal and small farmers (with less than 4 acres of landholding) should be encouraged to grow high-value crops such as medicinal plants, vegetables and fruits, and an appropriate system of collecting, processing and marketing of their produce (a system in which the farmers have a stake/share) involving the private sector should be evolved. It should be recognized that traceability of a farm product, or its having been grown organically (item N below), fetches significantly higher prices for the crop. An appropriate task force should be set up for popularizing our enormous repertoire of traditional fruits and vegetables; this should be done in collaboration with the private sector (e.g., our leading hotels) and ICAR. No import of any agriculture produce (unprocessed or processed) should be permitted except to meet a genuine demand that cannot be met from sources within the country. The role of traders in agro-products must be regulated to ensure that the maximum benefit comes to primary produce and processors. (7, 8, 14.3)
13. A national mission should be set up for ethical commercialization of our traditional creative, cultural and legacy industries, which will also bring work in these areas under various ministries (some 10 of them) under one umbrella. (8)
14. A set of new institutional mechanisms (perhaps corporations or cooperatives) should be set up to encourage organic farming (i.e., organic agriculture). ICAR should set up a separate institute as a national centre for research and development in organic

agriculture. Alternatively, ICAR could convert one of its existing institutes to an institute devoted to organic agriculture. The government should set up a group to define standards for products of organic agriculture for domestic market labelling. (8)

15. The government should set up a mission on post-harvest technologies to, among others, collect, collate, document and transmit relevant information to stakeholders; set phytosanitary standards; ensure traceability of products; set up appropriate training programmes; devise marketing strategies; identify investors; and ensure that the first step in post-harvest processing is taken by the primary producer and that they continue to be a stakeholder in all subsequent steps including marketing. This mission should also engage large business houses to invest in post-harvest processing, rather than in retail of primary agricultural produce which is currently destroying the livelihood of many. (8)

16. The nine new energy-saving technologies developed by ICAR so far should be promoted through an appropriate mechanism. The National Energy Policy should include energy generation from surplus biomass and crop residue, for the exploitation of which an appropriate consortium should be set up. The importance of continued use of biomass, like firewood, in the rural sector must be recognized, and mechanisms for increasing the efficiency and convenience of such use (like smokeless *chulahs*) and propagating them should be worked out. A well-thought-out programme of energy plantations (social forestry) should be implemented. A revolving fund for entrepreneurs (with a corpus of say ₹1,000 crores) should be set up for community biogas plants. (8)

17. Animal husbandry, fisheries, agriculture, fertilizers and other agrochemicals should be brought under a single department of the government. (8)

18. Steps must be taken to establish culture of mushrooms or orchid tissue culture industry (for both of which technologies are available in the country) to supplement farmers' income in states like Arunachal Pradesh. Special incentives should be provided to those setting up a marine biotechnology industry. Rural produce-based industries must be set up in the rural sector in a way that the primary producer has a stake in them, as also mentioned in item (O). (8, 11.4)

19. It should be ensured over a specified period (of say, 10 years) that every village child between the age of 6 and 18 is in a high-quality school of the standard of a good central school. Education in such schools must be free and compulsory, and must include trade training involving use of one's own hands (e.g., in agriculture in schools located in the rural sector), especially in the last 4–6 years of higher secondary school (10+2; to make this possible for the whole country, it is estimated that 400,000 central school-type schools would be needed, some 70% of which will need to be located in our villages). The number of vocational training institutions should be increased ten-fold (from about 5,000 to 50,000) with most of the new ones being located in rural areas. The number of vocations covered by such institutions should be increased several fold, and include those of relevance to rural communities, such as organic agriculture, use of fertilizers, preparation of organic manure, pest control, weaving and metal work. An appropriate system of empowering farmers through knowledge that would make them less prone to exploitation and more productive, on a continuing basis, must be evolved. This could include preparation and dissemination of information packages for panchayats as mentioned in Section III (x), setting up of village libraries in schools, establishing village resource centres as envisaged by the M S Swaminathan Research Foundation and setting up 50,000 knowledge clubs, each club taking care of a village cluster and having a budget of ₹1 lakh per year. (9.1, 9.2)

20. An effective national programme of credit, including micro-credit, for the marginal and small farmers and other self-employed rural communities should be instituted. It should be ensured that loans earmarked for the agriculture sector go primarily to marginal and small farmers. Self-help groups should be multiplied and supported, for example, through micro-credit. Priorities must be accorded to establishing connectivity of the rural sector with the urban sector through roads and telecommunication which would, for example, include tele-medicine. A three-tier rural medical and healthcare system along the lines mentioned in Section III (xii) should be set up, perhaps first on an experimental basis as a part of the existing rural health mission and medicare programme. The existing

mission to provide potable water to every resident of every village must be given top priority and made time bound. To provide better nutrition, the production of pulses should be substantially augmented. The public distribution system (PDS) should include them as well as grains other than those already included. It should be decentralized and brought under the local self-government to make it fair and efficient which it is not today. Steps (like those mentioned earlier) should be taken to make NREGS maximally effective and productive. All possible steps should also be taken to increase (double) the contribution of agriculture to GDP so that GDP growth decreases inequities. Goal-directed, project-based funding to the rural sector must be increased substantially. The funds released by withdrawal of fertilizer, power and seed subsidies could be used to finance some of the other support systems for the rural sector recommended in this chapter. (10, 11.1, 11.2, 11.3, 12)

21. ICAR should consider investing in research and extension work in selected areas listed in Annexure 3. Further, a suitable mechanism like an effective agriculture research development corporation (on the lines of the National Research Development Corporation should be set up to commercialize the results of agricultural research in the country. The value of setting up a national institute of agricultural design, with the help of National Institute of Design, Ahmedabad, should be examined. There is a need for revamping and restructuring (total reorganization, both qualitatively and quantitatively) of our rural extension programmes, keeping in mind that inappropriately done extension work can cause more harm than good. In the absence of any good governmental extension programme, this job is being done by multinational corporations to the great detriment of our agriculture security. It was the high quality and the massive extent of extension work done by ICAR that brought the first Green Revolution. ICAR today needs some 5,000 additional extension workers to optimally utilize its capabilities and output. ICAR must extend its Krishi Vigyan Kendras (KVKs) programme to cover every district. KVKs must not only be involved in proactively empowering the farmers with relevant knowledge and engage in extension work, but they must also identify and help solve district/region-specific

agriculture-related problems. The budget of ICAR should be increased sufficiently to enable it to implement the aforementioned recommendations. (13)

22. It must be ensured that our foreign agreements that relate to agriculture, like the ones mentioned earlier, are reviewed periodically and used transparently in our national interest. (14.4)

23. An agriculture disaster rapid action force should be set up. An effective flood control system should also be set up, learning lessons from successes in parts of the country like the Northeast. (15)

24. Land records must be fully straightened out and updated electronically in the entire country as has been done or is being done in some states such as West Bengal, Kerala and Andhra Pradesh. No agricultural land should be alienated to SEZs. On the contrary, a crash programme of bringing additional land (say, 5–10 million hectares per year) under cultivation should be started. This land could be given to marginal farmers (with a landholding of less than 2 hectares) around which new modern villages could come up. (16)

25. A strategy should be worked out to make our agricultural scientists, managers and policymakers become aware, on a continuing basis, of the use of, identification of and protection against agents of biological warfare against our agricultural crops, farm animals and poultry. The High Security Animal Lab of ICAR in Bhopal should be converted into a national centre for animal disease control, and a new centre for plant disease control should be set up to prevent the entry of in the country, identify and work out measures to combat, rare, exotic and emerging diseases affecting animals and plants. Our rules for importing plants (including seeds) and animals should be revisited, made appropriately stringent where they are not so and implemented strictly. (17, 18)

26. To address all the above, a high-power suitably empowered apex body chaired by the agriculture minister should be set up to examine in detail the aforementioned recommendations and work out mechanisms to implement those that are found to be worthy of implementation. One of the functions of the proposed apex body should be to put together every year reliable data on production (and productivity, e.g., per person, per animal, per unit land or per

rupee spent, as appropriate) as well as consumption per person of food grains, pulses, fruits, vegetables, milk, poultry, marine food and meat. This data should be presented to the government and the public along with the data for the preceding nine years and the population data. As a matter of policy, any obligatory import of food items recommended by the apex body should be 'compensated' for by at least an equivalent export of primary or value-added agro-product. Estimates should also be provided of food material wasted due to insects and pests, or on account of lack of storage, transport and processing facilities. The proposed apex body must take an integrated view of food security, farmer security, agriculture security and security of our rural sector, and take steps to ensure all of them. One of its major objectives should be to optimally utilize our national potential in the agriculture/rural sector and in the related traditional knowledge sector which is largely village based. It should, for example, determine the best manner in which the resources released by abolition of various subsidies (e.g., on power, seeds and fertilizers) and of FCI, and reorganization of PDS, can be used to meet the aforementioned objective. If all that is recommended here is done, our rural sector could account for more than 40 per cent of GDP in the next 10–12 years.

ANNEXURE 1

Employment and Wealth Generation Potential of Traditional Knowledge (TK)	
1. Employment Potential (Based on the 2001 Census)	
a. Non-workers	(Number, in Crores)
Total 62.64 crores	
44% (27.56 crores) can work	
40% of 27.56 crores can work in the TK sector	11.02
b. Agricultural workers: cultivators (10.10 crores)*	
20% of them can work in the TK sector	2.04

(Continued)

(Continued)

c. Agricultural workers: labour
(12.06 crores)[e]
One-sixth of them can work in the TK sector   2.01

d. Other workers: rural sector
(10.48 crores)
50% of them can work in the TK sector   5.24

e. Other workers: urban sector
(4.72 crores)
25% of them can work in the TK sector   1.18

    21.49
    (215 million)

Very conservative figure: 100 million

*approximate

2. Income Generation Potential per Year

	(₹ in crores)*
Plant-based drugs (10 × 10,000 crores)	100,000
(international market for one drug from *Phyllanthus amarus* estimated at $6–$18 billion, say $10 billion = 45,000 crores)	
Rainwater harvesting (100 × 100 crores)	10,000
(value ₹100 per person on an average, per year, including water for agriculture) (0.3 paise/litre, based on 100 litres/person/day)	
Preventable loss of agricultural produce due to pests using traditional methods (25% lost; 75% preventable)	100,000
Marketing of new (traditionally used) vegetables and fruits plus value addition by food processing (target 1 billion population at the rate of Euros 30 each/year)	150,000
20% value addition to 33% of our existing agriculture produce, through organic farming	35,000

(Continued)

(Continued)

New areas for tourism where traditional knowledge, traditional practices or cultural and creative work is exhibited (10 million tourists spending on an average 100 Euros extra)	5,000
Creative and cultural industries	200,000
Total	**600,000**
Note: Present value of marketed agricultural produce—approximately 20% of GDP of $600 billion or 2,700,000 crores	540,000

*approximate, rounded of values

ANNEXURE 2
On Foreign Control of Seed Production

1. Role of Seeds in the Power Game

   Food industry, based primarily on agriculture, is the largest industry in the world. Mankind can survive without arms, medicines or even housing (as it has done in the past) but cannot survive without food. Food security was the only security that primitive man worked towards; it is food security that made the human species survive on our planet. Therefore, those who control food production around the world would control the world. To control food production, one needs to control only seed production and agro-chemicals production. Table 1 gives some details of the major seed producers in the world. The effort of such foreign interests towards acquiring total control of our seed business is, therefore, something we must guard against.

2. How Do They Do It?

   a. Traditionally, farmers had total control over their seeds. They could keep them, barter them, sell them, or sow them themselves. Our recent Plant Varieties and Farmers' Rights Protection Act notified in 2005 allows the farmers to do exactly this. As long as farmers did so, there were no seed companies. They came into existence because of development of hybrid seeds,

Table 1 of Annexure 2

World's Top 11 Seed Companies

S. No.	Company	2004 Seed Sales (US millions)
1	Monsanto (USA) + Seminis (acquired by Monsanto 3/05)	$2,277 + $526 = 2,803
2	Dupont/Pioneer (USA)	$2,600
3	Syngenta (Switzerland)	$1,239
4	Groupe Limagrain (France)	$1,044
5	KWS AG (Germany)	$622
6	Land O' Lakes (USA)	$538
7	Sakata (Japan)	$416
8	Bayer Crop Science (Germany)	$387
9	Taikii (Japan)	$366
10	DLF-Trifolium (Denmark)	$320
11	Delta & Pine Land (USA)	$315

Source: ETC Group Global Seed Industry Concentration Report 2005.

the progeny of which cannot be reused (if reused, they will not give the same results as the original hybrids). Development of new hybrid seeds by seed companies is, therefore, one important way of acquiring control over seed production. If these companies are foreign companies or Indian companies controlled financially by foreign interests, and if their market share and our dependence on them progressively increases, we would also progressively lose agricultural security. As of today, their market share could be about 30 per cent which must ring an alarm bell.

b. The seed companies develop new technologies like genetically modified seeds and then they sell these technologies—as they have done in India—by persuading and influencing governments at various levels. They resort to bribery (as Monsanto did in Indonesia for Bt cotton seeds). They prevent indigenous development and break all laws of the land, as has happened in respect of Bt cotton in India (For details, see Bhargava 2003).

c. In the absence of an appropriate and effective regulatory and supervisory system in the country, seed companies have resorted to illegal plantation of unapproved crops like GM crops. There are many documented instances of such crops being planted in India (e.g., Navbharat's Bt cotton in Gujarat) which, in some cases, were uprooted by vigilant non-governmental organizations.

d. Another way is to contaminate the food chain in the country through illegal genetically manipulated food material. Since most of Europe and Japan have stringent laws about import and marketing of GM food, more than the prescribed percentage of GM food in the food product would prevent its export to Europe and Japan. A very well-known and highly publicized case was that of Zambia. When the country went through one of its worst famines recently, a developed country offered it GM corn. However, Zambia's government refused this corn and said they would appreciate if instead of corn, corn flour was sent. Their fear was that once the GM corn comes in, some farmers would be tempted to sow it and this could contaminate their own crops and other agricultural crops as well, the produce of which was being exported to Europe. This will have a serious repercussion on their exports. However, the donor country refused to donate corn flour instead of corn seed.

e. In fact, selling or taking any GM crop to any country is illegal under the Cartagena protocol, unless the recipient country is informed and has accepted to receive such GM food or crop; yet this practice has been widely resorted to. For example, when we had famine in Orissa and our government did not release grain in spite of the FCI godowns overflowing with 60 million tonnes of food grain, the US sent us soya bean flour which was eventually established to be flour prepared from GM soya bean and which could not be marketed in the host country. This was done without the Indian government's approval.

f. There is evidence that the foreign companies that operate, for example, in the area of seeds, fudge their data and propagate untruths about the results of their products. For example, what has been said about the success of Bt cotton is far from what the ground reality appears to be according to careful studies done by responsible non-governmental organizations as well as the government. In fact, there is strong documentary evidence that the 1,044 suicides of farmers in Vidarbha as of January last year were related to the failure of Bt cotton.

g. Foreign organizations concerned with agriculture also influence the governmental machinery in other ways. For example, when Monsanto's Bt cotton failed in parts of Andhra Pradesh, and the government finally accepted this failure, they asked the company to pay compensation to the farmers as per the rules. There is incontrovertible evidence available, which establishes that the data was fudged so that the compensation that the company had to pay to the farmers was much less than what they should have paid. Even this compensation has still (as of April 2007) not been paid.

h. The foreign interests that have entered into India in seed business have used false publicity to establish the superiority of their seeds, like Bt cotton. On this basis, they price their seeds very high. In the case of Bt cotton, the pricing by Monsanto was close to four times of that of non-Bt seeds. The difference was supposed to be the trait value. Again, after much vacillation and under pressure from farmers and responsible NGOs, the government took the case to the Monopolies and Restricted Trade Practices Commission which gave a verdict against the company; the company has agreed to cut its price by a factor of nearly two, but it is still much higher than what it should be.

ANNEXURE 3
Areas of Research/Extension Work to Meet Needs of Farmers

The following topics (randomly arranged) that relate to the felt needs of farmers are suggested for further research by ICAR and other organizations:

1. Post-harvest technology including technologies for value addition, like food processing.
2. Water harvesting using traditional technologies.
3. New agriculture product storage technologies, particularly for decentralized storage.
4. Veterinary genetics and pathology (including microbiology and virology), for example, sequencing of genomes of animals specially widely used in India, like buffaloes and developing genetically engineered vaccines for diseases such as FMV and rinderpest.
5. Organic agriculture and associated activities like vermiculture.
6. Developing methodologies for quick marker-aided selection.
7. Integrated pest management: to increase experience and range of applications and modifications where necessary.
8. Introduction of hybrid vigour into pure-breeding varieties.
9. Setting up of commercial DNA fingerprinting of plants and seeds. Also, documentation to help farmers ensure that they do not get spurious seeds.
10. Development of osmo-resistant varieties (collaboration with MSSRF at Chennai, and CCMB at Hyderabad) and encouragement of commercial plant tissue culture for producing products like vanillin.
11. Better weather prediction models (in collaboration with DST and MST Radar Facility of the Department of Space at Tirupati).
12. Identification of varieties of medicinal plants that would have high amounts of markers correlated with activity.
13. Development of technologies for use of agricultural waste products.
14. Technologies that could increase productivity and release time, labour and resources of farmers which could be used for additional employment.
15. Identification of avenues for additional employment and research on making them attractive and lucrative enough for farmers to engage in them.
16. A socio-economic analysis of the use of energy in agriculture, along with energy-saving mechanisms and strategies for energy management.
17. Development and propagation of technologies for controlled release of fertilizers and pesticides.

18. Systems approach towards commercialization of existing technologies like for orchid tissue culture in Arunachal Pradesh.
19. Metabolic engineering to generate more value (e.g., transferring genes of maize for enzymes such as phosphoenol pyruvate carboxylase/oxygenase and orthophosphate dikinase into rice for increasing yield).
20. An in-depth study of 'shifting agricultural practices', for example, in Arunachal Pradesh, to increase efficiency.

These areas should be pursued by carefully selected, competent and committed scientists in a mission mode, with clear time targets, appropriate funding based on milestones, freedom from bureaucratic hassles but professional, social and financial accountability. ICAR has already organized meetings in the areas marked with an asterisk, during 2005–2006, that have come up with specific recommendations, the more important of which are included in Section V.

REFERENCES

Bhargava, P. M. (2002, April 13). GMOs: Need for appropriate risk assessment system. *Economic & Political Weekly, 37*(15), 1402–1406.
Bhargava, P. M. (2003, August 23). High stakes in agro research: Resisting the push. *Economic & Political Weekly, 38*(34), 3537–3542.
Chatterjee, P. (2007). *The Lancet,* 369, 1417.
Cherian, D. (2007, June 10). Question galore about future of FCI. *Deccan Chronicle,* 7.
Economic Times. (2006, June 9).
Hyderabad Times. (2002, May 12).
Narayan, S., & Agarwal, A. (2001). *Making water everybody's business.* Centre for Science and Environment.

About the Editors and Contributors

SERIES EDITOR

Manoranjan Mohanty retired as Director, Developing Countries Research Centre and Professor of Political Science, University of Delhi in 2004. A political scientist, China scholar, and peace and human rights activist with special interest in China, India and global transformation, he is Editor of *Social Change* and Distinguished Professor, Council for Social Development, New Delhi. He is Chairperson, Development Research Institute, Bhubaneswar and Honorary Fellow and former Chairperson of the Institute of Chinese Studies, Delhi. He has taught or researched in many universities, including California, Oxford, Copenhagen, Moscow, Lagos and Beijing. He is the author of many publications, including *China's Transformation: The Success Story and the Success Trap, Ideology Matters: China from Mao Zedong to Xi Jinping* and edited or co-edited many publications, including *People's Rights, Class, Caste, Gender, India-Social Development Report, 2010, Exploring Emergent Global Thresholds* and *China at a Turning Point*.

VOLUME EDITOR

Prashant K. Trivedi, an Associate Professor at the Giri Institute of Development Studies, Lucknow, received his PhD in sociology from the University of Lucknow. His research interests include political economy of land reforms, rural studies and issues relating to Dalits, Muslims and women with a special focus on Uttar Pradesh, India. He has published articles on a variety of subjects including gender and law, caste and violence, and inequality in development in various journals including *Economic & Political Weekly, Journal of Indian School of Political Economy* and *Social Change*. His has co-authored *Backward and Dalit Muslims: Education, Employment and Poverty* and *Weapon of the Oppressed: An Inventory of People's Rights in India* and edited *The Globalisation Turbulence: Emerging Tensions in Indian Society*. Before joining the Giri

Institute, he was a faculty at the Council for Social Development (CSD), New Delhi. During this period, he was the book review editor of CSD's peer-reviewed journal *Social Change* published by SAGE.

CONTRIBUTORS

S. L. Batra was an honorary fellow at CSD, New Delhi.

Pushpa Mittra Bhargava was a scientist with a difference. Multifaceted, he was not only the architect of biotechnology in India but also worked tirelessly to inculcate a scientific temper in society. Professor Bhargava excelled in scientific discoveries and founded one of India's most well-known and respected scientific research institutes, the Centre for Cellular & Molecular Biology, Hyderabad. A doctorate from the University of Lucknow in Organic Chemistry, he also served as the vice chairman of the Knowledge Commission that was constituted by the Government of India in 2005. Outspoken, critical, highly influential and deeply interested in contemporary social problems, Professor Bhargava was closely associated with CSD.

Sulabha Brahme after finishing her schooling at Pune, received her PhD from the Gokhale Institute of Politics and Economics, Pune, an institute with which she had a long association. She served the institute both in academic and administrative capacities. At this institute, she wrote two major research reports, one on regional development of Marathwada and another on land use pattern in western Maharashtra, besides several other socially relevant study reports. She was also a member of the board of directors of the Bank of Maharashtra. She also founded the Shankar Brahme Samaj Vidnyan Granthalaya which provided platform to progressive intellectuals and activists. Sulabha Brahme wrote numerous popular books on contemporary issues besides contributing extensively to social science literature.

Swarup Dutta is an Assistant Professor in the TERI School of Advanced Studies and holds a PhD in social anthropology from the University of Delhi. He was a consultant in the Indian Council of Social Science Research, Ministry of Human Resource Development,

Government of India, in 2016–2017. He was nominated as Fellow of the Royal Anthropological Institute, Great Britain and Ireland. His research area largely falls in the area of agricultural and environmental anthropology, subaltern studies and gender. He has been a visiting faculty in the Department of Environmental Studies, University of Delhi, and the National Museum Institute of History of Arts, Conservation and Museology, Ministry of Culture, Government of India.

P. C. Joshi trained at the Lucknow School of Economics and Sociology under the guidance of legendry professor, Radhakamal Mukherjee. His major contributions were in the field of agrarian and development studies. Beginning with the doctoral dissertation on agrarian social structure in Uttar Pradesh, he continuously challenged artificial compartmentalization between social and economic. He served the Institute for Economic Growth for around three decades, both as professor and director. Apart from contributing to several policymaking government committees, he also served as the president of the Indian Sociological Society and the editor of its journal *Sociological Bulletin*.

Prodipto Roy after obtaining his master's and doctorate degrees from the Pennsylvania State University in rural sociology, taught at the Allahabad University, the Pennsylvania State University and the Washington State University. One of the founders of CSD, Roy's lifelong association with the institute as a general body member and emeritus professor among others lasted for more than four decades. His pioneering work in the field of child development formed the basis for the Integrated Child Development Scheme. His growth centre project (a part of which is included in this volume) provided the framework for a block-level planning manual in India. He is the author of many research articles and books dealing with agricultural innovation, community development and Adivasi issues, especially focusing on Jharkhand.

Ramesh Sharan an economist by training, is known for his critical comments and social activism and was the vice chancellor of the Vinoba Bhave University, Hazaribagh. He has also been a professor at the Economics Department of the Ranchi University. He also headed the department. He has done extensive research on land, agrarian, employment and Adivasi issues.

Amar Kumar Singh was executive chairperson of CSD, New Delhi. He is well known for his work on Adivasi issues and development of Jharkhand. He was also vice chancellor of the Ranchi University, besides being editor of *Social Change*, the social science journal brought out by the CSD.

Gurmanpreet Singh has been teaching in the Department of Evening Studies—Multi Disciplinary Research Centre, Panjab University, Chandigarh, for the past three years. He has obtained his master's degree, MPhil and PhD from the Department of Economics, Punjabi University, Patiala. His academic research interests and publications focus on production relations in Punjab agriculture, in general, and agricultural labour, in particular. He is currently working on the existence of untouchability and unfree production relations in Punjab's agriculture.

Kamaljit Singh is Professor and Head, Department of Economics, Punjabi University, Patiala. He has been teaching in the department for the past 28 years, also supervising three PhD students. He has written extensively on the labour and macroeconomic issues, and published and presented numerous articles. His book *International Migration in a Developing Economy* takes a critical look at the migration and advances an understanding of the impact of different migration policies.

Mahesh Pratap Singh obtained his PhD from the Centre for the Study of Regional Development, Jawaharlal Nehru University, New Delhi. He works in the field of big data, technological transformation and artificial intelligence.

R. A. P Singh was a student of sociology at the Centre for the Study of Social Systems, Jawaharlal Nehru University, New Delhi. For his doctoral thesis, he worked on social consequences of land reforms in Bihar under the supervision of the legendary professor, Yogendra Singh. Awarded Young Social Scientist Fellowship by the Indian Council for Social Science Research, he has taught sociology in Rajasthan.

Sukhpal Singh is Professor and Chairperson, Centre for Management in Agriculture, Indian Institute of Management Ahmedabad, Gujarat; former Director-General, Centre for Research in Rural and Industrial Development Chandigarh; and former Professor and Head, Agricultural Economic Research Unit, Institute of Economic Growth, New Delhi. He has been conferred the title of the Fellow of the Indian Society of Agricultural Economics for his contributions to the discipline and the society in 2018. Founding co-editor, *Millennial Asia*, an international journal of Asian studies, he has 12 books to his credit, the latest publication being *Institutional Innovations in the Delivery of Farmer Services in India* and more than 140 research papers in international/national journals/edited books. He is also on the boards of many non-profits working in the agriculture and rural space.

Meera Velayudhan has been involved in gender studies since its inception in India in the early 1980s, to an extent, conducted within the discipline of History. Her doctoral research focused on gender, caste, social reform, nationalism and popular movements in Kerala and her subsequent research has been on strategies of organization of women in varied contexts, both historical and contemporary. Coming from a family which has actively participated in the debate on citizenship, social policy and affirmative action in the 1930s and the 1940s and whose lives traversed several modernities—anti-caste, social reform, state people's movement and nationalist movements—she draws from her own social legacy. She has authored and edited numerous publications in English, Malayalam and Hindi. She is a policy analyst and President of Indian Association for Women's Studies.

C. K. Vijayasuryan works with Kerala State Planning Board, Thiruvananthapuram. He holds an MPhil in applied economics from the Centre for Development Studies, Kerala, India.

C. R. Yadu is a PhD scholar at the Centre for Development Studies, Kerala, India. He researches on agrarian political economy in India.

Index

agrarian structure, 101–105
  dynamics of growth, 109
  economic tendency, 109
  emerging capitalist sector and traditional peasant sector, 109
  existence of conflict, 108
  Mellor, John W.
    gap in assessment, 110–111
    point of view on considerable force and lucidity, 109–110
  Professor Dantwala's analysis, 111
    institutional reforms without technological progress, 111–112
    new technology, 111
    Poverty in India, 112–113
    questions of equitable distribution, 111
    weaknesses, 112
  Raja's argument, 117–118
  rural poor, 107–119
  spread effects from dynamic sub-sector, 108
agricultural backwardness under semi-feudalism
  Bhaduri, A.
    attention to in-built structural obstacles, 119
    model of semi-feudalism, 119
agricultural management, 162–165
  follow-through, 165
  quantities of wheat produced, 163–164
agricultural modernization in rural Maharashtra, 168–186
  methods of study, 170–172
  perspective, 169–170
  post-Independence India, 168
  Satara, 168, 172–177
agricultural production functions, costs and returns in India
  Rao's study, 118–119
agriculture in India. *see* small farms in India
agriculture management
  agricultural planning, 147–148
  characteristics of study area, 148–150
    Chamkaur Sahib Block, Punjab, 151
  growth centre
    concept, 141
    economically, 144
    educationally, 144–145
    health, 145
    objectives, 144
    operationally, 144
    political, 145
    questionnaires, 146
    recreation, 145
    religious centres, 145
  land utilization, 150–152
    Chamkaur Sahib block, Punjab, 151
  micro-regional partitions, 155–160
    quantities of wheat produced and marketed, 158–159
    three levels of spatial reach, 157
  micro-regional planning, 139–165
    Behrampur bet micro-region, 162
    crop production and marketing, 153–155
    growth centre, 141–146

Vohra, B. B.
  A Charter for Our Land, 140
  ERTS, 140–141
  lack of accurate soil and groundwater, 140
  wheat marketed and fertilizers purchased, 160–162
  distribution of fertilizer, 161
  NPK, 160
  sowing period, 162
agriculture security. *see* food security
antedated hukumnama
  form of sale of land in Dumka district, 48–51
  land sold to tribal after DC's permission, 48
  sada patta
    sale on plain paper, 47
    sale on plain papergift, 48
  through institution or SAR cases and fixation of compensation, 46–47
Association for Democratic Rights (AFDR), 206

badlanama, 48, 49
Behrampur bet micro-region, 162
benami/farzi transaction of land, 10
Bihar Military Police (BMP), 23
Bipartite CF model, 244

Central Place Theory, 141
Chakwars, 11
Chamkaur Sahib block
  crops produced and marketed in 1971-1972, 154
  land utilization, 151–152
  value of major crops produced and proportions sold, 155
chaparbandi, 28
chaparbandi method, 3
Chota Nagpur Tenancy (CNT) Act, 1908, 2

Chotanagpur and Santhal Pargana study covered, 21
Chotanagpur Tenancy (CNT) Act, 20
class interests, 2
Commission for Agricultural Cost and Prices (CACP), 189
53rd Conference of the Indian Economics Association, 111
Consult for Women and Land Rights (CWLR), 78
consumerism, 253
contextualizing women's rights
  Bina Agarwal argues about external constraints, 77
  CWLR, 78
  entitlement and usufruct rights in common land
    forest land, 84–86
  entitlements to land, 73–94
  Gujarat
    campaigns for land, 90–93
    changing land relations, 81–84
    changing land-use patterns, 87–90
    daughters married outside, 80
    family disputes and breakups, 80
    lead to land fragmentation, 79–80
    points highlighted, 80
    social biases, 93–94
  NANGOF, 78
  National Land Committee in South Africa, Kenya Land Alliance, 78
  National Land Forum in Tanzania, 78
  Rwanda Land Alliance, 78
  Uganda Land Alliance, 78
  Zambia National Land Alliance, 78
contract farming, 215
crop diversification programme, 254

Dalits, landownership in Kerala
  index of access for different social groups, 69

land inequality, 66–70
  caste and landholding, 67
  mean and median
    land cultivated across social groups, 69
    land owned across social groups, 68
  net accumulation of land, 64
  revenue generated from land transactions, 64
  share of different communities, 63
  situation defined by Omvedt, 54
  triple exclusion, 53–71, 54
    historical exclusion, 54–59
    land market, 62–66
    land reforms, 59–62
danpatra, 49
Demonstration scheme for crop specific mechanization' (DSCSM), 273
Dumka district, 48–51
  badlanama, 48
  ghairahi, 48
  gift or danpatra, 48
  land alienation of tribal public purpose, 23–25
  modes of sale
    badlanama, 49
    bhoodan land, 51
    danpatra, 49
    illegal conversion, 50
    kurfanama, 50–51
    land settled by pradhans, 51
    regularization under the SAR Act, 1969, 50
    sada patta, 50
  transfer of tribal land
    land temporarily transferred by bhugut bandha, 49
    temporary alienation on trust for cultivation, 49

Earth Resources Technical Satellite (ERTS), 140–141

The Economics of Land Reform and Farm Size in India
Khusro, A. M.
  land reform measures, 114
entitlement and usufruct rights in common land
Gujarat
  forest land, 84–86
  pasture land, 86–87

food security
  agriculture or agriculture-related, 303
  agrochemicals and organic agriculture, 307–309
  augmentation of income, 312–314
  bioterrorism, 319
  climate change, 319
  components, 307–308
  contract farming, 312
  crisis, 303–305
  disasters, 318
  external threats, 318
  immediate objectives of, 306
  increasing population and rising consumption, 305
  integrated pest management (IPM), 309
  knowledge empowerment, 314–315
  land records, 318
  loans, 315
  modern agricultural practices, 311
  Panchayat Raj, 311–312
  policy, 317
  rare, emerging, new and exotic diseases, 319
  recommendations, 319–327
  research needs, 317
  rural and urban sectors, integration of, 315–316
  seeds, 307
  soils, 310

traditional agricultural practices, 310
water and power, 309–310

ghairahi, 48
globalization era, 213–217
  Bhargava's schema, 217
    soil health, 216–217
    true-breeder seed varieties, 216
  contract farming, 215
  small farms, 214
green revolution, 188
  CACP report, 189
  changing nature of labour employment, 198–200
  Cleaver's view, 209
  contemporary agrarian situation in Punjab, 192–194
  decline in employment of Siri, 197–198
  Gandhi's argument, 189–190
  Gill and Singh's report, 190
  grain bowl of India, 189
  impact of globalization and liberalization, 201–202
  indebtedness and suicide in Punjab, 202–208
    AFDR study, 206
    arhtiyas, 204, 205
    IDC report, 206
    loan from PNB, 204
    profile of suicide victims, 207
  massive socio-economic crisis, 189
  methodology, 191–192
  Nadkarni's report, 189
  problem of reverse tenancy, 194–197
  Punjab and agricultural growth, 189
  rice cultivation, 189
  study area, 190–191
growth centre
  application of Location and Central Place Theory, 142
  Central Place Theory, 141

direct relevance of socialist literature, 142
literature, 141–142
research design, 142–147
sociological research, 142
total manpower and commodity management, 142
Gujarat
  campaigns for land, 90–93
  changing land-use patterns, 87–90
  contextualizing women's rights
    changing land relations, 81–84
    daughters married outside, 80
    family disputes and breakups, 80
    lead to land fragmentation, 79–80
  entitlement and usufruct rights in common land
    forest land, 81–84
    pasture land, 86–87
  learnings from grassroots field experiences, 78–81
  social biases, 93–94

heavy engineering corporation (HEC), 20
high-yielding varieties (HYVs), 147
  breakdown of acreages, 153
  maize and groundnut, 153
hukumnamas. *see* antedated hukumnama

Institute of Development and Communication (IDC), 206

Jharkhand region of Bihar
  land alienation of tribal, 19–51

kinship, land reform and conflict, 13–15
  abolition of zamindari, 13
  big ex-zamindar of Sukhyapur, 15
  Champapur, 15

ex-zamindar family head in
   Saritapur, 14
Kuberpur, 14
Land Ceiling Act, 13
Saritapur, 13, 14–15
kinship ties
   process of production, 11–12
kurfanama, 50–51

land, 74
   ownership by women, 75
   titles, 74
land alienation of tribal
   acquisition
      inbuilt rehabilitation package,
         with, 22–23
      rehabilitation package, without,
         23
   form of sale of land, 43–44
   individuals, 23, 25–26
   individuals by sample households,
      27
   legal framework, 21–22
   methods by sale to individuals, 43–44
      chaparbandi transactions, 45–46
      collusive title suits, 44
   mode, 29
      sample households, 30–32
   post-1970 phase, 33–39
      encroachment, 37
      post-mortgage status of
         mortgagee, 35, 36
      Ranchi, 34
      sale, 38
      Section 46 of the CNT Act, 34
   pre-1970 phase, 29–33
   public purpose, 24
      Dumka District, 23–25
      Ranchi district, 25
   quantum, 26–29
   sample households, 27
   sample households reasons
      due to sale, 41–43
      through mortgage, 40–41

study area and sample, 22
typology, 22
Land Ceiling Act, 10
   implementation, 13
land concentration
   Kinship basis, 9–11
land reform
   Sinha, J. N.
      transformation of subsistence into
         commercial farming, 119
land-based conflict, 12
   Champapur, 12
   kinship, land reform and conflict,
      13–15
   Kuberpur, 12
   Saritapur, 13
   Sukhyapur, 12
landed-class people, 8

Maharashtra
   agricultural modernization in rural
      areas, 168–186
      post-Independence India, 168
      Satara, 168
   agricultural modernization in
      Satara, 172–177
   Employment Guarantee Scheme,
      122
   impact of agricultural
      modernization at village level,
      177–185
      advent of agricultural
         modernization, 183
      combined effects, 184
      domination of large farmers, 185
      essential conditions for HYV,
         178
      labour system vs labour service,
         183
      percentage of transaction cost,
         183
      size class-wise distribution of
         attributes, 179–183
      type of labour, 184

Land to the Tiller, 122
peasant economy in capitalist development, 121–122
semi-permanent migration, 123
mass poverty
 eradication, 107
Modernizing Peasant Societies
 Guy Hunter
  emergence of dynamic sector in agriculture, 115
  growth of the dynamic sector, 115
  importance of security, 115
  vast majority, 115

Namibian NGO Federation (NANGOF), 78
new economic forces, 7
nitrogen, phosphorus and potassium (NPK), 160

Operation Barga Programme in West Bengal, 76

peasant economy in capitalist development
 Employment Guarantee Scheme, 122
 Land to the Tiller, 122
 Maharashtra state, 121–122
 role, 121–137
 semi-permanent migration, 123
 village Gulumb, 123–136
plough-based cultivation, 11
Poverty in India
 Dandekar and Rath, 112–113
  land policy, 113
   regulated capitalism in Indian agriculture, 113
   weakness, 113
pre-Green Revolution Punjab, 205
Punjab National Bank (PNB), 204

Quadpartite CF model, 246

raiyats, 9
Ranchi district
 land alienation of tribal
 public purpose, 25
Rural Poverty, Land Redistribution and Development
 Minhas, B. S.
 rural poor, 114–115
rural Punjab
 agrarian crisis, impact, 281
 agricultural labour forms, 280
 debt trap
  agricultural labourers, 296
  low level of income, 295
  non-institutional agencies, 295
 employment pattern
  economic status, 286
  gender laborers, 287
  kharif season, 289
  number of man-days, 288
  permanent and casual labourer, 288
  prevailing wage rate, 288–289
  rabi season, 288–289
  seasonal, 287–289
  wages, 288
 farming community, 280
 forms of bondage, 281
 green revolution's technological, 280
 household income, levels and pattern of, 285
 incidence of poverty
  defined, 291
  Planning Commission of India, 291–292
  Sen's 'P' measure of poverty, 292–295
 income and consumption, analysis
  average annual income, 284
  average propensity, 285
  consumption, 284–285
  levels and pattern of household income, 285
  levels of earning, 285–286

land reforms, 280
methodology
  agricultural labour households, 282
  random sampling method, 282
  studies, 283
  ownership of assets, 295
  dwelling houses, 297
siri, 281
social and economic feature, overview of
  drinking water, 283
  education level, 284
  Scheduled Castes, 284
social conditions
  economic-bondedness, victims, 298
  households, 298
  ownership of means of production, 298
  unemployment, 280
  wages, 280, 281–282
rural women
  entitlements to land, 74
  land ownership, 75
  secure property rights, 74

sada patta, 50
Santhal Parganas Tenancy (SPT) Act, 2, 21
Saritapur
  son becomes tenant of his father, 15–16
Satara, 168
  agricultural modernization in rural Maharashtra, 172–177
  time series information on agriculture, 173–175
Scheduled Area Regulation (SAR), 3
  regularization under, 50
Section 46 of the CNT Act, 34
Shifting pattern of agricultural space
  agreement, 253
  contract farming, 256–258, 266

allocation of areas to various extension agencies, 268–269
policy formulation, 272
credit and mechanization efforts
  demonstration scheme for crop specific mechanization' (DSCSM), 273
  new equipment for crops, 274–275
  PAFC, 273
crop diversification programme, 253
district-level staff, 271
high-yielding variety seeds, 272
modes of intervention, 260
MSP, 265
MSP purview, 272
multi-pronged methodology, 254
new development agenda, emergence of, 254–256
PAFC, 261–264, 266, 271
percentage distribution, 264
policy measures, aim of, 273
private expertise, 267
private firms, 270
purchase price (PP), 265
role of government institutions, 258–260
secretary-level meeting, 271
spread of consumerism, 253
study objectives, 253
transforming agriculture, 273
WTO norms, 272
Singh, R. A. P.
  changing social relations, transforming landownership structure, 1
Sixpartite (Networking) CF model, 246
small farms in India
  alternative marketing structures, relative benefits of, 234
  commercial farming, 224
  constraints of access
    agri-business companies, 239

Index | 347

collective action, 236
contracts, 238
corporate farming (CF), 237
  Fair Trade Commission, 237
  flexible production system, 237
  Model Producer Protection Act, 2000, of Iowa, 238
  practice of contracts, 238
  producers' organizations, 238
  trust, 239
corporate farming (CF), 228–232
crisis of sustainability, 223
crop diversification, 226
cropping pattern, 222
dairying accounts, 221
development agencies and projects, 235
distress, 225
diversification, 226
fair trade, 236
flower-cultivating, 227
globalization and trade liberalization, 225
globalized commercial agriculture
  dairy companies, 233
  market, 232
  new generation cooperatives (NGCs), 233
  right policy environment, 233
green revolution region, 224
grower contracts, 235
high-value products, 227
holdings, 220
input subsidies, 224
interlocking of markets, 222
international prices, 224
marginal holdings, 221
operational holding, 222
over-capitalization, 223
partnership, 236
procurement systems, 235
risk aversion, 227
risk dimension, 228
viability of smallholdings, 226

social revolution in Kerala village, 8, 13
state-led contract farming system, 245

taccavi loans, 205
The Challenge of World Poverty, drama, 109
The Economics of Land Reform and Farm Size in India
  Khusro, A. M., 114
The Social Framework of Agriculture
  Andre Beteille, 115–116
  general condition of uncertainty, 116
  quoting Schumpeter, 116
  uncertainty, 116–117
traditional knowledge (TK)
  areas of research/extension work to meet needs of farmers, 332–334
  employment and wealth generation potential, 327–329
  seed production, foreign control of, 339–332
tribal land alienation, 19–51
Tripartite CF model, 244

village Gulumb, 123–136
  1942, 123–136
    agriculture, 125–130
    changes in crop pattern adopted by cultivators, 127
    demographic characteristics, 125
    distribution of families by size of ownership holding, 129
    migration, 130
    occupational distribution of earners, 126
    population, 124
  1976, 130–131
    agriculture, 131–134
    migration, 135–136
village-level worker (VLW), 143

zamindari days, 9